T0119511

NAVAL & MARITIME HISTORY
An Annotated Bibliography

NAVAL & MARITIME HISTORY

An Annotated Bibliography

FOURTH EDITION
REVISED AND EXPANDED

————————————

ROBERT GREENHALGH ALBION

Gardiner Professor of Oceanic History and Affairs, Harvard University
Director, Munson Institute of American Maritime History
Sometime Historian of Naval Administration, Navy Department

Munson Institute
of American Maritime History

The Marine Historical Association, Incorporated
Mystic, Connecticut

1972

Library of Congress Catalog Card Number: 73-186863
Copyright 1972 by The Marine Historical Association, Incorporated
All rights reserved
First Edition published 1963. Fourth Edition 1972
Printed in the United States of America

Price: $15 cloth; $5.95 paper
Order from Seaport Stores
Mystic Seaport, Mystic, Connecticut 06355

Table of Contents

VI. NAVIES

Naval History by Chronological Periods

VII. SPECIAL TOPICS

Preface

The First Edition of this bibliography appeared privately and most informally in 1951, prepared primarily for use in my graduate and undergraduate courses in Oceanic History (maritime and naval) at Harvard. It originated in the desire to systematize the oral advice given down through the years to hundreds of students seeking suggestions as to how to get started on their term papers, senior theses, seminar reports or PhD theses. The effort has been to guide the student toward virgin subjects or at least toward topics that have not been done to death. Consequently, the sea history has been presented in its widest ramifications.

The impetus for the Second Edition in 1955 came from the wish to meet the needs of the new Munson Institute of American Maritime History at Mystic Seaport in Connecticut. The Third Edition was brought out in 1963, followed by two Supplements in 1966 and 1968. This present cumulative Fourth Edition combines those last three with new works appearing between 1968 and mid-1971.

Continuing public interest in things maritime and naval is evidenced by the fact that in the nine years since the Third Edition, the total entries have increased from around 3,000 to over 5,000. The fields of principal proportional gains in those nine years were West Africa and the Slave Trade (34 to 71); Red Sea and Persian Gulf (9 to 25); Latin America (57 to 87); National Naval Policy (20 to 50); Naval Procurement and Logistics (16 to 66); Naval, 1919-39 (36 to 66); and "Picture Books" (29 to 55).

Like the earlier editions, this is limited principally to *books in English* and PhD theses. That leaves out the important categories of periodical articles in English books and articles in foreign languages and unpublished manuscript material. If someone would take the time to undertake those, the results would be most welcome.

One particular purpose of this study has been to separate wheat and chaff in the maritime-naval field. Whether in card catalogs or on library shelves, the wide variety of books, good, bad, and indifferent presents a problem to the student. He may be bewildered by finding a half-trayful of cards on a general subject with no indication of their relative value. It has seemed best to divide them into three major categories—the shallow or superseded books not worth including, the large body of useful works, and the select minority of the most substantial and useful, indicated with a "*." Brief comments have been made on many of the books to indicate their scope or merit. The whole process has been highly subjective, like the passing of judgment on the relative merits of eating places. For all that, it is hoped that this will be somewhat more useful than a simple list of authors and titles.

One special complication in the field of maritime-naval history has been that the "romance" of the sea not only lures readers into the subject, but too often it also lures writers who feel that enthusiasm is an adequate substitute for research. They, and their publishers, know that a free-flowing style, a lively title, some well-selected pictures, and a striking paperback cover will often result in ample sales to uncritical readers, even though the book adds little if anything to what is known already. The most prolific exploiter of sea atmosphere, E. Keble Chatterton, ground out more than 40 books in 35 years, and there are several runners-up. The shelves are full of the "blow-by-blow" books of naval history and of what William McFee has termed the "yo-heave-ho" school of maritime history.

At the opposite extreme from such works are the PhD theses, published, microfilmed or still in typescript. Several hundred pertinent ones are included here, even though many of them are not strictly in the "books in English" category. Granting that most of the "atmosphere" books make better reading, there are some valid reasons for including the theses. They have all passed formal academic scrutiny and most of them have useful bibliographies, including original source material. Then, too, some apparent virgin subjects on which few if any published books are available will be found to have ample PhD coverage.

Originally, Columbia and several other universities required that all PhD theses be published, although Harvard never did. As time went on, the cost of publication rose so rapidly that an ingenious alternative developed. University Microfilms of Ann Arbor made it possible to adjust the supply and demand needs of author and reader at a reasonable rate with xerox copies in book form at less than five cents a page, while a brief summary was published in *Dissertation Abstracts,* all at a moderate charge to the author. Such theses are indicated here with a "DA", and the volume and page. Some universities which do not participate in this program have prepared abstracts on their own, and some have microfilm arrangements; students may find it feasible to secure copies of the bibliography if not the whole thesis. The definite guides to these PhD theses will be found in Section D. There has been no attempt to include MA (master of arts) theses on the same scale, but a few pertinent ones have been cited, especially from the Universities of Maine, New Brunswick and British Columbia, and Dalhousie University, which have emphasized maritime history. Also, there are some titles from Great Britain where PhDs were not common until after World War I nor in the Dominions until after World War II.

The material is divided into 72 sections, lettered from "A" to "BT"; many of those are further subdivided. Within each section and subsection, the items are arranged in alphabetical order.

I am indebted to Diana Whittle and Laurence C. Allin for their help in the preparation of this new edition.

R. G. A.

South Portland, Maine

viii

Abbreviations and Symbols

*   A work of particular significance or usefulness.

P   Paperback or other paperbound edition.

R   Reissue or revision of work cited in Third Edition.

PhD thesis, published:
> Fairchild, B. *Messrs. William Pepperell: Merchants at Piscataqua,* 1954 (PhD thesis, Princeton).

PhD thesis, University Microfilms, with volume and page reference to *Dissertation Abstracts:*
> Miller, R. *The New York Coastwise Trade 1865-1915* (PhD thesis, Princeton, 1940; DA v. 12, p. 47).

PhD thesis, manuscript:
> Perry, J.C. *Great Britain and the Imperial Japanese Navy, 1858-1905* (ms.PhD thesis, Harvard, 1962).

I   Reference Works

A   BIBLIOGRAPHY

*Albion, R.G. "Recent Writings in Maritime History" in quarterly issues of the *American Neptune,* 1952-58. Differs from this work in that it includes pertinent current periodical articles as well as books. See also Schultz, below.

*American Historical Association, *Guide to Historical Literature,* ed. G.F. Howe et al., 1961. Supersedes earlier 1931 and 1949 editions. Brief critical comments on principal works in all world history. See especially Sect. B, "General Reference Resources" for very helpful bibliographical guide, and Sect. U, "Expansion of Europe." Also consult index under Commerce, Military and Naval History, Ports, and Ships and Shipping.

*Anderson, R.C. *Mariner's Mirror: General Index to Volumes 1-35,* 1955. This is the excellent journal of the Society for Nautical Research in England.

Berio Library, Genoa, *Catalogue of the Columbus Collection,* 1965. Reproduction of 3,100 cards.

Bibliography of British History:
    C. Read, *Tudor Period, 1485-1603,* 1959. Pt. 7, sect. 7; pt. 8; and pt. 9.
    G. Davies, *Stuart Period, 1603-1714,* 1928. Pt. 3; pt. 5.
    S. Pargellis, *The Eighteenth Century, 1714-1789,* 1951. Pt. 6b; pt. 8. These are particularly useful because of the evaluation of the various items.

Blanchard, C.H., Jr. *Korean War Bibliography and Maps of Korea,* 1965. Lists 10,000 items.

Bowden, C.N., comp. *Catalogue of the Inland Rivers Library,* 1968.

British Museum, *Subject Index.* Every four years, this lists the books added to that great library. The most pertinent topics are Naval and Maritime Science, Trade, Shipbuilding and Ports, Harbours, Docks. Consult those same headings under the various countries and leading ports.

Callendar, G.A.R. *Bibliography of Naval History* (History Association Leaflets, Nos. 58, 61), P1924-25.

Cambridge History of the British Empire, 8 v. 1929-59. See Sect. T.
Cambridge History of India, 6 v. 1923-53.
New Cambridge Modern History, 12 v. 1957-
    These Cambridge works all have extensive bibliographies.

Cleveland Public Library, *Catalog of the Inland Rivers Library*, 1968.

Cox, E.G. *A Reference Guide to the Literature of Travel*, 2 v. 1935-49.

*Craig, H., Jr., comp. *A Bibliography of Encyclopedias and Dictionaries dealing with Military, Naval and Maritime Affairs, 1577-1970*, 4th ed. 1970.

*Gipson, L.H. *The British Empire before the American Revolution*, 15 v. 1958-70. See Sect. Z-2 for full contents. V.14, A Bibliographical Guide to the History of the British Empire, 1748-1776; v. 15, "A Guide to Manuscripts, 1748-1776."

Great Britain, Ministry of Defense, Naval Library, London, *Author and Subject Catalogues*, 5 v. 1967. Some 80,000 cards reproduced.

Hale, R.W. *Guide to Photographic Historical Materials in the United States or Canada*, 1961. Lists 11,137 collections held by 285 institutions.

Hanson, L.W. *Contemporary Printed Sources in British and Irish Economic History, 1701-50*, 1965. Includes sections on Colonies, Commerce and Transport.

Harvard Guide to American History, ed. O. Handlin et al., 1954. Comprehensive critical coverage. Consult helpful section on general sources, also on Federal documents and manuscripts. Consult index under Commerce, Navigation Acts, Navy, Shipping.

Knight, F. *The Sea Story, being a Guide to Nautical Reading from Ancient Times to the Close of the Sailing Ship Era*, 1958. Combines a running narrative with suggested readings under various heads. Useful principally as a guide to "illustrative fiction, contemporary and otherwise," not covered in this present bibliography.

*Larson, H.M. *Guide to Business History: Materials for the Study of American Business History and Suggestions for Their Use* (Harvard Studies in Business History, No. 12), 1948, R1970. Its 1,207 pages include a critical bibliography of some 5,000 items; particularly helpful in connection with commercial or shipping houses.

Lewis, C.L. *Books of the Sea, An Introduction to Nautical Literature*, 1943. More than half of it is devoted to novels, short stories and plays; relatively little touches on the economic side. Some chapters include critical descriptions but others are simply lists of titles.

Manwaring, G.E. *A Bibliography of British Naval History: A Bibliographical and Historical Guide to Printed and Manuscript Sources*, 1930, R1970. This is "not a guide to individual books," but to the "mass of naval material that lies buried in books, periodicals, magazines, transactions of learned societies," etc. Particularly useful for material in the Navy Records Society publications, the *Mariner's Mirror* and the *Journal* of the Royal United Service Institution.

*Marine Historical Association (Mystic Seaport), *Untapped Sources and Research Opportunities in the Field of American Maritime History: A Symposium Held at the G.W. Blunt White Library, October 8, 1966*, P1967.

*Mariners Museum (Newport News, Va.), *Dictionary Catalog of the Library,* 9 v. 1965. Reproduces 150,000 cards.
*———. *Catalog of Marine Photographs,* 5 v. 1965. 75,000 cards. See Sects. F, AS, AU-3, BK.
*———. *Catalog of Marine Prints and Paintings,* 3 v. 5,000 cards.
*———. *Catalog of Maps, Ships' Papers and Logbooks,* 1 v. 10,000 cards. This ambitious project was edited by John L. Lochhead, Librarian of the Museum, and published by G.K. Hall & Co.

Morrell, W.P. *A Select List of Books Relating to the History of the British Commonwealth and Empire Overseas,* 1944.

National Academy of Science. See Sect. K-7.

*National Maritime Museum, *Catalogue of the Library,* 2 v. 1968-70.

*Neeser, R.W. *Statistical and Chronological History of the United States Navy, 1775-1907,* 2 v. 1909. Vol. I is a painstaking, exhaustive list of thousands of items, including nearly all the printed documents. It is well indexed, but does not indicate relative values.

New York Times Index, quarterly 1913-29; annual since 1930. Highly useful for running down specific events or following play-by-play developments. Sometimes the index entries alone are sufficient; if not, they indicate where the full account can be found in the files.

*Parker, J. *Books to Build an Empire: A Bibliography of English Overseas Interests to 1620,* 1965. Analyzes some 267 titles and editions in science, navigation, travel narratives, etc., issued in England 1481-1620.

*Ragatz, L.J. *Guide for the Study of British Caribbean History, 1763-1834,* 1932. A model comprehensive, critical bibliography, with valuable descriptions of the various source collections; broader in scope than the title implies.

*Royal Empire Society, *Subject Catalogue of the Library of the Royal Empire Society, formerly the Royal Colonial Institute,* ed. E. Lewin, 4 v. 1930-37.
V. 1, British Empire, General, and Asia
V. 2, Australia-New Zealand, South Pacific, General Voyages and Travels, and Polar Regions
V. 3, Canada, West Indies, and Colonial America
V. 4, Mediterranean Colonies, Middle East, India, South and Southeast Asia, and Far East
Although it lacks critical comments or evaluation, it is invaluable for showing what has been written on particular subjects. It even shows the titles of particular volumes in collections and proceedings such as the Maine and Massachusetts Historical societies and the Essex Institute for the colonial period. The Society has once again been renamed; it is now the Royal Commonwealth Society.

*Schultz, C.R. *Bibliography of Maritime and Naval History, Periodical Articles during 1970,* 1971 (Marine Historical Assn.). Projected annual editions will be prepared by Pamela McNulty.

————. *Inventories of Papers in The Marine Historical Association Library, Mystic, Connecticut,* P1966-67: T.A. Scott Co., 1889-1927; Mallory Family Papers, 1808-1858; Lawrence & Co., 1822-1904; Silas Talbot Papers, 1767-1867. See also Sect. I.

Society of Naval Architects and Marine Engineers, *Index to Transactions, 1893-1943,* 1946, R1970.

The Times (London), *Palmer's Index,* quarterly since 1867; *Annual Index,* 1899-1913; *Official Index* since 1914.

Tremaine, M. *Arctic Bibliography,* 1967.

*Towle, E.L. *Bibliography on the Economic History and Geography of the Great Lakes-St. Lawrence Drainage Basin,* with Supplement, 1964. Includes many periodical articles and government reports.

U.S. National Archives, *List of National Archives Microfilm Publications,* 1965.

U.S. Naval History Division, *United States Naval History, Naval Biography, Naval Strategy and Tactics, A Selected and Annotated Bibliography,* 29 pp. 1959, 5th ed. 1969. The later editions are less spotty than the earlier ones.

U.S. Naval Institute, *General Index of the Proceedings, Nos. 1-100 (1874-1901),* 1902. Similar volume for Nos. 101-200.

Writings on American History . . . A Bibliography of Books and Articles Published during the year . . . with some memoranda on Canada and the British West Indies, ed. G.C. Griffin et al. Published under auspices of the American Historical Association. Annual since 1902. Particularly useful for locating periodical articles. Sections include "Military and Naval History," "Commerce and Industry," and "Communications-Transportation" as well as the separate regions and states.

In addition to the above mentioned general works, it is important to consult the bibliographies in the more scholarly books on specific subjects, and also the numerous PhD theses listed. Some of the major encyclopedia articles also include brief select bibliographies.

B ENCYCLOPEDIAS, DICTIONARIES, ETC.

B – 1 Current Major Works

Dictionary of American Biography ("D.A.B."), 21 v. 1928-37, with index and supplements. Also *The Concise Dictionary of American Biography,* ed. J.G. Hopkins et al. In a one-volume abridgement, it includes all 14,870 articles from the full "D.A.B."

Dictionary of National Biography ("D.N.B."), 63 v. 1885-1900, with supplements, epitomes, and index. The British counterpart of the "D.A.B." but not as up-to-date. Both give sketches of prominent deceased Americans and Britons respectively.

Encyclopedia Americana, various editions. A Harvard historian once remarked, "I don't know which man is more of a fool – the one who never uses the encyclopedia, or the one who never uses anything else." Its articles give a quick summary of the essentials; some of them, such as "Merchant Marine" and "Warships" are quite extensive.

Encyclopaedia Britannica, especially 11th ed. 1911. Many libraries still give prominent place to this edition, the last produced in Britain, particularly for its excellent historical coverage. The articles on "Ships" and "Shipbuilding" are particularly useful. *Collier's Encyclopedia* is also useful.

Encyclopedia of the Social Sciences, 15 v. 1930-35. Articles on general subjects such as Commerce, Merchant Marine, Ports and Harbors, Privateering, Seamen, Shipping, Shipbuilding, Smuggling, etc.

B – 2   Annuals

American Merchant Marine Conference – Proceedings. Numerous papers of varying merit read at annual meetings of the Propeller Club.

Americana Annual, since 1923, like *Britannica Book of the Year,* and *Collier's Year Book,* is useful for keeping track of current developments.

*Brassey's Naval Annual, 1886-1949. One of the most valuable single sources of modern naval history. Each issue contains articles on various aspects of naval development, in addition to factual data on ships of all navies; almost the only source in English, except Jane's, below, for adequate information on the navies of Continental Europe. From 1921 to 1935, it was expanded to include merchant shipping. In 1950, it became *Brassey's Annual: The Armed Forces Yearbook,* including armies and aviation.

*Jane's Fighting Ships, annual since 1898. Like Brassey, covers all the nations of the world, but with more details and diagrams of individual ships and classes, but with much less general critical comment. Original title, *All the World's Fighting Ships.*

Jane's All the World's Aircraft, annual since 1909. Includes naval aviation.

Jane's Weapons Systems, annual since 1969. Result of new missile development, etc.

The Journal of Commerce Annual Review (Liverpool). Articles on many aspects of maritime activity, interspersed with advertisements which also contain significant information.

Merchant Ships, World Built, annual since 1953. Data on all new ships of over 1,000 gross tons.

*The Naval Review, annual since 1963; an impressive "American Brassey's," edited by Frank Uhlig, Jr., for the U.S. Naval Institute at Annapolis. Wide variety of pertinent articles by authorities in their respective fields. Well illustrated.

New York Times Encyclopedic Almanac, annual since 1970.

The Shipping World Yearbook, annual since 1887. The original subtitle ran "A Desk Manual in Trade, Commerce, and Navigation." This was expanded to "General Maritime Information, Statutory Rules and Regulations, Statistical Tables, Classified World Directories of Shipowners, Shipbuilders, Towing Services, Marine Engine Builders, etc.; Training for the Merchant Marine; Shipping and Shipbuilding Organizations; 'Who's Who in the Shipping World.' " Emphasis strictly British.

*The Statesman's Yearbook: Statistical and Historical Annual of the World, annual since 1864. Wealth of data on exports, imports, navies and shipping of each country.

Whittaker's Almanac, annual since 1868. Similar but less specific data.

The World Almanac, annual since 1887. *The Statesman's Yearbook* and *Whittaker's* are British; the *World Almanac,* and *New York Times Encyclopedic Almanac,* American. *The Statesman's Yearbook* has the most useful collection of full statistics on the commerce, shipping, and navies of the various countries.

B - 3   Specialized Dictionaries and Glossaries

Ansted, A. *A Dictionary of Sea Terms, for the Use of Yachtsmen, Amateur Boatsmen and Others,* 1898.

Bradford, G. *A Glossary of Sea Terms,* 1927, 1942.

Falconer, A.F. *A Glossary of Shakespeare's Sea and Naval Terms, Including Gunnery,* 1965.

*Falconer, W. *A New and Universal Dictionary of the Marine,* 1804, R1970.
————. *Old Wooden Walls: An Abridged Edition of Falconer's Celebrated Marine Directory,* ed. C.S. Gill, 1930.

Firth, F.E., ed. *The Encyclopedia of Marine Resources,* 1969. 125 articles, from abalone to whaling, by recognized specialists.

Fruchtman, T. *Illustrated Ship's Dictionary: A Handy Compendium of the Most Commonly Used Terms,* 1951.

Garoche, P. *Dictionary of Commodities Carried by Ship,* 1952, R1970.

Gaynor, F., ed. *New Military and Naval Dictionary,* 1951.

Groener, L. *Illustrated Marine Encyclopedia,* 1948.

*(Hamersly, L.R. & Co., pub.), *A Naval Encyclopedia; Comprising a Dictionary of Nautical Words and Phrases; Biographical Notices, and Records of Naval Officers; Special Articles of Naval Art and Science . . . together with Descriptions of the Principal Naval Stations and Seaports of the World,* 1881.

Heinl, R.D., Jr., ed. *Dictionary of Military and Naval Quotations,* 1966.

*Homans, I.S. *A Cyclopedia of Commerce and Commercial Navigation,* 2 v. 1859-60, R1970.

Hunt, L.M. and Graves, D.C., eds. *A Glossary of Ocean Science and Undersea Technology Terms,* 1965.

Huxley, A.J. *Standard Encyclopedia of the World's Oceans and Islands,* 1963.

*Kerchove, R. de. *International Maritime Dictionary. An Encyclopedic Dictionary of Useful Maritime Terms and Phrases, together with their equivalents in French and German,* 1948. Its 946 pp. contain the most up-to-date and comprehensive coverage.

*Mason, H.B., ed. *Encyclopedia of Ships and Shipping,* 1908. Whereas the Hamersly emphasis is American, this is British. It includes details of individual steamship lines, with lists of ships; warships of various navies, alphabetically by individual names; biographies of prominent naval officers, shipowners, etc., and accounts of principal shipyards.

*McCulloch, J.R. *A Dictionary, Practical, Theoretical, Historical, of Commerce, and Commercial Navigation,* 2 v. 1837 ff. A British counterpart of the American Homans.

McEwen, W.A. and Lewis, A.H. *Encyclopedia of Nautical Knowledge,* 1954.

Montefiore, J. *A Commercial Dictionary; Containing the Present State of Mercantile Law, Practice and Custom,* 1804.

Mortimer, T. *A General Dictionary of Commerce, Trade and Manufactures, exhibiting their state in every part of the World,* 1810.

Noel, J.V., Jr. and Bush, T.J. *Naval Terms Dictionary,* 1952, RP1966.

*Postlethwayt, M. *Universal Dictionary of Trade and Commerce,* 4th ed., 2 v. 1774. His original version was based on the French dictionary of Savary; there was considerable international "borrowing" in those early days before copyright laws tightened. Like the other old dictionaries, this gives much contemporary information about various countries, ports, commodities, etc. not to be found in the later secondary volumes. This is particularly useful for the nations and ports of Continental Europe, about which there is amazingly little available in English.

Riverain, J. *Concise Encyclopedia of Explorations,* 1969.

U.S. Naval History Division, *Glossary of Naval Abbreviations,* 1945, R1970. Because the wartime naval documents and reports were sprinkled with such improvised abbreviations as "JOSCO," "JICPOA," "AdComPhibsPac" and "Nobduchar" which might be thoroughly unintelligible to later scholars, this compiler arranged, as part of the Navy's administrative history program, that they be gathered and translated while still intelligible. Lt. Cdr. D.E. Richard brought them together by the thousands, and did likewise in the *Glossary of Naval Code Names, World War II*, 1947.

B – 4   Manuals

Armstrong, W.E. *Purser's Handbook,* 1965.

*Blunt, J. *The Shipmaster's Assistant and Commercial Digest,* 1837 ff, R1970. Scope indicated by chapter headings: 1, Ships; 2, Navigation Acts; 3, Custom House Laws; 4, Fisheries; 5, Revenue Cutters; 6, Shipowners; 7, Shipmasters; 8, Seamen; 9, Consuls; 10, Freight; 11, General Average; 12, Salvage; 13, Bottomry and Respondentia; 14, Marine Insurance; 15, Factors and Agents; 16, The Navy; 17, Pensions; 18, Crimes; 19, Slaves; 20, Wrecks; 21, Quarantine; 22, Passengers; 23, Pilots; 24, Bills of Exchange; 25, Exchange; 26, Weights and Measures; 27, Harbor Regulations – U.S.; 28, Commercial Regulations – Foreign. American, while most of other old ones are British.

Hopkins, F.N. *Business and Law for the Shipmaster,* 1966.

Kirkaldy, A.W. *British Shipping,* 1914, R1970.

*McDowell, C.E. and Gibbs, H.M. *Ocean Transportation,* 1954. "Shipping industry techniques, practices and problems from the ship owners' and operators' point of view." Parts: 1, Shipping in the World Economy; 2, The Shipping Process; 3, The Finance of Shipping; 4, Admiralty, Insurance, and Regulations; 5, The Role of Government.

Pope, C., ed. *The Merchant Ship-Owner and Ship-Master's Import and Export Guide, comprising every species of authentic information relating to Shipping, Navigation and Commerce . . . .* 7th ed. 1838 ff. British.

*Rosenthal, M.S. *Techniques of International Trade,* 1954. "Export . . . from the start of the interior journey to overseas shipment, with special attention given to transportation." Chapters: 1, The Contract; 2, The Overseas Shipment; 3, Customs Procedure; 4, Marine Insurance; 5, Packing the Overseas Shipment; 6, Financing Export and Import Shipments; 7, Foreign Exchange; 8, Carriage of Goods by Air; 9, Communications.

Steel, D. *The Ship-Master's Assistant and Owner's Manual,* 6th ed. 1795.

*Thornton, R.H. *British Shipping,* 1939, R1959.

C   GOVERNMENT DOCUMENTS

The official publications of Great Britain and the United States can yield a wealth of material pertinent to maritime and naval history, once one masters the mystery of how to get at them. Instead of the usual clear-cut author arrangement for identifying particular works, the government anonymity is further complicated by arrangements resting more on tradition than upon logic. This section, which is a devilish one to compress into brief space, is designed to get the uninitiated within striking distance of the most useful sources.

C – 1 British Documents

a. Early Collections

G.B., Public Records Office, *Calendar of State Papers, Domestic Series (Cal. S.P., Dom.)*, 1558-(1704), 90 v. 1856-1924.

The phrase "calendar" means that the entries are arranged in chronological order. All these series are well indexed. Consult index under "Navy," "Ships," "Trade," etc.

G.B., *Calendar of State Papers and Manuscripts relating to English Affairs, existing in the Archives and Collections of Venice and other Libraries of North Italy (Cal.S.P., Venetian)*, 1202-1672, 37 v. Shrewd observations of Venetian diplomats on maritime matters of England, Holland, Spain, etc.
——————. *Calendar of State Papers, Colonial Series, East Indies*, etc. *(Cal.S.P., Col.,E.I.)*, 1513-1634, 5 v.
Vols. 2, 3, 4, 6, 8 of Colonial Series.
*——————. *Calendar of State Papers, Colonial Series, America and West Indies*, 1574-(1733), 35 v. *(Cal.S.P.,Col.,A. & W.I.)*. The numbering of the Colonial Series, totalling 40 so far, includes the five East India volumes noted above. The series contains a wealth of material on maritime subjects, with the opportunity for many good papers, covering in detail for a brief period of years either any colony from Massachusetts to Barbados, or any particular commodity.
——————. *Journals of the Commissioners of Trade and Plantations*, 1704-1782, 14 v. The journals of this colonial regulatory body were included in the above "A. & W.I." series until 1704; thereafter, they should be used in conjunction with that series in studying a particular subject.

b. Parliamentary Papers - General

Despite their obvious external differences in appearance and arrangement, the tall quarto volumes of the "Sessional Papers" and the chunkier octavos of the American Congressional Documents contain very much the same sort of basic material. Three particular categories in both series have a wealth of material valuable in the study of maritime and naval history:

(1) The reports of committees or commissions, especially when they were preceded by hearings. The hundreds of pages of testimony of witnesses, pro and con, can yield much in the way of facts and ideas on a given subject; attendant documents often further the utility of such sources.

(2) Basic reports and statistical tables, recurring year after year, constitute one of the two main features of value in the British "Accounts and Papers" and the American "Documents." By going through a succession of such sources, one can take off significant figures or trace particular developments.

(3) The other main feature of the "Accounts and Papers" and "Documents" consists of an even greater volume of miscellaneous matter, statistical or otherwise, varying from year to year. The indexes are particularly helpful for running down such scattered material.

The following analysis of the British and American legislative collections will center around that threefold distinction. Of the other elements in the series, the journals of the respective houses and the lists of bills are of concern only if one is tracing the course of a particular measure.

c. Parliamentary Papers – Organization

The most convenient guide to the British papers is H.B. Lees-Smith, *A Guide to Parliamentary and Official Papers*, 1924.

The present organization of the papers goes back to the formation of the United Kingdom in 1801. Some of the earlier papers were gathered into a collection of *Reports of the House of Commons, 1715-1803*, with an index. Thereafter, the volumes each year fell into four categories: "Bills," "Committee Reports," "Commission Reports," and "Accounts and Papers;" in 1890, those categories filled 9, 9, 22, and 44 volumes respectively. The normal method of citing, and thus enabling one to locate, a particular paper is to give: (1) the year of the session; (2) the serial number of the paper for that session, indicated at the bottom of each of its pages; (3) the volume in which it is located. Also, given in the index but not usually cited outside, the page in the volume. Thus, the "Naval Estimates" for 1890 would be cited: "*Parl. Papers*, 1890(70), XLIV." The chief exception to that normal system was that, after 1870, certain categories of papers became known as "Command Papers," with cumulative serial numbers, running through session after session, preceded by a "C," "Cd," "Cmd," and then "Comd."

d. Parliamentary Indexes

The system of indexes, essential to locating those needles in haystacks, is somewhat complicated. Since 1831, there has always been an annual index in the final volume for the session; one can always fall back on that. For the House of Commons series, there is an overall index for 1801-1852. After that, the cumulative indexes cover briefer periods:

Years Covered	Parl. Paper Location	Years Covered	Parl. Paper Location
1852-69	1870, v. 71	1890-99	1904, v. 112
1870-79	1880, v. 83	1900-09	1911, v. 104
1880-89	1889, v. 89	1910-19	1926, v. 31

The House of Lords has an initial index for 1801-59, with supplements for 1859-70 and 1871-85 but these are less useful than the Commons series. There is also an unofficial index, published by P.S. King, *Catalogue of Parliamentary Papers, 1801-1900*, by Hilda V. Jones, with supplements for 1901-10 and 1911-20, but it lacks the volume and serial citations.

e. Committee and Commission Reports

Unlike Congress, where much is delegated to permanent "standing" committees, Parliament has tended to utilize either temporary "select" committees ("S.C.") of its members, or Royal Commissions ("R.C.") of prominent outsiders. For the later, see A.H. Cole, *A Finding-List of British Royal Commission Reports: 1860 to 1935*, 1935. The hearings and report are in the same volume. Among the more pertinent and useful reports, rich in material for research, are:

1796-1801, *Reports . . . 1715-1803*, XIV – S.C. – London Port.

1802-06, S.C., "Committee of Naval Enquiry," 14 reports, scattered through regular series, also bound separately.

1806-09, S.C., "Committee of Naval Revision," 13 v., scattered; cf. index.

1831 (65,320) V-VI – S.C., Trade between G.B., the East Indies and China (preliminary to abolition of final Company monopoly, 1833).

1847 (2327) X – S.C., Navigation Laws; also 1847-48 (7), XX.

1859 (2469) VI – R.C., Manning the Navy.

1860 (530) XIII – S.C., Merchant Shipping.

1866 (3596) V – R.C., Unseaworthy Ships; also 1874 (1027), V (preliminary to Plimsoll reforms).

1878 (205) XXI – S.C., Merchant Seaman Bill.

*1886 (C4893) XXI-XXIII – R.C., "Depression of Trade and Industry," V. 9-11 (wealth of data on German competition, etc.).

1909 (Cd4668) XLVII-XLVIII – R.C., Shipping Rings and Deferred Rebates.

1929 (Cmd3282) VII, Committee on Industry and Trade ("Balfour Committee"), final report; see also its earlier detailed reports.

f. Special Accounts and Papers

1897 (C8449) LXI, Trade of British Empire and Foreign Competition: Despatch by Mr. Chamberlain to Governors of Colonies and Replies Thereto.

1899 (C9078) Foreign Trade Competition; Opinions of Her Majesty's Diplomatic and Consular Officers on British Trade Methods.

g. Continuing Documents

These reports, usually annual and sometimes changing wording of title from time to time, are sometimes also found outside the Parliamentary Papers; for location of such collections, and for many other titles beyond this brief list, see Winifred Gregory, ed., *List of the Serial Publications of Foreign Governments, 1815-1931*, 1932. Particularly useful are:

*Naval Estimates (detailed statement of Navy's need for coming year).

*Annual Statement of the Trade and Navigation of the United Kingdom with Foreign Countries and British Possessions.

*Annual Statement of the Navigation and Shipping of the United Kingdom.

Statistical Abstract for the several Colonial and other Possessions.

Statistical Abstract for the Principal Foreign Countries.

(The Statistical Abstracts consist of statistics for several years, instead of just one.)

*Reports of Consuls: Annual Series of Trade Reports.

h. Miscellaneous Accounts and Papers

These can cover almost everything; one is never sure as to what gems may be unearthed among the great mass of trivia. A few samples from 1890 include: Narrative of the Naval Maneuvers; Progress of British Merchant Shipping; Return of Ships arriving . . . from foreign ports with live cattle aboard, showing loss of human and animal life; Coal shipped coastwise and exported; and Statistical report of the health of the Navy, while, twenty years earlier, 1870 (255), XLIV was "Statement of the Custom of the Royal Navy and Marines as to wearing beards."

i. Legislative Process

For tracing the progress of a particular measure through Parliament, consult the *Journals* of Lords and Commons. The exchange of rival views on a subject can be found in the *Parliamentary Debates,* which bore the name of Hansard until 1912. The full text of all acts passed by Parliament can be found in the *Statutes at Large* to 1868; for later acts, see the *Statutes Revised* to 1899; then *Statutory Rules and Orders* to 1947; and *Statutory Instruments,* 1948 ff.

j. Manuscript Sources

The principal British official sources are located in the Public Records Office in London. The most useful guides to these include M.S. Giuseppi, *A Guide to the Records Preserved in the Public Records Office,* 2 v. 1923-24, and Charles Johnson, *The Public Records Office* (Helps to Students of History), 1918. Specific American maritime records will be found in *Abstract of English Shipping Records relating to Massachusetts Ports, 1686-1717,* from original records for Essex Institute; and Virginia Committee on Colonial Records, *The British Public Records Office, History, Description, of Record Groups, Finding Aids, and Materials for American History, with special reference to Virginia,* 1960.

C – 2   United States Documents

For general guidance, A.M. Boyd and R.E. Rips, *United States Government Publications,* 3rd ed. 1949, is probably the most helpful work.

a. Early Collections

In 1832, the Government began to publish many of the major documents since 1789 in a valuable series of folio volumes entitled:
American State Papers.   Documents, Legislative and Executive of the Congress of the United States.   Selected and edited under the Authority of Congress, 38 v. 1832-61.
    Class I. *Foreign Relations,* 1789-1828, 6 v. (A.S.P.,F.R.)
    Class IV. *Commerce and Navigation,* 1789-1823, 2 v. (A.S.P.,C.N.)
    Class VI. *Naval Affairs,* 1794-1836, 4 v. (A.S.P., Naval). At the front of each volume is a detailed table of contents, describing each document by title, so that a quick survey is easy.

b. Regular Congressional Series

A basic factor in the Congessional documents is the heavy emphasis upon each two-year Congress as a fundamental unit; on Capitol Hill, this is not 1972, but rather "92nd Congress, 2nd Session." The present system of organization dates from around 1817; before that, and even for a while afterward, it is more convenient to use the *American State Papers.* Once they took form, the Congressional documents fell into four major categories, aside from the Journals, which were integrated into the system. There were *Senate Reports, Senate Documents, House Reports, House Documents.* The Documents, roughly equivalent to the British

Accounts and Papers, were at times further divided into "Executive" and "Miscellaneous" series in one house or both. The standard citation of a particular paper had four essential parts: the Congress, session, series, and the number of the paper within that series for the session. Typical citations would be "40th Cong., 1st Sess. (or 40-1 for brevity), S.Doc. 123," or "50th Cong. 2nd Sess., H.Rep. 456." A fifth factor, convenient, not mandatory, developed later; to aid libraries, etc., in locating the books, each volume was assigned a cumulative serial number, starting in 1817 and running to the present; this is the quickest way to call for a desired volume.

c. Indexes

The American indexes nominally cover all Government documents. Virtually all the documents, however, even if issued by the executive departments, were included in the Congressional series at least until this century. Each of the four main Congressional series sometimes had its own index for the session. The first major index was *A Descriptive Catalogue of the Government Publications of the United States, September 5, 1774, to March 4, 1881, compiled by Benjamin P. Poore* (48-2,Sen.Misc.Doc. 67), 1885. That was followed by *A Comprehensive Index to the Publications of the United States Government, 1881-1893* (58-2,H.Doc.754), 2 v. 1905. Thereafter, indexing went on an annual basis, with the *Catalogue of the Public Documents of the United States,* commonly known as *Document Catalogue,* issued by the Superintendent of Documents for each two-year Congress, starting in 1893. The arrangement of these indexes makes it more difficult to run down major topics than in the British ones. Two further useful sources are the *Index to Reports of Committees,* compiled by T.H. McKee, 1887, and the *Checklist of U.S. Public Documents,* 1789-1909, issued by the Superintendent of Documents, 3rd ed., 1911. For a complete bibliography of all naval items in the Congressional Documents, see R.W. Neeser, *A Statistical and Chronological History of the United States Navy, 1775-1907,* 2 v. 1909, vol. I.

d. Committee Reports

Occasionally Congress appointed a "select" or "special" committee of the Parliamentary type to handle a specific task, but the bulk of its business was in the hands of permanent "standing" committees. Those most concerned with maritime-naval matters were Senate Naval Affairs, Senate Commerce, House Naval Affairs, and House Merchant Marine and Fisheries ("HMM&F" below). Whereas the British hearings almost invariably accompanied the reports, the Congressional hearings frequently went into the Documents series even in the old days. Gradually, around the turn of the century, they disappeared completely from the regular Congressional Documents series and became a distinct problem to locate. Some hearings for the previous decades are shelved according to their subject matter, rather than with the public documents. Full-dress hearings were not common before 1860. Among the most important in this field are:

1870   H.Sel.Com. on Causes of the Reduction of American Tonnage ("Lynch Report"), 41-2, H.Rep. 28.

*1876   House Naval Affairs, Naval Investigation, 3 v. 44-1, H.Exec.Doc. 170.
The most searching investigation to which the Navy was ever subjected. The exposure of inefficiency and corruption in the Shore Establishment helped to bring on the "New Navy" reforms.

1882   Joint Sel. Com. on American Shipbuilding, 47-2, H.Rep. 1827.
1890   HMM&F, American Merchant Marine in Foreign Trade, 51-1, H.Rep. 1210, "Farquhar Report."
1911   HMM&F, Seamen's Bill.
*1913-14   HMM&F, Shipping Combinations, 4 v.
1916   HMM&F, Creating a Shipping Board, etc.
1919   HMM&F, Government Control of Radio Communication.
*1921   Senate Naval Affairs, Subcom. Naval Investigation.
       The Sims-Daniels dispute over civilian vs. military control.
1944   H.Sel.Com. ("Woodrum"), on Post-War Military Policy.
       The opening gun in the Army-Air Force drive for a "merger."
*1946   Joint Committee on the Pearl Harbor Attack, 39 parts in 22 v.
       This "four-foot shelf" made public much that might otherwise have been locked in the files for years; opportunity for many interesting papers.
1947   Senate Armed Services, National Defense Establishment; similar final hearings on House Expenditures in Executive Departments.
*1949   House Armed Services, National Defense Program – Unification and Strategy.
       Dramatic airing of rival viewpoints; the Chief of Naval Operations was dismissed shortly after testifying.
1950   Sen. Interstate & For. Com., Merchant Marine Study and Investigation, 7 parts. Final Report (81 S.Rep. 2494).

e. Continuing Documents

Many, but not all, of these were at one time included in the Congressional series, but libraries often have separate copies. They are often listed in the card catalogue under "U.S." and then the particular bureau or office that issued them; e.g., "U.S., Bureau of Statistics." The Navy Department remained relatively unchanged, but the commercial series was affected by the creation of the Department of Commerce and Labor in 1903 and the Department of Commerce in 1913, as well as by the Shipping Board of 1916, becoming a Bureau of Commerce in 1933; the Maritime Commission in 1936, Maritime Administration in 1950 and Federal Maritime Commission in 1962. The references below indicate the original and latest issuing groups. (Abbreviations: "Bu" for Bureau; "F&DCom" for Foreign & Domestic Commerce.) The following are all useful:

*Annual Report of the Secretary of the Navy, since 1798.
       Early reports in A.S.P., Naval. Until 1933, included appendix with reports of bureaus and offices; irregular issues during World War II; since 1948 in Report of the Secretary of Defense.
Navy Register, since 1814. See Sect. E.
Navy Yearbook, 1904-21, Sen. Naval Affairs Com.
*(Foreign) Commerce and Navigation of the U.S., 1821-1954;
       Register of the Treas., BuCensus. "Foreign" added to title in 1888.
*United States Imports of Merchandise for Consumption (FT110), since 1954.
*United States Exports of Domestic and Foreign Merchandise (FT410), since 1954.
Annual Report of the Commissioner of Navigation, 1884-1923; BuNav. Not to be confused with Navy's BuNav.
Merchant Marine Statistics, since 1924; BuNav., BuMarine Insp. and Nav. See Sect. D for above three titles.
Statistical Abstract of the U.S., since 1878; BuStatistics, BuCensus. See Sect. D.
*Merchant Vessels of the U.S., since 1867; BuStatistics, BuMarine Insp. and Nav.

Ocean Going Merchant Fleets of Principal Maritime Nations, 1921-41; Shipping Board, Maritime Com.

*Commercial Relations of the U.S. with Foreign Countries, since 1856, State Dept., BuF&DCom. These consular reports, like those of the British series, are valuable for study of foreign nations or ports, as well as for general trade conditions.

Special Consular Reports, 1890-1923, id.

Special Agents Series, 1906-24; BuManufactures, BuF&DCom.

Miscellaneous Series, id.

*Trade Promotion Series, since 1924; BuF&DCom.

Formed by combining the above three series. The scores of substantial studies in these series are rich in material on a wide variety of commercial topics.

Foreign Relations of the U.S., since 1861; State Dept.

f. Other Documents

The practice of including so many of the general publications of the executive departments made the Documents series even more heterogeneous than the Parliamentary Accounts and Papers. Some of these were substantial books of real value. 32-1, Sen.Exec.Doc.112 was the *Report . . . on the Trade and Commerce of the British North American Colonies and upon the Trade of the Great Lakes and Rivers,* by Consul Israel D. Andrews, a fat work still valuable with its rich detail. Likewise 44-2, Sen.Exec.Doc. 27 was the *Report of Chief Engineer J.W. King, United States Navy, on European Ships of War and their Armament, Naval Administration and Economy, Marine Constructions, Torpedo Warfare, Dock-yards, etc.,* later successfully published privately as *The War-Ships and Navies of the World,* 1880. There were also useful collections of all the official documents in connection with such events as Commodore Jones's premature seizure of Monterey in 1842, the Perry expedition to Japan, the Samoan crisis of 1889, and many others. It was probably to separate the wheat from the chaff to some extent that the Documents were for a long time divided into the "Executive" and "Miscellaneous" series – the latter really was miscellaneous. As the fat "Document Catalogue" indicates, there is a tremendous volume of Government publication, much of it now outside the Congressional series. Its main drawback lies in the difficulty in locating and citing it, without the usual convenient author designation.

g. The Legislative Process

The American sources for this are almost identical in nature with those described for the British. The Senate and House Journals are incorporated in the regular series. The debates are in four successive series, *Annals of the Congress of the U.S. ("Annals of Congress"),* 42 v. 1789-1824; *Register of Debates in Congress (Congressional Debates),* 29 v. 1825-37; *Congressional Globe, Containing the Debates and Proceedings,* 108 v. 1833-73; and *Congressional Record,* since 1873. The full text of all the acts and resolutions can be found in the *Statutes at Large.*

h. Manuscript Sources

A valuable general guide to official American manuscript sources is *P.M. Hamer, *A Guide to Archival Manuscripts in the United States, compiled for the National*

Historical Publications Commission, 1961. For the National Archives, the American equivalent of the Public Records Office, the most useful publications are:

Guide to the Records in the National Archives, 1948.

Guide to Federal Archives Relating to the Civil War, 1962.

Handbook of Federal World War Agencies and their Records, 1917-1921, 1943.

Federal Records of World War II; vol. 1, *Civilian Agencies*, 1950; vol. 2, *Military Agencies*, 1951.

Preliminary Inventories (Each of these, in addition to indicating the various groups of records, gives a useful sketch of the agency.)
Navy Department: 6. Bureau of Medicine and Surgery, 1948; 10. Bureau of Yards and Docks, 1948; 26. Bureau of Aeronautics, 1951; 33. Bureau of Ordnance, 1951; 39. Hydrographic Office, 1952; 73. United States Marine Corps, 1954; 85. Office of the Chief of Naval Operations, 1955; 123. Bureau of Naval Personnel, 1960; 133. Bureau of Ships, 1961.
Other: 13. Naval Establishments Created Overseas During World War II, 1948; 20. Maritime Labor Board, 1949; 63. Special Committee of the Senate to Investigate Air-Mail and Ocean-Mail Contracts, 1953; 90. United States Antarctic Service, 1955; 91. Panama Canal, 1956; 97. United States Shipping Board, 1956; 105. Coast and Geodetic Survey, 1958; 116. U.S. District Court for the Southern District of New York, 1959; 121. Shipbuilding Stabilization Committee, 1959.

Preliminary Checklist of the Naval Records Collection of the Office of Naval Records and Library, 1775-1910, 1945.

D   GUIDES TO PhD THESES

The first general American list was the *List of American Doctoral Dissertations Printed in 1912* by the Library of Congress and continued annually until 1938. By that time, the H.W. Wilson Co. was publishing *Doctoral Dissertations accepted by American Universities*, annually, 1934-54, including unpublished as well as published theses. In 1938 appeared the first issue of *Microfilm Abstracts: A Collection of Abstracts of Doctoral Dissertations which are Available in Complete Form on Microfilm*, 1938-51, by University Microfilms of Ann Arbor, Mich. In 1951, continuing the same volume numbering, this became *Dissertation Abstracts, A Guide to Dissertations and Monographs Available in Microfilm*, with a summary of each thesis and the price for reproducing it in microfilm or Xerox. In 1955, the Wilson list of all theses, whether microfilmed or not, was coordinated with the above by University Microfilms as *Index to American Doctoral Dissertations*. In addition to the above series, the American Historical Association from time to time has issued a list of theses "in progress" and completed. For unpublished theses before 1938, it is necessary to consult the publications of the individual universities.

For British theses, masters' as well as doctoral, and even Oxford "B. Litt" titles, the Institute of Historical Research began to publish annual lists in *History*, 1920-28 and then, 1929-32, in its *Bulletin*. Since 1932, it has issued annual supplements of "Theses Completed" and "Theses in Progress." In addition, "Aslib" since 1950 has published an annual *Index to Theses Accepted for Higher De-*

grees in the Universities of Great Britain and Ireland. Numerous titles in maritime and naval history will be found among the MA theses not included in this bibliography. That is even more true of the Commonwealth universities where MA theses are very numerous and PhDs very rare.

E STATISTICS

E – 1 British and General

Allen, R.G.D. and Ely, J.E. *International Trade Statistics,* 1953.

Clark, G.N. *Guide to English Commercial Statistics, 1696-1782,* 1938.

*Great Britain, Board of Trade, "Annual Statement of the Trade and Navigation of the U.K." "Annual Statement of the Navigation and Shipping of the U.K." and "Statistical Abstracts." These annual statements in the Parliamentary Papers, just described, have been the basic source of figures on British foreign trade and shipping. For the major aspects, they have been ably adjusted and interpreted in the works of Mitchell and Deane and Schumpeter below, which are more reliable than the earlier works of James Marshall, John Macgregor, William Page and G.R. Porter. For specific details about particular regions, however, the earlier sources will furnish relatively accurate data.

Macpherson, D. *Annals of Commerce,* 4 v. 1805. Detailed annual tables of 18th century commerce with individual countries and colonies, to be used as suggested above.

*Mitchell, B.R. and Deane P. *Abstract of British Historical Statistics,* 1962. Like the similar volume of *Historical Statistics of the United States* noted below, this is a valuable addition to any general or private historical library. It "gives all the important economic statistics available for the United Kingdom over as long a historical period as possible. . . . The book will be a standard work for economists and historians. It relieves all who need to use British historical statistics from the labor of identifying and assessing original material and extracting comparable series; and it offers informed access to a very wide range of economic data." The following tables are particularly useful for maritime history: p. 217, Shipping Registered in the U.K., 1788-1938, distinguishing sail and steam; p. 220, Ships Built, 1787-1938, distinguishing sail and steam; p. 223, same, 1850-1908, also distinguishing wood, iron and steel hulls; p. 224, Index of Tramp Shipping Freights, 1869-1936; p. 279, Official Values of Overseas Trade, Imports, Domestic Exports, Re-exports, 1697-1804; p. 282, same, showing computed and official values, 1796-1956; p. 285, Official Values of Principal Imports (various commodities), 1700-1856; p. 293, same, Principal Domestic Exports, 1697-1829; p. 296, same, Principal Re-exports, 1800-1856; p. 298, Value at Current Prices of Principal Imports, 1854-1938; p. 302, same, Principal Domestic Exports, 1814-1938; p. 307, same, Principal Re-exports, 1854-1938; p. 309, Value of Imports, Domestic Exports and Re-exports by principal overseas regions, 1710-1938; p. 328, Indices of the Volume of Overseas Trade, 1796-1947; p. 333, Balance of Payments, 1816-1938. Also, special items: p. 47, Passengers to and from U.K. Ports; Wheat, pp. 94, 100; Coal, pp. 108, 112, 120; Metals, 139, 144, 161, 164, 169; Cotton, Wool and Textiles, 177, 180, 182, 190, 195, 201, 205, 209.

*Schumpeter, E.B. *English Overseas Trade Statistics, 1697-1808,* 1960.

The Statesman's Yearbook, annual since 1864. The most convenient summary of the basic maritime and naval figures for Britain and most other countries, right up to the present.

The World Almanac, annual since 1887. Less complete figures, but useful for world merchant fleets and a few other items.

E – 2 American

*Albion, R.G. *The Rise of New York Port, 1815-1860,* 1939, R1970. Appendix tables include for 12 principal ports, c1815-60: p. 389, relative maritime activity; p. 390, exports and imports; p. 392, tonnage entered and cleared; p. 402, tonnage registered, enrolled and licensed; p. 406, shipbuilding; p. 394, "Foreign and Coastwise Arrivals at New York, Boston and Philadelphia, 1835."

Homans, I.S. *An Historical and Statistical Account of the Foreign Commerce of the United States,* 1857, R1970. Convenient tables of the annual commerce of each state and with each foreign country, 1820-1856; also annual import and export tables of each colony, 1700-1776. More useful than the earlier private works of Adam Seybert and Timothy Pitkin.

Morison, S.E. *Maritime History of Massachusetts, 1783-1860,* 1921, P1961. Appendix tables include: p. 395, cod and mackerel fisheries of Mass., 1837-65; p. 396, arrivals from certain foreign ports at five U.S. ports, 1857; p. 397, foreign places whence vessels arrived at Mass. ports, 1857; p. 398, tonnage of shipping owned in each Mass. district and New York City, 1798-1860.

*U.S. Bureau of the Census, *Historical Statistics of the United States: Colonial Times to 1957,* 1960. Prepared with cooperation of the Social Science Research Council; supersedes 1949 edition. Like the Mitchell and Deane volume for Britain, a "must" for the scholar. Most useful tables: p. 444, documented merchant vessels, major classes and materials, 1789-1957; same, showing trade in which engaged; p. 450, tonnage entered and cleared, 1789-1957; p. 452, value of waterborne imports and exports, 1790-1946; p. 454, Great Lakes, Panama, and Canal traffic; p. 455, expenditures on rivers and harbors, 1822-1957; p. 542, value of exports and imports by commodities; p. 550, same by country of destination or origin. The tables are all kept up to date in the annual issues of the *Statistical Abstract of the United States.*

*U.S. Register of the Treasury, Bureau of the Census *(Foreign) Commerce and Navigation of the United States,* annual, 1821-1953. Counterpart of the British "Trade and Navigation" and "Navigation and Shipping" series. Indispensable for the study of particular seaports or commodities. Up to 1821, the national trade statistics were decidedly inadequate, particularly in respect to exports and the trade of individual districts. The tables of this series showed, for any one of the 90-odd customs districts, the value of imports and exports from or to each foreign country; the amount of particular commodities in such trade; and the tonnage entered or cleared from or to each country. One could also find the countries to which each of the nation's individual commodities were exported and from which particular import commodities were received. The only important gap in the figures was the lack of data on the domestic

18

coasting trade. A student working on a particular port or commodity could profitably work through these reports year by year, mining out significant tables on sheets of graph paper. Since 1954, the commercial statistics have been continued in two new Bureau of the Census series: *United States Imports of Merchandise for Consumption* (FT 110) and *United States Exports of Domestic and Foreign Merchandise* (FT 410). At first, *Commerce and Navigation* also showed the tonnage registered, enrolled and licensed in each district; the tonnage built; and by states, the number of ships, brigs, schooners, etc., built. That was taken over in 1884 by the *Annual Report of the Commissioner of Navigation* and then in 1924 by *Merchant Marine Statistics*.

U.S. Bureau of Statistics, *Exports of Manufactures from the United States and Their Distribution by Articles and Countries, 1800 to 1906*, 1907.

F   LISTS OF SHIPS

Albion, R.G. *Square-Riggers on Schedule: The New York Sailing Packets to England, France and the Cotton Ports*, 1938, R1965. Full tabular data on each vessel. See Sect. I.

*American Bureau of Shipping, *Record of American and Foreign Shipping*, annual since 1867, when it was established by the American Shipmasters' Association, with the title changed to above in 1898. A "classification" organization like Lloyd's Register and the Bureau Veritas, it gives full data on thousands of vessels.

American Lloyd's Registry of American and Foreign Shipping, started in 1857 as the *New York Marine Register*, changing to *American Lloyd's* in 1858 and continuing until about 1880 when it was absorbed by the *Record* above.

Anderson, R.C., et al. *Lists of Men-of-war, 1650-1700*, 5 parts, 1935-39. Part 1, English; 2, French; 3, Swedish; 4, Danish-Norwegian; 5, German. Anderson edited the English volume.

Blackman, R.V.V. *The World's Warships*, 4th ed. 1970. A compact work, by the editor of *Jane's Fighting Ships*.

Brassey's Naval Annual, See Sect. B-2. Less specific after it became *The Armed Forces Year-book* in 1950.

Brown, V.W. *Shipping in the Port of Annapolis, 1748-1775*, 1965. Includes list of every vessel that cleared Annapolis in those years, with name, rig, stern type, build, hailing port, master, and owners. Same table also included in *Naval Documents of the American Revolution*, ed. W.N. Clark, v. I, 1964.

*Colledge, J.J. *Ships of the Royal Navy: An Historical Index*, 2 v. 1969-70. V. 1, 13,000 major vessels, with tonnage, armament, builder, etc.; v. 2, Navy-built trawlers, drifters, tugs, etc.

Craig, R. and Jarvis, R. *Liverpool Registry of Merchant Ships* (Chetham Society), 1968. All Liverpool ships afloat in 1786 and for some years thereafter. See Sect. X-4d.

Cumpston, J.S. *Shipping Arrivals and Departures – Sydney, 1788-1825,* P1964.

Clowes, Sir W.L., ed. *The Royal Navy, A History from the Earliest Times to the Present,* 7 v. 1897-1903. Scattered through appropriate chapters are lists of the principal warships constructed, and of those participating in the various operations and engagements.

*Cutler, C.C. *Greyhounds of the Sea: The Story of the American Clipper Ship,* 1930, R1961. See Sect. I and also clipper studies of A.H. Clark, and O.T. Howe and F.C. Matthews.
* —————. *Queens of the Western Ocean, The Story of America's Mail and Passenger Sailing Lines,* 1961. See Sect. I.
—————. *Five Hundred Sailing Records of American Built Ships* (Marine Historical Assn.), 1952. Tables of passages on various runs.

Dowling, E.J. *The Lakers of World War I.* . . . P1967. See Sect. AE-2.

*Fahey, J.C. *The Ships and Aircraft of the U.S. Fleet.* . . . 1939 and various later editions; carries on after cessation of official *Ships' Data* volumes.

*Fairburn, W.A., et al. *Merchant Sail,* 6 v. 1945-55. See Sect. I. Numerous detailed tables of shipbuilding and ship performance.

Fay, L.G., ed. *Tanker Directory of the World,* 1959. Part 2, List of Tankers, showing tonnage, flag owners, builders and year built; also owners and managers.

*Great Britain, Admiralty, *Navy List,* annual or more frequent since 1814, giving details on all ships in commission.

Hegarty, R.B. *Returns of Whaling Vessels sailing from American Ports, 1876-1928, a Continuation of Alexander Starbuck's 'History of the American Whale Fishery'* 1959. Includes history of Hawaiian whalers, 1832-1880. See also Starbuck below.

*Hitchings, A.F. and Phillips, S.W. *Ship Registers of the District of Salem and Beverly, Massachusetts, 1789-1900,* 1906. These usually show the dimensions, owners and masters, based on original customs register. Similar lists, originally appearing in the *Essex Institute Historical Collections,* covered Newburyport, Gloucester, and Marblehead. These served as a prototype for the valuable series cited below under "U.S. Survey of Federal Archives (W.P.A.)."

Jane's Fighting Ships. See Sect. B-2; also see Weyer's, below.

Lancour, H. *Passenger Lists of Ships coming to North America, 1538-1825,* 1937, R1964. 3rd edition revised and enlarged by Richard Wolf with list of passenger arrival records.

Lloyd's Register of Shipping, annual since 1760. The records of this pioneer "classification society" give full data on thousands of merchant vessels of many nations, with their Lloyd's rating of "A-1" or otherwise. Many libraries have subscribed to the project of reproducing the 69 earliest volumes, from 1760 to 1833.

Lloyd's Register of Shipping, *Index of Merchant Vessels, 1940 to 1945,* 2nd ed. 1967.

*Lytle, W.M. *Merchant Steam Vessels of the United States, 1807-1868, "The Lytle List," Compiled by William M. Lytle from Official Merchant Marine Documents of the United States and other Sources,* ed. F.C. Holdcamper, et al. (Steamship Historical Society of America, Pub. No. 6), 1952. List consists of four parts: A. Merchant Steam Vessels of the U.S., 1807-1860; B. Losses, 1807-1867; C. Merchant Vessels converted to Steam, 1807-1867; D. Steam Vessels mentioned in Contemporary Newspapers or other Sources but not in Federal Records. Terminal date coincides with beginning of official annual *List of Merchant Vessels of the U.S.*

Manning, T.D. and Walker, C.F. *British Warship Names,* 1959. List of major vessels from earliest times, by officers in charge of naming vessels in World War II.

*Mariners Museum, *Catalogue of Marine Photographs,* 5 v. 1964. Wealth of detailed information about individual vessels, with date and place of construction, dimensions, ultimate fate, etc. Sect. PB, Steamships; PK, Sailing Vessels; PM, Ship Models; PN, U.S. Govenment Vessels; PNC, Confederate State Vessels; PY, Yachts and Yachting.

Mason, H.B. See Sect. B-3.

Merchant Ships, World Built, ed. A.J. Stewart, annual.

*Morison, S.E. *History of the U.S. Naval Operations in World War II,* 15 v. 1947-62. V. 15, pp. 25-111, "principal dimensions, armament, and so on for all vessels serving in the United States Navy and Coast Guard," June 27, 1940-Sept. 2, 1945. Also, throughout the previous volumes, lists of the major warships participating in particular operations.

"Navies of the Second World War" – See lists for the various national navies in Sect. BG-7.

Neeser, R.W. See Sect. A. Well indexed.

Smith, E.W. *Passenger Ships of the World, Past and Present,* 1963. This combines his previous *Trans-Atlantic Passenger Ships,* 1947 and *Trans-Pacific Passenger Ships,* 1953. See also the works of W.M. Angas, N.R.P. Bonsor, and C.R.V. Gibbs.

Somerville, K.F. and Smith, H.W., eds. *Ships of the United States Navy and their Sponsors,* 4 v. 1950-59.

*Starbuck, A. *A History of the Whaling Industry . . . to the Year 1876,* 1876, R1964. Data on the voyage of virtually every American whaler to that date. Continued to 1928 by R.B. Hegarty (Old Dartmouth Hist. Soc.), 1959.

Steel, D., pub. *Steel's Original and Correct List of the Royal Navy and Hon. East India Company's Shipping,* quarterly c1790-1814. Shows ships and their respective stations and, at the insistence of naval officers, records of their relative seniority. Prototype of British *Navy List* and American *Navy Register.*

Talbot-Booth, E.C. *Merchant Ships,* various editions since 1936.

*U.S. Bureau of Construction and Repair, *Ships' Data,* 1908-38. Full data on vessels of the New Navy.

*U.S. Bureau of Statistics, etc. *Merchant Vessels of the United States,* annual since 1867. Tabular lists of sail and steam vessels, showing date of building, tonnage, hailing port, and owners. Also table of ships lost during previous year.

U.S. Federal Writers Project (W.P.A.), *Whaling Masters, Voyages, 1731-1925,* 1938. Alphabetical list, showing separate sailings, with year, ship and port.

*U.S. Naval History Division, *Dictionary of American Fighting Ships,* 1959- Multi-volume work. Alphabetical list of vessels, with statistical data, brief history, and source of name. In addition, summary sections on major types of vessels.
————. *Submarine Losses, World War II,* 6th printing, 1964.

U.S. Navy Department, *Navy Register,* annual or semi-annual since 1814. Includes brief data on ships.

*U.S. Office of Naval War Records, *Official Records of the Union and Confederate Navies in the War of the Rebellion,* 30 v. 1894-1922. Series II, vol. I contains detailed data, of varying accuracy, on all ships of both navies.

*U.S. Survey of Federal Archives, (W.P.A.), *Ship Registers and Enrolments,* processed, 1939-42. Following the example of Hitchings and Phillips, above, this valuable "white collar" relief measure produced a highly useful series: Boston and Charlestown, Mass., 1789-95; New Bedford, Mass., 3 v.; Bristol-Warren, R.I., 1773-1939; Providence, R.I., 1773-1939; Philadelphis, Pa., A-D; New Orleans, La., 6 v. 1804-70; Machias, Me.; Saco, Me.; Barnstable, Mass.; Marshfield, Ore.; Portland, Ore.

Wallace, F.W. *Record of Canadian Shipping.* . . . 1929. Lists a large number of ships built in Canada.

Way, F., Jr. *Directory of Western Rivers Packets,* 1950.
————. *Way's Directory of Western River Steam Towboats,* 1954.

Weber, R.H. *Monitors of the U.S. Navy, 1861-1933,* 1969.

**Weyer's Warships of the World,* A. Bredt, comp. This had gone through 48 editions in German before it became eligible for inclusion here with the first edition in English in 1969. Lists nearly 7,000 ships with photographs and silhouettes. More details than Jane's in some respects.

G LISTS OF MEN

Albion, R.G. *Square-Riggers on Schedule,* 1938, R1965. Brief biographical data on many of the captains in the appendix.

Arthur, R.W. *Contact! Careers of U.S. Naval Aviators Assigned Number 1 to 2,000,* 1968.

*Baker, W.A. *A History of the Boston Marine Society, 1742-1967,* 1968. Lists the nearly 3,000 members, with dates of admission.

*Bonner-Smith, D. *The Commissioned Sea Officers of the Royal Navy, 1660-1815,* 3 v. processed, 1954.

Brown, V.W. See remarks, Sect. F.

Clowes, Sir W.L., ed. *The Royal Navy* . . . . 7 v. 1897-1903. Biographical data on the careers of all flag officers.

Dictionary of American Biography ("D.A.B."). See Sect. B-1.

Dictionary of National Biography ("D.N.B."). See Sect. B-1.

Dictionary of Shipowners, Shipbuilders, and Marine Engineers, annual since c1903. The shipowners' section, more than 400 pp., includes details of lines, etc. There are also sections of shipbuilders, ship repairers, marine engine builders, consulting naval architects, etc. Emphasis strongly British.

*Great Britain, Admiralty, *Navy List,* since 1814. Lists all commissioned officers by seniority within each rank. See Steel, below.

Hamersly, L.R., comp. *The Records of Living Officers of the United States Navy and Marine Corps,* various eds., 1870-1902. Hamersly, a former Marine lieutenant, wanted to be sure that the newspapers would have as much data as possible on naval and marine officers when their names appeared in the press.
* —————. *List of Officers of the Navy of the United States and of the Marine Corps from 1775 to 1900,* 1900, R1970.

Mason, H.B. See Sect. B-3.

Rasmussen, L.J. *San Francisco Ship Passenger Lists,* 3 v. 1965-70. A series which reports the names of passengers arriving by vessel in the Port of San Francisco, 1850-1875.

Steel, D., pub. *Steel's Original and Correct List of the Royal Navy* . . . . See Sect. F.

U.S. Naval Academy Alumni Association, *Register of Graduates,* annual since 1908. Data on every graduate since 1846, showing relative standing in class and highest regular rank achieved. Also lists non-graduates. Name later changed to *Alumni Register.*

U.S. Office of Naval Records and Library, *Register of Officer Personnel and Ships' Data, 1801-1807,* 1945. An additional volume to the *Naval Documents related to the United States Wars with the Barbary Powers.*

————. *Register of Officers of the Confederate States Navy, 1861-1865,* 1931.

Wentworth, H.L. *History of the Portland Marine Society,* processed, P1969. Includes list of the 531 members, 1796-1968.

Wood, R.G. and Dodge, E.S. See Sect. AL-1.

II Merchantmen and Warships

H GENERAL EVOLUTION OF SHIPS AND MARITIME ACTIVITY

Abell, Sir W. *The Shipwright's Trade,* 1948.

*Anderson, R. and R.C. *The Sailing-Ship: Six Thousand Years of History,* 1926, R1963. The standard overall work on sail.

*Bloomster, E.L. *Sailing and Small Craft Down the Ages,* 1940, R1969. As in Davis below, the distinctive features of each type are graphically shown in silhouette, to amplify the descriptions. Section on yachts.

*Chapelle, H.I. *The National Watercraft Collection* (U.S. National Museum Bulletin 219), 1960. Illustrations and descriptions of models in the Smithsonian collection originally established by Capt. J.W. Collins of Gloucester in 1884. Three parts: Merchant Sail, Merchant Steam, Fishing Craft. See Sect. I for Chapelle's other works.

Chatterton, K. *Sailing Ships and Their Story,* 1909. The first, and one of the best, of the 40-odd volumes turned out in 35 years by this most prolific exploiter of nautical atmosphere. Very well illustrated.

*Clowes, G.S.L. *Sailing Ships, Their History and Development as Illustrated in the Collection of Ship-Models in the Science Museum,* 2 v. 1930-32. Similar in its general nature to Chapelle above.

*Davis, C.G. *Shipping and Craft in Silhouette,* 1929. See also Bloomster above.

De la Varende, J. *Cherish the Sea: A History of Sail,* tr. M. Savill, 1956. Rambling informal account with special emphasis on French warships; "technical sketches" by the author.

Encyclopaedia Britannica, 11th ed., 1911. "Ships."

Gibson, C.E. *The Story of the Ship,* 1948. Readable popular summary of the gradual development of vessels, sail and steam.

*Landström, B. *The Ship, an Illustrated History,* tr. M. Phillips, 1967. Capable analysis of general development, with author's own drawings, not only of whole ships, but also of distinctive features. One of the most useful, as well as the most attractive, volumes on ship development.

————. *Sailing Ships in Words and Pictures from Papyrus Boats to Full-Riggers,* 1969. A concise edition of *The Ship.*

Spectorsky, A.C., ed. *The Book of the Sea,* 1954. Anthology of 83 selections in 488 pages, from Thucydides to Rachel Carson; 64 illustrations. New edition edited by A. de Selincourt, 1961.

Stackpole, E.A., ed. *Those in Peril on the Sea,* 1963. Consists of 18 first-person narratives of ocean exploits from the shipwreck of St. Paul to an atomic submarine under the North Pole.

*Tryckare, T., et al. *The Lore of Ships,* 1963. Significant components of all types of ships.

Underhill, H.A. *Sailing Ships and Rigging . . . .* 1956.

Van Metre, T.M. *Tramps and Liners,* 1931. Carries the evolution of freighters and passenger vessels far back of the normal connotation of the book's title.

*Villiers, A., ed. *Men, Ships and the Sea* (Story of Man Library, National Geographic Society), 1962. One of the most satisfactory popular introductions to maritime developments in general. Chapters by competent authorities on different stages and aspects; readable and very well illustrated.

H – 1 "Picture Books"

While many of the other works cited in this bibliography are well illustrated, the pictures are the principal feature of the following general works, with the text more or less written around them. In particular, several of the most attractive are based on the great Macpherson Collection at the National Maritime Museum at Greenwich.

Aymar, B. *A Pictorial Treasury of the Marine Museums of the World,* 1967.

*Baker, W.A. *The Engine-Powered Vessel: From Paddle-Wheeler to Nuclear Ship,* 1965. "A picture book, but not 'just another' picture book."

Barjot, P. and Savant, J. *History of the World's Shipping,* 1966. "This misnamed pictorial catchall is intriguing, for its shortcomings are balanced by unique offerings."

Beaver, P. *The Big Ship. Brunel's* Great Eastern, *a Pictorial Handbook,* 1969.

Bouquet, M. *West Country Sail . . . 1840-1960.* Pictures of small craft in little ports of England's west coast.

Bowen, F.C. *The Sea; Its History and Romance,* 4 v. 1925-26.
————. *From Carrack to Clipper: A Book of Sailing Ship Models,* 1927.

—————. *Sailing Ships of the London River,* 1936; later edition as *London Ship Types,* 1938.

—————. *America Sails the Seas, The History and Romance of America on the High Seas from the 15th to the 19th Century,* 1938. "170 full-page marine prints at a cost of little more than two cents apiece."

Braynard, F.O. *Lives of the Liners,* 1947.
—————. *Famous American Ships . . . .* 1956.
—————. *A Tugman's Sketchbook . . . .* 1965.

*Brewington, M.V. and D. *Kendall Whaling Museum Paintings,* 1966. 162 illustrations, with scholarly notes; the first of a projected series.
* —————. *The Marine Paintings and Drawings in the Peabody Museum,* 1968. Many excellent reproductions, well annotated. See also Sect. H-2.

Carse, R. *The Twilight of Sailing Ships,* 1965.

*Carver, G.G. *Sailing Ships – Sailing Craft* (Grosset All-Color Guides), 1970.

Casson, L. *Illustrated History of Ships and Boats,* 1968.

Chamier, J. *The Story of Sail,* v. 1, *1897-1914,* 1966. Large photographs of yachts, especially at Cowes.

Chatterton, E.K. *Old Ship Prints; with 18 illustrations in color and 95 in black and white, from the Macpherson Collection,* 1927, R1966.
—————. *Old Sea Paintings: The Story of Maritime Art as Depicted by the Great Masters,* 1928.

(Cook), *Captain Cook's Artists in the Pacific, 1769-1779,* 1969. Deluxe New Zealand volume, with "130 of the best."

Dolby, J. *The Steel Navy, A History in Silhouette,* 1962, R1965.

Dunn, L. *The Book of Ships,* 1968. Peabody Museum paintings; see also Brewington above.

Durant, J. and A. *A Pictorial History of American Ships on the High Seas and in Inland Waters,* 1953. Less substantial than Laing, below.

Fere-Cook, G., ed. *The Decorative Arts of the Mariner,* 1966. Pictures and essays, including charts and maps, navigational instruments, figureheads, scrimshaw, and ship models.

Gibbs, J.A. *Disaster Log of Ships,* 1971. See Sect. AD-1.

Greenhill, B. and Giffard, A. *The Merchant Sailing Ship: A Photographic History,* 1970.

Hailey, F.B. *Clear for Action! The Photographic History of Modern Naval Combat, 1898-1964,* 1964.

Hansen, H.J., ed. *Art and the Seafarer, A Historical Survey of the Arts and Crafts of Sailors and Shipwrights,* tr. J. and I. Moore, 1968.

Heyl, E. *Early American Steamers,* 6 v. with index, 1953-56. Drawings and brief histories; see also Stanton, below.

Hough, R. *Fighting Ships,* 1969. Comprehensive survey with nearly 200 illustrations.

*Jobe, J., ed. *The Great Age of Sail,* 1967. This Time-Life book has been called "a major enterprise of bookmaking in the maritime field."

*La Dage, J.H., et al. See Sect. J-6.

Laing, A. *American Sail: A Pictorial History,* 1961. "Over 500 illustrations," with text for each section; warships and merchantmen.

*Landström, B. *The Ship.* See Sect. H.
————. *Columbus,* 1967. See Sect. Q-2; "superbly illustrated."

Lee, R.E., ed. *Great Lakes Ships, 1925-1950,* P1966. Photographs from the Dessin Museum.

Macintyre, D., et al. *Man of War: A History of the Combat Vessel Down to the Present,* 1970. More than 300 illustrations.

Maloney, R.C. *Fifty Notable Ship Portraits at Mystic Seaport,* P1963.

McKnight, H. *Canal and River Craft in Pictures,* 1969.

Moeser, R.O. *U.S. Navy: Vietnam,* 1969. 192 photographs, by Navy chief journalist.

*Moore, Sir A. *Sailing Ships of War, 1800-1860, including the Transition to Steam,* 1926. A Macpherson picture book, but with valuable data on the various ships illustrated.

Murphy, R.C. *A Dead Whale or a Stove Boat,* 1967. Photographs by author on 1911-13 whaling voyage.

National Maritime Museum, *The Second Dutch War Described in Pictures and Manuscripts of the Time,* 1967.

Newell, G.R. See Sect. J-2.

Newry, E. *Grain Race,* 1968. Photographs of author's voyage on Finnish bark in 1939.

*Parker, H. and Bowen, F.C., eds. *Mail and Passenger Steamers of the Nineteenth Century; The Macpherson Collection, with Iconographical Notes,* 1929.

Parkinson, J., Jr. and Fortier, J. *Yachting on Narragansett Bay and Vineyard Sound*, 1968. 130 pictures by Fortier and text by Parkinson.

Peabody, R.E. *Models of American Sailing Ships. A Handbook of the Ship Model Collection in the Addison Gallery of American Art* (Phillips Academy, Andover, Mass.), 1961.

Penobscot Marine Museum, *Forty-four Ship Portraits at the . . . Museum*, 1963.

Perry, T.M. and Simpson, D.H., eds. *Drawings by William Westall, Landscape Artist, on board of H.M.S.* Investigator *during the Circumnavigation of Australia by Captain Matthew Flinders, R.N., in 1801-1803*, 1962.

Plowden, D. *Farewell to Steam*, 1966. Photographs of 20th-century steamboats and locomotives.

Ringwald, D.C. *Hudson River Day Line* . . . . See Sect. J-2.

Robinson, M.S. *A Pageant of the Sea: The Macpherson Collection of Maritime Prints and Drawings in the National Maritime Museum, Greenwich*, 1950.
*————. *Van de Velde Drawings. A Catalogue of Drawings in the National Maritime Museum*, 1958.

Roscoe, T., et al. *Picture History of the U.S. Navy from the Old Navy to the New (1776-1897)*, 1957.

Rosskam, E. and L. *Towboat Rivers*. See Sect. J-2.

*Stanton, S.W. *American Steam Vessels*, 1895. A collection of the various types of steamships and steamboats in American waters, with explanatory notes.
*————. *American Steam Vessels Series*, ed. E.S. Anderson, P1962 ff.
The drawings from the above book, together with others of his from private sources are being reproduced by his daughter in a series of paper-bound volumes, each dealing with a special type of steamer: 1, *Great Lakes Steam Vessels*, 1962; 2, *Long Island Sound and Narragansett Bay Steam Vessels*, 1962; *Ocean Steam Vessels*, 1963; *United States Navy*, 1963; *Hudson River Steamboats*, 1963; *Steam Vessels of Chesapeake and Delaware Bays*, 1967; *New York Bay Steam Vessels*, 1968. Other projected titles are Mississippi and Ohio Rivers; Southern and Western; Coastal Steam Vessels; Towboats and Tugs.

Swenson, S. *Sails Through the Centuries*, 1965. Drawings.

Tod, G.M. *The Last Sail Down East*, 1965. The last great fleets of commercial vessels, from big coal schooners to barges, with careers of the illustrated vessels.

U.S. Naval Academy Library, *The Henry Huddleston Rogers Collection of Ship Models*, 1954.

Wainwright, A.B. *Commodore James Biddle and His Sketch Book*, 1966. Drawings by E.C. Young, mostly based on Biddle's career.

Wilmersing, J.H. *A History of American Marine Painting*, 1968.

I   MERCHANT SAIL – SPECIAL TYPES

Adney, E.T. and Chapelle, H.I. *The Bark Canoes and Skin Boats of North America* (Smithsonian Institution), 1964.

*Albion, R.G. *Square-Riggers on Schedule: The New York Sailing Packets to England, France and the Cotton Ports,* 1938, R1965. More comprehensive than Lubbock's *Western Ocean Packets,* which dwells heavily on the brutality of Black Ball mates. C.C. Cutler's *Queens of the Western Ocean,* 1961, extends the subject to the lesser coastal packets. See also C.P. Wright, below.

*Baker, W.A. *The New* Mayflower: *Her Design and Construction, by Her Designer,* 1958. The author, like H.I. Chapelle below, is able to combine technical naval architecture with history. In his researches preceding the designing of the *Mayflower* replica, he made a thorough study of 17th-century ship design; this was amplified in the two following volumes.
——————. *Colonial Vessels: Some Seventeenth-Century Sailing Craft,* 1962. "Important contribution to nautical archaeology and technology." Includes pocketed set of three plans of a colonial bark.
——————. *Sloops and Shallops,* 1966.

Benham, H. *Last Stronghold of Sail: The Story of the Essex Sailing Smacks, Coasters and Barges,* 1948.

Bowker, F.E. *Hull-Down,* 1963. Enthusiastic account of a four-masted schooner, with details of the ship, her operation, and the way of life between the wars.

*Brewington, M.V. *Chesapeake Bay Log Canoes and Bugeyes,* 1963. Combined, revised and enlarged version of his *Chesapeake Bay Log Canoes,* 1937, and his *Chesapeake Bay Bugeyes,* 1941. See also his chapters on shipbuilding, sailing vessels, and bay craft in his *Chesapeake Bay: A Pictorial Maritime History,* 1953.

No attempt will be made here to record all the studies of British and other foreign small craft.

Brøgger, A.W. and Sheltig, H. *The Viking Ships: Their Ancestry and Evolution,* tr. K. John, 1951.

Carse, R. *The Twilight of Sailing Ships,* 1965.

*Casson, L. *The Ancient Mariners: Seafarers and Sea Fighters of the Mediterranean in Ancient Times,* 1959, R1967.

*Chapelle, H.I. *History of American Sailing Ships,* 1935. In 1921, S.E. Morison wrote "Until some competent naval architect makes a thorough study of American shipbuilding (and may that day come soon!) no one has a right to be dogmatic." Chapelle, followed by W.A. Baker, also a naval architect, has produced several books to meet that need. This study, less extensive in scope than the title indicates, deals primarily with ship design. The chapters include: 1, The Colonial Period; 2, Naval Craft; 3, Privateers and Slavers; 4, Revenue Cutters; 5, The American Schooner; 6, Merchant Craft; 7, Sailing

Yachts. He later expanded chapters 2 and 4 into a naval volume. See Sect. K-3.

————. *The Baltimore Clipper, Its Origin and Development*, 1930, R1969.

*————. *American Small Sailing Craft: Their Design, Development and Construction*, 1951. Deals mostly with boats less than 40 feet long; includes plans.

————. *The National Watercraft Collection*. See Sect. H.

*————. *The Search for Speed under Sail, 1700-1855*, 1967.

Chatterton, E.K. *The Old East Indiamen*, 1914.

*Clark, A.H. *The Clipper Ship Era: An Epitome of the famous American and British Clipper Ships, their Owners, Builders, Commanders and Crews, 1843-1869*, 1910, R1969. Ranks with Cutler, and Howe and Matthews as one of the three outstanding works on American clippers proper. (The Baltimore clippers were a separate account.) Clark's arrangement is topical; Cutler's, chronological, and Howe and Matthews', alphabetical.

Cotton, Sir E. *East Indiamen: The East India Company's Maritime Service*, 1949.

*Cutler, C.C. *Greyhounds of the Sea: The Story of the American Clipper Ship*, 1930, R1961. The best single account, combining spirited style with full factual data on construction, dimensions, owners, masters and speed performances of each ship. The author was founder and first curator of The Marine Historical Association in Mystic, Conn.

*————. *Queens of the Western Ocean: The Story of America's Mail and Passenger Sailing Lines*, 1961. Covers a wider range than the very "regular" major packets in Albion, above. In particular, gives full data on the small sailing coastal packets out of the major American ports, listing several thousand vessels and masters.

————. *Five Hundred Sailing Records of American Built Ships*, 1952.

Davis, D.J. *The Thames Sailing Barge: Her Gear and Rigging*, 1970.

Dorset, P.F. *Historic Ships Afloat*, 1967. "A guide to the obsolete preserved and exhibited ships in the United States, from seventeenth-century reproductions to World War II battleships."

*Dunn, C.D., et al. *The* Wavertree: *Being an Account of an Ocean Wanderer, and Particulars of a Voyage around the Horn in 1907-1908, from the Narrative of Captain George Spiers*, 1969. The ship was brought from Buenos Aires to New York to be the major exhibit at South Street Seaport.

*Fairburn, W.A., et al. *Merchant Sail*, 6 v. 1945-55 (Fairburn Marine Educational Foundation). The most comprehensive account of American sailing vessels, originally undertaken by Fairburn (1876-1947), a prominent ship designer and builder to 1908 before becoming head of the Diamond Match Co. The last four volumes were edited by Ethel M. Ritchie. V. 1, General Narrative, 1607-1812; v. 2, same, 1812-1865; v. 3, U.S. Merchant Sail – Types, Models, Rigs, Clippers and later Square-riggers; Speed of Sailing Vessels; Clipper Ship Era and California Trade; v. 4, Merchant Sail in China, Australia, Manila and India Trades. Development of Schooner Rigs and Coastwise Use; Last Days of Deep-Sea Sail; v. 5, Wooden Shipbuilders and Shipbuilding Centers through

19th Century, with particulars of Sailing Vessels; v. 6, Appendix 1, Owners of Clipper Ships and a Record of the Clippers that they owned, in New York; App. 2, *id.* Boston; App. 3, The Ship-Designing, Building, and Operating Experience of the Author; Index of 13,278 vessels mentioned in the text and appendices. The entire edition was distributed gratis to selected libraries and museums.

*Greenhill, B. *The Merchant Schooners: A Portrait of a Vanished Industry,* 2 v. 1951-57, R1968. The first edition had a much longer subtitle. Emphasis British.

Gropallo, T. *The Last Sail,* 1969.

Guthrie, J. *Bizarre Ships of the Nineteenth Century,* 1970.

Hennessy, M.W. *The Sewall Ships of Steel,* 1937. See Sect. L-5.

Howe, O.T. and Matthews, F.C. *American Clipper Ships, 1833-1858,* 2 v. 1926-27, R1969. See comments under Clark above.

Jones, H.A., ed. *It's a Friendship,* P1965. History of this celebrated Maine type; published by the Friendship Sloop Society. See also Roberts below.

Laing, A.K. *Clipper Ships and Their Makers,* 1966.

*Leavitt, J.F. *Wake of the Coasters,* 1970. (American Maritime Library). Important first-hand account of the little American coasting schooners which flourished in large numbers, especially from New England. The author, who spent several years on such schooners, has included many of his own drawings.

Le Scal, Y. *The Great Days of the Cape Horners,* tr. L. Ortgen, 1967.

Lubbock, B. *The Blackwall Frigates,* 1922, R1962. These big ships of the passenger lines to India and Australia in the period 1835-70 were a link between the old East Indiamen and the later P & O liners. Many of them were built in the big Blackwall Yard near London, whose owners operated some of the lines.
————. *The China Clippers,* 1914, R1968. These included the *Cutty Sark* and other crack British successors to the earlier American clippers of the 1850s. See also MacGregor below.
————. *The Colonial Clippers,* 1921, R1968. The big ships of the runs to Australia and New Zealand, one of the last major opportunities for crack sailing vessels. Includes emigrant ships, among which were some American vessels, and the later wool clippers.
————. *The Opium Clippers,* 1933, R1967. Fast little vessels, some from America, built to smuggle opium into China.
————. *Coolie Ships and Oil Sailors,* 1935, R1955. Carried "case oil" to the East and brought back indentured Chinese or Indians.
————. *The Nitrate Clippers,* 1932, R1966. One of the final opportunities for large sailing vessels, carrying nitrate around Cape Horn to Europe.
————. *The Down Easters, American Deep Water Sailing Ships, 1869-1929,* 1929, R1963. Large, fine ships built in Maine and elsewhere in New England,

less extreme than full clippers. Many of these vessels also appear in Matthews, below.

—————. *Last of the Windjammers*, 2 v. 1927, R1953-54.

—————. *The Western Ocean Packets*, 1925, R1956. Black Ball and other lines; see comment under Albion above.

Lubbock's works are somewhat spotty and undigested, but he brought together a great deal of useful information. Most of his volumes passed through several reprintings.

*MacGregor, D.R. *The Tea Clippers: An Account of the China Tea Trade and Some of the British Sailing Ships Engaged in It from 1849 to 1869*, 1952. Written by an architect, it includes diagrams and analyses of designs; also tables of passages and speed records. Similar to his later *The China Bird*, 1961. See also Shewan below.

*March, E.J. *Sailing Drifters. The Story of the Herring Luggers of England, Scotland and the Isle of Man*, 1953, R1969.

—————. *Sailing Trawlers. The Story of Deep-Sea Fishing with Long Line and Trawl*, 1953.

—————. *Spritsail Barges of Thames and Medway*, 1948, R1970.

—————. *Inshore Craft of Britain, in the Days of Sail and Oar*, 2 v. 1970.

Marsden, P.R.V. *A Roman Ship from Blackfriars, London*, 1966. Excavation and identification of the ancient vessel.

*Martinez-Hidalgo, J.M. *Columbus' Ships*, 1966. Account of the design and construction of the ships, their voyages, lists of crews, and chronology. Produced by direction of the Museo Maritimo in Barcelona.

*Matthews, F.C. *American Merchant Ships, 1850-1900*, 2 v. 1930-31, R1969.

Mayhew, D.R. *The Wooden Sailing Barges of Maine, 1886 to 1945* (ms. AM thesis, Maine, 1959).

*Mjelde, M.J. Glory of the Seas, 1970. Excellent detailed "biography" of big modified clipper, the last Donald McKay built, in 1869. This was the first volume in the new American Maritime Library series published for Mystic Seaport by Wesleyan University Press. The coasting volume by Leavitt, above, was the second.

*Moore, Sir A. *Rig in the North*, 1956.

*—————. *Last Days of Mast and Sail. An Essay in Nautical Comparative Anatomy*, 1925, R1970.

*Morris, E.P. *The Fore-and-Aft Rig in America, a Sketch*, 1927, R1970. Excellent survey.

Norton, P. *The End of the Voyage*, 1959. Reminiscences of experiences in British pilot cutters, prawners, hookers, oyster smacks and fishing boats.

Norton, W.J. Eagle *Ventures*, 1970. Training bark *Eagle* of the U.S. Coast Guard Academy, formerly German *Horst Wessel*. Well illustrated.

*Parker, J.P. *Sails of the Maritimes. The Story of the Three- and Four-Masted Cargo Schooners of Atlantic Canada and Newfoundland, 1859-1929* (Maritime Museum of Canada), 1960. For the square-riggers see Wallace below.

*Parker, W.J.L. *The Great Coal Schooners of New England, 1870-1909,* 1948.

*Parkinson, C.N. *Trade in the Eastern Seas, 1793-1813,* 1937. Ch. 5. The big ships of the East India Company were the aristocrats of the days of sail. See also Chatterton and Cotton.
*———— ed. *The Trade Winds,* 1948. Ch. 4. Discussion of the principal types of British merchantmen, 1793-1815.

Phillips-Birt, D. *Fore and Aft Sailing Craft and the Development of the Modern Yacht,* 1962.

Pullen, H.F. *Atlantic Schooners,* P1967. Prepared for Expo '67 by a Canadian admiral. Concentrates on a dozen Canadian Atlantic coast types.

Roberts, A., ed. *Enduring Friendships,* 1970. Maine Friendship sloops. See also Jones above.

Robinson, J. and Dow, G.F. *The Sailing Ships of New England, 1607-1907,* 3 v. 1922-28, R1969. See also Matthews, above.

Rogers, H.C.B. *Troopships and Their History,* 1963. A British colonel's account of their development since the Tangier occupation of 1662. Some of the later troopships, of course, were steamships.

Schultz, C.R. *Annotated Bibliography of American and British Clipper Ships,* (Marine Historical Assn., Information Bulletin 69-2), processed, P1969.

Shewan, A. *The Great Days of Sail,* 1927. Excellent on British tea clippers.

Story, D. *Hail* Columbia, 1970. "Perhaps the most beautiful of all racing Gloucestermen, the schooner *Columbia,* built by the author's father, A.D. Story, at his Essex shipyard in the winter of 1922-23."

Tod, G.M.S. See Sect. H-1.

Underhill, H.A. *Deep Water Sail,* 1952. Wide variety of sailing vessels of the 19th and 20th centuries, with nearly 200 illustrations, plates and plans.

*Villiers, A.J. *The Way of a Ship; Being Some Account of the Ultimate Development of the Ocean-Going Square-Rigged Vessel, and the Manner of Her Handling, Her Voyage-Making, Her Personnel, Her Economics, Her Performance and Her End,* 1953, R1970. Perhaps the most comprehensive account of "how things worked." Chapters include Pt. II, Technicalities: 4, Global Sailing Conditions; 5, Handling Square Sails; 6, Shiphandling under Sail; pt. III, The Men: 7, The Sailors; 8, The Masters; pt. IV: The Life; 9, Economics; 10, Standards of Conduct. Also case histories of the Laeisz ships of Hamburg and the *Cutty Sark.*

Wallace, F.W. *Wooden Ships and Iron Men; The Story of the Square-Rigged Merchant Marine of British North America,* 1924.

——————. *In the Wake of the Wind Ships,* 1927. Also Canadian ships.

Wright, C.P. *The Origins and Early Years of the Transatlantic Packet Ships of New York, 1817-1835* (ms. PhD thesis, Harvard, 1932).

J STEAM

J - 1 General Development

*Baker, W.A. *The Engine-Propelled Vessel from Paddle-Wheeler to Nuclear Ship,* 1966.

Culver, J.A. *Ships of the U.S. Merchant Marine,* 1963.

Fletcher, R.A. *Steam-Ships: The Story of Their Development to the Present Day,* 1910.

*Flexner, J.T. *Steamboats Come True, American Inventors in Action,* 1944; reissued as *Inventors in Action: The Story of the Steamboat,* P1962. Contributions and interplay of various inventors, American, British, and French, culminating in Fulton's ultimate success. See also Spratt below.

Fox, W.J. *Marine Auxiliary Machinery,* 1968.

Gregg, R. *The Exploitation of the Steamboat: The Case of Colonel John Stevens* (ms. PhD thesis, Columbia, 1951).

Gunderson, G.A. *The Social Saving of Steamships* (PhD thesis, U. of Washington, 1967; DA v. 28, p. 4864A).

*Hardy, A.C. *The Book of the Ship: An Exhaustive Pictorial and Factual Survey of the World's Ships, Shipping and Shipbuilding,* 1949. Best general picture of modern ships. Supersedes his earlier *Merchant Ship Types* (1924) and incorporates material from several of his other useful works, mentioned elsewhere in this bibliography. Describes all varieties of modern shipping, in relation to the functions for which the ships were designed.

Heyl, E. See Sect. H-1.

Jackson, C.G. *The Ship Under Steam,* 1927.

Kline, F.R. *When Steam Darkened the Sail: Some Economic, Geographic and Public Policy Factors affecting the Conversion from Sail to Steam Marine Power* (PhD thesis, Columbia, 1968; DA v. 31; p. 4366A).

Knauerhasse, R. *The Compound Marine Steam Engine: A Study in the Relationship between Technological Change and Economic Development* (PhD thesis, Pennsylvania, 1967; DA v. 28, p. 1194A).

*Lytle, W.M. See Sect. F.

Pudney, J. *The Golden Age of Steam,* 1967.

Rowland, R.T. *Steam at Sea,* 1971.

*Smith, E.C. *Short History of Naval and Marine Engineering,* 1938. An admirable survey of the main stages of development, presented in a manner intelligible to the non-technical reader.

*Society of Naval Architects and Marine Engineers, *Historical Transactions, 1893-1945,* 1945. Pertinent here are Part 2, special types; part 3, steam vessels of special regions; and part 6, development and history, including marine engines and boilers.

Spies, M.H. *Veteran Steamers: A Story of the Preservation of Steamships,* 1965.

*Spratt, H.P. *Handbook of the Collection Illustrating Marine Engineering; Part II, Descriptive Catalogue* (Science Museum, London) 1953.
*————. *The Birth of the Steamboat,* 1959. See also Flexner above.

*Stanton, S.W. See Sect. H-1.

Studley, M.V. *Guide to the Microfilm Edition of the Stevens Family Papers* (New Jersey Historical Society), 1968. John Stevens of Hoboken and his sons played prominent roles in the development of the steamboat.

Talbot, F.A.A. *Steamship Conquest of the World,* 1912.

U.S. Maritime Administration, *Ships of America's Merchant Fleet,* 1952 ff. Illustrations and descriptions of principal types.
————. *Merchant Fleets of the World – Seagoing Steam and Motor Ships of 1,000 Gross Tons and Over,* annual.
————. *A Statistical Analysis of the World's Merchant Fleets (Showing Age, Size, Speed, and Draft by Frequency Groupings),* 1967.

J – 2 Steamboats

*Albion, R.G. *The Rise of New York Port, 1815-1860,* 1939, R1970. Ch. 8, Steam on River, Sound and Bay.

Bernstein, H.T. *Steamboats on the Ganges (1828-1840),* 1960 (PhD thesis, Yale).

Blackstone, E.H. *Farewell Old Mount Washington: The Story of the Steamboat Era on Lake Winnipesaukee,* 1969.

*Bradlee, F.B.C. *Steam Navigation in New England,* 1920. Deals with the lines north of Boston, chiefly to Maine.

*Brown, A.C. *Steam Packets on the Chesapeake: A History of the Old Bay Line since 1840,* 1961. An extension of his *Old Bay Line,* 1940. An able, pleasing study of the Baltimore-Norfolk run.

36

Burgess, R.H. and Wood, G. *Steamboats out of Baltimore,* 1968.

Clegg, W.P. and Strying, J.S. *British Nationalized Shipping (1947-1968),* 1969. Deals especially with the cross-channel steamers, also covered in their *Steamers of British Railways and Associate Companies,* 1968. See C.L.D. Duckworth and G.E. Langmuir, *Railway and Other Steamers,* 2nd ed. 1968 and their *West Coast Steamers* and *West Highland Steamers.*

Covell, W.K. *Short History of the Fall River Line: The Story of an Era in American Inland Water Transportation,* 1947. See also McAdam below.

*Dayton, F.E. *Steamboat Days,* 1925, R1970. Delightful general survey of American steamboating.

De Barard, E.T. *Steamboats in the Hyacinths,* 1956. St. John's River, Florida, 1880-1900.

Douglas, B. *Steamboatin' on the Cumberland,* 1961.

Downs, N. *Paddlewheel on the Frontier: The Story of British Columbia Sternwheel Steamers,* V. 1, 1967. Navigation on the Fraser and other rivers.

Duncan, F. *History of the Detroit and Cleveland Navigation Company, 1850-1957,* 1954 (PhD thesis, Chicago). Appeared serially in *Inland Seas.*

Emmerson, J.C., comp. *Steam-Boat Comes to Norfolk Harbor,* 1949.
————. *Steam Navigation in Virginia and Northeastern North Carolina Waters, 1826-1836,* 1949.

Ewen, W.M. *Days of the Steamboats,* 1967.

Harlan, G. and Fisher, C. *On Walking Beams and Paddle Wheels: A Chronicle of San Francisco Bay Ferryboats,* 1951. See also Perry below.

Heyl, E. See Sect. H-1.

Hill, R.N. *Sidewheeler Saga: A Chronicle of Steamboating,* 1953. Readable, incomplete rehash, not as good as Dayton. Tells of efforts to keep old steamer going on Lake Champlain.

Hilton, G.W. *The Great Lakes Car Ferries,* 1962. "Scholarly and profusely illustrated."
————. *The Staten Island Ferry,* 1964.
*————. *The Night Boat,* 1968. Important passenger and freight services on coastal runs and Long Island Sound.

*Hunter, L.C. *Steamboats on the Western Rivers: An Economic and Technological History,* 1949, R1970. Admirable piece of sound research and able presentation of the significant aspects, in contrast to the "atmosphere" books such as Irving Anthony's *Paddle Wheels and Pistols.*

Ives, J.C. *Steamboat up the Colorado,* 1965.

Jacobus, M.W. *The Connecticut River Steamboat Story,* 1956.

Lane, W.J. *Commodore Vanderbilt: An Epic of the Steam Age,* 1942. Vanderbilt progressed through steamers on New York Bay, the Hudson River and Long Island Sound before graduating to ocean liners and the New York Central.

MacMullen, J. *Paddle Wheel Days in California,* 1944.

McAdam, R.W. *The Old Fall River Line,* 1937, R1955.
——————. *Salts of the Sound,* 1939, R1957.
——————. Priscilla *of Fall River,* 1947, R1956.
——————. Commonwealth, *Giantess of the Sound,* 1959.
    Like Covell above, these deal with the most celebrated of the Long Island Sound lines, 1847-1937, providing overnight passenger and freight service between Boston and New York via Fall River.

McNairn, J. and MacMullen, J. *Ships of the Redwood Coast,* 1945. Account of the unique lumber-carrying "steam schooners."

Meyer, D.J. *Excursion Steamboating on the Mississippi with Streckfas Steamers, Inc.* (PhD St. Louis Univ., 1967; DA v. 28, p. 3095A). Service started in 1901.

Mills, R.V. *Stern-wheelers up Columbia: A Century of Steamboats in the Oregon Country,* 1947.

Moran, E.F. and Reed, L. *Tugboat: The Moran Story,* 1957. The gradual development of the huge Moran fleet.

Morrison, J.H. *History of American Steam Navigation,* 1903, R1958. The revised edition has a foreword by F.O. Braynard. The book is a mine of factual detail, with little analysis, synthesis or style.

Mudie, I. *Riverboats,* 1961. Australian inland navigation.

Neville, B. *Directory of River Packets in the Mobile-Alabama-Warrior-Tombigbee Trades, 1818-1932,* P1962.

Newell, G.R. *Ships of the Inland Sea: The Story of the Puget Sound Steamboats,* 1951, R1960.
——————. *Pacific Tugboats,* 1957; *Pacific Steamboats,* 1958; *Pacific Coastal Liners,* 1959. These reproduce large numbers of photographs from the extensive Williamson Marine Collection; the third title alone has some 500 pictures of 300 vessels.

Patterson, A.J.S. *The Golden Years of the Clyde Steamers (1884-1914),* 1969.

Perry, J. *American Ferryboats,* 1957.

*Richardson, J.M. *Steamboat Lore of the Penobscot, An Informal Story of Steamboating in Maine's Penobscot Region,* 1941.

*Ringwald, D.C. *Hudson River Day Line: The Story of a Great American Steamboat Company,* 1965. Includes 270 pictures.

Rosskam, E. and L. *Towboat River,* 1948. Includes 244 photographs, with text, of towboats on western rivers.

Taylor, W.L. *A Productive Monopoly: The Effect of Railroad Control on the New England Coastal Steamship Lines, 1871-1916* (PhD Brown, 1968; DA V. 30, p. 261 A).

Way, F., Jr. See Sect. F.

Wellman, M.W. *Fastest on the River: The Great Race Between the* Natchez *and the* Robert E. Lee, 1957. Similar account by R.I. Barkhau, 1952.

Wilson, R.H. *The Application of Steam to the St. Lawrence Valley, 1809-1840* (ms. MA thesis, McGill, 1951).

J - 3   Steamships - General

The story of the crack transatlantic liners is one of the most overexploited fields in maritime history; only a few of the most useful titles will be noted here.

Angas, W.M. *Rivalry on the Atlantic,* 1939. The author, a naval civil engineer, throws particular light on the development of liner design and machinery.

*Bonsor, N.R.P. *North Atlantic Seaway,* 1955. With an arrangement by lines, gives minute details of some 1,300 vessels, with 150 scale drawings and 50 plates. Supplement issued in 1960. Most useful for reference purposes.

Dunn, L. *North Atlantic Liners, 1899-1913,* 1961. A long, narrow book, 20 by 10 inches, with 12 color plates and numerous silhouettes, giving generous data on the crack ships of that prewar period of important development.
————— . (foreword), *Soviet Merchant Ships, 1945-1968,* 1969.

Fellner, F.V. *Communications in the Far East,* 1934. Description of Japanese and Chinese shipping, and the foreign lines to East Asia.

Gibbs, V. *Passenger Liners of the Western Ocean,* 1952, R1957.
* ————— . *British Passenger Liners of the Five Oceans. A Record of Lines and Liners since 1840,* 1962. Data on some 1,300 ships.

Gregory, D. *Australian Steamships, Past and Present,* 1928.

*Isherwood, J.H. *Steamers of the Past,* 1966. 30 articles, with line drawings, selected from over 200 contributed to *Sea Breezes* since 1949. Vessels chiefly from 1900-1920 period.

Intergovernment Maritime Consultative Organization, *International Conference on Facilitation of Maritime Travel and Transport, 1965,* 1966.

*Kemble, J.H. *The Panama Route, 1848-1869,* 1943 (PhD thesis, Berkeley), R1970. The American subsidy lines from New York to San Francisco via the isthmus.

Lawson, W. *Pacific Steamers: The History, Rise and Development of Steamers on the Australian, New Zealand and Western American Coasts,* 1927. See also Gregory above.

*McClellan, W.C. *A History of American Military Sea Transportation* (ms. PhD thesis, American, 1953). Traces the separate Army and Navy transport services from 1898 up to their merger as "MSTS" in 1949.

Mitchell, W.H. and Sawyer, L.H. *British Standard Ships of World War I,* 1968.
————. *Empire Ships of World War II,* 1965. Over 1,300 strong, the "Empire fleet" was composed of captured enemy vessels, ships bought from the United States, and specially built wartime ships.
————. *Cruising Ships,* 1967.

*Parker, H. and Bowen, F.C. See Sect. H-1.

Pond, E.L. *Junius Smith, Pioneer Promoter of Transatlantic Steam Navigation* (Marine Historical Assn., 41), 1941.

Powell, L.H. *A Hundred Years On. History of the Liverpool Steam Ship Owners' Association, 1858-1958,* 1958.

Sawyer, L.H. and Mitchell, W.H. *The Liberty Ships: The History of the "Emergency" Type Cargo Ships constructed in the United States during World War II* (American Standard Ship Series), 1970.

Spratt, H.P. *Transatlantic Paddle Steamers,* 1951, R1967.

Stewart, C.L. *Flags, Funnels and Hull Colors,* 1953, R1963. Insignia of hundreds of world lines.

Stuart, C.B. *Naval and Mail Steamers,* 1853. Diagrams, pictures, statistics and rhetoric concerning American warships and subsidy liners, by the Engineer-in-Chief of the Navy.

*Tyler, D.B. *Steam Conquers the Atlantic,* 1939 (PhD thesis, Columbia). The most scholarly of the host of books on the transatlantic run; carries the story only to 1880. Consult also the appropriate portions of J.G.B. Hutchins, *The American Maritime Interests and Public Policy,* 1941 (PhD thesis, Harvard) and R.H. Thornton, *British Shipping,* 2nd ed. 1959.

Worker, C.F. *The World's Passenger Ships,* 1967, R1970.

J - 4 Individual Lines

Most of the British lines have at least one volume of history, in sharp contrast to the American situation.

a. British and Continental

*Anderson, R. *White Star,* 1964. See Oldham, below.

Babcock, F.L. *Spanning the Atlantic,* 1931. History of the Cunard Line.

Blake, G. *The B.I. Centenary, 1856-1956. The Story of the British India Steam Navigation Company,* 1957.
————. *The Ben Line: The History of William Thompson & Co. of Leith and Edinburgh and of the Ships Owned and Managed by Them, 1825-1925,* 1956. Starting with the exchange of Scottish coal and Canadian lumber, the line shifted around 1860 to the Far Eastern trade.

Bushell, T.A. *"Royal Mail," A Centenary of the Royal Mail Line, 1839-1939.* The Royal Mail Steam Packet Co., to the West Indies and South America.
————. *Eight Bells: Royal Mail Line's War Story, 1939-1945,* 1950.

*Cecil, L. *Albert Ballin: Business and Politics in Imperial Germany, 1888-1918,* 1967. The head of the Hamburg American Line, possibly the greatest of all shipping operators. See also Hulderman below.

Coons, R.E. See Sect. W-7. Austrian Lloyd.

Cornford, L.C. *A Century of Sea Trading, 1824-1924: The General Steam Navigation Company, Limited,* 1924. British coastwise service, later expanding to the Mediterranean, etc.

Crowdy, M. *Lyle Shipping Co., Ltd. 1827-1966,* P1966. Scottish service to South America, Africa and Australia.

Dennett, A.M. *The Donaldson Line: A Century of Shipping, 1854-1954,* 1960.

Duncan, R.E. *William Wheelwright, the Pioneer of Pacific Steam Navigation, 1825-1852* (ms. PhD thesis, Berkeley, 1960). Founder of the Pacific Steam Navigation Co., a British service to the west coast of South America. See also Kinsbruner below.

Ewart, E.A. (Boyd Cable, pseud.) *A Hundred Years of the P & O, Peninsular and Oriental Steam Navigation Co.,* 1937. A later history of the line is D. Divine, *These Splendid Ships: The Story of the Peninsular and Oriental Line,* 1960. Its World War II history is told in G.F. Kerr, *Business in Great Waters: The War History of the P & O, 1939-1945,* 1948.

Hamilton, J.H. *The "All-Red Route", 1893-1953: A History of the Trans-Pacific Mail Service between British Columbia, Australia, and New Zealand,* P1960.

(Harrison Line), *One Hundred Years of Progress: A Brief History of the Harrison Line, 1853-1953,* 1953.

*Hulderman, B. *Albert Ballin,* tr. W.E. Eggers, 1922. See also Cecil above.

*Hyde, F.E. and Harris, J.R. *Blue Funnel,* 1957. In contrast to some of the journalistic effusions, this is a well-executed and scholarly history of the service of Alfred Holt & Co., chiefly to the Far East. This progressive company was the first to shift to compound engines in the 1860s. The wartime experience of

Blue Funnel is recorded in S.W. Roskill, *A Merchant Fleet in War: Alfred Holt & Co., 1939-1945*, 1962.

John, A.H. *A Liverpool Merchant House: Being the History of the Alfred Booth Line to the Amazon*, 1959.

Keilhau, W. *Norway and the Bergen Line*, 1953.

Keir, D. *The Bowring Story*, 1962. Red Cross Line, 1884 until acquisition by Furness.

Kinsbruner, J. *The Business Activities of William Wheelwright in Chile, 1829-1960* (PhD thesis, New York Univ., 1964; DA v. 26, p. 328). This native of Newburyport founded the Pacific Steam Navigation Co.; see also Duncan above, and Wardle below.

LeFleming, H.M. *Ships of the Holland-American Line*, 1963.

McLellan, R.S. *Anchor Line, 1856-1956*, 1956.

Murray, M. *Ships and South Africa: A Maritime Chronicle of the Cape with Particular Reference to Mail and Passenger Liners, from The Earliest Days . . . (1825-1926)*, 1933.
————. *Union-Castle Chronicle, 1853-1953*, 1953. A merger of the Union and Castle Lines, with crack passenger service. Includes considerable material from the earlier volume.

Oldham, W.J. *The Ismay Line. The White Star Line and the Ismay Family Story*, 1961. Includes an account of the role of Bruce Ismay in the *Titanic* disaster, which he survived. See also Anderson above.

Sanderson, Lord. *Ships and Sealing Wax*, 1969. Autobiography of chairman of the Shaw, Saville service to Australia and New Zealand.

Stevens, E.F. *One Hundred Years of Houlders: A Record of the History of Houlder Brothers & Co., Ltd., from 1849 to 1950*, 1950. Eventually very prominent in the refrigerated meat trade.

Tregoning, K.G. *Home Port Singapore: A History of the Straits Steamship Co., Ltd. 1890-1965*, 1967.

Wardle, A.C. *Steam Conquers the Pacific. A Record of Maritime Achievement, 1840-1940*, 1940. The Pacific Steam Navigation Company; see also Duncan and Kinsbruner, above.

b. American

*Albion, R.G. *Seaports South of Sahara: The Achievements of an American Steamship Service*, 1959. History of Farrell Lines, which grew out of the American South African Line, acquired by the Farrells from the Shipping

Board in 1925. In 1947, they also acquired the American West African Line. Extensive appendix.

Armstrong, W. *The Collins Story,* 1957. Ambitious American-subsidized effort to beat the Cunarders in the 1850s. Ended after two disastrous shipwrecks. See A.C. Brown, Sect. BR.

*Baughman, J.P. *Charles Morgan and the Development of Southern Transportation,* 1968. Based on his Tulane PhD thesis, *The Maritime and Railroad Interests of Charles Morgan, 1837-1885, A History of the "Morgan Line."* Coastal service, New York to Gulf and later railroad service to interior.

Brown, G.T. *The Admiral Line and Its Competitors: The Zenith and Decline of Shipping Along the Pacific Coast* (ms. PhD thesis, Claremont, 1949).

Dugan, J. *American Viking: The Saga of Hans Isbrandtsen and His Shipping Empire,* 1963. Extensive services built up by this dynamic Dane who wrote his own rules.

Elliott, J.L. *Red Stacks over the Horizon: The Story of the Goodrich Steamboat Line,* 1967. Great Lakes.

Gilbert, H. *Awakening Continent: The Life of Lord Mount Stephen, 1829-1891,* V. 1, 1965. Founder of Canadian Pacific Railway and its fleets on the Atlantic and Pacific. See also Musk below.

McCoy, S.D. *Nor Death Dismay,* 1948. World War II experiences of American Export ships.

*Mellin, G.M. *The Mississippi Shipping Co. A Case Study in the Development of Gulf Coast-South American and West African Shipping, 1919-1953* (PhD thesis, Pittsburgh, 1955; DA v. 15, p. 1003). The "Delta Line."

(Moore-McCormack Lines), *A Profile of Maritime Progress, 1913-1963,* P1963. The story of "Moore-Mac" service to the east coast of South America, to the Baltic, and eventually to South and East Africa. Brief coverage also by R.C. Lee in Newcomen Society paper, 1957.

Musk, G. *Canadian Pacific Afloat, 1883-1968,* 1968. See also Gilbert above.

O'Brien, G.C. *The Life of Robert Dollar, 1844-1932* (PhD thesis, Claremont, 1969; DA v. 30, p. 1116A). After varied sea career, established Dollar Line, with large Shipping Board ships, named for American presidents, for Pacific and round-world service. Most valuable source was his diary, 1872-1932.

Proctor, R.C. *Fifty Years with the Prince Line, 1913-1963,* 1967.

Schultz, C.R. *Inventory of the Mallory Family Papers, 1808-1858,* P1964. Manuscripts in Mystic Seaport collection with details of the Mallory Line, a history of which is in preparation by J.P. Baughman, to be published in 1972.

*Sears, M.V. *The International Mercantile Marine Company,* P1953. Harvard Business School's case history of J.P. Morgan's unsuccessful "shipping trust."

c. Individual Steamships

Beaver, P. *The Big Ship: Brunel's* Great Eastern, *A Picture History,* 1969. See also Dugan, below.

Braynard, F.O. *S.S.* Savannah: *The Elegant Steam Ship,* 1963. Most complete account of ship which made pioneer crossing, partly under steam, in 1819.

*Brown, A.C. *Women and Children Last: The Loss of the Steamship* Arctic, 1961. Sinking of crack Collins liner in 1854 after collision in fog. Like the Hoehling and Lord titles below, contains description of the ship; also included later under Marine Disasters, Sect. BQ.

*Dugan, J. *The Great Iron Ship,* 1953. History of the huge *Great Eastern* of 1858, a "white elephant" far ahead of her time. So readable that it appeared in installments in the *New Yorker.* See also Beaver above.

Hoehling, A.A. and M. *The Last Voyage of the* Lusitania, 1956, RP1961. Crack Cunarder torpedoed May 7, 1915 off Ireland with loss of 1,198 lives; the sinking played its part in bringing the United States into World War I.

*Lord, W. *A Night to Remember,* 1955, RP1960. Sinking of great White Star liner *Titanic,* April 15, 1912 with loss of more than 1,500 lives after striking iceberg in fog. This book is important as a pioneer in popularizing the "mosaic" treatment of piecing together a detailed picture from hundreds of individual recollections. See also W.J. Oldham, Sect. J-4a.

Potter, N. and Frost, J. *The* Queen Mary, 1961. Full story of the designing, construction and services of the great Cunarder.

Stanford, D. Ile de France, 1960. Similar study of the popular French Line ship, 1926-58.

J – 5   Commercial Air Competition

Commercial aviation is important in connection with liners, because it has been steadily overtaking them in the oversea carriage of passengers, mail, and light cargo. Its progress became particularly serious after the jets cut the Atlantic crossing to five hours.

*Davies, R.E. *A History of the World's Airlines,* 1964.

Higham, R.S.S. *Britain's Imperial Air Routes, 1918 to 1939; the Story of Britain's Overseas Airlines,* 1961 (PhD thesis, Harvard).

Hurran, B.J. *Britain and World Air Transport,* 1943.

Josephson, M. *Empire of the Air,* 1944. The story of Pan American Airways and its early Latin American, Pacific and Atlantic expansion.

Sempill, Lord. *International Air Transport,* 1947.

Stuart, F.S. and Biard, H.C. *Modern Air Transport,* 1948. Chapters include: 6, British Empire Air Lines; 9, Transatlantic Air Routes; 10, Empire Trunk Routes.

Zachareff, L., ed. *Vital Problems of Air Commerce,* 1946.

J – 6   Other Merchant Steam – General

Albion, R.G. *The National Shipping Authority,* Ms, 1951. A study of the reactivation and utilization of some 500 Liberty ships from the laid-up fleet for service in the Korean crisis. Prepared for the Maritime Administration. Copies in libraries of the Department of Commerce and Harvard.

Bes, J. *Bulk Carriers,* 1965.

*Boczek, B.A. *Flags of Convenience: An International Legal Study,* 1962. The rapid rise of the "flags of necessity" or "flags of easy virtue" of the Panamanian, Liberian, and other "runaway" merchant marines, owned by outsiders. The book is confined almost entirely to the point of view of international law, for which it has a substantial bibliography. See also U.S. Maritime Administration, below.

Brady, E.M. *Tugs, Towboats and Towing,* 1967.

Braynard, F.O. *A Tugman's Sketchbook,* 1965.

Critchell, J.T. and Raymond, J. *A History of the Frozen Meat Trade,* 1912. Includes the development of the refrigerator ship by 1880. See also E.F. Stevens, Section J-4a.

*Hardy, A.C. *Bulk Cargoes: A Treatise on Their Carriage by Sea and Consequent Effect on the Design and Construction of Merchant Ships,* 1926. See also the appropriate sections of his *The Book of the Ship,* 1949.
———— . *Seafood Ships,* 1947.

*LaDage, J.H., et al. *Merchant Ships: A Pictorial Study,* 1955, R1968. Includes 1,160 photographs, under following major headings: 1, Living and working aboard ship; 2, Types of merchant ships; 3, Ship structure; 4, The handling and storage of cargo; 5, Deck operations; 6, Engines and operation; 7, Building and repairing the ship.

Rogers, H.C.B. *Troopships and Their History,* 1963.

U.S. Maritime Administration, *Ships Registered under the Liberian, Panamanian and Honduran Flags Deemed by the Navy Department to be Under Effective United States Control. . . .* P1968. Only an 8-page pamphlet, but material on this subject is rare. See also Boczek above.

Walsh, W.B. *A Ship Called* Hope, 1964. Unique philanthropy which fitted out a former hospital ship, with volunteer staff, to teach medical methods in various underdeveloped countries.

J – 7   Tramps

*Course, A.G. *The Deep Sea Tramp*, 1963. Evolution of tramp trade from early times; description of types and procedures; experience in World Wars, by a retired shipmaster. (Sir A. S. Hurd's *The Triumph of the Tramp Ship* and T.W. Van Metre's *Tramps and Liners* deal with merchant shipping in general, not simply the tramp ship proper.)

Fisser, F.M. *Tramp Shipping: Development, Significance, Market Elements*, P1958.

Gripaios, H. *Tramp Shipping*, 1960.

Hendry, F.C. *The Ocean Tramp*, 1938.

*Kirkaldy, A.W. *British Shipping*, 1914, R1970. Book 1, Ch. 10, The Modern Cargo Steamer; Book 3, Ch. 6, 24 Trading Voyages (1896-1913). The last-mentioned chapter gives a clear picture of the nature of tramp voyages, in contrast to "line" service on a regular route. See also R.H. Thornton, *British Shipping*, 1939, R1959.

*McFee, W. *Watch Below: A Reconstruction in Narrative Form of the Golden Age of Steam when Coal Took the Place of Wind and the Tramp Steamer's Smoke Covered the Seven Seas*, 1940. A semi-fictionalized, semi-autobiographical description of typical tramps and the "feel" of existence aboard them, by a prominent author, formerly an engineer aboard tramps.
——————. *In the First Watch*, 1946. A similar, but more directly autobiographical account.

Phillips, M.O. *Tramp Shipping: Its Changing Position in World Trade* (ms. PhD thesis, North Carolina, 1938).

J – 8   Tankers

See also Section BM-11, Commodities of Commerce - Oil.

Anderson, J. *East of Suez*, 1968. History of the British Petroleum Co. (BP), originally Anglo-Persian, since 1907.

Anderson, L.R. and Morrison, L.H. *The Tanker in Practice*, 1935.

Booker, F., et al. *The Wreck of the* Torrey Canyon, 1968. Inexcusable carelessness ran her on rocks, causing widespread pollution of coast of southwest England and western France. See also Cowan and Gill below.

Cowan, E. *Oil and Water: The* Torrey Canyon *Disaster*, 1968.

Crump, I. *Our Tanker Fleet*, 1952.

Frischauer, W. *Onassis*, 1968. The fabulous Greek operator whose immense tanker fleet was a major source of his huge fortune. More of the same in D. Lilly, *Those Fabulous Greeks: Onassis, Niarchos and Livanos*, 1970.

*Fry, L.G., ed. *Tanker Directory of the World*, 1959 ff. Sect. 1, General: Articles on principal British and Continental tanker fleets; Technical: useful articles on corrosion; maintenance, repairs, etc. Sect. 2, List of tankers of all flags, giving tonnage, owner and builder. Sect. 3, List of owners and managers.

Gade, H. *Loading Places for Tankers in the World*, 5th ed., 1966.

Gannett, E. *Tanker Performance and Cost: Measurement, Analysis and Management*, 1968.

Gill, C. *The Wreck of the* Torrey Canyon, 1967. See also Booker and Cowan above.

Hardy, A.C. *Oil Ships and Sea Transport*, 1931.

Jansen, P. *Sea Transport of Petroleum*, 1938.

Joestin, J. *The Giant Tanker Boom: A Global Survey and Analysis of the Worldwide Splurge in Super-Tanker Construction*, P1957.

Langebein, L.H. *International Movement of Petroleum Products* (ms. PhD thesis Pittsburgh, 1960).

Nielsen, R.S.M. *Ownership of Tankers: The Independents versus the Oil Companies* (ms. PhD thesis, Berkeley, 1958).

Standard Oil Company of New Jersey, *Ships of the Esso Fleet in World War II*, 1956.

U.S. Maritime Administration, *World Fleet of Liquefied Petroleum Tankers and Liquefied Natural Gas Tankers*, P1968.

White, H.J. *Oil Tank Steamers and Modern Motor Tankers: The Standard Manual of the Transportation of Oil*, 1935.

K WARSHIPS

K – 1 General

Naval developments are included in the surveys of the "General Evolution of Ships," just noted, and in the "Picture Books" of Landström and Lloyd in particular.

Browne, D.G. *The Floating Bulwark; The Story of the Fighting Ship, 1514-1945*, 1963. Readable but little new.

Fletcher, R.A. *Warships and Their Story*, 1911. Also popular.

*Lewis, M.A. *The Navy of Britain, A Historical Portrait*, 1948. Part II, Ships, from Round Ship to Battleship.

Macintyre, D., et al. *Man-Of-War* . . . . 1970. See Sect. H-1.

K – 2   Oars

*Anderson, R.C. *Oared Fighting Ships, from Classical Times to the Coming of Steam,* 1962. In addition to analyzing the various opinions on how the ancient galleys were rowed, devotes seven chapters to vessels of later periods, down to "Hybrids of the 17th and 18th Centuries" and "Oared Men-of-War in the Baltic."

*Casson, L. *The Ancient Mariners: Seafarers and Sea-Fighters of the Mediterranean in Ancient Times,* 1959, R1967. Likewise incorporates the theories of Rodgers, Torr and others, and presents the most readable account of the subject.

Morrison, J.S. and Williams, R.T. *Greek Oared Ships, 900-322 B.C.,* 1968.

K – 3   Sail

Archibald, E.H.H. *The Wooden Fighting Ship in the Royal Navy, A.D. 897-1860,* 1968.

Bugler, A. *H.M.S.* Victory, *Building, Restoration and Repair,* 1967.

*Chapelle, H.I. *History of the American Sailing Navy: The Ships and Their Development,* 1949. Full analysis, from viewpoint of a naval architect, of all the sailing warships and revenue cutters, 1775-1855, with remarks on the colonial period. Dozens of plans and diagrams and some comment on contemporary British types.

Cross, C.B., Jr. *The* Chesapeake – *A Biography of a Ship,* P1968. The Old Navy's "hard luck" ship, in view of encounters with the *Leopard* and *Shannon.*

Franzen, A. *The Warship* Vasa, 1966. See Ohrelius below.

Gardiner, J. *Warships of the Royal Navy,* First Series, Sail, 1968. Description of the major types.

Horgan, T.P. *Old Ironsides: The Story of the U.S.S.* Constitution, 1963. See also N. Richards, below.

Longridge, C.N. *The Anatomy of Nelson's Ships,* 1953. Five folding plans. Apparently written primarily for model builders.

Lundeberg, P.K. *The Continental Gunboat* Philadelphia, P1966. Reconstruction of survivor of Arnold's Lake Champlain flotilla.

*Moore, Sir A. *Sailing Ships of War, 1800-1860,* 1926. In addition to pictures from the Macpherson Collection, gives much useful information on the ships of the transitional period.

Ohrelius, B. Vasa, *the King's Ship,* tr. M. Michael, 1962. Description of Swedish ship of the line capsized at Stockholm, while new, in 1618, and recently salvaged. See Franzen above and R. Saunders, 1962.

Pengelly, C. *The First* Bellerophon: *The Life of a Famous Ship,* 1966. Carried Napoleon to St. Helena.

Richards, N. *The Story of Old Ironsides,* 1967. See also Horgan above.

K – 4   Steam and Iron-Steel – General

American Heritage, *Ironclads of the Civil War,* 1964.

*Baldwin, H. *The New Navy,* 1964.

*Baxter, J.P. *The Introduction of the Ironclad Warship* (PhD thesis, Harvard, 1933). Able study, by former president of Williams College, of the steps by which the French, British and other major European nations came to accept the idea of armored warships and even to adopt a few before the Civil War.

*Bennett, F.M. *The Steam Navy of the United States. A History of the Growth of the Steam Vessel of War in the United States Navy and of the Naval Engineer Corps,* 2 v. 1896.

Blackman, R.V. *The World's Warships,* 1956 ff, R1970. Compact summary by the editor of *Jane's Fighting Ships.*

Brassey's Naval Annual. See Sect. B-2.

*Brodie, B. *Sea Power in the Machine Age: Major Naval Inventions and Their Consequences on International Politics, 1814-1940,* 1940 (PhD thesis, Chicago), R1969. Valuable analysis of the transition to steam and steel.

Chapelle, H.I. and Pollard, L.D. *The* Constellation *Question,* 1970. Opposite views on whether the present ship was actually the 1797 frigate.

Dolby, J. *The Steel Navy. A History in Silhouette, 1860-1963,* 1962, R1965.

*Hovgaard, W. *Modern History of Warships, Comprising a Discussion of Present Standpoint and Recent War Experiences,* 1920. Authoritative analysis of the evolution of armored ships, including their battle performance. Author headed School of Naval Architecture and Marine Engineering at M.I.T.

Howard, J.L. *Our Modern Navy,* 1961. Competent American survey.

Jane's Fighting Ships. See Sect. B-2.

McBride, R. *Civil War Ironclads: The Dawn of Naval Armor,* 1962.

Melton, M. *The Confederate Ironclads,* 1968.

Penn, G. *Up Funnel, Down Screw, The Story of the Naval Engineer,* 1955. Like Bennett above, this British counterpart reveals the line officers' prejudices against the engineers. The title comes from the period of retractable propellers when the transitional cruisers could revert to sail.

*Sloan, E.W. *Benjamin Franklin Isherwood, Naval Engineer: The Years as Engineer-in-Chief, 1861-1869,* 1965. Based on Harvard PhD thesis, *Steam for the Union Navy.*

K – 5 Battleships

The original armored vessels were known as ironclads, but after steel supplanted iron by the 1880s, the word battleship took over.

Hough, R. *The Great Dreadnought,* 1967 (*The Great Battleship* in British edition). The huge *Agincourt* laid down in a British yard for Brazil, was shifted to Turkey and then taken over by the British in 1914; fought at Jutland.

*Parkes, O. *British Battleships,* Warrior *1860 to* Vanguard *1950: A History of Design, Construction and Armament,* 1958, R1966. A monumental 701-page quarto by a retired English physician. Goes into rich detail on all aspects, including some of the elusive discussions of design policy. Includes considerable material on foreign navies and also on cruisers, destroyers and other types. Wealth of statistics and diagrams. Not to be confused with the less impressive E.R. Pears, *British Battleships, 1892-1957,* 1957.

Roskill, S.W. *H.M.S.* Warspite, *The Story of a Famous Battleship,* 1958. Case study of one of the most successful of battleships which, with her sister ships *Barham, Malaya, Queen Elizabeth,* and *Valiant,* completed just at the outbreak of World War I, fought through that war and World War II as well.

Wilson, H.W. *Battleships in Action,* 2 v. 1926, R1968. Sequel to his *Ironclads in Action,* 2 v. 1896. Particularly useful for Russo-Japanese War.

K – 6 Destroyers

Alden, J.D. *Flush Decks and Four Pipers,* 1965. The 200-odd U.S. destroyers of World War I.

Kemp, P.K. *H.M. Destroyers,* 1956. Evolution from the torpedo boat of 1870, by the Admiralty librarian.

Manning, T.D. *British Destroyers,* 1961. Goes back to the *Havock* of 1893; includes some 150 photographs.

*March, E.J. *British Destroyers, 1893-1955,* 1967. "Contains an even greater volume of material than Parke's *British Battleships* and is a companion volume to it."

*Schofield, W.G. *Destroyer – 60 Years,* 1962. From *DD-1 Bainbridge,* 1902, to *DLG-N-25, Bainbridge,* 1962. Well illustrated.

(See also the World War II accounts by T. Roscoe and others.)

50

K – 7   Submarines

*Anderson, F. *Submarines, Submariners, Submarining. A Checklist of Submarine Books in the English Language . . . Author, Title and Subject,* 1963.

Best, A.C. *Underwater Warriors,* 1967.

Cope, H.G. *Serpent of the Seas, the Submarine,* 1942.

Douglas, L.H. *Submarine Disarmament, 1919-1931.* See Sect. BF.

Hoyt, E.P. *From the* Turtle *to the* Nautilus, 1963.

Jameson, W.S. *The Most Formidable Thing: The Story of the Submarine from Its Earliest Days to the End of World War I,* 1965. By a British admiral.

Lipscomb, F.W. *The British Submarine,* 1954.

*Morris, R.K. *John P. Holland, 1841-1914, Inventor of the Modern Submarine,* 1966. Scholarly research, well presented.

*National Academy of Science, National Research Council, *Bibliography of the Submarine, 1557-1963,* 1954. Prepared by the Committee on Undersea Warfare.

*Stafford, E.P. *The Far and the Deep: A Half Century of Submarine History,* 1967. "The most comprehensive history of the submarine to date."

Wagner, F. *Submarine Fighter of the American Revolution. The Story of David Bushnell,* 1963. Study on same subject by H.L. Abbott, 1966.

K – 8   Carriers and Aircraft

Berquist, F. *Aircraft Carriers in Action,* 1968.

Blundell, W.D.G. *British Aircraft Carriers,* 1969.

Boyle A. *Trenchard,* 1963. Biography of British Chief Air Marshal, whose widespread influence affected the Royal Navy's Air Service.

Cameron, J. *Wings of the Morning. The Story of the Fleet Air Arm in the Second World War,* 1962.

Duval, G.R. *British Flying Boats, 1909-1952,* 1965.

Higham, R.D. *The British Rigid Airship, 1908-1931. A Study in Weapons Evaluation,* 1961.

Kealy, J.D.F. *A History of Canadian Naval Aviation, 1918-1962,* 1965.

Larkins, W.T. *U.S. Navy Aircraft, 1921-1941,* 1960.

Lincoln, A. *The United States Navy and Air Power: A History of Naval Aviation, 1920-1924* (ms. PhD thesis, Berkeley, 1946).

Macintyre, D. *Aircraft Carriers: The Majestic Weapon,* P1968.

Mizrahi, J.V. *U.S. Carrier Fighters,* V. 1, 1960. U.S. planes in the 1920s and 1930s.

Nowara, H.J. *Marine Aircraft of the 1914-1918 War,* 1966.

Palmer, H.R., Jr. *The Seaplanes,* 1965. Military and civil.

Polmar, N. *Aircraft Carriers: A Graphic History of Carrier Aviation and Its Influence on World Events,* 1969. More than 500 photographs.

Popham, H. *Into Wind: A History of British Naval Flying,* 1969.

*Reynolds, C.G. *The Fast Carriers: The Forging of an Air Navy,* 1968 (PhD thesis, Duke). Valuable analysis of their new role.

*Roskill, S.W., ed. *Documents Relating to the Naval Air Service* (Navy Records Soc. V. 113), 1968.

Swanborough, G. and Bowers, P.M. *United States Navy Aircraft since 1911,* 1968.

Thetford, O. *British Naval Aircraft since 1912,* 1962, R1969.

*Turnbull, A.D. and Lord, C.L. *History of United States Naval Aviation,* 1949. Produced in Navy's administrative history program. Emphasis primarily on men and policies.

*Van Wyen, A.O. and Pearson, L.P. *United States Naval Aviation, 1910-60* (NavWeps 00-80P-1) 1960. Prepared under the direction of the Deputy CNO (Air) and Chief of Naval Weapons. Consists of month-by-month chronology of development.

K – 9   Weapons and Special Features

Annis, P.G.W. *Naval Swords: British and American Naval Edged Weapons, 1660-1815,* 1970.

Bracken, E.E. *The LSD – Landing Ship Dock,* P1965.

Brodie, B. *Sea Power in the Machine Age . . . .* 1940, R1969.

Bruzek, J.C. *The "IX" Dahlgren Broadside Gun,* P1964. Admiral Dahlgren, naval ordnance head, designed this popular Civil War gun.

Cole, R.H. *Underwater Explosions,* 1965.

Comprato, F.C. *The Age of Great Guns,* 1965. From the time of Napoleon, including naval guns.

Cowie, J.S. *Mines, Minelayers and Mine Laying,* 1949. See also Duncan and Lott below.

Dooly, W.G. *Great Weapons of World War I,* 1960.

*Duncan, R.C. *American Use of Sea Mines,* 1962. By the chief physicist of the Naval Ordnance Laboratory.

Durham, B. *Standard Boats of the United States Navy, 1900-1915,* 1963.

Garbett, H. *Naval Gunnery,* 1897.

Holley, A.L. *A Treatise on Ordnance and Armor,* 1865.

Hook, C. *Hydrofoils,* 1967.

Jane's Weapon Systems, annual.

*Lewis, E.R. *Seacoast Fortifications of the United States . . . .* 1970. See Sect. AS; evolution of coast artillery.

*Lewis, M.A. *The Armada Guns,* 1961. Comparison of English and Spanish naval artillery.

*Lott, A. *Most Dangerous Sea: A History of Mine Warfare and an Account of U.S. Navy Mine Warfare Operations in World War II and Korea,* 1959 and P.

May, W.E. and Kennard, A.M. *Naval Swords and Firearms,* 1962. British.

Norman, A.V.B. and Pottinger, D. *A History of War and Weapons, 449 to 1660. English Warfare from the Anglo-Saxons to Cromwell,* 1967. Includes naval guns.

Padfield, P. *Aim Straight, A Biography of Admiral Percy Scott,* 1967. Pioneer proponent of improved gunnery in the Royal Navy.

Peck, T. *Round Shot to Rockets. A History of the Washington Navy Yard and the Naval Gun Factory,* 1949.

Pope, D. *Guns,* 1965. "Guns of all nations, on land, at sea, and in the air" by one of the most prolific writers on naval subjects.

*Postan, M.M., et al. *Design and Development of Weapons,* 1964. Design, development and production of British weapons, and even some aircraft and ships, in World War II. In official history, civil series.

Reeman, D. *H.M.S.* Saracen, 1966. British monitor, 1915-1966.

*Robertson, F.L. *The Evolution of Naval Armament,* 1921, R1968.

*Rowland, B. and Boyd, W.B. *U.S. Navy Bureau of Ordnance in World War II,* 1953. "BuOrd" produced a similar official history in World War I.

Stevens, P.H. *Artillery through the Ages,* 1965.

Tennent, Sir J.E. *The Story of the Guns,* 1864.

Tucker, C.D. *Naval Guns, 1600-1850,* 1952. Typescript at Mariner's Museum, Newport News.

K – 10   Missiles and Nuclear Power

Anderson, W.R. and Blair, C., Jr. Nautilus *90 North,* 1959. Anderson commanded the first atomic submarine.

Barr, J. and Howard, W.I. Polaris! 1961.

Beach, E.L. *Around the World Submerged,* 1962. Beach, the author of *Submarine,* commanded the atomic *Triton* on an underwater circumnavigation in 1960.

Koliphkis, I.A. *Submarines in Arctic Waters,* 1966. Russian.

Kuenne, R.E. *The Attack Submarine: A Study in Strategy,* 1965.
————. *The Polaris Missile Strike. . . .*1967.

*Parson, N.A., Jr. *Missiles and the Revolution in Warfare,* 1962. An extensive amplification of his *Guided Missiles in War and Peace,* 1956.

Polmar, N. *Atomic Submarines,* 1963.

*Rees, E. *The Sea and the Subs,* 1961. Includes account of the development of the nuclear submarine and the Polaris missile.

Sokol, A.E. *Sea Power in the Nuclear Age,* 1959.

L   SHIPBUILDING AND NAVAL ARCHITECTURE

L – 1   General

Abell, Sir W. *The Shipwright's Trade,* 1948. Comprehensive account by former Chief Surveyor of Lloyd's. Emphasis largely British.

*Albion, R.G. *Forests and Sea Power, The Timber Problem of the Royal Navy, 1652-1862,* 1926, R1965. (PhD thesis, Harvard). Especially Ch. I., Trees and Ship Timber; ch. 2., Contracts, Conservatism and Corruption. Masts and naval stores were the principal critical strategic materials of the sailing ship era, as none of the maritime powers had an adequate domestic supply. England also eventually had to look overseas to replenish her diminishing supply of oak. Timber, like coal, had a strong maritime significance because its bulk required so much shipping.

Baker, W.A. *A History of the Department of Naval Architecture and Marine En-*

gineering, Massachusetts Institute of Technology: A History of the First 75 Years (Dept. Report No. 69-3), P1969.

*Bamford, P.W. *Forests and French Sea Power, 1660-1789,* 1956 (PhD thesis, Columbia). A companion work to Albion, above.

Baxter, B.N. *Naval Architecture,* 1967.

Biddlecomb, Sir G. *The Art of Rigging, Containing an Explanation of Terms and Phrases and the Progressive Methods of Rigging Expressly Adapted for Sailing Ships,* 1925.

*Brewington, M.V. *Shipcarvers of North America,* 1962, R1967.

*Chapman, F.H. *A Treatise of Ship-Building with Explanations and Demonstrations Respecting the Architectura Navalis Mercatoria,* 1820. A translation by J. Inman of the Swedish classical work on the subject, *Architectura Navalis Mercatoria,* 1768, R1957, 1967.

Charnock, J. *A History of Marine Architecture,* 3 v. 1800-02. A rambling miscellany.

Cobb, B. *Fiberglass Boats; Construction and Maintenance,* 1965.

*Comstock, J., ed. *Principles of Naval Architecture,* 1939, R1967. Cooperative "classic and unique treatise," prepared under the auspices of the Society of Naval Architects and Marine Engineers. Reflects tremendous amount of technical progress and ship design since the first edition in 1939.

*Fassett, F.G., ed. *The Shipbuilding Business in the United States of America,* 2 v. 1948, R1964, 1970. Another valuable publication of the Society of Naval Architects and Marine Engineers. Vol. 1, Ch. 2, History and Development of Shipbuilding, 1776-1944, by J.G.B. Hutchins; ch. 3, Shipyard Statistics, pp. 61-200, by H.G. Smith and L.C. Brown; giving a wealth of local detail. The rest of the work consists mainly of various business and technical details of modern shipbuilding.

Fincham, J. *Directions for Laying Off Ships on the Mould Loft Floor,* 1822.
————. *Treatise on Masting Ships and Mastmaking,* 3rd ed. 1851.
————. *History of Marine Architecture,* 1851.

Goldenberg, J.A. *The Shipbuilding Industry in Colonial America* (PhD thesis, North Carolina, 1969; DA v. 31, p. 338a).

*Griffiths, J.W. *A Treatise on Marine and Naval Architecture,* 1850 ff.
————. *The Shipbuilder's Manual and Nautical Referee,* 2 v. 1855. See also McKay below.

Halacy, D.S., Jr. *The Shipbuilders: From Clipper Ships to Submarines to Hovercraft,* 1966.

Hall, E.W. *Sailmaking in Connecticut Prior to 1800,* 1968.

*Hall, H. "Report on the Shipbuilding Industry of the United States" in *U.S. Report of the Tenth Census,* VIII, 1844, R1970. One of the most comprehensive accounts of American shipbuilding to that date, including a wealth of data on the various yards in specific localities.

Hammond, R. *The Making of a Ship,* 1965.

Hansen, H.J., ed. *Art and the Seafarer: A Historical Survey of the Arts and Crafts of Sailors and Shipwrights,* 1968. Over 300 pictures.

*Hardy, A.C. *From the Slip to the Sea: A Chronological Account of the Construction of Merchant Ships from the Laying of the Keel Plates to the Trial Trip, with over 134 Sketches and Illustrations,* 1916. The clearest play-by-play account of modern British steel construction, comparable to Lauchlan McKay for wooden ships.
————. *Bulk Cargoes: A Treatise on Their Carriage by Sea and Consequent Effect on the Design and Construction of Merchant Ships,* 1926.
————. *Shipbuilding: The Background of a Great Industry,* 1961.

Harvard Graduate School of Business Administration, *The Use and Disposition of Ships and Shipyards at the End of World War II,* 1945. Prepared for the use of the Navy Department and Maritime Commission.

Holden, D.A. *Men, Ships and the Sea: The Story of the Society of Naval Architects and Marine Engineers* (Newcomen Society), P1968.

*Hutchins, J.G.B. *The American Maritime Industries and Public Policy, 1789-1914,* 1941 (PhD thesis, Harvard), R1969. Able analysis of the relationship of shipbuilding conditions to maritime policy, particularly in connection with America's early abundant supply of timber and masts.

Institution of Naval Architects, *Transactions,* annual since 1860. British.

Jackson, G.W. and Sutherland, W.M. *Concrete Boatbuilding . . . .* 1969.

Knowles, J. *Elements and Practice of Naval Architecture,* 1822; based on D. Steel, *Elements and Practice of Naval Architecture,* 1805.

*LaDage, J.H., et al. *Merchant Ships: A Pictorial Study.* See Sect. J-6. Ch. 3, Ship Structure; ch. 7, Building and Repairing the Ship.

Laing, A.K. *Clipper Ships and Their Makers,* 1966.

*Lane, F.C., et al. *Ships for Victory: A History of the Shipbuilding under the U.S. Maritime Commission in World War II* (Historical Reports on War Administration, U.S. Maritime Commission), 1951.

Laughton, L.G. *Old Ship Figure-Heads and Sterns,* 1925, R1967. See also Brewington, above.

MacGregor, D.R. *Hey-Dey of Sail*, 1965. A study of the development of ships, 1815-75, based on ships' plans.

Manning, G.C. *The Theory and Technique of Ship Design: A Study of the Basic Principles and the Processes Employed in the Design of All Classes*, 1956. The author was Professor of Naval Architecture at M.I.T.

*Mattox, W.C. *Building the Emergency Fleet; A Historical Narrative of the Problems and Achievements of the United States Shipping Board Emergency Fleet Corporation*, 1920, R1970. The World War I counterpart of Lane.

*McKay, L. *The Practical Ship-Builder*, 1839, R1940, 1970. This, like the Griffiths volumes above, was written by a man prominent in the designing of American clippers, and gives detailed accounts of the processes involved in construction. Griffiths played an important designing role in the remarkable East River work at New York, while McKay was brother of the famous Donald.

Mitchell, W.H. and Sawyer, L.A. See Sect. J-4.

Munro-Smith, B. *Merchant Ship Design*, 1964.

*Neuhaus, H.M. "Fifty Years of Naval Engineering," *American Society of Naval Engineers Journal*, V. 50, 1938. Four parts, totalling 154 pages, covering the years 1888-1938.

Phillips-Birt, D.H.C. *The Naval Architecture of Small Craft*, 1958.

Pinckney, P.A. *American Figureheads and Their Carvers*, 1940, R1969. See also Brewington and Laughton.

Pollard, S. *The Economic History of British Shipbuilding, 1870-1914* (ms. PhD thesis, London, 1951).

Pollock, D. *Modern Shipbuilding and the Men engaged in it: A Review of recent progress in Steamship Design and Construction, together with Descriptions of Notable Shipyards . . . and Biographical Notes of Eminent Shipowners, Shipbuilders, Engineers and Naval Architects*, 1884.
————. *The Shipbuilding Industry: Its History, Practice, Science and Finance*, 1905. British emphasis in both.

Redlich, F. *The History of the Söderfors Anchor Works*, 1791, tr. L.H. Hedin (Kress Library Pub. No. 21), P1969.

Reed, E.J. *Shipbuilding in Iron and Steel*, 1869. Prominent British authority.

Russell, J.S. *The Modern System of Naval Architecture*, 3 v. 1865. Also prominent in that transitional period.

Sadler, S.B. *The Art and Science of Sailmaking*, 2nd ed. 1906.

*Society of Naval Architects and Marine Engineers, *Historical Transactions, 1893-*

1943, 1945. Collection of relatively short papers on many aspects of shipbuilding, including accounts of the various U.S. navy yards, part 1; the ten leading private shipyards, part 2; special types of vessels, part 3; naval vessels, part 4; vessels in particular areas, such as the Great Lakes, part 5; and general development and history, part 6. List of other pertinent articles in the Society's *Transactions*, pp. 455-66.

──────── . *Index to Transactions*, 1946, R1970.

Stackpole, E.A. *Figureheads and Ship Carvings at Mystic Seaport*, 1961.

(Steel, D.) *Steel's Elements of Mastmaking, Sailmaking and Rigging (from the 1794 edition), Arranged, with an introduction by Claude S. Gill*, 1958.

Still, W.N. *The Construction and Fitting Out of Ironclad Vessels-of-War within the Confederacy* (ms. PhD thesis, Alabama, 1964).

Sutherland, W. *Shipbuilder's Assistant*, 1711.

Webster, F.B., ed. *Shipbuilding Cyclopedia*, 1920.

L – 2   Regional – British and European

Banbury, P. *Shipbuilders of the Thames and Medway*, 1971.

Blake, G. *Down to the Sea: The Romance of the Clyde, Its Ships and Shipbuilders*, 1937.

Christensen, H.E., Jr. (Seeberg, E., pseud.) *Boats of the North: A History of Boatbuilding in Norway*, 1968.

Cormack, W.S. *An Economic History of Shipbuilding and Marine Engineering, with special reference to the West of Scotland* (ms. MA thesis, London 1937).

Crowther, S.J. *The Shipbuilding Industry*. . . . See Sect. L-3.

Dougan, D. *The History of North East Shipbuilding*, 1969. Tyneside and other parts of Northeast England.

Dunn, L. *Famous Liners of the Past: Belfast Built*, 1964.

Hickmore, M.A.S. *The Shipbuilding Industry on the East and South Coasts of England in the Fifteenth Century* (ms. MA thesis, London, 1937).

Landström, B. *Ships of the Pharoahs*, 1971. "4,000 years of shipbuilding in Egypt."

*Lane, F.C. *Venetian Ships and Shipbuilding of the Renaissance*, 1934 (PhD thesis, Harvard).

Mitchell, W.H. and Sawyer, L.A. See Sect. J-3.

Rebeck, D. *The History of Iron Shipbuilding at Belfast up to 1874* (ms. PhD thesis, Belfast, 1950).

Shields, J. *Clyde Built: A History of Ship-Building on the River Clyde,* 1949. See also Blake above.

Van Doorninck, F.H., Jr. *The Seventh Century Byzantine Ship at Yassi Ada: Some Contributions to the History of Naval Architecture* (PhD thesis, Pennsylvania, 1917, DA v. 28, p. 4078A). Sank near Bodrum, Turkey with 900 wine amphoras.

Wood, O. *The Development of the Coal, Iron and Shipbuilding Industries of West Cumberland, 1750-1914* (ms. PhD thesis, London, 1952).

L – 3   Regional – American

*Albion, R.G. *The Rise of New York Port, 1815-1860,* 1939, R1970. Ch. 14, The East River Yards. See also Morrison, below.

*Briggs, L.V. *History of Shipbuilding on the North River, Plymouth County, Massachusetts,* 1889, R1970. This little tidal stream had a tremendous output of sailing vessels.

Dowling, E.J. *The Lakers of World War I. . . .* P1967. See Sect. AE-2.

*Fairburn, W.A., et al. *Merchant Sail,* 6 v. 1945-55, Vol. 5, "Wooden Shipbuilders and Shipbuilding Centers through the 19th Century, with Particulars of Sailing Vessels." See Sect. L.

*Fischer, G.J., et al. *Statistical Summary of Shipbuilding under the Maritime Commission during World War II,* 1949.

*Hall, H. See Sect. L-1.

Herrick, R.B. *A Century of Shipbuilding in Blue Hill, Maine, 1792-1892* (ms. AM thesis, Maine, 1945).

Inches, H.C. *The Great Lakes Wooden Shipbuilding Era,* P1962.

Morrison, J.H. *History of the New York Shipyards,* 1909, R1970.

Rowe, W.H. *Shipbuilding Days in Casco Bay, 1727-1890,* 1929. Casco Bay extends eastward from Portland.
————. *The Maritime History of Maine: Three Centuries of Shipbuilding and Seafaring,* 1948, R1966.

Switzer, D.C. *Maritime Maine and the Union Naval Construction Effort 1861-1865* (ms. PhD thesis, Connecticut, 1970).

Tyler, D.B. *The American Clyde: A History of Iron and Steel Shipbuilding on the Delaware from 1840 to World War I,* 1958.

L – 4 Individual Designers, Builders and Yards – British

Barnes, E.C. *Alfred Yarrow, His Life and Work,* 1923. Naval construction, particularly torpedo boats and destroyers.

Brettle, R.E. *The* Cutty Sark. *Her Designer and Builder, Hercules Linton, 1836-1900,* 1969. The author married one of Linton's daughters and had access to his papers, drawings and photographs.

Bruce, A.B. *The Life of William Denny, Shipbuilder, Dumbarton,* 1889.

Carbel, J.L. (I.C. Leeds, pseud.) *Stephen of Linthouse: A Record of Two Hundred Years of Shipbuilding, 1750-1950,* 1951.

*Lubbock, B. *The Blackwall Frigates,* 1922, R1962. Part 1, The History of the Blackwall Yard, 1611-1836. See Sect. I. There is also a history of the yard by Henry Green and Robert Wigram, the two family names long associated with its operation.

Manning, F. *The Life of Sir William White,* 1923. The Royal Navy's Director of Naval Construction, 1885-1901.

*Pett, P. *The Autobiography of Phineas Pett,* ed. W.G. Perrin (Navy Records Society, No. 51), 1917. England's outstanding naval constructor of the 17th century, foremost among the numerous Petts in that field.

*Rolt, L.T.C. *Isambard Kingdom Brunel, A Biography,* 1957. Promoter and designer of the *Great Western,* the *Great Eastern* and other prominent early steamships, in addition to railway and bridge construction.

Scott, J.D. *Vickers: A History,* 1963.

Shields, J. *Two Centuries of Shipbuilding by the Scotts at Greenock,* 1920. The Scott Shipbuilding and Engineering Co. issued a later history, *The Scotts at Greenock,* 1961.

L – 5 Individual Designers, Builders and Yards – American

Balison, H.J. *Newport News Ships: Their History in Two Wars,* 1954. The Newport News Shipbuilding & Dry Dock Co. also produced *Three Generations of Shipbuilding, 1886-1961,* 1961.

*Bowen, H.G. *Ships, Machinery and Mossbacks: The Autobiography of a Naval Engineer,* 1954. Admiral Bowen was one of the last chiefs of the Bureau of Engineering and the first chief of the Office of Naval Research. His pugnacious persistence produced numerous important technological innovations, especially high-pressure, high-temperature steam aboard ship.

Braynard, F.O. *By Their Works Ye Shall Know Them,* 1968. An appreciation of William Francis Gibbs of Gibbs & Cox, one of the outstanding naval architects of this century.

Buell, A.C. *Memoirs of Charles H. Cramp,* 1906. With his great yard near Philadelphia, Cramp was the leading American shipbuilder at the turn of the century, producing many of the new warships. Some of Buell's statements need checking for accuracy.

Church, W.C. *Life of John Ericsson,* 2 v. 1890. A later biography of the developer of the screw propeller and the *Monitor* is R. White, *Yankee from Sweden,* 1960.

Clark, A.G. *They Built Clipper Ships in Their Back Yard,* P1963. The Shiverick yard at East Dennis on Cape Cod built eight ships (not all clippers) and four schooners, 1848-1863.

Eskew, G.L. *Cradle of Ships: A History of Bath Iron Works,* 1958. This Maine yard had built 338 vessels since 1885, including a quarter of the Navy's destroyers. One reviewer said of the book "the result is as if one were to leave a ship in frame with no planking, deck, inside fittings, rig, and machinery." A far more adequate comprehensive history of Bath shipbuilding is in preparation by W.A. Baker.

*Evans, H.A. *One Man's Fight for a Better Navy,* 1940. A naval constructor, Evans struggled to improve the efficiency of navy yard management. He finally resigned and became a successful private shipbuilder.

Finnie, R. *Marinship, the History of a Wartime Shipyard,* 1947. San Francisco Bay.

Hennessy, M.W. *Sewall Ships of Steel,* 1937. Most of the products of this famous Bath yard were of wood.

*Herreshoff, L.F. *Captain Nat Herreshoff: His Life and the Yachts He Designed,* 1954.

Isaacson, D.W. and Haggett, A.M., eds. *Phipsburg, Fair to the Wind,* P1964. Includes account of Minott yard which built the last square-rigged wooden ship in this Kennebec town below Bath.

Land, E.S. *Winning the War with Ships: Land, Sea and Air – Mostly Land,* 1958. Salty admiral who headed the Maritime Commission's tremendous shipbuilding program during World War II.

McKay, R.C. *Some Famous Sailing Ships and Their Builder, Donald McKay,* 1928, R1969.

Morison, S.E. *The Ropemakers of Plymouth: A History of the Plymouth Cordage Company, 1824-1949,* 1950.

Mylson, M. *The Babcock & Wilcox Co., 1867-1967* (Newcomen Society), P1967. Leading manufacturers of marine boilers.

Schultz, C.R. *Cost of Construction and Outfitting of the Ship* Charles W. Morgan, P1967. See Sect. AM-1.

Stevens, T.A. *George Greenman & Company: Shipbuilders of Mystic, Conn.* (Marine Historical Assn., 13), 1938.

*Swann, L.A. *John Roach, Maritime Entrepreneur: The Years as Naval Contractor, 1862-1886,* 1965 (PhD thesis, Harvard). An Irish immigrant, Roach first operated a New York marine engine works; moved to the Delaware and developed an "integrated" operation for building iron ships; and finally went into bankruptcy building the first four steel ships for the "New Navy."

*Webb, W.H. *Plans of Wooden Vessels . . . built by William H. Webb in the City of New York (1840-1869),* 2 v. 1895. The versatile Webb, producing packets, clippers, steamships, and warships, was perhaps the outstanding American shipbuilder of his time, a primacy later held in turn by Roach, Cramp, and Newport News.

Wright, R.J. *Freshwater Whales: A History of the American Shipbuilding Company and its Predecessors,* 1969. Builders of whalebacks and other vessels on the Great Lakes.

III   Captains and Crews

M   MERCHANT MARINE

M – 1   General

*Albion, R.G. *Square-Riggers on Schedule*, 1938, R1965. Ch. 4, "Tough Men," packet officers and crews, 1818-1848.

*Bullen, F.T. *The Men of the Merchant Service: Being the Polity of the Merchant Service for Longshore Readers*, 1900. The most useful picture of merchant marine personnel (British) in the transition period. Readable analysis and description of the status and duties of masters, mates, and various categories of crews, comparing conditions in sail and steam, and in liners and tramps.

Clark, A.H. *The Clipper Ship Era*, 1910.

Cornewall-Jones, R. *The British Merchant Service*, 1898, R1969.

Cotter, C.H. *The Master and His Ship*, 1962, "A series of twelve essays on seamanship topics. They cover the advanced kind of seamanship needed by a modern shipmaster."

Course, A.G. *The Merchant Navy, A Social History*, 1963. This received a mixed reception at the hands of the reviewers.

Dane, P. *The Seamen Are Down Below*, 1962. Life in the engine room and exploits ashore. Not of the same quality as McFee.

*Davis, R. *The Rise of the English Shipping Industry in the Seventeeth and Eighteenth Centuries*, 1963. Ch. 6, The Merchant Seaman; ch. 7, The Pay and Conditions of Merchant Seamen; ch. 8, Shipping Management and the Role of the Master.

Garbesi, G.C. *Consular Authority over Seamen from the United States Point of View*, 1968.

Hannay, D. *The Sea Trader: His Friends and Enemies*, 1912. Ch. 2, The Skipper and His Men; ch. 3, The Way of Life.

*Healy, J.C. *Foc's'le and Glory Hole: A Study of the Merchant Seaman and His Occupation*, 1936, R1970. Excellent. Limited to crew members whereas Bullen, above, emphasizes officers. Comprehensive and well-balanced analysis of many varied problems. Author, after service afloat, served many years as secretary of the Seamen's House at New York. Good bibliography.

Hohman, E.P. *History of the American Merchant Seamen*, 1956. Less comprehensive than the title indicates. Reprints of three separate articles: Pt. 1, Orientation and Background; pt. 2, Maritime Labor, 1790-1937; pt. 3, Merchant Seamen, 1937-52.

Hope, R., ed. *Seamen and the Sea*, 1965.

*Hugill, S. *Sailortown*, 1967. A composite of many ports, chiefly British, showing how seamen spent their time ashore. "Some of the prudish and narrow-minded may be inclined to discuss this book as a long chronicle of whoring, boozing, and debauchery, but . . . the book is nonetheless an important contribution to the social history of the seafarer."

Humiston, F.S. *Blue-Water Men – and Women*, 1966. A rambling collection of newspaper contributions, chiefly on 19th-century Maine seafarers, with more atmosphere than accuracy; indulges in imaginary conversations.

*McFee, W. *Watch Below*, 1940. Similar account in his *In the First Watch*. See Sect. J-7.

Parkinson, C.N., ed. *The Trade Winds . . . 1793-1815*, 1948. Ch. 5, Seamen.
————. *Trade in the Eastern Seas, 1793-1813*, 1937. Ch. 7, "The Maritime Service" shows the rich opportunities of commanders of East Indiamen.

Schull, J. *The Salt Water Men; Canada's Deep-Sea Sailors*, 1957.

*Villiers, A. *The Way of a Ship*, 1953, R1970. Pt. III, The Men. Ch. 7, The Sailors; ch. 8, The Masters. Pt. IV, The Life; ch. 9, Economics; ch. 10, Standards of Conduct.

M – 2   Maritime Labor Unions

Allbrecht, A.E. *The International Seamen's Union of America: A Study of Its History and Problems* (Bureau of Labor Statistics), 1923 (PhD thesis, Columbia).

*Goldberg, J.P. *The Maritime Story: A Study in Labor-Management Relations*, P1958 (PhD thesis, Columbia). Ch. 1, "The Seaman in 1900," a general description before going into play-by-play union developments. The National Maritime Union gave paperback copies to all its members.

Herzog, D.R. *A Study in Labor Relations relating to American Seamen in the Maritime Industry* (PhD thesis, Iowa State, 1955; DA v. 15, p.2046).

Lampman, R.J. *Collective Bargaining of West Coast Sailors, 1885-1947, a Case Study in Unionism* (ms. PhD thesis, Wisconsin, 1950).

Larrowe, C.P. *The Shape-Up and the Hiring Hall* (ms. PhD thesis, Yale, 1952).
————. *Maritime Labor Relations on the Great Lakes*, 1959.

Liebes, R.A. *Longshore Relations on the Pacific Coast, 1934-1942* (ms. PhD thesis, Berkeley, 1943).

Lovell, J.C. *Trade Unionism in the Port of London.* See Sect. BK-3.

Macarthur, W. *The Seamen's Contract*, 1915. Author collaborated with Andrew Furuseth.

Palmer, D.L. *Pacific Coast Maritime Labor* (ms. PhD thesis, Stanford, 1936).

Schneider, R.V. *Industrial Relations in the West Coast Maritime Industry*, P1958.

Stern, W.M. *The Porters of London*, 1960. Includes the organization and regulation of the "dockers" or longshoremen, from the 17th to the late 19th century.

Stockhan, J.M. *The Development of the Atlantic and Gulf Coast District of the Seafarers International Union of North America for the First Twenty Years, 1938-1958* (PhD thesis, New York Univ., 1963; DA v.27, p.4025A).

Swanstrom, E.E. *The Waterfront Labor Problem; A Study in Decasualization and Unemployment Insurance*, 1938 (PhD thesis, Berkeley).

Taylor, P.S. *The Sailors' Union of the Pacific*, 1923 (PhD thesis, Berkeley).

*Weintraub, H. *Andrew Furuseth: Emancipator of the Seamen*, 1959 (PhD thesis, UCLA). Life of the Norwegian-born labor pioneer (1846-1938) who organized the Coast Seamen's Union in 1885 and whose skillful, tireless lobbying led to the Lafollette Seamen's Act of 1915. See also Macarthur above.

White, D.J. *The New England Fishing Industry; A Study in Price and Wage Setting*, 1954 (PhD thesis, Harvard).

Wiseman, R.W. *The Maritime Industry; The Role of Federal Regulation in Establishing Labor and Safety Standards*, 1942 (PhD thesis, Columbia).

M – 3   Special Topics

Anson, P.F. *Church and the Sailor*, 1949.

Bridges, F.J. *Training Programs for Seafaring Personnel in the Maritime Industry* (ms. PhD thesis, Alabama, 1957).

Dillon, R.M. *Shanghaiing Days*, 1962.

Fisher, R. *The Ship's Orchestra*, 1966.

Gjerset, K. *Norwegian Sailors in American Waters: A Study in the History of Maritime Activity on the Eastern Seaboard*, 1933.

Henningsen, H. *Crossing the Equator, Sailors' Baptism and Other Initiation Rites*, 1961. See also Lydenburg, below.

*Lydenburg, H.M. *Crossing the Line*, 1957. Ceremonies during four centuries described by the librarian of New York Public Library.

Millington, E.C. *Seamen in the Making: History of Nautical Training*, 1933. See also Underhill below.

Moreby, P.H. *Personnel Management in Merchant Ships*, 1968.

Stackpole, E.A. *Scrimshaw at Mystic Seaport* (Marine Historical Assn.) P1958.

Underhill, H.A. *Sail Training and Cadet Ships*, 1956. See also Millington above.

Wallis, R. *Sailors and Sin*, 1969. See also Hugill, Sect. M-1.

Williams, J., et al. *Sea and Air: The Naval Environment*, 1968. (Original title, *Air and Water. . . .*)

Wright, L.G. *The Sailor's Wife*, 1967.

Zimmerman, J.F. *The Impressment of American Seamen*, 1925, R1966.

N NAVAL PERSONNEL

N – 1 General

Arnold-Forster, D. *The Ways of the Navy*, 1931. Modern British Navy.

Arthur, R.W. *Contact! Careers of U.S. Naval Aviators Assigned Numbers 1 to 2,000*, 1968.

Baynham, H. *From the Lower Deck: The Royal Navy 1780-1840*, 1969. "Journals, letters and anecdotes of the seamen who served in it."

Calvert, J.F. *The Naval Profession*, 1965.

Cope, H.F. *Command at Sea*, 1943, R1966.

*Goodrich, C. *Rope Yarns from the Old Navy* (Naval History Society), 1931. One of the very few adequate American counterparts of the rich British personnel literature. Admiral Goodrich was one of the most thoughtful and literate officers of his day.

Kemp, P. *The British Sailor: A Social History of the Lower Deck, 1588-1905*, 1971.

Laffin, J. *Jack Tar: The Story of the British Sailor*, 1969.

*Langley, H.D. *Social Reform in the United States Navy, 1798-1862*, 1967 (PhD thesis, Pennsylvania). The story of the recruiting, corporal punishment, religious, and temperance aspects.

*Lewis, M.A. *England's Sea Officers: The Story of the Naval Profession,* 1939. Like the next three works, admirable in research and presentation, by a professor at the Royal Naval Academy.

*————. *The Navy of Britain, a Historical Portrait,* 1948. In the personnel section, Pt. 2, Officers: Fighters and Seamen; pt. 3, Men: Seamen and Fighters.

*————. *A Social History of the Navy, 1793-1815,* 1960. Pt. 1, Origins: Social and geographical; pt. 2, Entry: Problems of Recruitment; pt. 3, The Profession: Prospects, Conditions of Service and Rewards; pt. 4, The Price of Admiralty: Action, Accident and Disease; The Cost in Ships; The Cost in Lives.

*————. *The Navy in Transition, 1814-1864, a Social History,* 1965. A sequel to the above 1793-1815 volume.

*Lloyd, C. *The British Seaman, 1200-1860: A Social Survey,* 1969. The author was also a professor at the Royal Naval Academy.

Lovette, L.P. *Naval Customs, Traditions and Usage,* 1939, R1959. Standard textbook on the subject, by the wartime Director of Public Relations.

Lowis, G.L. *Fabulous Admirals and Some Naval Fragments,* 1957. Delightful accounts of some eccentric Royal Navy personalities, before modern technical demands cut off the supply.

*Mahan, A.T. *Types of Naval Officers. Drawn from the History of the British Navy,* 1901, R1969. Studies of Hawke, Rodney, Howe, Jervis, Saumarez, Pellew.

*————. *From Sail to Steam: Recollections of Naval Life,* 1907, R1968. Like Goodrich above, gives good picture of later 19th-century navy.

Masefield, J. *Sea Life in Nelson's Time,* 1905, R1969. Until C.S. Forester wrote his fictional but technically accurate volumes on Horatio Hornblower, this was the most readable picture of conditions in the Royal Navy at that period.

Pack, S.W.C. *Britannia at Dartmouth,* 1967. History of the Royal Naval Academy, with cadet training since the 1850s.

Parkinson, C.N. *Portsmouth Point: The British Navy in Fiction, 1793-1815,* 1949. Clever use of passages from contemporary fiction to picture the status and role of the various ranks and ratings.

Robinson, C.N. *The British Fleet: The Growth, Achievements and Duties of the Navy of the Empire.* 1894. Pt. 4, Personnel. Superseded by Lewis volumes above.

N – 2 Special Topics

Broome, J. *Make a Signal,* 1955. A history of signaling at sea, with amusing examples of the British naval sense of humor.

Davies, J.A. *An Inquiry into Faction among British Naval Officers during the War of the American Revolution* (ms. MA thesis, Liverpool, 1964).

Drury, C.M. *History of the Chaplain's Corps, United States Navy*, 2 v. 1948-49.

Elder, R.E. *History of the Demobilization of the United States Navy Women's Reserve, 1945-46* (ms. PhD thesis, Chicago, 1948). Some of them, of course, stayed on in the Regular Navy as "permanent Waves."

Jarrett, D. *British Naval Dress*, 1960. "Naval uniform throughout the ages."

Jenny, A. *International Influence Processes in Navy Port Calls*, P1957. Human Science Research project analyzing "showing the flag" experiences.

Karsten, F.D. *The Naval Aristocracy: U.S. Naval Officers from the 1840s to the 1920s: Mahan's Messmates* (PhD thesis, Wisconsin, 1968; DA v. 29, p.543A).

Kreh, W.R. *Citizen Sailors*, 1969. The Naval Reserve.

Lyons, G.M. and Masland, J.W. *Education and Military Leadership.* . . . 1959.

*Masland, J.W. and Radway, L.I. *Soldiers and Scholars* . . . . 1957.

May, W.E. *The Dress of Naval Officers*, 1966. Royal Navy, since 1748.

McCall, V. *Navy Nurse*, 1968.

Molls, J. *Uniform of the Royal Navy during the Napoleonic Wars*, 1965.

*Penn, G. *Up Funnel, Down Screw*, 1955. See Sect. K-4.
————. *Snotty; The Story of the Midshipman*, 1957.

Rankin, R.H. *Uniforms of the Sea Services, A Pictorial History*, 1962. The United States Navy, Marine Corps and Coast Guard from the Revolution to the present, with some 300 sketches.

*Roskill, S.W. *The Art of Leadership*, 1965.

Scott, W.F. *The Naval Chaplian in Stuart Times* (ms. D Phil thesis, Oxford, 1935).

Smith, W.E.L. *The Navy and Its Chaplains in the Days of Sail*, 1961.
————. *The Navy Chaplain and His Parish*, 1967.

Stouppe, W. *Naval Air Reserve Training Command, 1916-1966*, 1967.

Tantum, W.H., et al. *Navy Uniforms, Insignia and Warships of World War II*, 1968. Attempts, with no great success, to cover 14 navies.

Tily, J.C. *The Uniform of the United States Navy*, 1964.

Vagts, A. *The Military Attaché: A History*, 1967.

Wieand, H.T. *The History of the Development of the United States Naval Reserve, 1889-1941* (ms. PhD thesis, Pittsburgh, 1953).

Wigby, F. *Stoker, Royal Navy*, 1967.

O BOTH MERCHANT MARINE AND NAVAL PERSONNEL

O – 1   Regulations and Mutiny

Avrich, P. *Kronstadt 1921*, 1970. Uprising of sailors at Kronstadt naval base near Petrograd; 16-day struggle checked by Soviet government.

Blunt, J. *The Shipmaster's Assistant*, 1837, R1970. Ch. 7, Shipmasters; ch. 8, Seamen.

Bullocke, J.G. *Sailors' Rebellion: A Century of Mutiny at Sea*, 1938. Various other popular works have covered the same subject.

Cleaver, S. *Under the Lash: A History of Corporal Punishment in the British Armed Forces*, 1954.

Cooper, J.F., ed. *Proceedings of the Naval Court-Martial in the Case of A.S. Mackenzie*, 1844. Mackenzie, commanding the brig *Somers* in 1842, hanged the ringleaders of an alleged mutiny plot, including the midshipman son of the Secretary of War. See also Van de Water, below.

Cooper, L. *The* Royal Oak *Affair*, 1970. In 1928, on flagship of Mediterranean Fleet, the affair "involved a strange cast among whom were an Admiral of the Fleet, a naval captain, a commander, and a bandmaster."

*Dana, R.H. *The Seaman's Friend*, 1845, R1970. The author of *Two Years Before the Mast*, later a successful Boston lawyer, here sought to aid the seamen by making them aware, in simple language, of their legal rights and duties.

Divine, D. *Mutiny at Invergordon*, 1970. See also Edwards below.

*Dugan, J. *The Great Mutiny*, 1965. The Spithead and Nore mutinies of 1797, with an account of their political backgrounds. See also Gill and Manwaring below.

Edwards, P. *The Mutiny at Invergordon*, 1937. Royal Navy, 1931, over reduction of pay.

Eisenstein, S. Potemkin, 1968.

Gill, C. *The Naval Mutinies of 1797*, 1913. See also Dugan above and Manwaring below.

*Great Britain, Admiralty, *Regulations and Instructions Relating to His Majesty's Service at Sea*, 9th ed., 1757 ff.

*Horn, D., ed. *War, Mutiny and Revolution in the German Navy*, 1967. Diary of Richard Stumpf who went through most of World War I on the battleship *Helgoland*.
————. *The German Naval Mutinies of World War I*, 1969.

Lay, W. and Hussey, C.M. *Mutiny on Board the Whaleship* Globe, 1828, RP1962. The reedition, in the American Experience Series, has an introduction by E. A. Stackpole.

*Manwaring, G.E. and Dobree, B. *The Floating Republic: An Account of the Mutinies at Spithead and the Nore in 1797*, 1935, R1966. See also Dugan and Gill above.

Martin, C. *The* Amistad *Affair*, 1970. Mutiny of kidnapped free Nigerians on slave ship; seizure at sea by American authorities, and acquittal of mutineers by Supreme Court. Story also told in "quasi-novel" form in W.A. Owens, *Slave Mutiny: The Revolt on the Schooner* Amistad, 1953.

McArthur, J. *Principles and Practice of Naval and Military Courts Martial*, 4th ed., 2 v. 1813. Description of the British system, which was closely followed by the American.

*Nordhoff, C. and Hall, C.N. *Mutiny on the* Bounty, 1932 ff. Rising on British naval vessel in 1789 after loading breadfruit plants at Tahiti; Captain Bligh made long open-boat trip to Timor. Though presented in fictionalized form, this was based on thorough research, as were the sequels, *Men Against the Sea* and *Pitcairn's Island*. All three were issued in 1945 in a single volume, as *The* Bounty *Trilogy*. See also G. Mackaness, *The Life of Vice Admiral William Bligh*, 2 v. 1931; O. Rutter, ed., *The Court Martial of the* Bounty *Mutineers*, 1931; and A. McKee, *H.M.S.* Bounty, 1962.

*Norris, M.J. *The Law of Seamen*, 1951, 3rd ed. 1970. The first work since Dana's "to cover all the American laws involving seamen and other personnel sailing on the ocean, lakes and inland waterways."

Pack, S.W.C. *The* Wager *Mutiny*, 1965. Trouble among castaway crew of one of Anson's ships, wrecked on the coast of Patagonia in 1741.

Pope, D. *The Black Ship*, 1963. A blow-by-blow account of the bloody uprising on the British frigate *Hermione*, Sept. 21, 1797, with 10 of the 14 officers killed. The mutineers turned the ship over to the Spaniards, but she was recovered by a bold cutting-out action. Many of the mutineers were eventually run down and hanged for their part in "the worst mutiny in the history of the Royal Navy."

Rawson, G. Pandora's *Last Voyage*, 1964. In the sequel to the *Bounty* mutiny, the frigate *Pandora* was sent out in 1790 to capture the mutineers at Tahiti; those who had not gone on to Pitcairn's Island were apprehended and, although the *Pandora* was wrecked on Great Barrier Reef, some of them were hanged on reaching England.

Rosen, J.J. *Strike or Mutiny: An Evaluative Analysis of Sanctions Applicable to Concerted Activities of Maritime and Shoreside Labor* (ms. PhD thesis, New York Univ., 1954).

Snedeker, J. *Military Justice Under the Uniform Code*, 1953.
————. *A Brief History of Courts Martial*, P1954.

*U.S. Bureau of Navigation (Treasury), *Laws of the United States Relating to Navigation and the Merchant Marine*, 1895 ff. Includes the text of laws affecting the status of officers and crews; roughly the equivalent of "Navy Regs."

U.S. Congress, *Laws Relating to Shipping and the Merchant Marine*, 1960. Covers period 1916-60; compiled by G.G. Udell.

*U.S. Navy Dept., *Naval Courts and Boards*, 1917 ff. Later modified by the new "Uniform Code" for the three services.

*U.S. Navy Dept., *Regulations for the Government of the Navy of the United States*, 1818 ff. Popularly known as "Navy Regs," this code was originally copied by John Adams in 1775 fairly direct from the British code. It has been the legal basis for naval discipline, spelling out the duties and responsibilities of all naval personnel. Gradually expanding in scope, it ultimately became a fat volume.

Van de Water, F.F. *The Captain Called It Mutiny*, 1954. The *"Somers* Affair" of 1842; see also Cooper, above.

Webb, C. *The* Ann and Hope *Mutiny*, 1966.

O – 2   Seamanship

Beck, S.E. *The Ship: How She Works*, 1953.

*Brady, W. *The Kedge-Anchor; or Young Sailor's Assistant, appertaining to the Practical Evolutions of Modern Seamanship, Rigging, Knotting, Splicing . . . and other miscellaneous matters applicable to Ships of War and Others*, 5th ed., 1850, R1970.

Cotter, C.H. *The Master and His Ship*, 1962. See comments, Sect. M-1.

Crenshaw, R.S. Jr. *Naval Shiphandling*, 3rd ed. 1965.

Fawcett, R.F., et al. *The Rules of the Nautical Road*, rev. ed. 1957. See also Will, below.

Hartle, M.C., et al. *Elementary Seamanship*, 1958.

Hogan, W.C., et al. *The Coast Guardsman's Manual*, 5th ed. 1967.

Hutchinson, W. *Treatise on Practical Seamanship*, 1787.

*Knight, A.M. *Modern Seamanship*, 1901, 14th ed. 1966.

*Luce, S.B. *Seamanship*, 1862 ff. There have been many other manuals of seamanship, British and American; all explain the details of watchkeeping and other parts of the standard shipboard ritual. Brady, Luce and Knight, however, represent the successive works used in training American naval officers, and many merchant shipmasters as well. Luce and Knight later became distinguished rear admirals; Luce was connected with naval training all the way from tying knots to the Naval War College which he founded. His work was the standard Annapolis text until, by 1901, sail was so completely out of the picture that it seemed desirable to start afresh.

MacDonald, E.A. *Polar Operations*, 1969. Guide to shiphandling in polar regions.

*Riesenberg, F. *Standard Seamanship for the Merchant Service*, 1922, 1936.

Smith, H.G. *The Arts of the Sailor*, 1953. "A handbook of instructions in all of the skills involving rope and canvas which are necessary to the average boat owner." There are numerous other useful manuals for yachtsmen.

*U.S. Bureau of Navigation (later Naval Personnel), *The Bluejacket's Manual*, 1920, 11th ed. 1960. This was for the enlisted man what Knight was for the officer.

*Villiers, A. *The Way of a Ship*, 1953, R1970. Ch. 4, Global Sailing Conditions; ch. 5, Handling Square Sails; ch. 6, Shiphandling under Sail.

Will, O.W. *Simplified Rules of the Nautical Road*, 1963.

O – 3   Medicine and Health

Allison, R.S. *Sea Diseases*, 1943. Historical study of the causes and attempted cures of the prevalent sea diseases – scurvy, typhus, malaria, yellow fever, dysentery, etc.

Foltz, C.S. *Surgeon of the Seas: The Adventurous Life of Surgeon General Jonathan M. Foltz in the Days of Wooden Ships*, 1931. Disappointingly little on the medical side of his career. See Pugh below.

Gordon-Pugh, P.D. *Nelson and His Surgeons*, 1968. Nelson had some 25 surgeons attend him in the course of his career.

Great Britain, Official History of the Second World War, Medical Series, especially *Royal Navy Medical Services*, 2 v. 1, Administration; 2, Operations.

*Keevil, J.J., et al. *Medicine and the Navy, 1200-1900*, 4 v. 1956-63. An ambitious but somewhat uneven coverage in detail of the whole subject. Surgeon-Commander Keevil, RN, had, before his death, completed the first two volumes, 1200-1649, 1649-1714. The last two, 1714-1815 and 1815-1900 were the work of C. Lloyd and J.L.S. Coulter, and are often catalogued under their names. The final volume, for instance, includes chapters on the Medical Department, Hygiene, Ventilation, Sea Diseases, Naval Hospitals, Nursing Services, Crimean War, Arctic Voyages, West African Squadron, and Convict Ships.

Lloyd, C., ed. *The Health of Seamen: Selections from the Works of .Dr. James Lind, Sir Gilbert Blane and Dr. Thomas Trotter* (Navy Records Society), 1965.

*————. *The Navy and the Slave Trade* . . . . 1949, R1968. Tables and discussion of relative mortality on the various overseas stations, with West Africa the worst. See also Keevil above.

Mason, F. Van W. *Manila Galleon*, 1961, P1962. A detailed account of Anson's great voyage of 1740-44 during the War of Jenkin's Ear. Fictionalized but based on solid research, it gives a wealth of grim detail on the terrific ravages of scurvy. Not to be confused with W.L. Schurz, *Manila Galleon*, 1939, a general survey of the Manila-Acapulco service.

Miles, S. *Underwater Medicine*, 1966. Problems of environment and diving, by a British Surgeon Rear Admiral.

Parkinson, C.N., ed. *The Trade Winds* . . . *1793-1813*, 1948. Ch. 6, Health and Sickness.

Pugh, H.L. *Navy Surgeon*, 1959. Autobiography of former Surgeon General, USN.

*Roddis, L.H. *James Lind: Founder of Nautical Medicine*, 1950. Lind wrote a *Treatise on Scurvy* in 1753 and did much to improve health conditions afloat. Captain Cook, profiting by his recommendation of anti-scorbutics, kept his crews remarkably free from scurvy on his lengthy exploring voyages.

*Straus, R. *Medical Care for Seamen: The Origin of the Public Medical Service in the United States*, 1950.

Tredree, H.L. *The Strange Ordeal of the* Normadier, 1958, & P (*Blackwater* in the British edition). British tramp, bound from French West Africa to Canada late in 1918, was rescued by American destroyer. Most of the officers and crew were dead or dying from Blackwater disease, contracted at Dakar. The author, then wireless operator, was one of two survivors.

Walsh, W.B. *A Ship Called* Hope, 1964. See Sect J-4.

Watson, P.K. *The Commission for Victualling the Navy, the Commission for Sick and Wounded Seamen and Prisoners of War and the Commission for Transport, 1702-1714* (ms. PhD thesis, London, 1965).

O – 4 Sea Language and Songs

Chase, G.P. *Sea Terms Come Ashore* (Univ. of Maine Studies), 1942. See also Colcord below.

*Colcord, J.D. *Roll and Go, Songs of American Sailormen*, 1921, R1938. One of the best collections of American sea chanteys. The 1938 title omitted the "Roll and Go."

————. *Sea Language Comes Ashore*, 1945. Miss Colcord, a distinguished social service worker, was born at sea aboard the Down Easter of her father, a Searsport sea captain. See also Chase above.

Doerflinger, W.M. *Shanteymen and Shanteyboys: Songs of the Sailor and Lumberman*, 1951. Chiefly from Maine and the Maritimes.

Firth, C.H., ed. *Naval Songs and Ballads* (Navy Records Society), 1906.

Granville, W. *Sea Slang of the Twentieth Century*, 1949, R1962. British.

Greenleaf, E.B., ed. *Ballads and Sea Songs of Newfoundland*, 1968.

*Harlow, F.P. *Chanteying aboard American Ships*, 1962.

Healy, J.N. *Irish Ballads and Songs of the Sea*, 1968.

*Hugill, S. *Shanties from the Seven Seas: Shipboard Work-Songs and Songs used as Work-Songs from the Great Days of Sail*, 1961.
————. *Shanties and Sailor Songs*, 1969.

Huntington, G. *Songs the Whalemen Sang*, 1968.

Ives, B. *Sea Songs of Sailing, Whaling and Fishing*, P1956. Includes "68 songs with melody and guitar chords."

Mackenzie, W.R. *Ballads and Sea Songs from Nova Scotia*, 1964.

Rawls, R. *Modern Sea Ballads: The Mire to the Mist*, 1966.

Shay, E., ed. *American Sea Songs and Chanteys*, 1948, R1969. A revision of *Iron Men and Wooden Ships*.

Trident Society, U.S. Naval Academy, *The Book of Navy Songs*, 1926. "Over 90 old and new songs."

O – 5 Memoirs Illustrative of Shipboard Life

Literally hundreds of mariners – navy and merchant marine officers and foremast hands – have broken into print with reminiscences of varying color and value. Someone remarked that maritime history consists of crossing sailors' yarns with customs records. The following list is a highly selective one, to illustrate varying experiences and viewpoints; it naturally omits many other titles virtually as good. Except for the delightful Gardiner volume, most of the memoirs of naval officers are given later in connection with the chronological naval coverage. Much colorful material can also be found in the 200-odd volumes of the Hakluyt Society.

Barlow, E. *Barlow's Journal of His Life at Sea in King's Ships, East and West Indiamen and other Merchantmen from 1659 to 1703*, ed. B Lubbock, 2 v. 1934. Also edited by A.G. Course, under title *A Seventeenth Century Mariner*, 1966.

Bisset, Sir J. *Ship Ahoy!* 1932; *Sail Ho!* 1958; *Tramps and Ladies*, 1959. Memoirs of a former Cunard commodore. See Grattidge below.

Borden, N.E., Jr., ed. *Dear Sarah: New England Ice to the Orient and other incidents from the Journals of Captain Charles Edward Barry to his Wife*, 1966.

Bowker, F.E. *Hull Down*, 1964. See Sect. I.

Bradford, G. *In with the Sea Wind*, 1962. Twenty independent chapters on maritime life, by the author of *Yonder Is the Sea* and *Life Afloat as Certain Men Have Found It.*

Bradley, W. *A Voyage to New South Wales; the Journal of William Bradley RN, of H.M.S.* Sirius, *1786-1792*, 1969.

Briggs, L.V. *Around Cape Horn to Honolulu on the Bark* Amy Turner, 1880, R1926, 1970.

Cary, T.G. *Memoir of Thomas Handasyd Perkins, containing extracts from his Diaries and Letters*, 1856. RP1969. Early voyaging of future great Boston merchant around 1790s, to St. Domingue, Canton and France.

*Cobb, E. *Elijah Cobb, 1768-1848, A Cape Cod Skipper*, ed. R.D. Paine, 1925, R1970.

*Coggeshall, G. *Voyages to Various Parts of the World*, 1851 ff. R1970. (Several different editions, with varying number of voyages.) Like the more compact reminiscences of Cobb, full of excellent "case histories" of trading adventures both during the hectic period of neutral trade and later tramp voyaging, in Coggeshall's case, chiefly to Latin America.

Coxere, E. *Adventures by Sea*, ed. E. Meyerstein, 1952. Experiences in English and Dutch warships and merchant shipping, mid-17th century.

*Dana, R.H. *Two Years before the Mast*, 1840 ff. One of the classics of the sea. Dana interrupted his undergraduate career at Harvard to sail around the Horn to California in a Boston brig, returning in a ship. Vivid picture of "how things worked" aboard a square-rigger. New edition, 1964, "from the original manuscript and from the first edition with journals and letters of 1834-36 and 1859-60" by J.H. Kemble. See also *The Journal of Richard Henry Dana, Jr.,* ed. R.F. Lucid, 3 v. 1968.

Davies, D.W. *Elizabethans Errant, The Strange Fortunes of Thomas Sherley and His Three Sons, as well in the Dutch Wars as in Muscovy, Morocco, Persia, Syam and the Indies*, 1967.

Duncan, F.B. *Deepwater Family*, 1969. Reminiscences of life aboard father's Down Easter in 1890s.

Evans, A.A. See Sect. BA-4.

*Forbes, R.B. *Personal Reminiscences*, 1878, R1970. He was a versatile Boston mariner-merchant who served at Canton in the tea trade, dabbled in steam, took a warship to famine-stricken Ireland with relief grain, and agitated for safety at sea.

Gallery, D.V. *Now Hear This!* 1964. Yarns by a prominent admiral.

*Gardiner, J.A. *Above and Under Hatches, being Naval Recollections in Shreds and Patches with Strange Reflections,* ed. C. Lloyd, 1955. Delightfully intimate picture of old Royal Navy. Originally published by the Navy Records Society as *The Recollections of Commander James Anthony Gardiner, 1775-1814,* ed. R.V. Hamilton and J.K. Laughton, 1906. See also Hervey below.

*Garner, S., ed. *The Captain's Best Mate: The Journal of Mary Chipman Lawrence on the Whaler* Addison, *1856-1860,* 1966.

Garrison, J.H. *Behold Me Once More: The Confessions of James Holley Garrison, Brother of William Lloyd Garrison,* ed. W.M. Merrill, 1954. Experiences of a persistent seagoing alcoholic in the American merchant marine, the Royal Navy and the United States Navy, c1818-1839.

Grattidge, H., et al. *Captain of the Queens: The Autobiography of Captain Henry Grattidge, former Commodore of the Cunard Lines,* 1957. Similar memoirs, starting in sail and rising to high liner command, have been written by Sir James Bisset, D.W. Bone and others.

Harlow, F. *The Making of a Sailor or Sea Life Aboard a Yankee Square-Rigger* (Marine Research Society), 1928.

Hartog, J. de. *A Sailor's Life,* 1956. Varied modern aspects, well told.

Hay, R. *Landsman Hay: The Memoirs of Robert Hay, 1790-1847,* 1953. This young Scot ran away to sea at 13 and served before the mast during the Napoleonic wars in the Royal Navy and in merchantmen.

*Hervey, A.J. *Augustus Hervey's Journal: Being the Intimate Account of the Life of a Captain in the Royal Navy Ashore and Afloat,* ed. D. Erskine, 1953. Covers the years 1746-59. In addition to naval actions, gives vivid tactical details of the "wife in every port" aspect of naval life. Hervey became Earl of Bristol.

Karlsson, E. *Mother Sea,* 1964. Description, based on long experience, of conditions on Baltic sailing vessels.

Kemble, J.H., ed. *To California and the South Seas: The Diary of Albert G. Osbun, 1849-1851,* 1966.

King, R. *Sailor in the East,* 1956. British below decks career; "so gentle a touch that a Japanese brothel sounds like a Bloomsbury tea party."

*Leavitt, J.F. *Wake of the Coasters,* 1970. See Sect. I.

Lindsey, J.M. *Sailor in Steam,* 1966.

Lubbock, B. *Round the Horn Before the Mast*, 1902. One of the first of his many books; similar accounts of initiation in square-riggers in F. Riesenberg, *Under Sail*, 1918; D.W. Bone, *The Brassbounder*, 1921, and A.J. Villiers, *Falmouth for Orders*, 1929.

Merrill, J.M. *Quarter Deck and Fo'c'sle*, 1963. Source collection, chiefly naval, from letters, log books, reports and essays, from the Revolution to the present.

Munger, J.F. *Two Years in the Pacific and Arctic Oceans and China. Being a Journal of a Whaling Voyage*, 1852, R1967.

*Nordhoff, C. *Life on the Ocean: Being Sketches of Personal Experience in the United States Naval Service, the American and British Merchant Marine, and the Whaling Service*, 1874, R1970. Valuable because of one man's opportunity to compare at first hand the way of life in those different services. The naval portion was published first as *Man-of-War Life*, 1851, and the naval and whaling portions, edited by his grandson of the same name, as *In Yankee Windjammers*, 1940. Herman Melville had a similar variety of experience, recounted in fictional form as *White Jacket, Redburn, Typee*, and *Moby Dick*.

*Parr, C.M. *The Voyages of David DeVries: Navigator and Adventurer whose writings reveal why the Dutch lost America to the English*, 1969. Prominent roles both at Batavia and New Amsterdam.

*Samuels, S. *From the Forecastle to the Cabin*, 1887, R1970. Lively range of experiences, losing nothing in the telling, ranging from service as a boy on a Philadelphia collier to command of a clipper-packet, including some mutinies.

Sargent, H.J. *The Captain of the* Phantom, *The Story of Henry Jackson Sargent, Jr., 1834-1862, as revealed in Family Letters* (Marine Historical Assn.) P1967. Young "proper Bostonian" who had held clipper commands before he went missing at 28.

*Slocum, J. *The Voyages of Joshua Slocum*, ed. W.M. Teller, 1958. The first complete collection of his writings; the most celebrated portion, *Sailing Alone Around the World*, had first appeared in 1900. Teller also wrote *The Search for Captain Slocum*, 1959.

Stackpole, E.A. *Those in Peril on the Sea*, 1963. Anthology of brief excerpts from first-hand accounts (18 in 272 pages) down through the centuries.

*Teller, W.M. *Five Sea Captains: Their Own Accounts of Voyages under Sail*, 1960. 1, Amasa Delano, Voyage in the Ship *Perseverance*, 1799-1802; 2, Edmund Fanning, First Voyage Round the World in *Crusader*, 1797-1799; 3, Richard Cleveland, First Voyage, 1797-1801; 4, George Coggeshall, Voyage in the Pilot Boat Schooner *Sea Serpent*, 1821-22; 5, Joshua Slocum, The Voyage of the *Aquidneck*, 1886-88. See also Slocum above.

Teonge, H. *Diary of Henry Teonge, 1675-79*, ed. G.E. Manwaring, 1927. An amusing account of life afloat, by a chaplain.

Wetherell, J. *The Adventure of John Wetherell,* ed. C.S. Forester, 1953. "The authentic diary of a 19th-century British seaman, impressed into His Majesty's service to fight Bonaparte." Drawings by the author. Covers years 1803-15.

*Whidden, J.D. *Ocean Life in the Old Sailing Ship Days, from Forecastle to Quarter-Deck,* 1908 ff. The 1925 edition had the title *Old Sailing Ship Days.*

IV   Maritime Science, Exploration
and Expansion

P   MARITIME SCIENCE

P – 1   Navigation

Bedini, S.A. *Early American Scientific Instruments and Their Makers* (Smithsonian Institution, Museum of History and Technology), P1964.

Branch, W.J.V. and Brooks-Williams, E. *A Short History of Navigation*, 1942.

*Brewington, M.V. *The Peabody Museum Collection of Navigation Instruments with Notes on their Makers*, 1963. Includes 57 pages of collotype illustrations.

Calahan, H.A. *The Sky and the Sailor; A History of Celestial Navigation*, 1952.

*Campbell, J.F. *History and Bibliography of the* New American Practical Navigator *and the* American Coast Pilot, 1964. By a mariner and sometime Panama Canal pilot who had long collected editions of Bowditch and Blunt.

Collinder, P.A. *A History of Marine Navigation*, 1954.

Cotter, C.H. *History of Nautical Astronomy*, 1968.

Gould, R.T. *The Marine Chronometer: Its History and Development*, 1923.

Harding, L.A. *History of the Art of Navigation*, 1952.

Hewson, J.S. *History of the Practice of Navigation*, 1952.

Hill, H.O., et al. *Instruments of Navigation: A Catalogue of Instruments at the National Maritime Museum, with notes upon their use*, 1958.

Hitchins, H.L. and May, W.E. *From Lodestone to Gyro-Compass*, 1953.

Howse, D. and Hutchinson, B. *The Clocks and Watches of Captain James Cook, 1769-1969*, 1969. Reprinted from *Antiquarian Horology*.

Parramore, T.C. *Anson's Voyage and the Dawn of Scientific Navigation* (PhD thesis, North Carolina, 1965; DA v.26, p. 3912).

Petze, C.L. *History of Celestial Navigation*, 1948.

Quill, H. *John Harrison: The Man who Found Longitude*, 1966.

Smith, R.A. *Radio Aids to Navigation*, 1947.

Stanford, A. *Navigator: The Story of Nathaniel Bowditch*, 1927.

*Taylor, E.G.R. *The Mathematical Practitioners of Tudor and Stuart England*, 1966. Includes short biographies and extensive bibliography, with much valuable material on the early development of navigation.

*————. *Mathematical Practitioners of Hanoverian England*, 1966. A sequel.

*————. *The Haven-Finding Art: A History of Navigation from Odysseus to Captain Cook*, 1967. By far the most authoritative general survey; Miss Taylor is professor of geography at the University of London.

————ed. *A Regiment for the Sea and other Writings in Navigation by William Bourne, a Gunner, of Gravesend* (c1535-1582). Edited by E.G.R. Taylor for the Hakluyt Society, 1963.

*Taylor, E.G.R. and Richey, M.W. *The Geometrical Seaman: A Book of Early Nautical Instruments*, 1963. Shows "interaction between practical seamanship, mathematics and astronomy." See also Hill above.

*Waters, D.W. *The Art of Navigation in England in Elizabethan and Early Stuart Times*, 1958. Takes story to 1640. Same high quality of scholarship as in Taylor above. Based on several years of research made possible by a grant from Henry C. Taylor who had assembled a remarkable collection of navigational history.

Wright, M.D. *A History of Aerial Navigation to 1941* (PhD thesis, Duke, 1970; DA v. 31, p. 2862A).

Wroth, L.C. *The Way of a Ship: An Essay on the Literature of Navigational Science*, 1937.

————. *Some American Contributions to the Art of Navigation*, 1947.

P – 2 Cartography, Hydrography, Oceanography, Etc.

*Bagrow, L. *History of Cartography*. Revised and enlarged by R.A. Skelton, 1964. Well illustrated.

Bell, B.H. and E.F. *Old English Barometers*, 1952.

*Blewitt, M. *Survey of the Seas: A Brief History of British Hydrography*, 1957. Comprehensive, elaborate and expensive, including reproductions of original charts by Cook, Vancouver, Dalrymple, MacKenzie, etc.

Bricker, C. *Landmarks of Mapmaking: An Illustrated Survey of Maps and Mapmakers*, 1968. Includes more than 250 reproductions.

*Brown, L.A. *The Story of Maps*, 1949. Comprehensive survey from the earliest times, "equally concerned with the cartography of land and sea."

Brundze, R. *The Rise and Fall of the Seas: The Story of the Tides*, 1964.

*Burstyn, H.L. *At the Sign of the Quadrant: An Account of the Contribution to American Hydrography made by Edmund March Blunt and His Sons* (Marine Historical Assn.), 1957. The Blunts developed the *American Coast Pilot*, finally taken over by the Government.

Campbell, J.F. See Sect. P-1.

*Carson, R. *The Sea Around Us*, 1951, P1954. Best seller introduction to oceanography.
————. *Under the Sea-Wind, a Naturalist's Picture of Ocean Life*, 1952. Miss Carson has been honored as a pioneer in calling attention to the threats against natural conditions.

Chapin, H. and Smith, F.G.W. *The Ocean River*, 1952. The Gulf Stream.

Coker, R.E. *The Great and Wide Sea. An Introduction to Oceanography and Marine Biology* (Science Library), 1947, RP1962.

Cole, A.B., ed. *Yankee Surveyors in the Shogun's Seas: Records of the U.S. Surveying Expedition to the Pacific Ocean, 1853-1856*, 1947, R1969.

Coleston Research Society, *Submarine Geology and Geophysics*, 1965.

Colman, J.S. *The Sea and Its Mysteries*, 1950.

Cousteau, J-Y., with J. Dugan, *The Living Sea*, 1962. Adventures in underwater oceanographic exploration.

*Cowen, R.C. *Frontiers of the Sea: The Story of Oceanographic Exploration*, 1960, R1969. Starts with the voyage of H.M.S. *Challenger*, 1872-76.

*Crone, G.R. *Maps and Their Makers: An Introduction to the History of Cartography*, 1953, R1966. By the map curator of the Royal Geographical Society.

Davis, C.H., Jr. *The Life of Charles Henry Davis, Rear Admiral, 1807-1877*, 1899. The elder Davis established and edited the *Nautical Almanac* and was first chief of the Navy's Bureau of Navigation, started as a scientific bureau.

Dawson, L.S. *Memoirs of Hydrography*, 1969. Britain's Naval Surveying Service, 1750-1885.

*Day, Sir A. *The Admiralty Hydrographic Service, 1795-1919*, 1967.

Deacon, G.E.R., ed. *Seas, Maps and Men*, 1962. By the Director of the National Institute of Oceanography.

De la Rue, E.A. *Man and the Winds*, 1956.

Dodge, E.S. *Beyond the Capes . . . .* See Sect. AL-2.

Dunn, G.E. and Miller, B.I. *Atlantic Hurricanes*, 1960, R1964. A study in "tropical meteorology."

Edgell, J. *Sea Surveys*, P1965. Hydrography since 1865.

Ericson, D.B. and Wollin, G. *The Ever-Changing Sea*, 1967. "A much-needed, wide-ranging popularization of the relatively new science, oceanography."

Evans, G.N.D. *Uncommon Obdurate: The Several Public Careers of J.F.W. Des Barres*, 1969. Based on Yale PhD thesis, *North American Soldier, Hydrographer, Governor*. Made surveys of Maritime Provinces and published the *Atlantic Neptune*.

*Fairbridge, R.W. *Encyclopedia of Oceanography*, 1966. Vol. 1 of the *Encyclopedia of Earth Sciences*.

Fry, H.T. *Alexander Dalrymple, Cosmographer and Servant of the East India Company* (ms. PhD thesis, Cambridge, 1967).

Galey, M.E. *The Intergovernmental Oceanographic Commission of UNESCO: Its Capacity to Implement the International Decade of Ocean Exploration* (PhD thesis, Pennsylvania, 1970; DA v. 31, p.5491A).

Guberlet, M.L. *Explorers of the Sea: Famous Oceanographic Expeditions*, 1964.

Hapgood, C.H. *Maps of the Ancient Sea Kings . . . .* 1966.

Harding, E.T., et al. *Heavy Weather Guide*: Pt. 1, *Hurricanes*; pt. 2, *Typhoons*, 1965. See also Ludlum below.

Hardman, W.A. *Founders of Oceanography and Their Work . . . .* 1925.

Hardy, A.C. *Great Waters: A Voyage of Natural History to Study the Whales, Plankton and the Waters of the Southern Ocean in the Old Royal Research Ship* Discovery, *with the results brought up to date by the findings of the RRS* Discovery II, 1967.

Ingleton, G.C. *Charting a Continent: A Brief Memoir on the History of Marine Exploration and Hydrographical Surveying in Australian Waters*, 1944. The British naval surveyors included the celebrated Cook, Vancouver, Flinders and Bligh. See Sect. AL-2.

Jahns, P. *Matthew Maury and Joseph Henry: Scientists of the Civil War*, 1961.

Lewis, C.L. *Matthew Fontaine Maury, the Pathfinder of the Seas*, 1937, R1969.

Lewis, O. *George Davidson: Pioneer West Coast Scientist*, 1954. Davidson, active for many years in the U.S. Coast Survey and author of the *Pacific Coast Pilot* is said to have "helped more than any one man to make travel by water safe along the coast."

Long, E.J., ed. *Ocean Sciences*, 1964. Fifteen chapters, each by an expert in his field of oceanography.

Ludlum, D.M. *Early American Hurricanes, 1492-1870*, 1963. Monograph No. 1 in the American Meteorological Society's series on the History of American Weather.

Macmillan, P.H. *Tides*, 1966.

Manley, S. and Lewis, G., eds. *The Oceans*, 1967.

*Marx, W. *The Frail Ocean*, 1967, P1969. A forceful and able argument for conservation against threats of encroachment and pollution.

*Maury, M.F. *Explanations and Sailing Directions to Accompany the Wind and Current Charts*, 1851 ff. Maury's analyses of thousands of log books enabled him to recommend the most effective sea routes to take advantage of winds and currents.
*————. *The Physical Geography of the Sea*, 1855 ff, R1963.

Mellersh, H.E. *Fitzroy of the* Beagle, 1968. In command of the celebrated Darwin voyage. Later governor of New Zealand and an active oceanographer. See also next title.

*Moorehead, A. *Darwin and the* Beagle, 1969.

Ommanney, F.D. *The Ocean*, 1949. Emphasis on the biological side.

Putnam, G.R. *Nautical Charts*, 1908.

Raitt, H. *Exploring the Deep Pacific*, 1956. Account of the Scripps-Capricorn Expedition, 1952-53.

Ritchie, G.S. Challenger: *The Life of a Survey Ship*, 1958. By the captain of the namesake of the pioneer survey vessel, 1931-53. See also Spry below.
*————. *The Admiralty Chart. British Naval Hydrography in the Nineteenth Century*, 1967. See also Day above.

*Robinson, A.H.W. *Marine Cartography in Britain: A History of the Sea Chart to 1855*, 1962 (PhD thesis, London). Unlike Blewitt above, this is limited to charts of the British Isles "from the earliest manuscript charts of the 16th century to the Grand Survey of the British Isles." Includes 42 full-page reproductions.

Rogers, F.M. *Official English Maritime Exploration, 1660-1780: A Study of the Beginnings of Scientific Exploration* (ms. PhD thesis, Texas, 1958).

Shipman, J.C. *William Dampier, Seaman-Scientist*, P1962.

*Skelton, R.A. ed. *James Cook, Surveyor of Newfoundland, being a Collection of Charts of the Coast of Newfoundland and Labrador drawn from the Original Survey taken by James Cook and Michael Lane*, 1965. Ten large folio charts reproduced in facsimile, with introductory sketch by Skelton, superintendent of the Map Room, British Museum.

*————. *Explorers' Maps: Chapters in the Cartographic Record of Geographic Discovery*, 1958.

*————. *Captain James Cook, After Two Hundred Years*, 1969.

Sprang, W.A. *Surveying and Charting the Indian Ocean: The British Contribution, 1750-1838* (ms. PhD thesis, London, 1966).

*Spry, W.J.J. *The Cruise of H.M.S.* Challenger, 1877. The ship cruised five years in all seas on pioneer oceanographic work. This account by her captain is less scientific than that of Sir C.W. Thompson, *The Voyage of the* Challenger, 2 v. 1878. For the later similar work of the second *Challenger,* see Ritchie above.

*Stewart, H.B. *The Global Sea,* P1963. "A non-technical presentation of current oceanographical knowledge, thought and research" by the Chief Oceanographer of the U.S. Coast & Geodetic Survey.

Stommel, H. *Science of the Seven Seas,* 1949.

Taylor, J. DuP., ed. *Marine Archaeology: Developments during 60 years in the Mediterranean,* 1966.

Tooley, R.V. *Maps and Map Makers,* 1949. See also Brown and Crone, above.

Towle, E.L. *Science and Commerce: The Navy in the Seafaring Frontier (1842-1861). The Role of Lieutenant M.F. Maury and the U.S. Naval Hydrographic Office in Naval Exploration, Commercial Expansion and Oceanography before the Civil War* (PhD thesis, Rochester, 1966 DA v.27, p.173A).

Tyler, D.B. *The Wilkes Expedition; The First U.S. Exploring Expedition (1838-1842).* (Memoirs of the American Philosophical Society, v. 73), 1968. See also Wilkes below.

*Waters, D.W. *The Rutters of the Sea: The Sailing Directions of Pierre Garcie. A Story of the First English and French Printed Sailing Directions. With Facsimile Reproductions,* 1967.

Weber, G.A. *The Coast and Geodetic Survey: Its History, Activity and Organization,* 1925. Emphasizes administrative rather than operational aspects. He produced similar studies of the Hydrographic Office and Naval Observatory in 1926. See also Wraight below.

Wheat, J.C. and Brun, C.T. *Maps and Charts Published in America before 1800: A Bibliography,* 1969.

*Wilkes, C. *Narrative of the United States Exploring Expedition, 1838-1842,* 6 v. 1845. Lt. Wilkes, who commanded the expedition, engaged in various aspects of scientific work and also contributed the studies on *Hydrography* and *Meteorology* in the multi-volume report. Some of the Wilkes charts were still being used by the Navy a century later in World War II. See also Tyler above and D. Henderson, *The Hidden Coasts,* 1953, a life of Wilkes.

*Williams, F.L. *Ocean Pathfinder; A Biography of Matthew Fontaine Maury*, 1966. Supersedes the earlier biographies by D.F.M. Corbin, 1888; C.L. Lewis, 1927; J.A. Caskie, 1928; and J.W. Wayand, 1930.

Wraight, A.J. and Roberts, E.B. *The Coast and Geodetic Survey, 1807-1957; 150 Years of History*, 1957. More comprehensive and interesting than Weber, above. The Survey charted the adjacent waters while the Hydrographic Office charted distant seas.

Wroth, L.C. *The Early Cartography of the Pacific*, 1944 (Papers of the Bibliographical Society of America, v. 38, no. 2).

Q   EXPLORATION

See also the above scientific exploration; some of the regional exploration is included in the local sections of commerce and shipping, particularly for the Pacific, Sect. AL-2.

Q – 1 General

*Baker, J.N.L. *History of Geography*, 1931, R1963. The first edition had the title, *A History of Geographical Discovery and Exploration*.

*Beazley, C.R. *The Dawn of Modern Geography: A History of Exploration and Geographical Science* 3 v.1897-1906. Covers the period 300-1420 A.D. Useful, but somewhat "dated" background for the explorations just beginning in 1420. Heawood and Penrose, below, carry on the story into later periods, as do several others.

Brendon, J.A. *Great Navigators and Discoverers*, 1930, R1967.

Cameron, I. *Lodestone and Evening Star: The Epic Voyages of Discovery 1493 BC-1896 AD*, 1966.

Carletti, F. *My Voyage Around the World. The Chronicles of a 16th Century Florentine Merchant*, tr. H. Weinstock. "How the world from the Canary Islands to Japan looked, ate, traded, warred and made love."

*Cary, M.C. and Warmington, E.H. *The Ancient Explorers*, P1963.

Crone, G.R. ed. *The Explorers: Great Adventurers Tell Their Own Stories of Discovery*, 1962. British title: *An Anthology of Discovery*.

*Debenham, F. *Discovery and Exploration: An Atlas History of Man's Wanderings*, 1960, R1968. Because of its ingenious and admirably executed devices, this is the most useful geographical reference work for any library. The major text includes many illustrations and relief maps. Particularly useful are the 244 pp. of brief chronological tables for individual explorers, with small sketch maps showing the routes of 197 of them. Also, sketch maps showing the progress of exploration in six continents at four periods, 1700-1900.

Elliott, J.H. *The Old World and the New, 1492-1652* (Cambridge Studies in Early Modern History), 1970. A brilliant analysis of the impact.

Gay, P. *The Age of Exploration* (Time-Life, Great Ages of Man), 1967. Paintings, charts, etc.

Gillespie, J.E. *A History of Geographical Discovery (1400-1800)*, 1933.

*Hakluyt, R. *The Principal Navigations, Voyages, Traffiques and Discoveries of the English Nation*, 1589 ff – various editions, often in 8 to 12 volumes. This Elizabethan gathered and published all the seafarers' tales he could find, and played his part in stimulating national interest in exploration and colonization. He did not limit himself to English accounts, having the tales of various foreign explorers translated. Both his original 1589 and multi-volume 1598-1600 editions were reissued in 1965, the former in a lithographic facsimile edited by D.B. Quinn and R.A. Skelton, the latter reproduced from the 20-volume Glasgow edition of 1903-05. Hakluyt's work was carried on, less effectively, by Samuel Purchas, whose *Purchas his Pilgrims* in 20 volumes appeared in 1625.

*Hakluyt Society, *Publications*. More than 200 volumes since 1847. See Sect. R.

*Heawood, E. *History of Geographical Discovery in the Seventeenth and Eighteenth Centuries*, 1912, R1969.

*Landström, B. *The Quest for India: A History of Discovery and Exploration . . . in Words and Pictures*, 1964. Covers the years 1493 B.C. to 1498 A.D. Beautifully illustrated with author's own colored pictures, but the text makes it more than just a "picture book."

*Outhwaite, L. *Unrolling the Map: The Story of Exploration*, 1935, R1971. Useful map-shading device, showing areas opened by each exploration; story brought up to date, with space developments, in revised edition.

*Penrose, B. *Travel and Discovery in the Renaissance, 1420-1620*, 1955. Fills the gap between Beazley and Heawood in the chronological general exploration coverage.

Rose, J.H. *Man and the Sea: Stages in Maritime and Human Progress*, 1936.

Skelton, R.A. *Explorers' Maps*. See Sect. P-1.

Smith, E.S. *The Law of Maritime Exploration* (ms. PhD thesis, George Washington, 1954).

Sykes, Sir P. *A History of Exploration from the Earliest Times to the Present Day*, 1935, RP1961. This British general tends to overemphasize Asia and British efforts.

Warmington, E.H. and Cary, M. *Ancient Explorers*, P1963.

Arcinegas, G. *Amerigo and the New World: The Life and Times of Amerigo Vespucci*, tr. H. de Onis, 1955. Emphasizes his distinguished Renaissance background and his reaching the mainland of America ahead of Columbus.

*Beazley, C.R. *Prince Henry the Navigator, the Hero of Portugal and of Modern Discovery, 1394-1460 A.D.*, 1895, R1968.

Berio Library, Genoa, *Catalog of the Columbus Collection*, 1963. Reproduction of 3,100 cards.

Bradford, E. *A Wind from the North: The Life of Henry the Navigator*, 1960. (*Southward the Caravels* in British edition.)

*Diffie, B.W. *Prelude to Empire: Portugal Overseas before Henry the Navigator*, 1960. Discusses political and military factors, including the English alliance, which influenced Portugal in addition to shipping and trade.

Hart, H.H. *Sea Road to the Indies: An Account of the Voyages and Exploits of the Portuguese Navigators, together with the Life of Vasco da Gama*, 1950.

Jayne, K.G. *Vasco da Gama and His Successors, 1460-1580*, 1910, R1970.

*Landström, B. *The Quest for India* . . . . 1964. See Sect. Q-1.
* —————. *Columbus*, 1967. See Sect. H-1.

Link, E.A. and M.C. *A New Theory on Columbus's Voyage* (Smithsonian Misc. Coll. v.135, no. 4), 1958. Argument that his "San Salvador" landfall was on Caicos rather than Watling Island.

*Martinez-Hidalgo, J.M. *Columbus's Ships*, 1966. See Sect. I.

*Morison, S.E. *Admiral of the Ocean Sea: A Life of Christopher Columbus*, 1942 ff. Based on the author's sailing the actual route of Columbus, this won a Pulitzer Prize. Original 2 v. edition, with extensive footnotes, was followed by one-volume edition. After further contraction and reappraisal, it was cut from 680 pp. to 234 as *Christopher Columbus, Mariner*, 1955, P1956.
————— . *Portuguese Voyages to America* . . . . 1940. Refutes claim that the Portuguese already knew about America before Columbus sailed.
————— .ed. *Journals and Other Documents on the Life and Voyages of Christopher Columbus*, 1963.

*Parr, C.M. *Ferdinand Magellan, Circumnavigator*, 1953, R1964. The first edition was entitled *So Noble a Captain*.

*Pigafetta, A. *The Voyage of Magellan: The Journal of Antonio Pigafetta*, tr. P. Soa, 1968. Based on copy in the Clements Library, Ann Arbor. Originally edited by Lord Stanley in Hakluyt Society Pub., Series I, no. 52, 1874. Also, with two lesser accounts, in C.E. Nowell, ed., *Magellan's Voyage Around the World: Three Contemporary Accounts*, 1962.

*Pike, R. *Enterprise and Adventure: The Genoese in Seville and the Opening of the New World*, 1966 (PhD thesis, Columbia). Genoa was the capital of Catholic finance, just as Amsterdam was the capital of Protestant finance.

Pohl, F.J. *Atlantic Crossings before Columbus*, 1961. Deals with some highly controversial theories.

*Prestage, E. *The Portuguese Pioneers*, 1930.

Renault, G. *The Caravels of Christ*, tr. R. Hill, 1959. Henry the Navigator and his captains; too uncritical concerning Portuguese religiosity – "more on how they preyed than how they prayed."

Quinn, D.B. *Sebastian Cabot and Bristol Exploration* (Univ. History Assn. no. 21) 32 pp., P1969.

Rogers, F.M. *The Travels of the Infante Dom Pedro of Portugal*, 1961. The brother of Prince Henry the Navigator, with an estimate of his influence in connection with Portuguese expansion.

Romoli, K. *Balboa of Darien, Discoverer of the Pacific*, 1953.

Sanceau, E. *Henry the Navigator; The Story of a Great Prince and His Times*, 1947, R1969. Seems better than Renault but not as good as Bradford or Beazley.

Waldman, G. *The Voyages of Christopher Columbus*, 1964.

*Williamson, J.A. *Maritime Enterprise, 1485-1558*, 1913.
*————. *The Voyages of the Cabots and the English Discovery of North America under Henry VII and Henry VIII*, 1929.
*————. ed. *The Cabot Voyages and Bristol Discovery under Henry VII* (Hakluyt Society, Second Series, 120), 1962.

*Wright, L. *Gold, Glory and the Gospels*. See Sect. T.

Wroth, L.W. *The Voyages of Giovanni Da Verrazzano, 1524-1528*, 1970.

Q - 3   Elizabethan Seafaring

In the remarkable activity of the "Sea Dogs," exploration, colonization, trade, informal raiding, and war were so intertwined that it seems feasible to cite the various aspects together here; the naval activity proper will also be noted in the chronological 1500-1650 (AW) section of naval history. See also Sect. R-3.

*Adamson, J.H. and Folland, H.F. *The Shepheard of the Ocean: Sir Walter Ralegh and His Times*, 1969.

Anderson, M.S. *Britain's Discovery of Russia, 1553-1815*, 1959.

*Andrews, K.R. *Elizabethan Privateering: English Privateering during the Spanish War, 1585-1603*, 1964 (PhD thesis, London).

*Barbour, P.L. *The Three Worlds of Captain John Smith,* 1964.
——————. ed. *The Jamestown Voyages under the First Charter, 1606-1609* (V. 1 and 2, Hakluyt Society, Second Series, 136, 137), 1969.

Bradford, E. *The Wind Commands Me: A Life of Sir Francis Drake* (*Drake* in the British edition), 1965.

*Corbett, Sir J.S. *Drake and the Tudor Navy, with a History of the Rise of England as a Maritime Power,* 2 v. 1899, R1965. The old classic.
——————. *The Successors of Drake* (1589-1603), 1900, R1970.

Cruickshank, C.G. *The Organisation and Administration of the Elizabethan Foreign Military Expeditions, 1585-1603* (ms. DPhil thesis, Oxford, 1940). Ch. 8, Transport.

Davies, D.W. *Elizabethans Errant,* 1967. See Sect. 0-5.

Deardorff, N.R. *English Trade in the Baltic during the Reign of Elizabeth,* 1912 (PhD thesis, Pennsylvania).

Dietz, B. *Privateering in North West European Waters, 1568 to 1572,* 1959. This was chiefly under Protestant Dutch or Huguenot flags.

Fowler, E.W. *English Sea Power in the Early Tudor Period, 1485-1558,* 1965. Progress up to the accession of Elizabeth.

Gerson, A.J. *The Origin and Early History of the Muscovy Company,* 1912 (PhD thesis, Pennsylvania).

Gookin, W.F. and Barbour, P.L. *Captain Bartholomew Gosnold: Discoverer and Planter, New England, 1602, Virginia, 1607,* 1963.

Hughes, C.E. *Wales and Piracy: A Study in Tudor Administration, 1500-1640* (ms. MA thesis, Swansea, 1937).

Kilfeather, T.P. *Graveyard of the Spanish Armada,* P1967. "Details of the fate of men and ships on the Irish coast."

*Lewis, M.A. *The Spanish Armada* (British Battles Series) 1959, R1968.
*——————. *The Armada Guns,* 1961.

Lloyd, C. *Sir Francis Drake,* 1957.

Manhart, G.B. *The English Search for a Northwest Passage in the Time of Queen Elizabeth,* 1924 (PhD thesis, Pennsylvania).

*Mattingly, G. *The Armada,* 1959, P1963. Half the book is devoted to the Counter Reformation background of bitter Catholic-Protestant rivalry.

Means, P.A. *The Spanish Main, Focus of Envy, 1492-1700,* 1935, R1965.

*Monson, Sir W. *The Naval Tracts of Sir William Monson,* ed. M. Oppenheim (Navy Records Soc. v. 22, 23, 43, 45, 47), 5 v. 1902-14.

Mood, F.F. *The Influence of Robert Thorne on English Maritime History, 1527-1607* (ms. PhD thesis, Harvard, 1929). Bristol merchant, author of influential propaganda for overseas empire.

Moore, R.O. *Some Aspects of the Origin and Nature of English Piracy, 1603-1625* (PhD thesis, Virginia, 1960; DA v. 21 p. 2600).

*Parker, J. *Books to Build an Empire: A Bibliographical History of English Overseas Interests to 1620,* 1966.

*Parks, G.B. *Richard Hakluyt and the English Voyages,* 1928 (PhD thesis, Columbia). See also Hakluyt, Sect. Q-1.

*Quinn, D.B. *Raleigh and the British Empire,* P1962. See also Wallace below.

*Rabb, T.K. *Enterprise and Empire: Merchant and Gentry Investment in the Expansion of England, 1575-1630,* 1967. Compares and analyzes more than 6,000 investors who helped to finance the beginnings of England's overseas empire.

Raleigh, Sir W. (II), *The English Voyages of the Sixteenth Century,* 1910. By the namesake of *the* Sir Walter.

Rowse, A.L. *Sir Richard Grenville of the* Revenge: *An Elizabethan Hero,* 1937, R1962.
*————. *The Expansion of Elizabethan England,* 1956. The second part deals with the Sea Dogs, the colonization of America, and the war with Spain.
*————. *The Elizabethans and America,* 1959.

Sellman, R.R. *The Elizabethan Seamen,* 2nd ed., 1963.

Uden, G. *Drake at Cadiz,* 1969.

Unwin, R. *The Defeat of John Hawkins: A Biography of His Third Slaving Voyage,* 1960, P1961. Lively story, well told.

Wagner, E.R. *Sir Francis Drake's Voyage Around the World,* 1967.

Wallace, W.M. *Sir Walter Raleigh,* 1959. In addition to Adamson and Folland, 1969, above, other recent works include D.B. Quinn, P1962, above; E. Ecclestone, P1941; and P. Edwards, 1953.

*Willan, T.S. *The Early History of the Russia Company, 1553-1603,* 1956.

*Williamson, J.A. *Sir John Hawkins, the Time and the Man,* 1927. A shorter, more popular version in 1949 had the title *Hawkins of Plymouth.* R1969.
*————. *The Age of Drake,* 1938, R1961, RP1962. The new edition had the title *Sir Francis Drake.*

Q – 4   Major Regional Exploration
(For the Pacific see Sect. AL-2)

Allen, E.S. *Arctic Odyssey: The Life of Rear Admiral Donald B. MacMillan*, 1963.

*Anderson, B. *Surveyor of the Seas: The Life and Voyages of Captain George Vancouver*, 1960, R1967. The new edition has the title *The Life and Voyages of Captain George Vancouver*. (PhD thesis, Harvard.)

Anderson, J.L. *Vinland Voyage*, 1967. One of several new works of speculation about the Vikings in the western Atlantic.

Armstrong, T. *The Northern Sea Route: Russian Exploration of the North East Passage*, 1952.

Bakeless, J. *The Eyes of Discovery: The Pageant of North America as Seen by the First Explorers*, 1950, R1961.

*Brebner, J.B. *The Explorers of North America, 1492-1806*, 1933.

Buller, J. *Our Navy Explores Antarctica*, 1966.

Cameron, H.C. *Sir Joseph Banks, KB, PRS, the Autocrat of Philosophers*, 1952. Wealthy amateur scientist, President of the Royal Society, and wire-puller extraordinary who promoted Cook's voyages and much else.

Casewell, J.E. *Arctic Frontiers*, 1957. Based on his Stanford PhD thesis, *U.S. Scientific Expeditions to the Arctic, 1850-1909*.

Crouse, N.M. *In Quest of the Western Ocean*, 1928. Search for the Northwest Passage.
————. *The Search for the North Pole*, 1947.

*Debenham, F. *Antarctica: The Story of a Continent*, 1961. Excellent survey by the author of the overall *Discovery and Exploration*. Debenham was one of the youngest members of the ill-fated Scott expedition.

*Dodge, E.S. *Northwest by Sea*, 1961. One of the most readable and useful summaries of the quest for the Northwest Passage, by the Director of the Peabody Museum.

Dolan, E.F. *Explorers of the Arctic and Antarctic*, 1968.

Dutilly, A.A. *Bibliography of Bibliographies on the Arctic*, 1945. Since space forbids citing more than a few titles on Arctic exploration here, this and *H. B. Collins, *Arctic Bibliography*, 1953, will be useful guides to the extensive literature.

*Ingstad, H. (tr. from the Norwegian by E.J. Friis), *Westward to Vineland: The Discovery of Pre-Columbian Norse House Sites in North America*, 1969.

*Jones, G. *The Norse Atlantic Saga: Being the Norse Voyages of Discovery and Settlement to Iceland, Greenland, America,* 1964.

*Kearns, W.H. and Britton, B. *The Silent Continent,* 1954. Contains "the complete stories of more than thirty Antarctic expeditions."

*Kemp, N. *Conquest of the Antarctic,* 1957.

*Morison, S.E. *The European Discovery of America: I, The Northern Voyages,* 1971.

Newcomb, C. *Explorer with a Heart: The Story of Giovanni da Verrazzano,* 1969.

(Scott, R.F.) *Scott's Last Expedition: The Journals of Captain R.F. Scott,* ed. L. Humphrey, 1913, RP1957.

Shackleton, Sir E. *South: The Story of Shackleton's Last Expedition, 1914-1917,* 1920, RP1962.

Stackpole, E.A. *The Voyage of the* Huron *and the* Huntress: *The American Sealers and the Discovery of the Continent of Antarctica* (Marine Historical Assn.), 1955.

Van Loon, H.W. *The Golden Book of the Dutch Navigators,* 1916. Deals with the Dutch explorers; one of the few accounts in English.

Weems, J.E. *Peary: The Explorer and the Man,* 1967.

Williams, G. *The British Search for the Northwest Passage in the Eighteenth Century,* 1962.

R   ORIGINAL SEAFARING ACCOUNTS (HAKLUYT SOCIETY)

A wealth of first-hand source material on exploration and early seafaring has been made available in English by the Hakluyt Society, with some 200 volumes since 1847. This British "guinea a year" society (now two guineas) was formed to publish important accounts of voyages, travels, expeditions and other geographical records. It has averaged about two volumes a year, each well edited, and, where necessary, translated. The titles up to 1946 have been listed in *A List of Publications of the Hakluyt Society,* but for convenience, the more pertinent works are summarized below, by nations. Incidentally, the explorers are listed under the flags for which they sailed rather than by their nativity – Henry Hudson, to be sure, was a "tramp athlete" sailing for Holland as well as his native England. Many of the works deal with shore-based activities and are not included. For those who can handle Dutch, a similar valuable series has been published by the Linschoten Society. The citations below indicate first the Series (I, 1847-1898; II, since 1898; and Ex, extra series), and then the volume number in that series; where the volume was later reissued, both numbers are given.

R – 1   Portuguese

Travels of Ludovico di Varthema, Egypt, Syria, Persia, India, Ethiopia, 1503-08. I, 32.

*The Book of Duarte Barbosa, An Account of the Countries Bordering on the Indian Ocean, I, 35; II, 44, 49.

*The Three Voyages of Vasco da Gama, I, 42; First Voyage, I, 99. 62, 69. In the absence of an adequate biography of the remarkable founder of the Portuguese empire, these are very useful.

*Chronicle of the Discovery and Conquest of Guinea, Gomes Eannes de Azurara. This has been the chief source of the various books on the voyages of Henry the Navigator's captains. I, 95, 100.

Peter Floris, His Voyage to the East Indies, 1611-15, II, 74.

The Voyages of Cadamosto, II, 80. He was the principal Italian navigator in the service of Henry the Navigator.

The Voyage of Pedro Alvares de Cabral to Brazil and India, II, 81.

The Tragic History of the Sea, 1589-1622; Narratives of the Shipwrecks of the Portuguese East Indiamen . . . and the Journies of the Survivors in East Africa, by B. Gomes de Brito. II, 112.

R – 2   Spanish

Select Letters of Christopher Columbus, I, 2; 43. *The Journal of Christopher Columbus during His First Voyage*, I, 86; *Voyages of Columbus. Select Documents illustrating the Four Voyages*, II, 65, 70.

The Discovery and Conquest of Terra Florida, de Soto. I, 9.

The Travels of Pedro Cieza de Leon, 1532-50. "From the Gulf of Darien to the City of La Plata." I, 33.

The Proceedings of Pedrarias Davila in Tierra Firma . . . and the Discovery of the South Seas and the Coasts of Peru and Nicaragua, I, 34.

*The First Voyage Around the World by Magellan, 1518-21, by Pigafetta et al., I, 52.

The Conquest of LaPlata, 1535-55, I, 81.

The Letters of Amerigo Vespucci and other Documents Illustrative of His Career, I, 90.

Narratives of the Voyages of Pedro Sarmiento de Gamboa to the Straits of Magellan, 1579-80. This was at the time when Drake had just passed through the Straits on his great world raid.

The Voyage of Mendana to the Solomon Islands in 1568, II, 7-8.

The Voyage of Captain Don Felipe Gonzales to Easter Island, 1770-71, II, 13.

The Voyages of Pedro Fernandez de Quiros, 1595-1606, II, 14-15.

The Guanches of Teneriffe . . . With the Spanish Conquest and Settlement, Alonso de Espinosa, II, 21.

Magellan's Strait, Early Spanish Voyages, II, 28.

The Quest and Occupation of Tahiti, 1772-76, II, 32, 36, 43.

R – 3   English, 1558-1603

The Observations of Sir Richard Hawkins . . . South Seas, 1593. This son of John Hawkins was very active and prominent in his own right, I, 1, 57.

The Discovery of Guiana, Sir Walter Raleigh, 1595, I, 3 (reprint 1963).

Sir Francis Drake, His Voyage, 1595, I, 4; *The World Encompassed*, I, 16; *New Light on Sir Francis Drake*, II, 34.

Russia at the Close of the Sixteenth Century, Giles Fletcher, Sir Jerome Horsey, I, 20.

The Three Voyages of Sir Martin Frobisher in Search of a Passage to Cathaia and India by the North-West, George Best, I, 38 (reprint 1963).

The Voyages of Sir James Lancaster to Brazil and the East Indies, 1591-1603, I, 56; II, 85. After preliminary scouting, Lancaster made the first voyage for the East India Company, capturing a huge carrack.

The Voyages and Works of John Davis the Navigator, I, 59. This highly respected Sea Dog not only left his name on the Arctic map with Davis Strait but was finally killed by Japanese pirates in the East after writing valuable navigational treatises.

Early Voyages and Travels to Russia and Persia, by Anthony Jenkinson and other Englishmen; most of their travel was overland, I, 72-73.

The Voyage of Robert Dudley to the West Indies and Guiana in 1594, II, 3.

English Voyages to the Caribbean, 1527-68. selected from the Spanish archives at Seville, II, 62. Similar, 1569-80, II, 71; 1583-94, II, 99.

The Roanoke Voyages, 1584-1590: Documents to Illustrate the English Voyages to North America Made under the Patent Granted to Sir Walter Raleigh in 1584, II, 104.

The Cabot Voyages and Bristol Discovery under Henry VII, II, 120.

R – 4   English, 1603-1650

The Historie of Travaille into Virginia Britannia, by William Strachey, 1612, I, 6; II, 103. Propaganda for colonization.

Memorials of the Empire of Japan, I, 8. Letters of Will Adams, the first Englishman in Japan, 1611-17.

The Voyage of Sir Henry Middleton to Bantam and the Molucco Islands. The second voyage of the East India Company, I, 19; II, 88.

Henry Hudson the Navigator, 1607-13, I, 27. Hudson was sailing for Holland in 1609 when he discovered the Hudson River, and for his native England when he found Hudson's Bay and was cast adrift there.

The Voyages of William Baffin, 1612-1622, I, 63. Baffin was another who left his name on the Arctic map.

Hystorye of the Bermudaes or Summer Islands, I, 65.

The Diary of Richard Cocks, "Cape Merchant in the English Factory in Japan," I, 66-67.

Early Voyages and Travels in the Levant, 1599-1679, I, 87.

The Voyages of Captain Luke Fox, of Hull, and Captain Thomas James of Bristol, in search of a N.W. Passage, 1631-32, et al. I, 88-89.

The Embassy of Sir Thomas Roe to the Court of the Great Mogul, 1615-19, II, 1-2. This diplomatic mission for the East India Company was important at a time when most Europeans were in India on Mogul suffrance.

The Voyage of Captain John Saris to Japan in 1613, II, 5.

The Strange Adventures of Andrew Battell of Leigh in Essex, II, 6.

John Jourdain's Journal of a Voyage in the East Indies, 1608-1617, II, 16.

Robert Harcourt's Voyage to Guiana in 1613, II, 60.

R – 5   English, after 1650

The Geography of Hudson's Bay, Captain W. Coats, 1727-51, I, 11.

The Diary of William Hedges, during his Agency in Bengal, 1681-87, I, 74-75, 78.

The Countries Round the Bay of Bengal, Thomas Bowrey, 1669-79, II, 12.

A New Account of East India and Persia, being nine years' travels, 1672-81, John Freyer, II, 19, 20, 39.

Journal of William Lockerby in Fiji, 1808, II, 52.

Colonising Expeditions to the West Indies and Guiana, 1623-67, II, 56.

R – 6 Dutch

The Three Voyages of William Barents to the Arctic Regions, in 1594, 1595, and 1596, by Gerrit de Veer, I, 13, 54. Includes the discovery of Spitzbergen and ten months in Novaya Zemlya.

*The Voyages of John Huyghen van Linschoten to the East Indies, I, 70-71. One of the most significant works in the whole Hakluyt series. Written by a young Dutchman in the service of the Archbishop of Goa, it gave a brilliant description of the Portuguese empire in the 1590s, showing how rich and rotten it was, and virtually giving directions for attacking it. It did much to stimulate the Dutch and English to seize the Portuguese holdings. Should be reprinted.

Early Dutch and English Voyages to Spitzbergen in the Seventeenth Century, II, 11.

East and West Indian Mirror, by Joris van Spillbergen, II, 18. Account of voyage around the world in 1614-17.

The Rise of British Guiana, from despatches of Storm van's Gravesande, II, 26-27.

R – 7 French

Narrative of a Voyage to the West Indies and Mexico, 1599-1602, by Samuel Champlain, I, 23.

The Canarian, or Book of the Conquest and Conversion of the Canarians in the year 1402, by Jean de Bethencourt, I, 46.

The Voyage of Francois Pyrard, of Laval, to the East Indies . . . and Brazil, I, 76-77, 80.

The Voyage of Francois Leguat, of Brasse, 1690-98, to Rodruguez, Mauritius, Java, and the Cape of Good Hope, c.1700, I, 82-83.

R – 8 Miscellaneous

Narratives of Voyages towards the North-West, 1496 to 1631, I, 5.

Notes upon Russia, Baron Sigmund von Herberstein, I, 10, 12.

A Collection of Documents on Spitzbergen and Greenland, I, 18.

History of the New World, G. Benzoni of Milan. "Showing his travels in America from 1541 to 1556," I, 21.

India in the Fifteenth Century, I, 22.

Early Voyages to Terra Australis, now called Australia, c.1500-1769, I, 25.

The Voyages of the Venetian Brothers, Nicolo and Antonia Zeno to the Northern Seas in the Fourteenth Century, I, 50.

Danish Arctic Expeditions, 1605 to 1620, I, 96-7.

The Life of the Icelander, Jon Olaffson, I, 53, 68.

Europeans in West Africa, 1450-1560, Portuguese, Spaniards, and Englishmen, I, 86-7.

The Voyage of Captain Bellingshausen to the Antarctic Seas, 1819-1821, II, 91-2.

The Red Sea and Adjacent Countries at the Close of the Seventeenth Centuries, three narratives, II, 100.

South China in the 16th Century, three narratives, II, 106.

Travels of Ibn Batuta, A.D.1325-1354, II, 110, 117.

R – 9   Extra

*Beaglehole, J.C. *The Journals of Captain Cook on His Voyages of Discovery*, 4 v. 1955-67. This "monumental" project makes available the pure original text of the Cook journals, which had been altered by the early official efforts of Hawkesworth and Douglas to "improve" them. The work is enriched by the very ample annotation of Beaglehole, assisted by J.A. Williamson, J. W. Davidson, and by R.A. Skelton, who edited a portfolio of "Charts and Views." Vol. 1, The Voyage of the *Endeavour*, 1768-70 (1955); v. 2, The Voyage of the *Resolution* and *Adventure*, 1772-75; v. 3, The Voyage in the *Resolution* and *Discovery*, 1776-80 (Cook was killed in Hawaii in 1778); v. 4, Essays and Lists Bearing on Cook's Life and Voyages.

S   SEA ROUTES, COMMUNICATIONS, ETC.

Allen, C.R. *Travel and Communication in the Early Colonial Period, 1607-1720* (ms. PhD thesis, Berkeley, 1956).

Ardehall, A. *The Suez Canal; Its History and Economic Development* (ms. PhD thesis, Clark, 1952).

Armstrong, T. *The Northern Sea Route: The Russian Exploration of the North-East Passage*, 1952 (PhD thesis, Cambridge). See also Krypton below.

Beatty, C.R.L. *De Lesseps of Suez: The Man and His Times*, 1957 (*Ferdinand de Lesseps* in British edition, 1956).

Broome, J. *Make a Signal*, 1955. See Sect. N-2.

Brownback, P.E. *The Acquisition of the Nicaragua Canal Route: The Bryan-Chamorro Treaty* (ms. PhD thesis, Pennsylvania, 1952). See also Folkman below.

Burrow, M. *The First Trans-Pacific Postal Service* (ms. MA thesis, Victoria College, New Zealand, 1937).

Canal Zone Library-Museum, *Subject Catalog of the Panama Collection*, 1964.

*Chidsey, C.B. *The Panama Canal: An Informal History of Its Concept, Building and Present Status*, 1970.

Clarke, A.C. *Voice Across the Sea: The Story of Deep Cable-Laying, 1858-1958*, 1958.

DeCrespigny, M.C. *The Overseas Mail Service of the Colony of South Australia, 1836-1901* (ms. MA thesis, Melbourne, 1947).

Dixon, J.T. *The Problem of Imperial Communications during the Eighteenth Century between Britain and Colonial America* (ms. MA thesis, Leeds, 1964).

*Du Val, M.P. *Cadiz to Cathay: The Story of the Long Diplomatic Struggle for the Panama Canal*, 1940, R1947.
*————. *And the Mountains Will Move: The Story of the Building of the Panama Canal*, 1947, R1969.

Fellner, F.V. *Communications with the Far East*, 1934. "Development of all forms in the last century."

Fletcher, M.E. *Suez and Britain: An Historical Study of the Effects of the Suez Canal on the British Economy* (ms. PhD thesis, Wisconsin, 1957).

Folkman, D., Jr. *Westward via Nicaragua: The United States and the Nicaragua Route, 1821-1869* (PhD thesis, Utah, 1966; DA v. 27, p. 1914A). See also Brownback above.

Hallberg, C.W. *The Suez Canal, Its History and Diplomatic Importance*, 1931.

Hammond, R. and Lewin, G.J. *The Panama Canal*, 1966. Technical and political analysis of detailed schemes for building a new canal.

*Hancock, H.E. *Wireless at Sea: The First Fifty Years*, 1950. See also Schroeder below.

*Hardy, A.C. *Seaways and Sea Trade: Being a Maritime Geography of Routes, Ports, Rivers, Canals, and Cargoes*, 1927 ff. "The first definite attempt to interpret trade routes and the cargoes carried on them in terms of maps." The 1941 title was prefixed with the words "World Shipping."

Harris, N.G. *Lifelines of Victory*, 1922. Discussion of the importance of communications in war, based on World War I experience.

Herring, J.M. and Gross, G.C. *Telecommunications: Economics and Regulation*, 1936. Ch. 2 "Growth and Development of Submarine Telegraphy" is one of the best accounts of the world cable net.

*Horrabin, J.F. *An Atlas of Empire*, 1937.

*Hoskins, H.L. *British Routes to India*, 1928 (PhD thesis, Pennsylvania), R1966. Relationship of sea and overland routes.

Howeth, L.S. *History of Communications-Electronics in the U.S. Navy*, 1964.

Kirkaldy, A.W. *British Shipping*, 1914, R1970, Pt. 3, Trade Routes.

Krypton, C. (pseud.) *The Northern Sea Route and the Economy of the Soviet North*, 1956. See also Armstrong above.

*Lewin, P.E. *Select List of Publications . . . illustrating the Communications of the British Empire*, 1927.

*Marlowe, J. *World Ditch: The Making of the Suez Canal*, 1964.

*Maury, M.F. *Explanations . . . .* See Sect. P-2.

Pudney, J. *Suez: DeLesseps' Canal*, 1968.

Pumphrey, R.S. *Marine Signalling Methods*, 1966.

Reade, L. *Marconi and the Discovery of Wireless*, 1963.

Reid, W.J. *The Building of the Cape Cod Canal, 1627-1914*, 1961 (PhD thesis, Boston Univ.).

*Rimington, C. *Merchant Fleets*, 1944. Ch. 3, Sea Routes, by R.G. Albion.

*Robinson, H. *Carrying British Mails Overseas*, 1964.
————. *A History of the Post Office in New Zealand*, 1964.

Rydell, R.A. *Cape Horn to the Pacific: The Decline of an Ocean Highway*, 1951 (PhD thesis, UCLA).

*Sargent, A.J. *Seaways of the Empire: Notes on the Geography of Transport*, 2nd ed. 1930. See also Hardy above.

Schonfeld, H.J. *The Suez Canal in World Affairs*, 1953.

*Schroeder, P.B. *Contact at Sea: A History of Maritime Radio-Communications*, 1967. The first comprehensive history of the art of maritime communication by wireless-radio, etc.

Sidebottom, J.K. *The Overland Mail: A Postal Historical Study of the Mail Routes to India*, 1948. See also Hoskins above.

Smith, D.H. *The Panama Canal: Its History, Activities and Organization*, 1927. Administrative details.

Smith, J. *Telecommunications: Their Significance as a Factor in Economic Developments* (ms. PhD thesis, London, 1946).

*Smith, W.D. *Northwest Passage: The Historic Voyage of the S.S.* Manhattan, 1970. Pioneer traversing of the Passage, westbound and eastbound by huge tanker to test the practicability of carrying out Alaska oil by sea.

*Staff, F. *The Transatlantic Mail*, 1957. Postal history, beginning with the government mail brigs and the New York packets.

Tascher, H. *American Foreign Policy in Relation to the Selection of the Trans-Isthmian Canal Route* (ms. PhD thesis, Illinois, 1933).

U.S. Hydrographic Office, *Table of Distances between Ports by the Shortest Navigable Routes* (H.O.No. 117), 1900 ff.

*Wakely, A.V.T. *Some Aspects of Imperial Communications*, 1924, Ch. 2, The Great Sea Routes; ch. 3, The Defence of Sea Communications; ch. 4, Air Routes of the Empire; ch. 8, Sea Cables and Land Lines; ch. 9, Wireless Intercommunication. Excellent maps.

Williams, M.W. *Anglo-American Isthmian Diplomacy, 1815-1915*, 1916, R1965.

Zukowski, W.H. *The Panama Canal: A Public Venture* (PhD thesis, Clark, 1956; DA v. 16, p. 1611).

T COLONIAL EXPANSION

The following works deal only with the broadest aspects; further references will be found in Part V (Commerce and Shipping) in connection with the particular regions, such as Spain in Latin America, Portugal in India, Holland in Indonesia, and Britain everywhere.

Boxer, C.R. *Four Centuries of Portuguese Expanison, 1415-1825, A Succinct Survey*, 1962, R1970.
*————. *The Portuguese Seaborne Empire, 1415-1825*, 1969.
*————. *The Dutch Seaborne Empire, 1600-1800*, 1965. These two excellent volumes, along with Parry below, are part of a series edited by J.H. Plumb. Boxer, with his command of Portuguese and Dutch, has also written several more specialized studies, noted later in connection with both empires.

Cambridge History of the British Empire, 8 v. 1929-40. Vol. 1, The Old Empire to 1783; v. 2, New Empire, 1783-1870; v. 3, Empire-Commonwealth, 1870-1939; v. 4-5, India; v. 6, Canada-Newfoundland; v. 7, Australia-New Zealand; v. 8, South Africa. Vols. 4-5 are identical with vols. 5-6 of the *Cambridge History of India*. Extensive bibliographies.

*Carrington, C.E. *The British Overseas: The Story of a Nation of Shopkeepers,* 1950, R, Pt. 1, 1968.

Cippola, C.M. *Guns, Sails and Empires: Technological Innovations and the Early Phases of European Expansion, 1400-1700* (In British edition, *Guns and Sails in the Early Phases of European Expansion*), 1966. "Overextended."

*Gipson, L.H. *The British Empire Before the American Revolution,* 9 v. 1936-54; revised edition, 15 v. 1958-70, plus bibliography. See Sect. Z-2.

Hall, W.P., Albion, R.G. and Pope, J.B. *History of England and the Empire-Commonwealth,* 1938 ff, R. 5th ed., 1971.

Knowles, L.C.A. *The Economic Development of the British Overseas Empire,* 3 v. 1924-36. Vol. 1, General; v. 2, Canada; v. 3, South Africa.

*Masselman, G. *The Cradle of Colonialism* .... 1963. See comments, Sect. AJ-3.

*Moon, P.T. *Imperialism and World Politics,* 1926. Stimulating, detailed account of the period c1870-1925, with a rather anti-imperialistic bias. More useful for commercial aspects than W.L. Langer's excellent diplomatic study.

Newton, A.P. *A Hundred Years of the British Empire* (1837-1937), 1940.

Nowell, C.E. *The Great Discoveries and the First Colonial Empires,* 1954, RP1960.

*Parry, J.H. *The Age of Reconnaissance: Discovery, Exploration and Settlement 1450 to 1650,* 1963. The most adequate comprehensive one-volume account of the early stages of expansion. It was preceded by his briefer *Europe and a Wider World, 1415-1715,* 1950 (in American edition, *The Establishment of the European Hegemony,* P1960). See also Wright below.
————. ed. *The European Reconnaissance, Selected Documents,* 1968.
*————. *The Spanish Seaborne Empire,* 1966.
*————. *Trade and Dominion: The European Overseas Empires in the Eighteenth Century,* 1971.

Prebble, J. *The Darien Disaster: A Scots Colony in the New World, 1698-1700,* 1969. Its failure made the Scots more ready to join England in 1707.

Priestly, H.I. *France Overseas: A Study in Modern Imperialism,* 1938, R1966.

*Rabb, T.K. *Enterprise and Empire.* .... 1967. See Sect. Q-3.

Rich, E.E. and Wilson, C.H. *The Economics of an Expanding Europe* (Vol. 4 of the *Cambridge Economic History of Europe*), 1967.

Townsend, M.E. *European Colonial Expansion since 1871,* 1941.
————. *The Rise and Fall of Germany's Colonial Empire, 1884-1918,* 1930.

Trevor-Roper, H.R., ed. *Age of Expansion, Europe and the World, 1559-1660,* 1968.

*Vlekke, B.H.M. *The Story of the Dutch East Indies*, 1945.

Williams, G. *The Expansion of Europe in the Eighteenth Century: Overseas Rivalry, Discovery and Exploration*, 1967.

*Wright, L.B. *Gold, Glory, and the Gospel*, 1970. Concentrates on individuals from Henry the Navigator to the Elizabethans, whereas Parry, for similar period, puts more emphasis on institutions.

V Commerce and Shipping

U GENERAL

There are no fully adequate overall accounts of commerce or shipping as a whole, although the British part of the story has been fairly well covered, as noted shortly in connection with Britain. In addition to the following few titles which give partial coverage, consult some of the standard, full-dress economic histories such as T.S. Ashton, J.H. Clapham, C.R. Fay, E. Lipson, H. Heaton, and S.B. Clough and C.W. Cole.

*Alexandersson, G. and Norstrom, G. *World Shipping: An Economic Geography of Ports and Seaborne Trade*, 1963.

Armstrong, R. *History of Seafaring*, 3 v. 1968-69.

Colby, C.C. *North Atlantic Arena: Water Transport in the World Order*, 1966.

Condliffe, J.B. *The Commerce of Nations*, 1950. Relatively slight "salt water content" but useful on basis of commercial policy and London money market. Pt. 1, Historical to 1800; 2, The 19th Century; 3, The World Wars; 4, Current Problems.

Day, C. *History of Commerce*, 1907 ff. Simple textbook survey, but far out of date.

Fayle, C.E. *A Short History of the World's Shipping Industry*, 1933. Useful material on crews, shipowning, shipping methods and general maritime activity, but not well organized. The works of A.W.Kirkaldy and R.H.Thornton,mentioned later, are better for modern period.

Lindsay, W.S. *History of Merchant Shipping and Ancient Commerce*, 4 v. 1874-76, R1965. The first two volumes, to 1815, have been thoroughly superseded but there is considerable of interest in the last two, as the author was active in various shipping affairs. Vol. 4 deals with steam navigation.

Macpherson, D. *Annals of Commerce*, 4 v. 1805. Chronological, year-by-year arrangement, well indexed for particular topics. Contains a wealth of scattered information and useful annual statistical tables of British commerce. Parts 2 and 3, 1492-1760, are taken virtually intact from Adam Anderson, *An Historical and Chronological Deduction of the Origin of Commerce*, new ed., 1787-89.

*Mance, O. *International Sea Transport*, 1945.

Scott, M.F. *A Study of United Kingdom Imports*, 1963 (National Institute of Economic and Social Research).

V COMMERCIAL THEORY AND POLICY

V – 1   Mercantilism and Laissez-Faire

Child, Sir J. *A New Discourse of Trade*, 1668 ff. Like Mun below, a classic statement of English mercantilism by a prominent merchant-economist who was head of the East India Company.

*Cole, C.W. *Colbert and the Century of French Mercantilism*, 1939.
*————. *French Mercantilism, 1683-1700*, 1943, R1964. Two excellent studies by the former president of Amherst College.

*Harper, L.A. *England's Navigation Laws: A Seventeenth Century Experiment in Social Engineering*, 1939, R1964. Carries the story through the two centuries (1651-1849) of constant modification to the final repeal.

*Heckscher, E.F. *Mercantilism*, tr. M. Shapiro, 2 v. 1935. More useful than the older work by G. Schmoller.

Langsdorf, W.B., Jr. *The Commercial Policy of the Landed Aristocracy in England, 1714-1740* (ms. PhD thesis, Berkeley, 1936).

*Lipson, E. *Economic History of England*, 3 v. 1915-31, R1961-62.

McCord, N. *Free Trade: Theory and Practice from Adam Smith to Keynes*, 1970.

*Mun, T. *England's Treasure by Forraign Trade*, 1664 ff. "The classic of mercantilism." For the other very numerous mercantilist writings, which incidentally throw considerable light on the Dutch and English commerce of the time, see the footnote citations in Lipson, v. 3, ch. 4.

Patrick, J.B. *The Privy Council and Trade and Industry, 1588-1603* (PhD thesis, Wisconsin, 1957; DA v. 20, p. 280).

Prouty, R. *The Transformation of the Board of Trade, 1830-1855; A Study of Administrative Reorganization in the Heydey of Laissez Faire*, 1958 (PhD thesis, Columbia).

See, H. *Modern Capitalism: Its Origin and Evolution*, tr. H.B. Vanderblue and G.F. Doriot, 1928, R1968. See especially chapters 4-7 on the interplay of commercial, colonial and financial factors in the 16th to 18th centuries.

*Smith, A. *An Enquiry into the Nature and Causes of the Wealth of Nations*, 1776 ff, RP1960. Normally cited as the *Wealth of Nations*. Highly influential pioneer classic of laissez-faire.

V – 2   British Colonial Policy

a. General

Beer, G.L. *The Old Colonial System, 1660-1754*, 1913.
——————. *British Colonial Policy, 1754-65*, 1907.

Cambridge History of the British Empire, 8 v. 1929-40. Vol. 1, to 1783, for all colonies, thereafter separate regional volumes.

Egerton, H.E. *A Short History of British Colonial Policy*, 1897.

Kammen, M. *Empire and Interest: The American Colonies and the Politics of Mercantilism*, 1970.

Knorr, K.E. *British Colonial Theories, 1570-1850*, 1944, R1963.

Knowles, L.C.A. *The Economic Development of the British Overseas Empire*, 3 v. 1924-36.

b. to 1776

Adolf, L.A. *The Operation of the English Navigation System in Colonial Pennsylvania, 1681-1750, a Case Study* (ms. PhD thesis, U. of Washington, 1953).

Albion, R.G. *Forests and Sea Power, the Timber Problem of the Royal Navy, 1652-1862*, 1926 (PhD thesis, Harvard), R1965. Ch. 5, The Broad Arrow in the Colonies. See also Malone below.

*Andrews, C.M. *The Colonial Period of American History*, 4 v. 1934-38, R1964. Vol. 4, *England's Commercial and Colonial Policy*, is an outstanding treatment of the subject.

Bilson, G. *English Committees and Councils of Trade and Plantations, 1600-1675* (PhD thesis, Stanford, 1970; DA v. 31, p. 5975A).

*Dickerson, O.M. *The Navigation Acts and the American Revolution*, 1951, R1970.

Doty, J.D. *The British Admiralty Board as a Factor in Colonial Administration, 1689-1763*, 1930 (PhD thesis, Pennslyvania).

Giesecke, A.A. *American Commercial Legislation before 1789*, 1910, R1970.

*Gipson, L.H. See Sect. Z-2.

Guthridge, G.H. *The Colonial Policy of William III in America and the West Indies*, 1923, R1967.

Hall, M.G. *Edward Randolph and the American Colonies, 1676-1703*, 1960, RP1969.

Haywood, C.R. *Mercantilism: Theory and Practice in the Southern Colonies, 1700-1763* (ms. PhD thesis, North Carolina, 1956).

Hemphill, J.M. *Virginia and the English Commercial System, 1689-1733. Studies in the Development and Fluctuations of a Colonial Economy under Imperial Control* (PhD thesis, Princeton; DA v. 25, p. 3536).

Henretta, J.A. *The Duke of Newcastle, English Politics and the Administration of the American Colonies, 1724-1754* (ms. PhD thesis, Harvard, 1967).

Kammen, M.G. *A Rope of Sand: The Colonial Agents, British Politics and the American Revolution*, 1968.

*Labaree, B.W. *The Boston Tea Party*, P1964. Detailed analysis of the 18th-century tea trade and British policy in connection with it.

*Malone, J.J. *Pine Trees and Politics.* . . . 1964. See Sect. AA-2.

Manning, F.J. *The Duke of Newcastle and the West Indies: A Study in the Colonial and Diplomatic Policies of the Secretary of State for the Southern Department, 1713-1754* (PhD thesis, Yale, 1925; DA v. 30, p. 5389A). See also Henretta above.

Mullen, F.F. *Rhode Island and the Imperial Reorganization of 1763-1766* (PhD thesis, Fordham, 1955; DA v. 26, p. 2166).

Sosin, M. *Agents and Merchants: British Colonial Policy and the Origins of the American Revolution*, 1965.

Steele, I.K. *Politics of Colonial Policy. The Board of Trade in Colonial Administration, 1696-1720*, 1968 (PhD thesis, London).

Thomas, P.J. *Mercantilism and the East India Trade: An Early Phase of the Protection vs. Free Trade Controversy*, 1926, R1963.

Ubbelohde, C. *The Vice-Admiralty Courts and the American Revolution, 1763-1778*, 1960 (PhD thesis, Wisconsin).

There is no room here to indicate further the extensive, and often controversial, literature on the general causes of the Revolution.

c. Since 1776

Burt, A.L. *The United States, Great Britain and British North America (1783-1815)*, 1940, R1961.

*Graham, G.S. *British Policy and Canada, 1774-1793, a Study in 18th Century Trade Policy*, 1930 (PhD thesis, Cambridge).
*————. *Sea Power and British North America, 1783-1820: A Study in British Colonial Policy*, 1941, R1969.

*Harlow, V.T. *The Founding of the Second British Empire, 1763-1793*, 2 v. 1952, 1964. Vol. 1, Division and Revolution; 2, Discovery and Changing Values. Harlow died in 1961 and the second volume was completed by F.M. Madden.

Johnston, C.M. *Charles Jenkinson, Lord Hawkesbury, at the Committee for Trade, 1784-1792: A Study in Commercial and Colonial Policy* (ms. PhD thesis, Pennsylvania, 1954). By a very embarrassing coincidence, a very similar study was written three thousand miles away: C.B. Ferguson, *The Colonial Policy of Charles Jenkinson, Baron Hawkesbury and the First Earl of Liverpool, as President of the Committee for Trade, 1784-1800* (ms. DPhil thesis, Oxford, 1952).

Lingelbach, A.L. *Application of the British Navigation Acts to Intercourse with America, 1783-1815* (ms. PhD thesis, Pennsylvania, 1916).

*Manning, H.T. *British Colonial Government After the American Revolution, 1782-1820*, 1933, R1966.

Platt, D.C.M. *Finance, Trade, and Politics in British Foreign Policy, 1815-1914*, 1968.

*Schuyler, R.L. *The Fall of the Old Colonial System, A Study in Free Trade*, 1945, R1966.

V – 3   Shipping Policy

a. British

Clegg, W.P. and Styring, J.S. *British Nationalized Shipping, 1947-1968*, 1968.

Cornewall-Jones, R.J. *The British Merchant Service: Being a History of the British Merchant Marine from the Earliest Times to the Present Day*, 1887, R1969.

*Davis, R. *The Rise of the English Shipping Industry in the Seventeenth and Eighteenth Centuries*, 1962 (PhD thesis, London). See comments, Sect. Y-3.

Dyos, H.J. and Aldecraft, D.H. *British Transport: An Economic Survey from the Seventeenth Century to the Twentieth*, 1969.

*Harper, L.A. See Sect. V-1.

Hunter, H.C. *How England Got Its Merchant Marine*, 1935. Simply a compilation of legislation from the earliest times.

Hurd, Sir A.S. *British Maritime Policy; Decline of Shipping and Shipbuilding*, 1939.

*Kirkaldy, A.W. *British Shipping, Its History, Organisation and Importance*, 1914, R1970. Useful comprehensive work, not completely supplanted by Thornton below.

MacDonagh, O. *The Passenger Acts*. See Sect. BO-2.

Moyse-Bartlett, H. *A History of the Merchant Navy*, 1937.

Otterson, J.E. *Foreign Trade and Shipping*, 1945. A comparison of British and American policy, for the American Maritime Council.

*Saletan, L. *State Subsidies to the British Merchant Marine, 1900-1950*, 1954.

*Thornton, R.H. *British Shipping*, 1939, R1959. Best general brief survey of all aspects.

Tomlinson, H.M. *The Foreshore of England, or Under the Red Ensign*, 1927 ff. First part of title dropped in later edition.

b. American

*Albion, R.G. *Seaports South of Sahara: The Achievements of an American Steamship Service*, 1959. Includes analysis of United States merchant marine policy since 1914, especially in Chaps. 1 and 5.

American Institute of Merchant Shipping, *The United States Merchant Marine in National Perspective*, 1970.

*Bentinck-Smith, J. *The Forcing Period: A Study of the American Merchant Marine, 1914-1917* (ms. PhD thesis, Radcliffe, 1958). Able analysis of the pre-1914 dependence on foreign shipping, resulting in a desperate shortage of American-flag seagoing tonnage. This situation led to the creation of the Shipping Board, and, combined with U-boat losses, to the building of the Emergency Fleet.

Dickinson, E.H. *The United States Merchant Marine as an Arm of National Policy* (PhD thesis, St. Louis Univ., 1968; DA v. 29, p. 1485A).

(*Fortune*) *Our Ships, An Analysis of the United States Merchant Marine* by the Editors of *Fortune*, 1938. Valuable articles on various aspects, amplifying their special "Shipping Issue" of 1937.

Franklin, F.E. *The Economic Impact of Flag Discrimination on Ocean Transportation* (PhD thesis, American Univ., 1968; DA v. 29, p. 1022A).

Georgetown University School of Foreign Service, *Government Aid to Shipping, Foreign and United States*, 1954. Good bibliography.

Gorter, W. *United States Shipping Policy* (Council on Foreign Relations Pub.), 1956. Extreme "internationalist" opposition to current policy, naturally highly unpopular in American shipping circles.

*Harvard Graduate School of Business Administration, *The Use and Disposition of Ships and Shipyards at the End of World War II*, 1945. Its recommendations were influential in postwar legislation on the disposal of war-built ships.

*Hutchins, J.G.B. *The American Maritime Industries and Public Policy, 1789-1914*, 1941, R1969. One of the most important single studies of the subject. Extensive bibliography.

*Jones, G.M. *Government Aid to Merchant Shipping: A Study of Subsidies, Subventions and Other Forms of State Aid in Principal Countries of the World* (U.S. Bureau of Foreign and Domestic Commerce, Special Agents Series, No. 119), 1916.

*Lawrence, S.A. *United States Merchant Shipping Policies and Politics* (Brookings Institute), 1966. Most useful work on the recent decades.

Mandeville, M.J. *The American Merchant Marine Problem: Its Development from 1920 to 1932* (ms. PhD thesis, Illinois, 1935).

Marx, D. *The United States Maritime Commission, 1936-1940* (ms. PhD thesis, Berkeley, 1947).

Matsushita, M. *The Application of United States Anti-Trust Laws to Foreign Commerce* (ms. PhD thesis, Tulane, 1962). See also Simmons below.

Meeker, R. *History of Shipping Subsidies*, 1905.

Miller, B.O. *The American Merchant Marine Policy and the Protective Tariff* (ms. PhD thesis, Virginia, 1937).

Neverson, R.C. *American Maritime Policy Since the Second World War* (ms. PhD thesis, Harvard, 1959).

Northwestern University, Transportation Center, *Economic Value of the American Merchant Marine*, 1961. Prepared under a grant from the Committee of American Steamship Lines. Wealth of statistics.

Patterson, J.M. *The Federal Promotion of Ocean Shipping* (PhD thesis, Cornell, 1961; DA v. 22, p. 2059).

Pierson, W.W. *Regulation of Foreign Commerce by the Interstate Commerce Commission*, 1908 (PhD thesis, Pennsylvania).

*Renninger, W.D. *Government Policy in Aid of American Shipbuilding: A Historical Study of the Legislation*, 1911.

Safford, J.J. *The United States Merchant Marine and American Commercial Expansion, 1860-1920* (PhD thesis, Rutgers, 1968; DA v. 29, p. 3961A).

Simmons, A. *Application of the Sherman Anti-Trust Act to the Foreign Trade of the United States* (ms. PhD thesis, London, 1960). See also Matsushita above.

U.S. Congress. (See list of major reports and hearings on merchant marine policy, Sect. C-2d.)
* ————. House Committee on Merchant Marine and Fisheries, *Merchant Ma-*

rine Act, 1936, Revised, 1951. Includes full edited text of the acts of 1916, 1920, 1928 and 1936, as well as other basic legislation.

*U.S. Maritime Commission, *Economic Survey of the American Merchant Marine,* 1937, R1970. Thorough analysis of shipping needs.
*————. *Survey of Coastwise and Intercoastal Shipping,* 1939.
————. *Report Describing Essential Foreign Trade Routes and Services Recommended for U.S. Flag Operation,* 1949.

U.S. Maritime Administration, *Ships Registered under the Liberian, Panamanian and Honduran Flags Deemed by the Navy Department to be under Effective United States Control.* . . . 1968 (8 pp.).
————. *Maritime Subsidies,* 1969. Lists the assistance given by 88 governments to their merchant marines.

Zeis, P.M. *American Shipping Policy,* 1938 (PhD thesis, Princeton).

COMMERCE AND SHIPPING BY REGIONS

W   SOUTHERN EUROPE AND EASTERN MEDITERRANEAN

W – 1   Ancient

Amit, M. *Piraeus and the Sea-People of Athens in the Fourth and Fifth Centuries, B.C.* (ms. PhD thesis, London, 1958).

Armstrong, R. *The Early Mariners,* 1967.

Bass, G.F. *Cape Gelidonya: A Bronze Age Shipwreck,* 1967. Archaeological investigation of the wreck of a "Canaanite merchantman," which sank on the coast of present-day Turkey around 1200 B.C., with details of cargo.

*Boulnois, J. *The Silk Road,* 1966. The overland path across Asia "from the moment the Romans first glimpsed Chinese silk in 53 B.C."

*Casson, L. *The Ancient Mariners: Seafarers and Sea Fighters of the Mediterranean in Ancient Times,* 1959, P1967. Sound and readable, the best book to read first. Emphasizes naval more than commercial aspects.

Culican, W. *The First Merchant Venturers: The Ancient Levant in History and Commerce,* 1966.

Edgerton, W.F. *Ancient Egyptian Ships and Shipping,* 1923 (PhD thesis, Chicago).

Frost, H. *Under the Mediterranean: Marine Antiquities,* 1963. Like Bass above and McKee, Taylor and Throckmorton below this reflects the fast-growing "marine archaeology," with its diving and dredging for old wrecks.

Grant, M. *The Ancient Mediterranean,* 1969.

Hapgood, C.H. *Maps of the Ancient Sea Kings,* 1966.

Herman, Z. *Peoples, Seas and Ships*, 1966. History of the eastern Mediterranean from the Egyptians through the Phoenicians.

Hyde, W.W. *Ancient Greek Mariners*, 1947.

Linder, E. *The Maritime Texts of Ugarit: A Study in Late Bronze Age Shipping* (PhD thesis, Brandeis, 1970; DA v. 31, p. 2822A). The Ugarit economy reached its peak in the 14th century B.C. " . . . serving the interests of both the Egyptians and the Hittites."

Loane, H.J. *Industry and Commerce of the City of Rome (50 B.C.-200 A.D.)*, 1938 (PhD thesis, Johns Hopkins).

McKee, A. *History Under the Sea*, 1969. Marine archaeology.

Meiggs, R. *Roman Ostia*, 1960. Seaport of Rome at the mouth of the Tiber.

*Miller, J.I. *The Spice Trade of the Roman Empire, 29 B.C. to A.D. 641*, 1969 (DPhil thesis, Oxford). Describes spices and practically all aspects of Roman trade with the Far East and East Africa. The subject is also well covered in Boulnois above and in E.H. Warmington, *Commerce Between the Roman Empire and India*, 1928.

Morrison, J.S. and Williams, R.T. *Greek Oared Ships, 900-322 B.C.*, 1968.

Moscati, S. *The World of the Phoenicians*, tr. A. Hamilton (History of Civilization Series), 1968. See also D. Hardens, *Phoenicians*, 1962.

Rideout, E.S.F. *The Commercial Law of Ancient Athens to 323 B.C.* (ms. PhD thesis, London, 1935).

*Taylor, J. duP., ed. *Marine Archaeology: Developments during 60 Years in the Mediterranean*, 1966. See also Frost above.

Throckmorton, P. *The Lost Ships: An Adventure in Undersea Archaeology*, 1964.

Young, G.P. *The Historical Background of Phoenician Expansion into the Mediterranean in the Early First Millenium, B.C.* (PhD thesis, Brandeis, 1970; DA v. 31, p. 1173A).

W – 2 Medieval

Argenti, P.P. *The Occupation of Chios by the Genoese, 1346-1566*, 3 v. 1959. The last two volumes consist of documents.

Bloomquist, T.W. *Trade and Commerce in Thirteenth Century Lucca* (PhD thesis, Minnesota, 1966; DA v. 28, p. 3006A).

Byrne, E.H. *Commercial Contacts of the Genoese in the Syrian Trade of the Twelfth Century*, 1916 (PhD thesis, Wisconsin).

—————. *Genoese Shipping in the Twelfth and Thirteenth Centuries*, 1930, 1971.

Chambers, D.S. *The Imperial Age of Venice, 1380-1580*, 1970.

Hughes, D.D. *Antonio Pesagno, Merchant of Genoa* (PhD thesis, Yale, 1968; DA v. 29, p. 534A). Trade and finance with England at the time of Edward II.

*Ibn Batuta. *Travels, A.D. 1325-1354*, tr. Sir H.A.R. Gibb (Hakluyt Soc. Pub. 2nd series, Nos. 110, 117), 2 v. 1958-61.

Kedar, B.Z. *Merchant Communities in Crisis: Changes in the Mood of Genoese and Venetian Merchants and Citizens, 1270-1400* (PhD thesis, Yale, 1969; DA v. 30, p. 3384A).

Krueger, H.C. *Genoese Trade with Northeast Africa in the Twelfth Century*, 1933 (PhD thesis, Wisconsin).

*Lane, F.C. *Venetian Ships and Shipbuilding of the Renaissance*, 1934 (PhD thesis, Harvard).
*—————. *Andrea Barbarigo, Merchant of Venice, 1418-1449*, 1944, R1967.
*—————. *Venice and History – The Collected Papers of Frederic C. Lane*, 1966. A convenient variation from the traditional *Festschrift*.

*Lewis, A.R. *Naval Power and Trade in the Mediterranean, A.D. 500-1100*, 1951, R1970. Analyses of the interplay of the Byzantine, Arab and Western elements in this valuable contribution to a neglected period of maritime history.

*Lopez, R.S. and Raymond, I.W. *Medieval Trade in the Mediterranean World: Illustrative Documents Translated with Introduction and Notes*, 1955, R1970. A valuable demonstration of "how things worked."

Lucki, E. *History of the Renaissance (1350-1550)*; Book I, *Economy and Society*, 1963. Ch. 2, Commerce and Business.

Mallett, M.E. *The Florentine Galleys in the Fifteenth Century, with the Diary of Luca di Maso Degli Albizzi, Captain of the Galleys, 1429-30*, 1967. An attempt to copy the long-standing Venetian galley system, with voyages around the Mediterranean as well as to Flanders and England.

Mitchell, R.J. *The Spring Voyage: The Jerusalem Pilgrimage in 1458*, 1964.

*Origo, I. *The Merchant of Prato: Francesco di Marco Datini, 1325-1410*, 1952, RP1963. Detailed account of a big businessman of Tuscany, with chapters on the cloth trade, trading companies, etc.

Perroni, A.G. *The Florentine Merchant and the Profit Motive* (PhD thesis, Univ. of Washington, 1968; DA v. 30, p. 475A).

Pike, R. *Enterprise and Adventure*. . . . 1966. See Sect. Q-2.

*Pirenne, H. *Economic and Social History of Medieval Europe*, tr. H. Clegg, 1936,

RP1960. A long-established authority in the field. Part 1, The Revival of Commerce; part 5, International Trade at the End of the 13th Century.

Reinert, R.G. *Genoese Trade with Provence, Languedoc, Spain and the Balearics in the Twelfth Century* (ms. PhD thesis, Wisconsin, 1938).

Sapori, A. *The Italian Merchant in the Middle Ages*, tr. P.A. Kennan, 1970.

Tenenti, A. *Piracy and the Decline of Venice, 1580-1615*, 1967.

Van Doorninck, F.H., Jr. *The Seventh Century Byzantine Ship at Yassi Ada. . . .* See Sect. L-2.

Watson, W.B. *A Common Market in Fifteenth Century Europe: The Structure of Genoese, Venetian, Florentine and Catalan Trade with Flanders and England* (ms. PhD thesis, Harvard, 1962).

W – 3   Modern Period – General

Fisher, Sir G. *Barbary Legend: War, Trade and Piracy in North Africa 1415-1830*, 1958. Considerable detail on British commerce of the Levant Company, which maintained the Barbary consulates; too tolerant of the pirates.

Harvey, M.L. *The Development of Russian Commerce on the Black Sea and Its Significance* (ms. PhD thesis, Berkeley, 1938).

Ibrahim Pasha, N.N. *Foreign Trade and Economic Development of Syria*, 1951 (PhD thesis, Columbia).

Mitchell, M. *The Maritime History of Russia, 1848-1948*, 1949, R1969. Falls far short of its promising title; very little on seaborne trade.

Monk, W.F. *Britain and the Western Mediterranean*, 1950. Both the commercial and naval aspects, especially for period 1688-1900.

Poyser, E.R. *Anglo-Italian Trade from the Reign of Elizabeth to the French Revolution, with special reference to the Port of Leghorn* (ms. PhD thesis, Cambridge, 1951).

Shillington, V.M. and Chapman, A.B.W. *The Commercial Relations of England and Portugal*, 1907. See also Fisher and Francis, Sect. W-6.

Stillman, N.A. *East-West Relations in the Islamic Mediterranean in the Early Eleventh Century – A Study in the Genza Correspondence in the House of Ibn Awaki* (PhD thesis, Pennsylvania, 1970; DA v. 31, p. 2827A). "One of the oldest, if not the oldest, collections of commercial correspondence from the Mediterranean world during the Middle Ages. The Commercial Revolution had reached its height in the Islamic and Byzantine worlds and was fast developing in the city states of the Italian peninsula."

Wood, A.C. *A History of the Levant Company*, 1935 (DPhil thesis, Oxford).

W – 4   16th Century

Carletti, F. *My Voyage Round the World: The Chronicles of a 16th Century Florentine Merchant*, tr. H. Weinstock, 1964.

*Connell-Smith, G. *Forerunners of Drake*, 1953 (PhD thesis, London). English trade with Spain and Spanish America in the early Tudor period.

*Usher, A.P. *Facts and Figures in Economic History*, 1932. Section on details of "Spanish Ships and Shipping in the 16th and 17th Centuries."

W – 5   17th Century

Bamford, P.W. *Forests and French Sea Power, 1660-1789*, 19t6 (PhD thesis, Columbia).

*Cole, C.W. *Colbert and a Century of French Mercantilism*, 1938.

W – 6   18th Century

*Davis, R. *Aleppo and Devonshire Square: English Traders in the Levant in the Eighteenth Century*, 1967.

Fisher, H.E.S. *Anglo-Portuguese Trade, 1700-1770* (ms. PhD thesis, London, 1961).

Francis, A.D. *The Methuens and Portugal*, 1966. Anglo-Portuguese diplomatic and commercial relations, 1691-1708. The Methuen Treaty is credited with giving English aristocrats gout by substituting port for lighter French wines.

Gharaybeh, A.K.M. *English Traders in Syria, 1744-1791* (ms. PhD thesis, London, 1952).

Matterson, C.H. *English Trade in the Levant, 1693-1753* (ms. PhD thesis, Harvard, 1936).

McLachlan, J.O. *War and Trade with Old Spain*, 1940, based on his PhD thesis, Cambridge, *Anglo-Spanish Diplomatic and Commercial Relations, 1731-59*.

Norton, W.B. *The Commercial Policy of the English Board of Trade toward France, 1696-1714* (ms. PhD thesis, Yale, 1938).

Viles, P. *The Shipping Interest of Bordeaux, 1774-1793* (ms. PhD thesis, Harvard, 1965).

W – 7   19th-20th Centuries

Boxer, B. *Israel Shipping and Foreign Trade*, 1957.

Coons, R.E. *Steamships and Statesmen: Austria and the Austrian-Lloyd, 1836-1948* (ms. PhD thesis, Harvard, 1966).

Dunham, A.L. *The Anglo-French Treaty of Commerce of 1860 and the Progress of the Industrial Revolution in France*, 1950 (PhD thesis, Harvard).

Field, J.A., Jr. *America and the Mediterranean World, 1776-1882*, 1969. "More attention is given to American naval contacts, maritime trade and missionary activity than to traditional diplomatic relations." Emphasis chiefly on eastern Mediterranean.

Finnie, D.H. *Pioneers East: The Early American Experience in the Middle East* (Harvard Middle East Studies), 1967.

Gendebein, A.W. *Commercial Relations Between the Kingdom of Sardinia and the United States of America, 1820-1848* (ms. PhD thesis, American Univ., 1951).

Glazier, I. *The Foreign Trade of Lombardy and Venetia, 1815-1865* (ms. PhD thesis, Harvard, 1964).

Walker, W.H. *Franco-American Commercial Relations, 1820-1850*, 1931 (PhD thesis, Iowa).

Walmsley, F.S. *The Economic Geography of Cyprus, 1878-1900* (ms. MA thesis, Liverpool, 1964).

X NORTHERN EUROPE

X – 1 Medieval

Brondsted, J. *The Vikings*, P1960, RP1965.

Colvin, I.D. *The Germans in England, 1066-1598*, 1915.

Dilley, J.W. *The German Merchants and Scotland, 1295-1327* (ms. PhD thesis, UCLA, 1946).

*Dollinger, P. *The German Hansa*, 1970. All aspects, during five centuries.

Finlayson, W.H. *The Scottish Nation of Merchants in Bruges* (ms. PhD thesis, Glasgow, 1951).

Foote, P.G. and Wilson, D.M. *The Viking Achievement, A Comprehensive Survey of the Society and Culture of Early Medieval Scandinavia*, 1970.

Gade, J.A. *The Hanseatic Control of Norwegian Commerce during the Middle Ages* (ms. PhD thesis, Columbia, 1950).

Horn, A.H. *German Merchants in England during the First Half of the Fourteenth Century* (ms. PhD thesis, UCLA, 1943).

Jellema, D.W. *Frisian Trade to 1100* (ms. PhD thesis, Wisconsin. 1952).

Keller, E.F. *The Historical Geography of Bruges, Belgium* (PhD thesis, Penn. State, 1964; DA v. 12, p. 7196).

Kendrick, T.D. *A History of the Vikings*, 1930, R1968.

Kerling, N.J.M. *The Commercial Relations of Holland and Zeeland from the Late 13th Century to the Close of the Middle Ages*, 1954 (PhD thesis, London).

Kirchner, W. *Commercial Relations between Russia and Europe, 1400 to 1800. Collected Essays*, 1966.

Leighton, A.C. *Early Medieval Transport* (ms. PhD thesis, Berkeley, 1964; DA v. 25, p. 4098).

*Lewis, A.R. *The Northern Seas: Shipping and Commerce in Northern Europe, A.D. 300-1100*, 1958. A companion work to his Mediterranean study for the same neglected period, based on archaeology and numismatics in addition to written sources. Differs from Pirenne on some interpretations.

*Marcus, G.J. *Ocean Navigation of the Middle Ages in Northern Waters* (ms. DPhil thesis, Oxford, 1955). Parts of this have appeared in journals.

Morey, G. *The North Sea*, 1968. "From pre-history to the present."

Munro, J.H.A. *Wool, Cloth and Gold. Bullionism in Anglo-Burgundian Commercial Relations, 1384-1478* (PhD thesis, Yale, 1965; DA v. 26, p. 1981).

Nash, E.G. *The Hansa*, 1929. Supersedes H. Zimmern, *The Hanse Towns*, 1889.

Peek, G.S. *The Anglo-Flemish Conflict (1270-1274) and Its Effects* (PhD thesis, Univ. of Washington, 1959; DA v. 20, p. 276).

*Pirenne, H. *Economic and Social History of Medieval Europe*, 1936, P1960. See comments, Sect. W-2.

Sawyer, P.H. *The Age of the Vikings*, 1962. Ch. 4, The Ships; 7, The Settlements; 8, Towns and Trade.

Tonning, O. *Trade and Commerce on the North Atlantic from 830 to 1350, Including Ireland, Scotland, Iceland, Greenland, England and Norway*, 1936 (PhD thesis, Minnesota).

*Van der Wee, H.A. *The Growth of the Antwerp Market and the European Economy (14th to 16th Centuries)*, 3 v. 1963. Vol. 1, Statistics; v. 2, Interpretation; v. 3, Graphs.

X – 2   16th Century

Deardorff, N.R. *English Trade in the Baltic during the Reign of Elizabeth* (in

Studies in the History of Commerce in the Tudor Period, pp. 215-332), 1912 (PhD thesis, Pennsylvania).

Gerson, A.J. *The Origin and Early History of the Muscovy Company* (in *ibid.*, pp. 1-122), 1912 (PhD thesis, Pennsylvania).

Kirchner, W. See Sect. X-1.

Lassen, A.P. *Commerce in the Baltic from 1500 to 1700 with special reference to the Decline of the Hanseatic League* (ms. PhD thesis, Berkeley, 1934).

*Willan, T.S. *The Muscovy Merchants of 1555*, 1953, R1969.
*————. *The Early History of the Russia Company, 1553-1603*, 1956.

X – 3   17th-18th Centuries

*Albion, R.G. *Forests and Sea Power: The Timber Problem of the Royal Navy, 1652-1862*, 1926 (PhD thesis, Harvard), R1963. Ch. 4, Baltic Timber and Foreign Policy; ch. 5, Penury and the Dutch Wars. The Navy received much of its plank, its smaller masts and its naval stores from the Baltic or Norway; it tried to cut off such supplies from its rivals. See also the companion work, P.W. Bamford, *Forests and French Sea Power, 1660-1789*, 1956 (PhD thesis, Columbia).

*Barbour, V. *Capitalism in Amsterdam in the 17th Century*, 1950, R1963. Ch. 5, Capitalism in Commerce. Emphasizes the great advantage of low interest rates and easy credit. She has also written several excellent articles in this field.

*Boxer, C.R. *The Dutch Seaborne Empire, 1600-1800*, 1965. A long-hoped-for study by the man best qualified to write it, dealing with the great days of Holland at sea. Deals not only with shipping, commerce, naval strength and colonies but also with the Dutch background.

*Davis, D.W. *A Primer of Dutch Seventeenth Century Overseas Trade*, 1961. Its 160 pages include chapters on the Herring Fishery, Sweden, Russia, Baltic, France, Spain and the Dislocation of the Westward Trade; Mediterranean; Indonesia, China and Formosa; Japan and Malay Peninsula; India, Ceylon and Burma; Arabia and Persia; Australia; West Indies and Guiana; Brazil; New Netherland; and Iceland.

Deen, L.D. *Anglo-Dutch Relations from 1660 to 1688* (ms. PhD thesis, Radcliffe, 1936).

Edmundson, G. *Anglo-Dutch Rivalry in the First Half of the Seventeenth Century*, 1911.

Fox, F. *Franco-Russian Commercial Relations in the Eighteenth Century and the Franco-Russian Commercial Treaty of 1787* (PhD thesis, Delaware, 1966; DA v. 28, p. 4985A).

Gideonse, M. *Dutch Baltic Trade in the Eighteenth Century* (ms. PhD thesis, Harvard, 1932).

Hautala, K. *European and American Tar in the English Market during the Eighteenth and Early Nineteenth Centuries*, tr. from the Finnish, 1963.

*Hinton, R.W.K. *The Eastland Trade and the Common Weal*, 1959 (PhD thesis, Cambridge). Gradual shift, in the Baltic trade, from monopolistic chartered company to the broader scope of the Navigation Acts; useful tables of traffic passing the Sound at the entrance to the Baltic.

Kent, H.S.K. *Anglo-Scandinavian Economic and Diplomatic Relations, 1755-1763* (ms. PhD thesis, Cambridge, 1956).

Kirchner, W. See Sect. X-1.

Kohlmeier, A.L. *The Commercial Relations Between the United States, the Netherlands and Dutch West Indies, 1783-1789* (ms. PhD thesis, Harvard, 1921).

*Oddy, J.J. *European Commerce, Showing New and Secure Channels of Trade with the Continent of Europe, Detailing the Produce, Manufactures and Commerce of Russia, Prussia, Sweden, Denmark and Germany*, 1805. Valuable tables of port statistics not included in American edition, 2 v. 1807.

*Price, J.M. *The Tobacco Adventure to Russia: Enterprise, Politics and Diplomacy in the Quest for a Northern Market for English Colonial Tobacco, 1676-1722*, 1961.

Smith, T.C. *The Overseas Trade of Scotland, with particular reference to the Baltic and Scandinavian Trades, 1660-1707* (ms. PhD thesis, Cambridge, 1960).

Sven-Erik, A. *From Cloth to Iron. The Anglo-Baltic Trade in the Seventeenth Century, Part 1, The Growth, Structure and Organization of the Trade*, tr. from the Finnish, 1963.

Warner, O. *The Sea and the Sword. The Baltic, 1630-1945*, 1965. Despite the title, has very meager maritime content.

Wilson, C.H. *Anglo-Dutch Commerce and Finance in the 18th Century*, 1941.
——————. *Profit and Power; A Study of England and the Anglo-Dutch Wars*, 1957.

X – 4   19th-20th Centuries

Beckerman, W. *Some Aspects of Monopoly and Monopsony in International Trade as Illustrated in Anglo-Danish Trade, 1921-1938* (ms. PhD thesis, Cambridge, 1952).

*Cecil, J. *Albert Ballin*. See Sect. J-4.

Chee-hsien, W. *Two Decades of Soviet Foreign Trade* (ms. PhD thesis, Harvard, 1947).

*Crosby, A.W., Jr. *America, Russia, Hemp and Napoleon. . . .* 1965.

Fridlizius, G. *Swedish Corn Export in the Free Trade Era: Pattern in the Oats Trade, 1850-1880*, 1957. Meticulous detail on the "boom and bust" episode.

Galpin, W.F. *The Grain Supply of England during the Napoleonic Period*, 1925 (PhD thesis, Pennsylvania).

Harbron, J.D. *Communist Ships and Shipping*, 1962.

Hauser, H. *Germany's Commercial Grip on the World: Her Business Methods Explained*, 1917. World War I propaganda. See Hoffman below.

*Heckscher, E.F. *The Continental System, an Economic Interpretation*, 1922. See also Galpin, Melvin, Ruppenthal and the titles in the 1793-1815 warfare section.

*Hoffman, R.J.S. *Great Britain and the German Trade Rivalry, 1875-1914*, 1933 (PhD thesis, Pennsylvania), R1964. Interesting and important analysis of the factors which enabled Germany to make heavy inroads into Britain's foreign markets. A more substantial work than Hauser above or E.E. Williams, *Made in Germany*, 1896.

Hulderman, B. *Albert Ballin*. See Sect. J-4.

Krypton, C. (pseud.) *The Northern Sea Route. . . .* 1956. See Sect. S.

Melvin, F.E. *Napoleon's Navigation System: A Study of Trade Control during the Continental Blockade*, 1919 (PhD thesis, Pennsylvania).

Ruppenthal, R.G. *Denmark and the Navigation System* (ms. PhD thesis, Wisconsin, 1939).

Woodward, D. *The Russians at Sea: A History of the Russian Navy*, 1965.

Y GREAT BRITAIN

Y – 1 General

*Ashton, T.S. *An Economic History of England*, 1956. Ch. 4, Overseas Trade and Shipping. One of the best overall summaries.

Bradford, E. *Wall of England: The Channel's Two Thousand Years of History*, 1966. See also Hargreaves below.

Cornewall-Jones, R.J. *The British Merchant Service*, 1887, R1969.

*Fay, C.R. *Great Britain from Adam Smith to the Present Day*, 1928, R1950. Part II, Ch. 7, "The Course of Foreign Trade" is a particularly lucid summary of the later period.

Hargreaves, R. *The Narrow Seas: A History of the English Channel, Its Approaches and Its Immediate Shores*, 1959. Fairly similar, in its broad, loosely defined scope, involving navies, merchant shipping, and seaports down through the centuries, to J.A. Williamson, *The English Channel: A History*, which also appeared in 1959. See also Bradford above.

*Kirkaldy, A.W. *British Shipping, Its History, Organisation and Importance*, 1914, R1970.

Knowles, L.C.A. *The Economic Development of the British Overseas Empire*, 3 v. 1924-36.

*Lipson, E. *Economic History of England*, 3 v. 1915-38, R1961-62. Particularly good on the earlier period; v. 2, ch. 2 contains an excellent account of the early trading companies.

Moyse-Bartlett, H. *A History of the Merchant Navy*, 1937.

*Thornton, R.H. *British Shipping*, 1939, R1959. Part I, successive periods since 1801. Part II, The Ship and Its Job; Sea Carriage; Dockside; The Ship; The Office; Passengers; The Men; Watch-keepers; The Voyage; Competition and Combination; The Business of Shipowning.

Williamson, J.A. *The Ocean in English History*, 1941.

Y – 2   Medieval

Beardwood, A. *Alien Merchants in England, 1300 to 1377; Their Legal and Economic Position*, 1931 (DPhil thesis, Oxford).

Bridbury, A.R. *The Import Trade in Salt into England in the Fourteenth and Fifteenth Centuries* (ms. PhD thesis, London, 1953).

Burwash, D. *English Merchant Shipping, 1460-1540*, 1947 (PhD thesis, Bryn Mawr), R1969. Full details of ships and crews but little on cargoes.

*Carus-Wilson, E. *Medieval Merchant Venturers*, 1953, R1967.
*——————— and Coleman, O. *England's Export Trade, 1275-1547*, 1963.

James, M.K. *The Non-Sweet Wine Trade in England During the Fourteenth and Fifteenth Centuries* (ms. PhD thesis, London, 1953).

Jenckes, A.L. *The Origin, the Organization and the Location of the Staple of England*, 1908 (PhD thesis, Pennsylvania).

Lingelbach, W.E. *The Internal Organization of the Merchant Adventurers of England*, 1902 (PhD thesis, Pennsylvania).

Martin, G.H. *The Borough and the Merchant Community of Ipswich, 1312-1422* (ms. DPhil thesis, Oxford, 1956).

*Power, E. and Postan, M.M. *Studies in English Trade in the Fifteenth Century*, 1933, R1966.

Ruddock, A.A. *Italian Merchants and Shipping in Southampton, 1270-1600*, 1951 (PhD thesis, London, 1938).

*Salzman, L.F. *English Trade in the Middle Ages*, 1931, R1964.

*Schenck, F. *London Merchants in the Reign of Edward I* (ms. PhD thesis, Harvard, 1918).

Thrupp, S.L. *The Merchant Class of Medieval London (1300-1500)*, P1962. Emphasis on the social context in which the activities took place.

Veale, E.M. *The English Fur Trade in the Later Middle Ages*, 1966.

Willey, C.F. *History of the English Wine Trade under John and Henry III* (ms. PhD theesis, Yale, 1941).

Wilson, K.P., ed. *Chester Customs Accounts, 1301-1566* (Record Society of Lancashire and Cheshire), 1970.

Y – 3   Modern

See also the preceding sections on Southern and Northern Europe for subjects involving Britain.

Aldercroft, D.H., ed. *The Development of British Industry and Foreign Competition, 1875-1914*, 1967.

Bowden, P.J. *The Wool Trade in Tudor and Stuart England*, 1962.

Clapp, B.W. *John Owens: Manchester Merchant*, 1967. Textile exporter.

*Clark, Sir G. *The Seventeenth Century*, 1929, R1947, RP1961. Ch. 4, Commerce and Finance; ch. 13, Colonies.

Cullen, L.M. *Anglo-Irish Trade, 1660-1800*, 1969 (PhD thesis, London).

*Davis, R. *The Rise of the English Shipping Industry in the Seventeenth and Eighteenth Centuries*, 1962 (PhD thesis, London). One of the most valuable contributions to British maritime history, filling an important gap. Thorough research has made possible valid conclusions in place of former vagueness. Ch. 1, Widening of Horizons, 1560-1689; 2, Consolidation, 1689-1775; 3-4, Ships and Shipbuilding; 5, The Shipowners; 6-7, The Merchant Seamen; 8, Shipping Management and the Role of Master; 9, Shipping and Trade; *Trades*: 10, Nearby and Northern European; 11, Southern European and Mediterranean; 12, East Indian; 13, American and West Indian; 14, The Government and the Shipping Industry; 15, War and the Shipping Industry; 16, Four Ships and their Fortunes; 17, Was It a Profitable Business? 18, Conclusion. Appendix A, Note on Shipping Statistics, 1686-1788; B, Sources. Many of these topics are carried into the next period in Parkinson below.

————. *A Commercial Revolution* (Historical Assn., Pamphlet, No. 64, 24 pp.), P1967. The century between the Restoration and the Industrial Revolution.

*Deane, P. and Cole, W.A. *British Economic Growth, 1688-1959; Trends and Structure*, 1962. Also, as a companion work, *Mitchell, B.R. and Deane, P. *Abstract of British Historical Statistics*, 1962; see detailed list of contents, Sect. E-1.

*Ehrman, J. *The British Government and Commercial Negotiations with Europe, 1783-93*, 1962.

Gipson, L.H. *The British Empire before the American Revolution*, 15 v. 1958-70. V. 1, Great Britain and Ireland.

Meyer, F.V. *Britain's Colonies in World Trade*, 1948. Useful for the period between the World Wars.

Minchinton, W.E. *The Growth of English Overseas Trade in the 17th and 18th Centuries*, 1969.

Page, W. *Commerce and Industry: A Historical Review of the Economic Condition of the British Empire (1815-1914)*, 1919, 2 v. 1968. Vol. 2 contains a wide variety of statistical tables.

*Parkinson, C.N., ed. *The Trade Winds: A Study of British Overseas Trade during the French Wars, 1793-1815*, 1948. A very useful cooperative study of many phases of maritime activity. Ch. 1, Shipowning and Marine Insurance; 2, Seaports; 3, Employment of British Shipping; 4, Ships of the Period and Developments in Rig; 5, Seamen; 6, Health and Sickness; 7, East India Trade; 8, West India Trade; 9, American Trade; 10, Newfoundland Trade; 11, Slave Trade; 12, Post Office Packets; Glossary of Marine Terms.

Payne, A.N. *The Relation of the English Commercial Companies to the Government, 1660-1715*, 1930 (PhD thesis, Illinois).

*Ramsay, G.D. *English Foreign Trade during the Centuries of Emergence*, 1957. Summarizes well the widespread research on the character and organization of trade between about 1450 and 1750, starting with the Netherlands and extending to other regions.

Ramsey, P.H. *The Merchant Adventurers in the First Half of the Seventeenth Century* (ms. DPhil thesis, Oxford, 1958).

*Saul, S.B. *Studies in British Overseas Trade, 1870-1914*, 1960 (PhD thesis, Birmingham). Analyzes the system of international trade and payments, the changes in structure, the special policies for Empire trade, and the causes for decline, particularly the failure to adopt new techniques and areas of trade.

Schlote, W. *British Overseas Trade, from 1700 to the 1930s*, tr. W.O. Henderson, et al., 1952. Statistical analysis.

*Schumpeter, E.B. *British Overseas Trade Statistics, 1692-1808*, 1960.

Silverman, A.G. *The International Trade of Great Britain, 1880-1913* (ms. PhD thesis, Harvard, 1930).

Smart, W. *Economic Annals of the Nineteenth Century*, 2 v. 1910-17. Like Page, above, based chiefly on Parliamentary papers and debates.

Smout, T.C. *Scottish Trade on the Eve of Union, 1660-1707*, 1963. Analysis of conditions leading the Scots to agree to union with England.

Supple, B.E. *Commercial Crisis and Change in England, 1600-1642*, 1960, R1969.

*Willan, T.S. *The English Coasting Trade, 1600-1750*, 1938 (DPhil thesis, Oxford), R1967.

Y – 4   British Seaports

For medieval activity of particular ports, see above, G.H. Martin, A.A. Ruddock, F. Schenck, S.L. Thrupp.

a. General

*Bird, J. *The Major Seaports of the United Kingdom*, 1963.

Carter, C.G. *The Forgotten Ports of England*, 1954.

Course, A.G. *Docks and Harbours of Britain*, 1964. Brief popular account of 69 modern ports.

Oram, R.B. *The Story of Our Ports*, 1969.

*Owen, Sir D.J. *The Origin and Development of the Ports of the United Kingdom*, 1939. Owen was general manager of the Port of London Authority.

Rees, H. *British Ports and Shipping*, 1958.

Victoria History of the Counties of England, 141 v. 1903-61. Wealth of information on local ports and coastal areas.

Walmsley, L. *British Ports and Harbours* (Britain in Pictures), 1942, R1946.

b. London

Banbury, P. See Sect. L-2.

Bell, A. *Port of London, 1909-34*, 1934.

Bird, J. *The Geography of the Port of London*, 1957.

*Broodbank, Sir J. *History of the Port of London*, 2 v. 1921.

Davis, D.J. *The Thames Sailing Barge*, 1970.

Elmer, J. *A Scientific, Historical and Commercial Survey of the Harbour and Port of London*, 1838.

Herbert, J. *The Port of London* (Britain in Pictures), 1947.

Jones, J.R. *London's Trade with France during the Reign of Elizabeth* (PhD thesis, Pennsylvania, 1944). A 44-page summary privately printed, 1944.

Jones, L.R. *The Geography of London River*, 1932. Historical evolution of the Thames estuary.

Lang, R.G. *The Greater Merchants of London in the Early Seventeenth Century* (ms. DPhil thesis, Oxford, 1963).

LeFleming, H.M. *Ships of the London River*, P1964.

Lovell, J.C. *Trade Unionism in the Port of London*. See Sect. BK-3.

McManus, J.P. *The Trade and Market in Fish in the London Area in the Early 16th Century, 1485-1563* (ms. MA thesis, London, 1952).

Millard, A.M. *The Import Trade of London, 1600-1640* (ms. PhD thesis, London, 1956).

Owen, Sir D.J. *The Port of London, Yesterday and Today*, 1927.

Sutherland, L.S. *A London Merchant, 1695-1774*, 1963. William Braund, engaged in Portuguese ventures, East India shipping, and marine insurance.

c. Bristol

Ballard, M. *Bristol, Seaport City*, 1966.

Farr, G.E. *Wreck and Rescue in the Bristol Channel, II – The Story of the Welsh Lifeboats* (Wreck and Rescue Series, V), 1967.

*MacInnes, C.M. *Bristol: A Gateway of Empire*, 1939, R1968. A history of Bristol.

Marcy, P.T. *A Chapter in the History of the "Bristol Hogs:" A Social and Economic History of Bristol, 1740-1780* (PhD thesis, Claremont, 1965; DA v. 27, p. 4024A).

Minchinton, W.E., ed. *Politics and the Port of Bristol in the Eighteenth Century: The Petitions of the Society of Merchant Venturers 1698-1803* (Bristol Records Soc. Pub. v. 23), 1963.

Neale, W.G. *At the Port of Bristol*, 2 v.; v. II, *The Turn of the Tide, 1900-1914* (Port of Bristol Authority), 1971.

Savadge, W.R. *The West Country and the American Colonies, 1763-1783; with special reference to the Merchants of Bristol* (ms. DPhil thesis, Oxford, 1951).

Sherborne, J.W. *The Port of Bristol in the Middle Ages*, P1965. A 30-page pamphlet of the Bristol branch of the History Association.

Winstone, R. *Bristol as It Was, 1866-1874*, 1966.

d. Liverpool

Banbury, P. See Sect. L-2.

*Chandler, G. *Liverpool Shipping*, 1960.

*Craig, R. and Jarvis, R. *Liverpool Registry of Merchant Ships* (Chetham Society), 1968. "Starting from the earliest Act of General Registry in 1786, Craig has transcribed the registries of Liverpool ships then afloat and also for a representative period thereafter." Jarvis provides an historical introduction and account of the development of the registry law and practice.

Harris, J.R., ed. *Liverpool and Merseyside: Essays in the Economic and Social History of the Port and Its Hinterland*, 1969.

Hughes, J.Q. *Seaport: Architecture and Townscape in Liverpool*, 1967.

Hyde, F.E., ed. *Shipping Enterprise and Management, 1830-1939: Harrisons of Liverpool*, 1967.
—————. *Liverpool and the Mersey: The Development of a Port, 1700-1970* (Ports of the British Isles), 1971.

Marriner, S. *The Rathbones of Liverpool, 1845-73*, 1961. An essay in business history. Imports of cotton and breadstuffs from the United States, Brazil coffee, and China tea.

Muir, R. *A History of Liverpool*, 2nd ed. 1907.

Neal, F. *Liverpool Shipping, 1815 to 1835* (ms. MA thesis, Liverpool, 1963).

Parkinson, C.N. *The Rise of the Port of Liverpool*, 1952. Carries the story through the eighteenth century.

Poole, B. *The Commerce of Liverpool*, 1854. Each of its 24 chapters deals with a commodity handled at the port.

Powell, L.H. *One Hundred Years of the Liverpool Steamship Owners Association, 1858-1958*, 1958.

*Williams, G. *History of Liverpool Privateers and Letters of Marque with an Account of the Liverpool Slave Trade*, 1897, R1966.

e. Other West Coast

Armour, C. *The Trade of Chester and the State of the Dee Navigation 1600-1800* (ms. PhD thesis, London, 1957).

Bouquet, M. *West Country Sail . . . 1840-1860*, 1968, R1971. See Sect. H-1.

*Clark, E.A.G. *The Ports of the Exe Estuary, 1660-1860: A Study in Historical Geography*, 1960 (PhD thesis, London), R1968. Until 1760, Exeter was active outlet for Devonshire woolens but then declined rapidly because of railroads and shallow channel.

Davies, L.N.A. *The History of the Barry Dock & Railways Company in the Development of the South Wales Coalfield* (ms. MA thesis, Cardiff, 1939). See also Hodges below.

Hodges, T.M. *History of the Port of Cardiff in Relation to Its Hinterland, with special reference to the Years 1830-1914* (ms. MEcon. thesis, London, 1946).

Hughes, H. *Immortal Sails*, 1969. Schooners from Portmadoc, Wales to Newfoundland.

Lucking, J.H. *The Great Western & Weymouth: A Railway and Shipping History*, 1970.

Makey, W.H. *The Place of Whitehaven in the Irish Coal Trade, 1600-1750* (ms. MSc thesis, London, 1952). See also Williams below.

Rees, J.F. *The Story of Milford (Milford Haven)*, 1954.

Williams, J.E. *The Growth and Decline of the Port of Whitehaven, Cumberland, 1650-1900* (ms. MA thesis, Leeds, 1951). See also Makey above.

Wood, O. *The Development of the Coal, Iron and Shipbuilding Industries of West Cumberland, 1750-1914* (ms. PhD thesis, London, 1952).

Woodward, D.M. *The Trade of Elizabethan Chester*, 1970.

f. South Coast

Andrews, J.H. *Geographical Aspects of the Maritime Trade of Kent and Sussex, 1650-1750* (ms. PhD thesis, London, 1954).

Carter, C. *Cornish Shipwrecks: The North Coast*, v. II, 1970. See Larn, below.

Dell, R.F., ed. *Rye Shipping Records, 1561-1590* (Sussex Records Society, v. 64), 1966.

Dunn, L. *Ships of Southampton*, P1964.

Farr, G.E. *Wreck and Rescue on the Coast of Devon: The Story of the South Devon Lifeboats* (Wreck and Rescue Series), 1968.

Foster, B., ed. *The Local Port Book of Southampton for 1435-36*, 1963.

Gill, C. *Plymouth, A New History, Ice Age to the Elizabethans*, 1967.

126

Hull, F., ed. *A Calendar of the White and Black Books of the Cinque Ports, 1432-1965*, 1966.

*Jessup, R.F. and F. *The Cinque Ports*, 1952.

Knowles, B. *Southampton, the English Gateway*, 1951.

Larn, R. *Cornish Shipwrecks: The Isles of Scilly*, v. III, 1971. See Carter, above.

Larn, R. and Carter, C. *Cornish Shipwrecks: The South Coast*, 1969. See also Noall below.

Lipscomb, F.W. *Heritage of Sea Power: The Story of Portsmouth*, 1967.

Noall, C. and Farr, G.E. *Wreck and Rescue Round the Cornish Coast*, 3 v. 1964-66. See also Larn and Carter above.

*Oppenheim, M. *The Maritime History of Devon* (reprint from *Victoria County History of Devon*, 1908), 1968.

Pannell, J.P.M. *Old Southampton Shores*, 1967.

Pearse, R. *The Ports and Harbours of Cornwall, an Introduction to the Study of Eight Hundred Years of Maritime Affairs*, 1963.

Perry, P.L. *A Geographical Study of the Trade of the Dorset Ports, 1815-1914* (ms. PhD thesis, Cambridge, 1963).

Sillick, C.B.M. *The City-Port of Plymouth – An Essay in Geographical Interpretation* (ms. PhD thesis, London, 1938).

Stephens, A.E. *Plymouth Dock, a Survey of the Development of the Royal Dockyard in Hamoaze during the Sailing Ship Era* (ms. PhD thesis, London, 1940).

Wiggs, J.L. *The Seaborne Trade of Southampton in the Second Half of the Sixteenth Century* (ms. MA thesis, Southampton, 1954).

Wright, M. *The Cinque Port Towns: A Comparative Geographical Study* (ms. PhD thesis, London, 1965).

g. Other East Coast

Allen, B.H. *The Administrative and Social Structure of the Norwich Merchant Class, 1485-1660* (ms. PhD thesis, Harvard, 1951). Though scarcely a seaport proper, Norwich was long important as a center of the wool staple.

Benham, H. *Last Stronghold of Sail: The Story of the Essex Sailing-Smacks, Coasters and Barges*, 1948.

Elliott, N.R. *Tyneside, a Study in the Development of an Industrial Seaport* (ms. PhD thesis, Durham, 1956).

Gillett, E. *A History of Grimsby*, 1970. Major fishing port.

Hall, B. *The Trade of Newcastle-upon-Tyne and the North-East Coast, 1600-1640* (ms. PhD thesis, London, 1933).

Harris, G.G. *The Trinity House of Deptford, 1514-1660*, 1969.

Jackson, G. *The Economic Development of Hull in the Eighteenth Century* (ms. PhD thesis, Hull, 1960).

Philpott, D.R.E. *Dover: The Historical Geography of the Town and Port since 1750* (ms. MA thesis, London, 1964).

Roche, T.W.E. *Ships of Dover, Folkestone, Deal and Thanet*, P1964.

Storey, A. *Trinity House of Kingston-upon-Hull*, 1967.

Webb, J. *Great Tooley of Ipswich* (Suffolk Records Soc.), 1963. Based primarily on account book of an early Tudor merchant "trading to the ports of Biscay, the Low Countries and Iceland."

h. Scotland and Ireland

Christie, G. *Harbours of the Forth*, 1955.

Cooke, S. *The Maiden City and the Western Ocean*, 1961. Londonderry and its relations with North America.

Cullen, L.M. *Anglo-Irish Trade, 1660-1800*, 1969 (PhD thesis, London).

Forbes, H.A.C. and Lee, H. *Massachusetts Help to Ireland during the Great Famine*, 1967. See Sect. AA-3.

Hughes, J.S. *Harbours of the Clyde*, 1955.

LeFleming, H.M. *Ships of the Clyde*, P1964.

Monaghan, J.J. *A Social and Economic History of Belfast during the First Quarter of the Nineteenth Century* (ms. PhD thesis, Belfast, 1940).

Nicol, N. *Glasgow and the Tobacco Lords*, 1967.

Owen, Sir D.J. *A Short History of the Port of Belfast*, 1917.

Paterson, A.J.S. *The Golden Years of the Clyde Steamers, 1889-1914*, 1969.

Reid, J.M. *A History of the Merchants' House of Glasgow*, 1967.

Worsley, S. *An Investigation of the Changing Trade between Ireland and England in the Eighteenth Century* (PhD thesis, Univ. of Washington, 1968; DA v. 29, p. 3276A). See also Cullen above.

Z SHIPPING AND COMMERCE – UNITED STATES

In contrast to the British situation, the United States still has no adequate overall maritime studies for the nation as a whole, though it is rich in local regional studies of commerce and shipping. Useful background will be found in the general textbooks in American economic history.

Z – 1 General Surveys

*Albion, R.G. and Pope, J.B. *Sea Lanes in Wartime: The American Experience, 1775-1945*, 1942, R1968. Effect of wartime activity on merchant shipping.

Bryant, S.W. *The Sea and the States: A Maritime History of the American Merchant Marine*, 1947, R1967. A not-too-successful attempt to combine the maritime and naval story in a single volume; leaves too many "blind spots."

*Hutchins, J.G.B. *The American Maritime Industry and Public Policy, 1789-1914*, 1941, R1969. See comments, Sect. V-3.

Johnson, E.R., et al. *History of Domestic and Foreign Commerce of the United States*, 2 v. 1915, R1922. Cooperative work, very uneven.

Marvin, W.L. *The American Merchant Marine, Its History and Romance from 1620 to 1902*, 1902. Despite its age and its propaganda in the later period, still useful.

Spears, J.R. *The Story of the American Merchant Marine*, 1915. Like Marvin, still fairly useful.

Z – 2 Colonial Period

*Andrews, C.M. *The Colonial Period of American History*, 4 v. 1934, R1964 and P. See comments on v. 4, Sect. V-2.

*Barrow, T.C. *Trade and Empire: The British Customs Service in Colonial America, 1660-1775*, 1967.

Bever, V.M. *The Trade in East Indian Commodities to the American Colonies, 1690-1775* (ms. PhD thesis, Iowa, 1941).

*Bridenbaugh, C. *Cities in the Wilderness: Urban Life in America, 1625-1742*, 1938 (PhD thesis, Harvard), R1955, R1964. Studies of five leading colonial seaports: Boston, Newport, New York, Philadelphia and Charleston.
*———. *Cities in Revolt: Urban Life in America 1743-1776*, 1955, R1964. The same five, to the Revolution.

Carse, R. *Ports of Call*, 1967. Sketches of early American seaports, from Castine to New Orleans.

Cederberg, H.R., Jr. *An Economic Analysis of English Settlements in North America, 1583 to 1635* (PhD thesis, Berkeley, 1968; DA v. 30, p. 1102A).

Dawson, J.L. *The Effect of the Discovery of the American Frontier on English Shipping, 1650-1688* (ms. PhD thesis, Edinburgh, 1956).

Dixon, J.T. *The Problem of Imperial Communications.* . . . 1964. See Sect. S.

*Gipson, L.H. *The British Empire before the American Revolution,* 9 v. 1936-54; R15 v. 1958-70. In this series, the word "before" means "just before." This monumental work centers on the period 1748-1776. Vol. 1, Great Britain and Ireland; 2, Southern Plantations (including West Indies); 3, Northern Plantations (including Maritimes, Newfoundland, Hudson Bay); 4-5, Zones of International Friction, 1748-64 (including New France and India); 7-8, The Great War for the Empire (Seven Years War); 9-12, The Triumphant Empire; 9, New Responsibilities, 1763-68; 10, Thunder Clouds Gather in the West, 1753-68; 11, The Rumble of the Coming Storm; 1766-70; 12, Britain Sails into the Storm, 1770-76; 13, The Empire Beyond the Storm, 1770-76; 14, Bibliography, 1748-1776; 15, Manuscripts.

Goldenberg, J.A. *The Shipbuilding Industry in Colonial America* (PhD thesis, North Carolina, 1969; DA v. 31, p. 338A).

Hautala, K. *European and American Tar.* . . . 1963. See Sect. X-3.

Mishkin, D.J. *The American Colonial Wine Industry. An Economic Interpretation* (PhD thesis, Illinois, 1966; DA v. 27, p. 1997A).

Savadge, W.R. *The West Country and the American Colonies.* . . . 1951. See Sect. Y-4c.

*Schlesinger, A.M., Sr. *The Colonial Merchants and the American Revolution, 1773-1776,* 1918 (PhD thesis, Columbia), R1957.

Ubbelohde, C. *The Vice Admiralty Courts and the American Revolution, 1763-1776,* 1960 (PhD thesis, Wisconsin).

Walton, G.M. *A Quantitative Study of American Colonial Shipping* (PhD thesis, Univ. of Washington, 1966; DA v. 27, p. 2712A).

Wright, J.L., Jr. *English-Spanish Rivalry in North America, 1492-1763* (PhD thesis, Virginia, 1958; DA v. 19, p. 1361).

Z – 3   1783-1860

*Buck, N.S. *The Development of the Organization of Anglo-American Trade, 1800-1850,* 1925 (PhD thesis, Yale), R1969.

Ellenstone, D.L. *America and the World Economy of the 1780s; A Study of Mercantile Behavior* (PhD thesis, Kansas, 1965; DA v. 26, p. 3039).

Frederickson, J.W. *American Shipping in Foreign Commerce, 1789-1860* (ms. PhD thesis, Chicago, 1953).

*Gilchrist, D.T., ed. *The Growth of the Seaport Cities, 1790-1825*, P1967. Proceedings of a symposium of the Eleutherian Mills-Hagley Foundation on the various factors affecting the relative growth of Boston, New York, Philadelphia and Baltimore.

Green, C.M. *American Cities in the Growth of the Nation*, 1957. Ch. 1, Seaboard Cities at the Opening of the Nineteenth Century: Boston, New York, Philadelphia, Charleston; ch. 4, The River Cities: Cincinnati, St. Louis, New Orleans.

*Hidy, R.W. *The House of Baring in American Trade and Finance* (Harvard Studies in Business History), 1949 (PhD thesis, Harvard), R1970.

*Nettels, C.P. *The Emergence of a National Economy, 1775-1815*, 1962, R1969.

Nute, G.L. *American Foreign Commerce, 1825-1850* (ms. PhD thesis, Radcliffe, 1921).

Roberts, G.H. *The Foreign Commerce of the United States during the Confederation* (ms. PhD thesis, Harvard, 1904).

Rubin, J. *Canal or Railroad? Imitation and Innovation in Response to the Erie Canal*, 1961.

Setser, V.G. *The Commercial Reciprocity of the United States, 1774-1839*, 1937 (PhD thesis, Pennsylvania).

Shineberg, D. *They Came for Sandalwood: A Study of the Sandalwood Trade in the Southwest Pacific, 1830-1865*, 1968.

Z – 4   Since 1861

*Albion, R.G. *Seaports South of Sahara*. . . . See Sect. V-3b.

*Bentinck-Smith, J. *The Forcing Period: A Study of the American Merchant Marine, 1914-1917*. See Sect. V-3b.

Carse, R. *Ocean Challenge: The New United States Merchant Marine*, 1967.

*Dalzell, G.W. *The Flight from the Flag: The Continuing Effect of the Civil War on the American Carrying Trade*, 1940. Summary of Confederate raiding; continues with the transfer of many American-flag ships to foreign registry to avoid high war risk rates resulting from the raiding of the *Alabama*, et al.

*Gilchrist, D.T., ed. *Economic Change in the Civil War Era. Proceedings of a Conference on American Economic Institutional Change, 1850-1873, and the Impact of the Civil War*, P1965. An Eleutherian Mills-Hagley Foundation symposium.

Harbeson, R.W. *The Atlantic Port Differentials: A Problem in Railway Rates* (ms. PhD thesis, Harvard, 1931).

Henry, A.K. *The Panama Canal and Intercoastal Trade*, 1929 (PhD thesis, Pennsylvania).

Schonburger, H.S. *Transportation to the Seaboard: A Study in the "Communication Revolution" and American Foreign Policy, 1860-1900* (ms. PhD thesis, Wisconsin, 1967).

Ullman, E.L., et al. *Flow Maps of American Coastal and Foreign Ocean Traffic*, 1955.

U.S. Board of Engineers for Rivers and Harbors and U.S. Shipping Board, *Transportation Lines on the Atlantic, Gulf and Pacific Coasts*, P1940 ff.

U.S. Maritime Administration, *Participation of U.S. Flag Ships in Overseas Trade, 1921-1951*, P1952.

AA   NEW ENGLAND

AA – 1   General

*Albion, R.G., Baker, W.A. and Labaree, B.W. *New England and the Sea* (American Maritime Library), 1972. History from Colonial times to the present.

*Bailyn, B. *The New England Merchant in the Seventeenth Century* (Studies in Entrepreneural History), 1954 and P. (PhD thesis, Harvard).

*Bennett, N.R. and Brooks, G.E., eds. *New England Merchants in Africa: A History through Documents 1802 to 1865* (Boston Univ. African Research Studies), 1965.

Carroll, C.T. *The Forest Civilization of New England: Timber Trade and Society in the Age of Wood, 1607-1688* (PhD thesis, Brown, 1970; DA v. 31, p. 6509A).

*Clark, C.E. *The Eastern Frontier: The Settlement of Northern New England, 1610-1763*, 1970. Ch. 1, The Forest and the Sea; ch. 2, Our Main End Was to Catch Fish.

*Dodge, E.S. *New England and the South Seas*, 1965.

Dorsey, P.M. *The Resumption of Anglo-American Trade in New England, 1783-1794* (ms. PhD thesis, Minnesota, 1956; DA v. 16, p. 1891).

*Kirkland, E.C. *Men, Cities and Transportation, a Study in New England History, 1820-1900*, 2 v. 1948. Covers period 1820-1890; emphasis chiefly on railroads, but gives one of rare accounts of coastwise trade, I, Ch. 1; II, ch. 19-21.

Lord, E.L. *Industrial Experiments in the British Colonies of North America*, 1898 (PhD thesis, Byrn Mawr), R1969. Particular emphasis on naval stores.

Moloney, F.X. *The Fur Trade in New England, 1620-1676*, 1931, R1967. See also Roberts below.

Morse, S.G. *New England Privateering in the Revolution* (ms. PhD thesis, Harvard, 1941).

*Pares, R. *Yankees and Creoles: The Trade between North America and the West Indies before the American Revolution*, 1955, R1968.

Roberts, W.I. *The Fur Trade of New England in the Seventeenth Century* (ms. PhD thesis, Pennsylvania, 1958). See also Moloney above.

Robinson, J. and Dow, G.F. *The Sailing Ships of New England, 1607-1907*, 3 v. 1922-28, R1969.

Taylor, W.L. *A Productive Monopoly: The Effect of Railroad Control on the New England Steamship Lines, 1877-1916* (PhD thesis, Brown, 1968; DA v. 30, p. 261A).

Tod, G.M.S. *The Last Sail Down East*, 1965. See comments, Sect. I.

AA – 2   Maine-New Hampshire

*Albion, R.G. *Forests and Sea Power*, 1926 (PhD thesis, Harvard), R1965. Ch. 6, The Broad Arrow in the Colonies; ch. 7, Masts and American Independence. See also Malone below.

Biscoe, M.W. *Damariscotta-Newcastle Ships and Shipbuilding* (ms. AM thesis, Maine, 1957). A number of Maine masters' theses are included here, as Orono has had an active interest in maritime history. These are available at the university library.

Black, F.F., ed. *Searsport Sea Captains* (Penobscot Marine Museum), 1960. Includes 28 photographs of captains from the Museum collection.

Blackistone, E.H. *Farewell Old Mount Washington: The Story of the Steamboat Era on Lake Winnepesaukee*, 1969.

Boone, M.P. *Chronicles of Calais and Vicinity* (ms. AM thesis, Maine, 1945).

Coro, B.A. *The Maritime Enterprise of a Kennebunk Shipowner, William Lord, 1820-1860* (ms. AM thesis, Maine, 1970).

Davis, H.A. *An International Community on the St. Croix (1604-1930)* (Univ. of Maine Studies, 2nd Series, 1964). Includes maritime activities of Eastport and Calais on the American side and St. Stephen and St. Andrews on the Canadian.

Drewett, B.K. and Spear, A.P., eds. *From Warren to the Sea, 1827-1852: Letters from the Counce and McCallum Families* (Warren Historical Society), 1970. Shipbuilders and sea captains of Warren, Maine; includes numerous letters written from sea.

Dunn, W. *Casco Bay Steamboat Album*, 1969. Photographs and brief history of the steamboats that plied the waters of Casco Bay, just east of Portland.

Everson, J.G. *Tidewater Ice on the Kennebec River* (Maine Heritage Series V.1), 1971.

*Fairchild, B. *Messrs. William Pepperrell: Merchants at Piscataqua*, 1954 (PhD thesis, Princeton). Careers of Col. William Pepperrell, Sr., c1647-1734, who settled at Kittery c1675; and his son Sir William Pepperrell, Bart., 1696-1759, captor of Louisburg. Wealth of detail on their widespread commercial activity.

Flaherty, P.A., Jr. *The Effect of the Civil War on Portland, Maine* (ms. AM thesis, Maine, 1956). See also Switzer below.

Gould, A.T. *The St. George's River*, 1950.

Grindle, L.G. *Quarry and Kiln: The Story of the Maine Lime Industry*, 1971 (PhD thesis, Maine). Lime, for plastering, was an important but inflammable coastal cargo.

*Hale, R.W. *The Story of Bar Harbor*, 1949. Fuller account than S.E. Morison, *The Story of Mount Desert Island, Maine*, 1960.

Hauk, Z.W. *The Stone Sloops of Chebeague and the Men Who Sailed Them*, 1949, R1953. Island in Casco Bay, near Portland.

Herrick, R.B. *A Century of Shipbuilding in Blue Hill, Maine, 1792-1892* (ms. AM thesis, Maine, 1945).

Isaacson, D.W. and Haggett, A.M. *Phippsburg, Fair to the Wind*, 1964. Town on Kennebec below Bath; site of 1607 Popham colony and later shipbuilding.

Jordan, W.B., Jr. *A History of Cape Elizabeth, Maine*, 1965 (AM thesis, Maine).

*Malone, J.J. *Pine Trees and Politics: The Naval Stores and Forest Policy in Colonial New England*, 1964 (PhD thesis, London). Centered mostly in New Hampshire and Maine. See also Albion above.

Mayhew, D.R. *The Wooden Sailing Barges of Maine, 1886 to 1945* (ms. AM thesis, Maine, 1959).

McKinley, S.J. *The Economic History of Portsmouth, N.H. from Its First Settlement to 1830, Including a Study of Price Movements There, 1723-1770 and 1804-1810* (ms. PhD thesis, Harvard, 1931).

Peck, H.A. *Seaports in Maine: An Economic Study*, 1955.

Pillsbury, D.B. *The History of the Atlantic and St. Lawrence Railroad Company* (ms. AM thesis, Maine, 1962). The American portion of the Grand Trunk Portland-Montreal run.

Preston, R.A. *Gorges of Plymouth Fort, Governor of New England and Lord of the Province of Maine*, 1953.

*Prince, H., Jr. *The Diaries of Hezekiah Prince, Jr.*, ed. A.P. Spear, 1965. For years 1822-28; includes record of movements of coastal shipping at Thomaston; appendix gives details of each vessel mentioned.

*Richardson, J.M. *Steamboat Lore of the Penobscot, an Informal History of Steamboating in Maine's Penobscot Region*, 1944.

Rowe, W.H. *The Maritime History of Maine: Three Centuries of Shipbuilding and Seafaring*, 1948, R1966. Less comprehensive than title indicates. It concentrates on sail and wooden shipbuilding, neglecting steam navigation and Portland's long role as winter port of Montreal.
——————. *Shipbuilding Days in Casco Bay, 1727-1890*, 1929, expanding an original study of the yards of North Yarmouth.

*Saltonstall, W.G. *Ports of Piscataqua: Soundings in the Maritime History of the Portsmouth, N.H. Customs District*, 1941, R1968. A delightful work, by the former headmaster of Phillips Exeter Academy.

Sherman, R.B. *The Bangor & Aroostook Railroad and the Development of the Port of Searsport* (ms. AM thesis, Maine, 1965).

Short, V. and Sears, E.B. *Sail and Steam along the Maine Coast*, 1954, R1967.

Smith, D.C. *A History of Lumbering in Maine, 1860-1930*, 1970 (PhD thesis, Cornell).

*Stahl, J.J. *A History of Old Broad Bay and Waldoboro*, 2 v. 1956. A model study of local maritime history; v. 1 covers the colonial and federalist periods; v. 2, the 19th and 20th centuries.

Stanley, R.D. *The Rise of the Penobscot Lumber Industry to 1860* (ms. MA thesis, Maine, 1958).

*Switzer, D.C. *Maritime Maine and the Union Naval Construction Effort, 1861-1865* (ms. PhD thesis, Connecticut, 1970).

*Wasson, G.S. *Sailing Days on the Penobscot: The Story of the River and the Bay in the Old Days*, 1932, R1949, 1970. The first edition includes a useful list of vessels, compiled by Lincoln Colcord.

Wentworth, H.L. *History of the Portland Marine Society*, P1969. Includes a list of the 531 members, 1796-1968.

Wilson, R.P. *An Inquiry into the Use the English Inhabitants of Colonial Maine made of the Fish and Game Resources of that Region* (ms. AM thesis, Maine, 1951).

Winn, R.H. *The Maine that Was: Legends of Cape Neddick*, 1964.

*Bailyn, B. and L. *Massachusetts Shipping, 1697-1714. A Statistical Survey*, 1959. An "IBM" analysis of 1,621 vessels registered at Boston, resulting in 33 tables showing the size and composition of the merchant fleet, its ownership, and much else.

*Baker, W.A. *The History of the Boston Marine Society, 1742-1967*, 1968. Lists the nearly 3,000 members, with dates of admission.

*Baxter, W.T. *The House of Hancock: Business in Boston, 1724-1775* (Harvard Studies in Business History), 1945. Valuable detail on "how things worked."

Cary, T.G. *Memoir of Thomas Handasyd Perkins . . . His Diaries and Letters*, 1856, RP1969. After early voyaging to Canton and elsewhere became one of Boston's outstanding merchants. See Sect. O-5.

Clapp, E.J. *The Port of Boston*, 1916. Modern problems.

Connolly, J.B. *The Port of Gloucester* (Seaport Series), 1940. See other Gloucester studies in Fishing section, AM-3.

Copeland, M.T. and Rogers, E.C. *The Saga of Cape Ann*, 1960, RP1967.

Corbett, S. and Zira, M. *The Sea Fox: The Adventures of Cape Cod's Most Colorful Rumrunner*, 1956.

Coughlin, M. *Boston Merchants on the Coast, 1787-1821; An Insight into the American Acquisition of California* (PhD thesis, So. California, 1970; DA v. 31, p. 2837A).

Dalton, J.W. *The Life Savers of Cape Cod*, 1902, R1967.

Forbes, H.A.C. and Lee, H. *Massachusetts Help to Ireland during the Great Famine*, 1967. As part of the generous philanthropic effort Capt. R.B. Forbes took over a cargo of flour.

Forbes, J.D. *The Port of Boston, 1783-1815* (ms. PhD thesis, Harvard, 1937).

Gregory, F.W. *Nathan Appleton, Yankee Merchant, 1779-1861* (ms. PhD thesis, Radcliffe, 1949).

Hauk, Z.W. *T Wharf*, 1952. History of one of Boston's most celebrated piers.

Hawes, C.B. *Gloucester by Land and Sea*, 1923, R1970.

Kittredge, H.C. *Shipmasters of Cape Cod – A Chronicle of the Great Days of Sail*, 1935.

*Labaree, B.W. *Patriots and Partisans: The Merchants of Newburyport, 1764-1815*, 1962 (PhD thesis, Harvard).

*————. *The Boston Tea Party*, 1964, R1968. Gives the background of tea trade and smuggling in addition to the local events.

McAvoy, M.G. *Boston Sugar Merchants Before the Civil War* (PhD thesis, Boston Univ., 1967; DA v. 28, p. 1768).

McKey, R.H., Jr. *Elias Hasket Derby, Merchant of Salem, Massachusetts, 1739-1799* (PhD thesis, Clark, 1961; DA v. 22, p. 2776).

*Morison, S.E. *The Maritime History of Massachusetts, 1783-1860*, 1921, RP1960. One of the classics of maritime literature, combining original approach, sound scholarship, and delightful style. Its topical arrangement covers various aspects ashore as well as the different spheres of distant activity.

Phillips, J.D. *Salem in the Seventeenth Century*, 1933.
————. *Salem in the Eighteenth Century*, 1937.
*————. *Salem and the Indies: The Story of the Great Commercial Era of the City*, 1947. The most comprehensive studies of this most history-conscious seaport, already the subject of a number of good books and articles. Other Salem items are cited in the section on South and Southeast Asia.

*Porter, K.W. *The Jacksons and the Lees: Two Generations of Massachusetts Merchants, 1765-1844* (Harvard Studies in Business History), 2 v. 1937, R1969.

Reid, W.J. *The Building of the Cape Cod Canal, 1627-1914*, 1961 (PhD thesis, Boston Univ.).

Reindehl, J.H. *The Impact of the French Revolution and Napoleon upon the United States as Revealed by the Fortunes of the Crowninshield Family of Salem* (PhD thesis, Michigan State, 1953; DA v. 14, p. 794).

Roberts, C. *The History of the Middlesex Canal* (ms. PhD thesis, Harvard, 1927).

Robinson, R.H. *The Boston Economy during the Civil War* (ms. PhD thesis, Harvard, 1958).

Ross, G.D. *The Crowninshield Family in Business and Politics, 1790-1930* (PhD thesis, Claremont, 1965; DA v. 28, p. 4103A).

Small, I.M. *Shipwrecks on Cape Cod*, 1928, R1967.

Spalding, R.V. *The Boston Mercantile Community and the Promotion of the Textile Industry in New England* (PhD thesis, Yale, 1963; DA v. 30, p. 1097A).

Starbuck, A. *The History of Nantucket*, 1924, R1969.

*Story, D. *Frame Up! The Story of Essex, Its Shipyards, and Its People*, 1964.

*U.S. Federal Writers Project, WPB, *Boston Looks Seaward: The Story of the Port, 1630-1940*, 1941, R1970. One of the best organized and best presented products of that WPB program; much better than the New York study.

Warden, G.B. *Boston, 1689-1776*, 1970.

Whitehill, W.M. *Captain Joseph Peabody, East India Merchant of Salem, (1757-1844)*, 1962.

AA – 4   Rhode Island – Connecticut

Anderson, V.B. *Maritime Mystic* (Marine Historical Assn., 39), P1962. See also earlier study by C.C. Cutler.

Bigelow, B.M. *The Commerce of Rhode Island with the West Indies* (PhD thesis, Brown, 1930; DA v. 30, p. 1490A). Pt. 1, History, Revolution; pt. 2, Commercial Organization and Practices. Includes chapter on "The Rhode Island Merchant and His Commercial Organization," based on types in Newport and Providence.

Chyer, S.F. *Lopez of Newport: Colonial Merchant Prince*, 1970.

Colby, J.P. *Mystic Seaport: The Age of Sail*, 1970.

Coleman, P.J. *The Transformation of Rhode Island, 1790-1860*, 1963.

Decker, R.O. *The New London Merchants, 1645-1907: The Rise and Decline of a Connecticut Port* (PhD thesis, Connecticut, 1970; DA v. 31, p. 6496A).

Hall, E.W. *Sailmaking in Connecticut Prior to 1860*, 1968.

*Hedges, J.B. *The Browns of Providence Plantation* (Harvard Studies in Economic History), 2 v. 1951, 1968. This admirable study dominates Rhode Island maritime history just as the Brown family, whose rich collection of family papers has been utilized, dominated it commercially. The first volume deals with the colonial period, the second comes down into the nineteenth century.

Lippincott, B. *Indians, Privateers and High Society: A Rhode Island Sampler*, 1961.

Longhorn, M. *The Rise of the Merchant Class in Rhode Island* (ms. PhD thesis, Wisconsin, 1937).

Martin, M.E. *Merchants and Trade of the Connecticut River Valley*, 1939 (PhD thesis, Columbia). See also Jacobus, Sect. J-2.

Palmer, H.R., Jr. *Stonington by the Sea*, 1957.

Tanner, E.C. *The Early Trade of Providence with Latin America* (ms. PhD thesis, Harvard, 1950).

VanDusen, A.E. *The Trade of Revolutionary Connecticut* (PhD thesis, Pennsylvania, 1948; DA v. 10, p. 99).

138

AB   MIDDLE ATLANTIC STATES

AB – 1   New York

*Albion, R.G. *The Rise of New York Port, 1815-1860*, 1939, R1961, 1970. Comprehensive topical treatment, including geographical setting, relations with hinterland, business and port organization, rivalry with other ports, and various spheres of coastal and overseas activity. Extensive appendix includes statistics of chief rival ports; see Sect. E. See also McKay below for plagiarism.

Armour, D.A. *The Merchants of Albany, New York, 1686-1760* (PhD thesis, Northwestern, 1965; DA v. 26, p. 3271).

Axelrod, D. *Government Covers the Waterfront: An Administrative Study of the Background, Origin, Development and Effectiveness of the Bistate Waterfront Commission of New York Harbor, 1953-1966* (DPA thesis, Syracuse, 1967; DA v. 29, p. 25B).

Bloch, J., et al. *An Account of Her Majesty's Revenue in the Province of New York, 1701-09*, 1966. Reproduction of the customs records of the Port of New York with several introductions, indices and appendices.

Boyle, R.H. *The Hudson River: A Natural and Unnatural History*, 1969.

Cohen, I. *The Auction System in the Port of New York, 1817-1837* (PhD thesis, N.Y. Univ., 1969; DA v. 31, p. 1183A).

Condon, T.J. *New York Beginnings: The Commercial Origin of New Netherland*, 1968. Examines relationship between the Company and the colony in the context of the Company's interests scattered over half the world.

Davison, R.A. *Isaac Hicks: New York Merchant and Quaker, 1767-1820* (Harvard Studies in Business History), 1964.

Forner, P.S. *Business and Slavery: The New York Merchants and the Irrepressible Conflict*, 1941 (PhD thesis, Columbia). Complications arising from the "cotton triangle."

Gabriel, R.H. *The Evolution of Long Island: A Study of Land and Sea*, 1921 (PhD thesis, Yale).

Griffith, J.L. *The Port of New York* (Institute of New York Area Studies), 1959. Description of various port functions, with statistical data on trade, etc.

*Harrington, V.D. *The New York Merchant on the Eve of the Revolution*, 1935 (PhD thesis, Columbia), R1964.

Horlick, A.S. *Countinghouses and Clerks: The Social Control of Young Men in New York, 1840-1860* (PhD thesis, Wisconsin, 1969; DA, v. 31, p. 708A).

*Hough, C.M. *Reports of Cases in the Vice Admiralty of the Province of New*

York and in the Court of Admiralty of the State of New York, 1715-1788, 1925. Such printed American records are very rare.

Johnson, H.A. *The Law Merchant and Negotiable Instruments in Colonial New York, 1664-1730,* 1963.

Kinsella, T. *The Development of Albany as a Modern World Port* (ms. PhD thesis, Clark, 1938).

Lemisch, L.J. *Jack Tar vs. John Bull: The Role of New York Seamen in Precipitating the Revolution* (ms. PhD thesis, Yale, 1962).

*Luke, M.E. *The Port of New York, 1800-1810: The Foreign Trade and the Business Community* (ms. PhD thesis, N.Y. Univ., 1950).

*Lydon, J.G. *The Role of New York in Privateering Down to 1763* (PhD thesis, Columbia, 1956; DA v. 16, p. 1436).

McKay, R.C. *South Street: A Maritime History of New York,* 1934, R1969. Covers years 1789-1860. A shameless scissors-and-paste compilation, it was withdrawn by the publishers after attention was called to its extensive plagiarism. Despite that, another publishing house has brought out a reissue 35 years later.

*Miller, R. *The New York Coastwise Trade, 1865-1915,* 1970 (PhD thesis, Princeton). One of the very few studies of this important subject.

Mitchell, J. *The Bottom of the Harbor,* 1959. "Little known scenes of life" in New York, originally appearing in the *New Yorker.*

Murray, J.E. *The Fur Trade in New France and New Netherland Prior to 1645* (ms. PhD thesis, Chicago, 1937); brief 13-page summary, 1938.

Palmer, W.R. *The Whaling Port of Sag Harbor* (PhD thesis, Columbia, 1959; DA v. 20, p. 655).

Parr, C.M. *The Voyages of David DeVries. . . .* 1969. Prominent Dutch navigator active for a while at New Amsterdam and in Connecticut.

Port of New York Authority, *A Selected Bibliography of the Port of New York, 1921-1956,* 1956.

*Porter, K.W. *John Jacob Astor, Business Man* (Harvard Studies in Business History), 1931 (PhD thesis, Harvard), R1966.

Rubin, I.I. *New York State and the Long Embargo* (PhD thesis, N.Y. Univ., 1961; DA v. 23, p. 612).

Stanton, S.W. *American Steam Vessels.* See Sect. H-1.

Trelease, A.W. *Indian Relations and the Fur Trade in New Netherland, 1600-1664* (ms. PhD thesis, Harvard, 1955), expanded into *Indian Affairs in Colonial New York in the Seventeenth Century,* 1960.

U.S. Federal Writers Project, WPB, *The Maritime History of New York*, 1941. The only coverage of the whole three centuries, but it falls far short in quality of the Program's Boston study, *q.v.*

Verplanck, W.E. and Collyer, M.W. *The Sloops of the Hudson: An Historical Sketch of the Packet and Market Sloops of the Last Century with a Record of Their Names. . . .* 1908, R1968.

*White, P.L. *The Beekmans of New York in Politics and Commerce, 1647-1877*, 1956.
————. ed. *The Beekman Mercantile Papers, 1746-1799*, 3 v. 1957. V. 1, Gerard G. Beekman Letter Book, 1746-1770; v. 2-3, James Beekman, Mercantile Correspondence, 1750-1799.

AB – 2 Pennsylvania

Adolf, L.A. *The Operation of the English Navigation System in Colonial Pennsylvania, 1681-1750, A Case Study* (PhD thesis, Univ. of Washington, 1953; DA v. 13, p. 771).

*Alberts, R.C. *The Golden Voyage: The Life and Times of William Bingham, 1752-1804*, 1969. Philadelphian with widespread financial interests, including connections with the Barings.

Arena, C.R. *Philadelphia-Spanish New Orleans Trade, 1789-1803* (PhD thesis, Pennsylvania, 1959; DA v. 21, p. 2242).

Balderston, M., ed. *James Claypoole's Letter Book, London and Philadelphia 1681-1686*, 1967. Record of business correspondence, chiefly during his last years in London before migrating to Philadelphia in 1683.

Bert, H.D. *Merchants and Mercantile Life in Colonial Philadelphia, 1748-1763* (ms. PhD thesis, Iowa, 1941).

Burt, S. *Philadelphia, Holy Experiment* (Seaport Series), 1945. Like too many other volumes in the Doubleday, Doran "Seaport Series," this devotes much less attention to the seaport proper than to the city in general.

Crowther, S.J. *The Shipbuilding Industry and the Development of the Delaware Valley, 1681-1776* (PhD thesis Pennsylvania, 1970; DA v. 31, p. 5010A).

Doll, E.D., ed. *Index to the Pennsylvania Magazine of History and Biography Volumes 1-75 (1877-1951)*, 1953. Includes many maritime items.

Duvall, R.F. *Philadelphia's Maritime Commerce with the British Empire, 1783-1789* (PhD thesis, Pennsylvania, 1960; DA v. 23, p. 861).

Gares, A.J. *Stephen Girard's West Indian Trade from 1789 to 1812* (ms. PhD thesis, Temple, 1947).

*Jensen, A.L. *The Maritime Commerce of Colonial Philadelphia*, 1963.

Kauffman, J.L. *Philadelphia Navy Yards, 1801-1948* (Newcomen Society), P1948.

Klopfer, H.L. *Statistics of the Foreign Trade of Philadelphia, 1700-1860* (ms. PhD thesis, Pennsylvania, 1936).

Larsen, G.H. *Profile of a Colonial Merchant: Thomas Clifford of Pre-Revolutionary Philadelphia* (PhD thesis, Columbia, 1955; DA v. 26, p. 326).

Livingood, J.W. *The Rivalry of Philadelphia and Baltimore for the Trade of the Susquehanna Region* (ms. PhD thesis, Princeton, 1936).

Martin, A.S. *The Port of Philadelphia, 1763-1776; A Biography* (ms. PhD thesis, Iowa, 1941).

Neel, J.L.C. *His Britannic Majesty's Consul General, Phineas Bond, Esq.* (ms. PhD thesis, Bryn Mawr, 1963; DA v. 25, p. 1178). American Loyalist, first British consul at Philadelphia.

Oaks, R.F. *Philadelphia Merchants and the American Revolution, 1765-1776* (PhD thesis, So. California, 1970; DA v. 31, p. 3448A).

Powell, H.B. *Coal, Philadelphia and the Schuylkill* (PhD thesis, Lehigh, 1969; DA v. 29, p. 1349A).

Romanek, C.L. *John Reynell: Quaker Merchant of Colonial Philadelphia* (PhD thesis, Penn. State, 1969; DA v. 30, p. 4924A). In Philadelphia 1728-1784.

Tolles, F.B. *Meeting House and Counting House: The Quaker Merchants of Colonial Philadelphia, 1682-1763*, 1948 (PhD thesis, Harvard), R1963.

Tooker, E. *Nathan Trotter, Philadelphia Merchant, 1787-1853* (Harvard Studies in Business History), 1955.

Turner, M.K. *Commercial Relations of the Susquehanna Valley during the Colonial Period* (ms. PhD thesis, Pennsylvania, 1916).

Tyler, D.B. *The Bay and River Delaware: A Pictorial History*, 1955. In the same series as Brewington's Chesapeake Bay and Kemble's San Francisco.
————. *The American Clyde: A History of Iron and Steel Shipbuilding on the Delaware from 1840 to World War I*, 1958.

Walzer, J.F. *Transportation in the Philadelphia Trading Area, 1740-1775* (PhD thesis, Wisconsin, 1968; DA v. 29, p. 202A).

Wax, D.D. *The Negro Slave Trade in Colonial Pennsylvania* (ms. PhD thesis, Univ. of Washington, 1962; DA v. 24, p. 272).

AB – 3   New Jersey – Delaware

Hanna, M.A. *The Trade of the Delaware District before the Revolution*, 1917 (PhD thesis, Bryn Mawr).

Hunter, W.C. *The Commercial Policy of New Jersey under the Confederation, 1783-1789*, 1922 (PhD thesis, Princeton).

Krotee, W. and R. *Shipwrecks Off the New Jersey Coast*, P1966. Written primarily for scuba divers; locates over 400 wrecks and describes circumstances of loss.

Lane, W.C. *From Indian Trail to Iron Horse: Travel and Transportation in New Jersey, 1620-1860*, 1939 (PhD thesis, Princeton).

Marvil, J. *Pilots of the Bay and River Delaware.* . . . 1965.

Miller, M.E. *The Delaware Oyster Industry: Past and Present* (ms. PhD thesis, Boston Univ., 1962).

Moss, G.H., Jr. *Nauvoo to the Hook: The Iconography of a Barrier Beach*, 1966. History of the New Jersey coast from Sea Bright to Sandy Hook.
——————. *Steamboat to the Shore: A Pictorial History of the Steamboat Era in Monmouth County, N.J.*, 1967. Documentation of 147 years of steamboat service between New York and the Jersey shore.

Pierce, A.D. *Smugglers' Woods.* . . . 1960. Smuggling in the late colonial period and privateering in the Revolution between the Mullica River and Cape May in New Jersey.

AC SOUTHERN STATES

AC – 1 General

*Albion, R.G. *Square-Riggers on Schedule: The New York Sailing Packets to England, France and the Cotton Ports*, 1938. R1965. Ch. 3, Enslaving the Cotton Ports, and appendix for typical cargoes.
*——————. *The Rise of New York Port, 1815-1860*, 1939, R1970. Ch. 6, The Cotton Triangle; detailed appendix statistics of the cotton ports.

*Baughman, J.P. *Charles Morgan and the Development of Southern Transportation*, 1968. See Sect. J-4b.

Booker, H.M. *Efforts of the South to Attract Immigrants, 1890-1900* (ms. PhD thesis, Virginia, 1965).

Brown, A.C. *The Dismal Swamp Canal*, 1967.

*Bruchey, S., ed. *Cotton and the Growth of the American Economy, 1790-1860, Sources and Readings*, 1967.

Cutler, C.C. *Queens of the Western Ocean*, 1961. Wealth of detail on coastal sailing packet service to major southern ports. See Sect. I.

Eisterhold, J.A. *Lumber and Trade in the Seaboard Cities of the Old South, 1607-1860* (PhD thesis, Mississippi, 1970; DA v. 31, p. 2816A).

Gipson, L.H. *The British Empire before the American Revolution*. See Sect. Z-2; v. 2, Southern Plantations. Detailed picture of the Southern colonial economy.

Haywood, C.R. *Mercantilism, Theory and Practice, in the Southern Colonies, 1700-1763* (ms. PhD thesis, North Carolina, 1956).

Hazard, J.L. *The Crisis in Coastal Shipping: The Atlantic-Gulf Case* (Univ. of Texas, Bureau of Business Research, Monograph No. 16), 1955 (PhD thesis, Texas).

Howard, R.W., ed. *This Is the South*, 1959. Ch. 23, Sea Lure, by R.G. Albion.

Pares, R. *Merchants and Planters* (Economic History Review, Supplement No. 4), 1960. Analyzes the planter-trader relationship in the tobacco colonies and the Caribbean.

Wright, G. *The Economy of Cotton in the Antebellum South* (PhD thesis, Yale, 1969; DA v. 31, p. 915A).

AC – 2   Maryland – Virginia

Beitzell, E.W. *Life on the Potomac River*, 1968.

Bornholt, L.A. *Baltimore as a Port of Propaganda for South American Independence* (ms. PhD thesis, Yale, 1945).

*Brewington, M.V. *Chesapeake Bay: A Pictorial Maritime History*, 1953. Chapters, with brilliant concise summaries, include: The Explorers and Settlers; Shipbuilding; Sailing Vessels; Steamboats; Ferries; Baycraft; The Ports; Commerce and Trade; Maritime Artisans; Oysters, Crabs and Fish; Pilots; Privateering, Piracy and War; The Bay's Maritime Museum; Sports.

*Brown, A.C. *Steam Packets on the Chesapeake: A History of the Old Bay Line since 1840*, 1961. Amplification of his original *The Old Bay Line*, 1940.

Brown, V.W. *Shipping in the Port of Annapolis, 1748-1775*, 1965. Includes list of "every vessel that cleared customs at Annapolis," 1748-75, with details about each vessel.

Bruchey, S.W. *Robert Oliver, Merchant of Baltimore*, 1956 (PhD thesis, Johns Hopkins).

Burgess, R.H. *This Was Chesapeake Bay*, 1963. A collection of historical articles, many of which originally appeared in local papers.

Byron, G. *The War of 1812 in Chesapeake Bay*, 1964. See also Muller below.

Clark, M.C. *The Coastwise and Caribbean Trade of Chesapeake Bay, 1696-1776* (PhD thesis, Georgetown, 1970; DA v. 31, p. 2297A).

Coakley, R.W. *Virginia Commerce during the American Revolution* (ms. PhD thesis, Virginia, 1949).

Coulter, C.B., Jr. *The Virginia Merchant* (PhD thesis, Princeton, 1944; DA v. 12, p. 286). The role of the Scots traders, handling a large part of the tobacco trade, who contributed much to the economic foundation of Virginia's "golden age."

DeGast, R. *The Oystermen of Chesapeake Bay*, 1970. Includes 180 photographs in addition to history and present situation.

Forner, P.S. *Business and Slavery: The New York Merchants and the Irrepressible Conflict*, 1941.

Gray, R.D. *A History of the Chesapeake and Delaware Canal, 1760-1960* (PhD thesis, Illinois, 1962; DA v. 23, p. 333).

Hemphill, J.M., II. *Virginia and the English Commercial System, 1689-1733. Studies in the Development and Fluctuations of a Colonial Economy under Imperial Control* (PhD thesis, Princeton, 1964; DA v. 25, p. 3536).

Livingood, J.T. See Sect. AB-2, *The Rivalry of Philadelphia and Baltimore.* . . .

Marsh, C.F., ed. *The Hampton Roads Communities in World War II*, 1951.

Mason, F.N. *John Norton & Sons, Merchants of London and Virginia, Being the Papers from Their Counting House for the Years 1750 to 1795*, 1937, R1968. Basis for Rosenblatt thesis, below.

*Middleton, A.P., Jr. *Tobacco Coast: A Maritime History of Chesapeake Bay in the Colonial Era*, 1953 (PhD thesis, Harvard).

Moriss, M.S. *Colonial Trade of Maryland, 1689-1715*, 1914 (PhD thesis, Bryn Mawr).

Muller, C.B. *The Darkest Day, 1814: The Washington-Baltimore Campaign* (Great Battles), 1963.

Owen, H. *Baltimore on the Chesapeake* (Seaport Series), 1941. See comments on Burt's Philadelphia, Sect. AB-2.

Peale Museum (Municipal Museum of Baltimore), *Harbor, 1854-1955: A Century of Photographs of the Port of Baltimore*, 1955.
————. *Baltimore's Harbor, A History in Photographs since 1850* (Pub. no. 11), 1963. Some pictures are the same as in the earlier work.

Potter, F.R. *The South American Trade of Baltimore.*

Quittmeyer, C.L. *The Seafood Industry of Chesapeake Bay States of Maryland and Virginia, a Study in Private Management and Public Policy* (PhD thesis, Columbia, 1955; DA v. 16, p. 473).

Rosenblatt, S.M. *The House of John Norton & Sons: A Study of the Consignment Method of Marketing Tobacco from Virginia to England* (PhD thesis, Rutgers, 1960; DA v. 21, p. 2525). Based in part on the papers in Mason above.

Sargent, C.W. *Virginia and the West Indian Trade, 1740-1765* (PhD thesis, New Mexico, 1964; DA v. 26, p. 6007).

Schlegel, M.W. *Conscripted City: Norfolk in World War II*, 1951. See also Marsh above.

*Stewart, P.C. *The Commercial History of Hampton Roads, Virginia, 1815-1860* (ms. PhD thesis, Virginia, 1967).

*Tawes, L.S. *Coasting Captain*. . . . 1967. See Sect. O-5 for Baltimore-Rio coffee trade, etc.

Thompson, R.P. *The Merchant in Virginia, 1700-1775* (ms. PhD thesis, Wisconsin, 1956).

Wertenbaker, T.J. *Norfolk, Historic Southern Port*, 1931, R1962. M.W. Schlegel collaborated in the second edition which carries the story forward 30 years.

*Whedbee, T.C. *The Port of Baltimore in the Making, 1828 to 1878*, 1953. Originally a Princeton senior thesis.

AC – 3   The Carolinas – Georgia

Cate, M.D. *Early Days of Coastal Georgia*, 1955. Photographs with explanatory text.

Clowse, C.D. *The Charleston Export Trade, 1717-1737* (ms. PhD thesis, Northwestern, 1962).

Crittenden, C.C. *The Commerce of North Carolina, 1763-1789*, 1936.

Dunbar, C.S. *Geographical History of the Carolina Banks* (Coastal Studies Institute, LSU), 1956. Like the works of MacNeill and Stick below, this deals with the unique story of the sandy, storm-swept angle of the "Outer Banks," culminating in Cape Hatteras.

Helwig, A.B. *The Early History of Barbados and Her Influence upon the Development of South Carolina* (ms. PhD thesis, Berkeley, 1931).

Hoffman, N.J., Jr. *Godfrey Barnsley, 1805-1873: British Cotton Factor in the South* (ms. PhD thesis, Kansas, 1964; DA v. 26, p. 1005). Cotton trade in antebellum Savannah.

Landon, C.E. *The North Carolina State Ports Authority*, 1963.

Lee, L.E., Jr. *The History of Lower Cape Fear; The Colonial Period* (ms. PhD thesis, North Carolina, 1956).

MacNeill, B.D. *The Hatterasman*, 1958. See also Dunbar above and Stick below.

Merrens, H.R. *Colonial North Carolina in the Eighteenth Century, a Study in Historical Geography*, 1964.

146

Reese, T.R. *Colonial Georgia: A Study in British Imperial Policy in the Eighteenth Century*, 1963.

*Sellers, L. *Charleston Business on the Eve of the American Revolution*, 1934 (PhD thesis, Columbia), R1970.

*Stick, D. *Graveyard of the Atlantic: Shipwrecks of the North Carolina Coast*, 1952. See also Dunbar and MacNeill above.
*————. *The Outer Banks of North Carolina, 1584-1958*, 1958. The history of this desolate region included the "Lost Colony" and other Raleigh colonizing ventures, and also the Wrights' pioneer air flight at Kitty Hawk, in addition to the terrific shipwreck story.

AC – 4   Florida – Alabama

Neville, B. *Directory of River Packets on the Mobile-Alabama-Warrior-Tombigbee Trades, 1818-1932*, P1962. These river steamers brought Black Belt cotton for Mobile's thriving antebellum commerce.
————. *Steamboats on the Coosa River in the Rome, Georgia, Gadsden-Greenport Alabama Trades, 1845-1920s*, 1966.

Summersell, C.G. *Mobile: History of a Seaport Town*, 1949.

Ullman, E.L. *Mobile, Industrial Seaport and Trade Center*, 1945.

Varney, C.B. *Economic and Historical Geography of the Gulf Coast of Florida: Cedar Keys to St. Marks* (ms. PhD thesis, Clark, 1962).

White, L. and Smiley, N. *History of Key West*, P1961.

AC – 5   Louisiana

Arena, C.R. *Philadelphia-Spanish New Orleans Trade, 1789-1803* (PhD thesis, Pennsylvania, 1959; DA v. 20, p. 2242).

Babin, C.H. *The Economic Expansion of New Orleans before the Civil War* (ms. PhD thesis, Tulane, 1954).

*Baughman, J.P. See Sect. AC-1.
————. "Gateway to the Americas," in H. Carter, ed. *The Past as Prelude: New Orleans, 1718-1968*, 1968.

Baughn, W.H. *The Impact of World War II on the New Orleans Port-Mississippi River Transportation System*, 1950.

Caughey, J.W. *Bernardo de Galvez in Louisiana, 1776-1783*, 1934. Based on his PhD thesis, Berkeley, 1929, *Louisiana under Spain, 1762-1783*.

Conway, A.A. *New Orleans as a Port of Immigration, 1820-1860* (ms. MA thesis, London, 1949).

LeBreton, P.P. *The Organization and Post-war Administration Policies of the Port of New Orleans* (ms. PhD thesis, Illinois, 1953).

Lowrey, W.M. *Navigational Problems at the Mouth of the Mississippi River, 1698-1880* (PhD thesis, Vanderbilt, 1956; DA v. 16, p. 1436).

*Mellen, G.M. *The Mississippi Shipping Co.: A Case Study in the Development of Gulf Coast-South American and West African Shipping, 1919-1953* (PhD thesis, Pittsburgh, 1955; DA v. 15, p. 1002). The "Delta Line."

Nasatir, A.P. *Spanish War Vessels on the Mississippi, 1792-1796*, 1947.

Padgett, H.R. *The Marine Shell Fisheries of Louisiana* (PhD thesis, Louisiana State, 1960; DA v. 21, p. 588). The Louisiana coast has become one of the leading shrimp areas.

Parkman, F. *The French in Louisiana, 1690-1712* (ms. PhD thesis, Harvard, 1930).

Rabin, C.C. *Voyage to Louisiana, 1803-1805*, 1966.

Roeder, R.E. *New Orleans Merchants, 1790-1837* (ms. PhD thesis, Harvard, 1959).

Sibley, M.M. *The Port of Houston, a History*, 1968. Emphasizes social and political aspects.

Sinclair, H. *The Port of New Orleans* (Seaport Series), 1942.

Surrey, N.M. *The Commerce of Louisiana during the French Regime, 1689-1763*, 1916 (PhD thesis, Columbia), R1969.

Thibodeaux, E.C. *The New Orleans-Houston Rivalry* (PhD thesis, Columbia, 1952; DA v. 12, p. 500).

Trump, R.M. *The Port of New Orleans with special reference to Its Foreign Trade* (ms. PhD thesis, Ohio Univ., 1948).

AC – 6   Texas

Fornell, E.W. *Island City: The Story of Galveston on the Eve of Secession, 1850-1860* (ms. PhD thesis, Rice, 1956).

Graf, L.P. *The Economic History of the Lower Rio Grande Valley, 1820-1875* (ms. PhD thesis, Harvard, 1942). Includes account of the shipping connections with the New Orleans entrepôt.

Hartrick, W.J. *Foreign Trade through Texas Ports* (ms. PhD thesis, Texas, 1943).

Irby, J.A. *Line of the Rio Grande: War and Trade on the Confederate Frontier, 1861-1865* (PhD thesis, Georgia, 1969; DA v. 30, p. 5360A).

McComb, D.G. *Houston, The Bayou City* (ms. PhD thesis, Texas, 1968; DA v. 30, p. 2926A).

O'Brien, L. *The Curving Shore: The Gulf Coast from Brownsville to Key West*, 1957. Description and some history.

Thibodeaux, E.C. See above section.

Weems, J.E. *A Weekend in September*, 1957. The destructive combination of wind and high water that struck Galveston on Sept. 8, 1900.

AD   WEST COAST AND ALASKA

AD – 1   General

*Bancroft, H.H. *Works*, 39 v. 1882-90. Contains a wealth of scattered detail about maritime activity, particularly his *History of the Pacific States*.

Benson, R.M. *Steamships and Motorships of the West Coast*, 1968.

*Brown, G.T. *Ships That Sail No More: Marine Transportation from San Diego to Puget Sound, 1910-1940*, 1966 (PhD thesis, Claremont). Pacific coastal steamers, especially the Admiral Line and other major lines.

Caster, J.G. *The Earliest Spanish Exploration of the Pacific Northwest* (PhD thesis, New Mexico, 1969; DA v. 30, p. 4906A).

Coughlin, M. *Boston Merchants on the Coast: 1787-1821; An Insight into the American Acquisition of California* (PhD thesis, So. California, 1970; DA v. 31, p. 2837A).

Cox, T.R. *Sails and Sawmills: The Pacific Lumber Trade to 1900* (PhD thesis, Oregon, 1969; DA v. 30, p. 3392A).

Crockatt, P.C. *Trans-Pacific Shipping since 1914* (ms. PhD thesis, Berkeley, 1922).

Gibbs, J.A. *Disaster Log of Ships*, 1971. 333 photos, 5 maps and drawings of shipwrecks and ships (sail and steam) wrecked on the coasts of California, Oregon, Washington, British Columbia and Alaska from 1859 to the present. Heaviest emphasis on 20th century.

Gorter, W. and Hildebrand, G.H. *Pacific Coast Maritime Shipping Industry 1930-1948*, 2 v. 1952-54. V. 1, *An Economic Profile*; v. 2, *An Analysis of Performance*.

Gough, B.M. *The Royal Navy on the North-West Coast of North America, 1810-1910* (ms. PhD thesis, London, 1969).

Graebner, N.A. *Empire on the Pacific: A Study in American Continental Expansion*, 1955. Extension of control over the West Coast in the 1840s.

Hammelton, R.L. *New Port Cities in Western America and Their Effect on Economic Development* (ms. PhD thesis, So. California, 1964; DA v. 26, p. 147). Special emphasis on Sacramento and Stockton.

Hull, A.H. *Spanish and Russian Rivalry in the North Pacific Regions of the New World, 1760-1812* (PhD thesis, Alabama, 1966; DA v. 27, p. 1757A). See also Polich below.

Kirshner, H.I. *Anglo-Russian Rivalry in the Pacific Northwest, 1790-1867* (PhD thesis, Cornell, 1970; DA v. 31, p. 6519A).

Liebes, R.A. *Longshore Relations on the Pacific Coast, 1934-1942* (ms. PhD thesis, Berkeley, 1943). The beginnings of the Harry Bridges impact. See also Palmer and Schneider below.

Martin, F. *Sea Bears: The Story of the Fur Seal,* 1960.

Mears, E.G. *Maritime Trade of the Western Trade of the Western United States,* 1935. Much less comprehensive than the title would indicate – largely statistical and mostly on the 20th century.

Newell, G. and Williamson, J. *Pacific Lumber Ships,* 1960. Sail and steam; profusely illustrated.

Palmer, D.L. *Pacific Coast Maritime Labor* (ms. PhD thesis, Stanford, 1936).

Polich, J.L. *Foreign Maritime Intrusion on Spain's Pacific Coast, 1786-1810* (PhD thesis, New Mexico, 1968; DA v. 30, p. 665A). See also Hull above.

Schneider, R.V. *Industrial Relations in the West Coast Maritime Industry,* P1958.

Sluiter, E. *The Dutch on the Pacific Coast of America, 1598-1621* (ms. PhD thesis, Berkeley, 1937).

Spoehr, A., ed. *Pacific Port Towns and Cities* (Bishop Museum, Honolulu), 1963.

AD – 2   California

*Bateson, C. *Gold Fleet for California: Forty-niners from Australia and New Zealand,* 1964. More than 7,000 people in more than 200 ships, 1849-50; sailings listed in appendix. See also Monaghan below.

Baresnes, R.W. *The Maritime Development of San Pedro Bay, California, 1821-1921* (ms. PhD thesis, Minnesota, 1963; DA v. 25, p. 6558). Part of the port of Los Angeles.

Coy, O.C. *The Humboldt Bay Region, 1850-1875; A Study in the American Colonization of California,* 1929 (PhD thesis, Berkeley).

Dallas, S.F. *The Hide and Tallow Trade in Alta California, 1822-1846* (PhD thesis, Indiana; DA v. 15, p. 2435).

*Dana, R.H. *Two Years Before the Mast,* 1840 ff. See Sect. O-5. Includes description of the above hide and tallow trade.

Dillon, R.H. *Embarcadero: Being a Chronicle of True Sea Adventures from the Port of San Francisco,* 1959. A lively collection of tall yarns.

Galvin, J., ed. *A Journal of Exploration Northward Along the Coast from Monterey in the Year 1775,* 1964. Small Spanish naval expedition under Hezeta to find out if any foreign settlements had been made. One of the last episodes of Spanish colonial expansion.

Grady, H.F. and Carr, R.M. *The Port of San Francisco: A Study of Traffic Competition, 1921-33,* 1933.

Hardeman, N.P. *History of the Inland Seaport of Stockton, California* (ms. PhD thesis, Berkeley, 1953).

Huff, B.F. *The Maritime History of San Francisco Bay* (ms. PhD thesis, Berkeley, 1956).

*Kemble, J.H. *The Panama Route, 1848-1869,* 1943 (PhD thesis, Berkeley), R1970. Chiefly on the Pacific Mail line, from Panama to San Francisco.
* ————. *San Francisco Bay, A Pictorial Maritime History,* 1957. Comprehensive annotated coverage: pre-1846 San Francisco waterfront; bay and river ports; shipbuilding and repairing; fishing and whaling; local, coastal, and deep-water shipping; naval; sports; maritime museum. More substantial than H. Gilliam, *San Francisco Bay,* 1957.

Leader, H.A. *The Hudson's Bay Company in California* (ms. PhD thesis, Berkeley, 1928).

Lewis, O. *Sea Routes to the Gold Fields: The Migration by Water to California in 1849-1852,* 1949. For the ships, see also the clipper studies of A.H. Clark, C.C. Cutler, O.T. Howe and F.C. Matthews.

Longstreet, S. *The Wilder Shore: Rise of a Great Seaport – A Gala Social History of San Francisco, Sinners and Spenders, 1849-1906,* 1968. "Racy, violent and vibrant."

MacMullen, J. *Paddle-Wheel Days in California,* 1944.

McNairn, J. and MacMullen, J. *Ships of the Redwood Coast,* 1945. A study of the unique lumber-carrying "steam schooners."

Mears, E.G. *San Francisco Trans-Pacific Shipping,* 1929.

Miller, M. *Harbor of the Sun: The Story of San Diego* (Seaport Series), 1940. See also Pourade below.

Monaghan, J. *Australians and the Gold Rush: California and Down Under, 1849-1854,* 1966. See also Bateson above.

*Ogden, A. *The California Sea-Otter Trade, 1784-1848,* 1942 (PhD thesis, Berkeley).

Pomfret, J.E., ed. *California Gold Rush Voyages, 1848-1849: Three Original Nar-*

ratives, 1954. Two Cape Horn voyages and the journals of Capt. Fobes of the SS *California*.

Pourade, R.F. *The History of San Diego*, 5 v. 1960-67. See also Miller above and Stewart below.

Rasmussen, L.J. *San Francisco Ship Passenger Lists*. See Sect. G.

Riesenberg, F., Jr. *Golden Gate: The Story of San Francisco Harbor*, 1940.

Rockwell, M.M. *California's Sea Frontier: Part I, The Channel Coast*, 1962.

Ryder, D.W. *Memories of the Mendocino Coast*, 1948. Details of lumber shipments from rugged "dogholes" on the northern California coast.

Stewart, D.A. *Frontier Port: A Chapter in San Diego's History*, 1966. Covers period from the 1640s to the early 1880s.

Thurman, M.E. *The Naval Department of San Blas: New Spain's Bastion for Alta California and Nootka, 1767 to 1798*, 1967. See also V. Tate, *The Founding of San Blas*, Sect. AH-2.

Voget, L.M. *The Waterfront of San Francisco, 1863-1930; A History of Its Administration by the State of California* (ms. PhD thesis, Berkeley, 1943).

Wheelock, W. *Ferries of the South*, 1964. Southern California.

AD – 3   Oregon – Washington

Andrews, D.W. and Kirwin, H.A. *This Was Seafaring: A Sea Chest of Salty Memories*, 1955. More than 200 photographs of the Pacific Northwest.

Binns, A. *Northwest Gateway: The Story of the Port of Seattle* (Seaport Series), 1941, R1949.

Brewer, S.H. *The Comparative Position of Seattle and Puget Sound Ports in World Trade*, P1963.

Brier, H.M. *Sawdust Empire: The Pacific Northwest*, 1958.

*Coman, E.T. and Gibbs, H.M. *Time, Tide and Timber: A Century of Pope and Talbot*, 1949, R1968. Excellent account of one of the great lumbering and shipping companies.

Conant, R. *Mercer's Belles: The Journal of a Reporter*, ed. L.A. Deutsch, 1960. Account of 1866 voyage from New York around Cape Horn to Washington Territory with a large group of well-chaperoned maidens as prospective wives for the settlers.

Cox, R. *The Columbia River*, ed. E. J. Stewart, 1957. Account by a clerk in the Astor expedition, 1811.

Finger, N.R. *Henry L. Yester's Seattle Years, 1852-1892* (PhD thesis, Univ. of Washington, 1969; DA v. 29, p. 3555).

Franchere, G. *Adventure at Astoria, 1810-1814*, 1967. Author of diary went from Montreal to New York and thence to Astoria on Astor's *Tonquin*; after her loss, organized trading post. Translated and edited by H.C. Franchere.

Holbrook, S.H. *The Columbia* (Rivers of America), 1955.

*Irving, W. *Astoria, or Anecdotes of an Enterprise beyond the Rocky Mountains*, 2 v. 1836 ff, also P. Account by one of America's leading early literary figures of the fur-trading post near the mouth of the Columbia, established by John Jacob Astor in 1811, falling into British hands during the War of 1812.

*Johansen, D.O. and Gates, C.M. *Empire of the Columbia: A History of the Pacific Northwest*, 1957, R1967. The most substantial scholarly work on the region. See especially ch. 2, Spain and England; ch. 3-4, Maritime; ch. 7, Nor'western and Astoria; ch. 25, Harvests from the Sea.

Meany, E.S., Jr. *The History of the Lumber Industry of the Pacific Northwest to 1917* (ms. PhD thesis, Harvard, 1936).

Nesbit, R.C. *"He Built Seattle," A Biography of Judge Thomas Burke*, 1961. Initiative in developing the city, 1875-1910, including maritime aspects.

Newell, G. *Ships of the Inland Sea: The Story of Puget Sound Steamboats*, 1951, R1960.
————. *Pacific Steamboats*, 1958. Reproduces more than 500 illustrations depicting more than 300 steamers, from the Joseph Williamson Maritime collection. Also a volume on *Pacific Tugboats*.
————. *S.O.S. North Pacific*, 1955. Shipwrecks off Washington, British Columbia and Vancouver.
———— and Williams, J. *Pacific Coastal Liners*, 1959.

Peckham, E.T. *The Halibut Fishery of the Pacific Northwest* (ms. PhD thesis, Harvard, 1954).

Sirridge, A.T. *Spanish, British and French Activities in the Sea Otter Trade of the Far North Pacific, 1774-1790* (ms. PhD thesis, St. Louis, 1954).

Stevens, W.E. *The Northwest Fur Trade, 1763-1800*, 1928 (PhD thesis, Illinois).

Stewart, C.L. *Martinez and Lopez de Haro on the Northwest Coast, 1788-1789* (ms. PhD thesis, Berkeley, 1937).

Stewart, W.K. *Steamboats on the Columbia: The Pioneer Period, 1850-1869* (ms. PhD thesis, Berkeley, 1948).

Throckmorton, A.L. *Oregon Argonauts: Merchant Adventurers on the Western Frontier*, 1961.

Andrews, C.L. *The Story of Sitka: The Historic Outpost of the Northwest Coast, the Chief Factory of the Russia American Company*, 1922.

Bancroft, H.H. *History of Alaska, 1730-1885*, 1890 (*Works*, v. 33), R1967.

Bixby, W. *Track of the* Bear, *1875-1963*, 1965. Built at Glasgow, served 40 years on Bering Sea patrol and later on Antarctic expeditions. See Ransom below.

*Chevigny, H. *Lord of Alaska: Baranov and the Russian Adventure*, 1942, R1951.
*——————. *Russian America, the Great Alaskan Venture, 1741-1867*, 1965.

Hulley, C.C. *Alaska, 1741-1953*, 1953. Reissued as *Alaska: Past and Present*.

McCracken, H. *Hunters of the Stormy Sea*, 1958. Russian sea otter hunters, 1740-1840.

Murphy, J.F. *Cutter Captain: Life and Times of John C. Cantwell* (ms. PhD thesis, Connecticut, 1968). Service 1882-1920, especially Alaska.

Ransom, M.A. and Engle, E.K. *The Sea of the* Bear, 1964. Experiences on a 1921 cruise on the celebrated old revenue cutter. See also Bixby above.

West, E.L. *Captain's Papers, a Log of Whaling and other Sea Experiences*, 1965. See Sect. O-5.

Wheeler, M.E. *The Origins and Formation of the Russian-American Company* (PhD thesis, North Carolina, 1965).

AE   GREAT LAKES AND INLAND WATERWAYS

AE – 1   Great Lakes – General

*Andrews, I.D. *Report . . . on the Trade and Commerce of the British North American Colonies, and upon the Trade of the Great Lakes and Rivers* (U.S. Congress, 32-1, Sen. Exec. Doc. 112), 1853. This exhaustive report, by an American consul, on the eve of reciprocity with Canada, is a mine of information. Part II, pp. 45-262, contains much data on the trade of the lakes in general and each port in particular.

Beasley, N. *Freighters of Fortune: The Story of the Great Lakes*, c1930.

Buehr, W. *Ships of the Great Lakes*, 1956.

Curwood, J.O. *The Great Lakes and the Ships that Plough Them*, 1967. Ships, owners, crews and cargoes.

Cuthbertson, G.A. *Freshwater: A History and Narrative of the Great Lakes*, 1931.

*Havighurst, W. *The Long Ships Passing: The Story of the Great Lakes*, 1942, RP1961.

*Towle, E.L. *Bibliography on the Economic History and Geography of the Great Lakes-St. Lawrence Drainage Basin, with supplement.* P1964.

AE – 2   Great Lakes – Specific

Baylis, J.E. and E.M. *River of Destiny: The St. Mary's*, 1955. The Soo Canal (Sault Ste. Marie) between Lakes Superior and Huron has at times carried heavier annual traffic than the Panama or Suez canals. See also Dickinson below.

Boyle, D. *Ghost Ships of the Great Lakes*, 1968. Narrative of 17 of the many ships that have "gone missing."

Brownell, G. *The Role of the Lake Package Freighters, Southwestern Ontario* (ms. MA thesis, Western Ontario, 1951). See also Fletcher below.

Carter, J.L. *Voyageur's Harbor, Grand Marais*, 1967.

Derby, W.E. *A History of the Port of Milwaukee, 1835-1910* (PhD thesis, Wisconsin, 1963; DA v. 24, p. 2695).

Dickinson, J.N. *The Canal at Sault Ste. Marie, Michigan: Inception, Construction, Operation, and the Canal Grant Lands* (ms. PhD thesis, Wisconsin, 1967).

Dowling, E.J. *The Lakers of World War I: The Story of the Contribution of the Great Lakes Shipyards to the Defense Effort of Our Country in the First World War*, P1967.

Draine, E.H. *Import Traffic of Chicago and Its Hinterland* (ms. PhD thesis, Chicago, 1963).

Duncan, F. *History of the Detroit & Cleveland Navigation Company, 1850-1951* (PhD thesis, Chicago). This appeared serially in various editions of *Inland Seas*.

Fletcher, D.G. *A Study of Package Freight Carriers on the Great Lakes* (PhD thesis, Michigan, 1960; DA v. 21, p. 2137).

Frederickson, A.C. and L.F. *Pictorial History of the C & O Train and Auto Ferries and Pere Marquette Line Steamers*, 1955. See Hilton below.

Gjerset, K. *Norwegian Sailors on the Great Lakes, a Study in the History of Inland Transportation*, 1928.

Hamming, E. *The Port of Milwaukee*, 1954.

*Hilton, G.W. *The Great Lakes Car Ferries*, 1962.

Inches, H.C. *The Great Lakes Wooden Shipbuilding Era*, P1962.

Lindblad, A.F. *A Critical Analysis of the Factors Affecting Safety and Operation of the Bulk Freight Vessels of the Great Lakes*, 1924 (PhD thesis, Michigan).

McPhedran, M. *Cargoes on the Great Lakes*, 1952.

Odle, T.D. *The American Grain Trade of the Great Lakes, 1825-1873* (PhD thesis, Michigan, 1952; DA v. 12, p. 180).

Rapp, M.A. *The Port of Buffalo, 1825-1880* (ms. PhD thesis, Duke, 1948).

Steadman, T.P. *The Regulation of Commerce and Navigation on the Great Lakes* (ms. MA thesis, Queens, 1938). British and Canadian regulation, 1768-1846.

U.S. Board of Engineers for Rivers and Harbors, and U.S. Shipping Board, *Transportation on the Great Lakes*, 1926 ff.

Wright, R.G. *Freshwater Whales: A History of the American Shipbuilding Company and Its Predecessors*, 1969 (PhD thesis, Kent State). Title apparently an allusion to the "whaleback" type of lake freighters.

Young, A.G. *Great Lakes Saga: The Influence of One Family in the Development of Canadian Shipping on the Great Lakes, 1816-1931*, 1965. Three generations of the Gildersleeve family of Kingston, Ontario.

AE – 3   Inland Waterways – General

Bowden, C.N., comp. *Catalogue of the Inland Rivers Library*, 1968.

Case, L.S. *Estimation of Production Cost Functions for Inland Waterway Transportation* (PhD thesis, Northwestern, 1968; DA v. 29, p. 3278A).

Clowes, E.S. *Shipways to the Seas: Our Inland and Coastal Waterways*, 1929.

DeSalvo, J.S. *Longhaul Process Functions for Rail and Inland Waterway Transportation* (PhD thesis, Northwestern, 1968; DA v. 29, p. 1998A).

*Havighurst, W. *Voices on the River: The Story of the Mississippi Waterways*, 1964.

Johnson, E.R. *Inland Waterways: Their Relation to Transportation*, 1893 (PhD thesis, Pennsylvania).

Johnson, J.A. *Pre-Steamboat Navigation on the Lower Mississippi River* (PhD thesis, Louisiana State, 1963; DA v. 24, p. 5320).

Muller, H.N., III *The Commercial History of the Champlain-Richelieu River Route, 1760-1815* (PhD thesis, Rochester, 1969; DA v. 30, p. 3616A).

See Sect. S for Suez and Panama canals.

Albion, R.G. *The Rise of New York Port*, 1939, R1970. Ch. 5, Hinterland and Canal.

Brown, A.C. *The Dismal Swamp Canal*, 1967.

Byzyski, A.J. *The Lehigh Canal and Its Effect on the Economic Development of the Region through which It Passed, 1818-1875* (PhD thesis, N.Y. Univ., 1957; DA v. 21, p. 3305).

Carter, H.H. *A History of the Cumberland and Oxford Canal* (ms. AM thesis, Maine, 1950). Inland from Portland, Maine.

Cranmer, H.J. *The New Jersey Canals; State Policy and Private Enterprise, 1820-1832* (ms. PhD thesis, Columbia, 1955). See also Goodrich below.

Goodrich, C., et al. *Canals and American Development*, 1961. Pt. 1, The Political Decision, J. Rubin and H.J. Cranmer; pt. 2, The Economic Impact, H.H. Segal.
*————. *Governmental Promotion of American Canals and Railroads, 1800-1890*, 1960.

Gray, R.D. *The National Waterway: A History of the Chesapeake and Delaware Canal, 1769-1965*, 1967 (PhD thesis, Illinois).

Miller, N. *"The Enterprise of a Free People;" Canals and the Canal Fund in the New York Economy, 1792-1838* (PhD thesis, Columbia, 1960; DA v. 24, p. 261).

O'Hara, J.E. *Erie's Junior Partner: The Economic and Social Effects of the Champlain Canal upon the Champlain Valley* (PhD thesis, Columbia, 1951; DA v. 11, p. 663).

Poinsette, C.R. *Fort Wayne, Indiana during the Canal Era, 1828-1855* (PhD thesis, Notre Dame, 1964; DA v. 25, p. 1880).

Roberts, C. *The History of the Middlesex Canal* (ms. PhD thesis, Harvard, 1927). From near Boston to the Merrimac River.

Rubin, J. *Canal or Railroad? Imitation or Innovation in the Response to the Erie Canal*, 1961 (PhD thesis, Columbia). See also Goodrich above.

Shaw, R.E. *Erie Water West: A History of the Erie Canal, 1792-1854*, 1966. Details of social and political history, but little on the "market economy."

Stewart, W.H., Jr. *The Tennessee-Tombigbee Waterway: A Case Study in Inland Water Transportation* (PhD thesis, Alabama, 1968; DA v. 29, p. 3657A).

Wakefield, M.B. *Coal Boats to Tidewater*, 1965. History of the Delaware and

Hudson Canal, carrying coal from Honesdale, Pa. to Rondout Creek near New York, with some 240 illustrations and more than 30 maps. Some of this anthracite was distributed by schooners to New England.

Ward, G.W. *Early Development of the Chesapeake and Ohio Canal Project* (ms. PhD thesis, Johns Hopkins, 1897).

Whitford, N.E. *A History of the Canal System of the State of New York*, 1921.

Wilcox, F.N. *The Ohio's Canals*, 1969.

AE – 5   River Traffic

Baldwin, L.D. *The Keelboat Age on Western Waters*, 1941, R1960.

Barkhau, R.I. *The Great Steamboat Race between the* Natchez *and the* Robt. E. Lee, 1952. Similar account by M.W. Wellman below.

Bates, D.L. *The Western River Steamboat Cyclopedia of American River Boats*, 1968.

Carse, P.M. *The River Men*, 1969. Canadian and American.

Donovan, F. *River Boats of America*, 1966. "Flatboats, keelboats, paddlewheel freight and passenger boats, showboats, circus boats, and luxurious floating palaces."

Dorsey, F.L. *Master of the Mississippi: Henry Shreve and the Conquest of the Mississippi*, 1941.

Drago, H.S. *The Steamboaters: From the Early Side-Wheelers to the Big Packets*, 1967.

Droze, W.H. *Tennessee River Navigation: Government and Private Enterprise since 1932* (PhD thesis, Vanderbilt, 1960; DA v. 21, p. 2687).

Hartley, J.R. *Economic Effects of Ohio River Navigation*, P1959.

*Hunter, L.C. *Steamboats on the Western Rivers: An Economic and Technological History*, 1949. Admirable piece of sound research and able presentation of the significant aspects, in contrast to such "atmosphere" books as Irving Anthony's *Paddle Wheels and Pistols*. For authentic atmosphere, of course, Mark Twain's *Life on the Mississippi* is still the classic.

Klein, B.F., ed. *Ohio River Atlas*, 1954. Old maps and charts, back to 1714.

Lass, W.E. *A History of Steamboating on the Upper Missouri*, 1962.

Leland, E.A. *An Administrative History of the Inland Waterways Corporation* (PhD thesis, Tulane, 1960; DA v. 21, p. 235). See also McCartney below.

Lloyd, J.T.T. *Lloyd's Steamboat Directory and Disasters on the Western Rivers*, 1856. Lists of vessels and accounts of scores of disasters.

*Maass, A. *Muddy Waters: The Army Engineers and the Nation's Rivers*, 1951 (PhD thesis, Harvard).

Martinez, R.J. *Steamboat Days on the Mississippi*, 1965.

McCartney, K.H. *Government Enterprise: A Study of the Inland Waterways Corporation* (PhD thesis, Minnesota, 1959; DA v. 20, p. 123). See also Leland above.

Meyer, D.J. *Excursion Steamboating in the Mississippi with Streckfas Steamers, Inc.* (PhD thesis, St. Louis Univ., 1967; DA v. 28, p. 3095). Started in 1901.

Petersen, W.J. *Steamboating on the Upper Mississippi*, 1868, Rc1968. Facsimile reproduction with new introduction and pictures.

U.S. Board of Engineers for Rivers and Harbors and U.S. Shipping Board (Transportation Series), *Transportation on the Mississippi River System*, 1945 ff.

Way, F., Jr. *Directory of Western Rivers Packets*, 1950; revision of his *Steamboat Directory*, 1944.
————————. *Way's Directory of Western River Steam Towboats*, 1954.

AF   BRITISH NORTH AMERICA

AF – 1   General

*Andrews, I.D. *Report . . . on the Trade and Navigation of the British North American Colonies. . . .* See Sect. AE-1.

Burt, A.L. *The United States, Great Britain and British North America, 1785-1815*, 1940, R1961. See also Graham below.

Cambridge History of the British Empire, 8 v. 1929-40. V. 1, to 1783; v. 6, since 1783.

*Creighton, D.C. *The Empire of the St. Lawrence, 1760-1850*, 1937.

Croil, J. *Steam Navigation and Its Relation to the Commerce of Canada and the United States*, 1898.

Graham, G.S. *British Policy and Canada, 1774-1791: A Study in 18th Century Trade Policy*, 1930 (PhD thesis, Cambridge).
*————————. *Sea Power and British North America, 1783-1820: A Study in British Colonial Policy*, 1941, R1968.
*————————. *Empire of the North Atlantic: The Maritime Struggle for North America*, 1950, R1958. One of the most important analyses of the importance of Britain's maritime advantages over France.

159

Heaton, H. *A History of Trade and Commerce, with special reference to Canada*, 1939.

Knowles, L.C. *The Economic Development of the British Overseas Empire*, 3 v. 1924-36. V. 2, Canada.

Lawrence, M.L. *Canadian Trade with the British West Indies, 1937-1950* (ms. MA thesis, Queens, 1952).

Lower, A.R.M. *The North American Assault on the Canadian Forest*, 1938, R1969. The "timber trade," as the British called it, was long a mainstay of the Canadian economy and employed a large quantity of marginal shipping. (Based on MA thesis, Toronto and PhD thesis, Harvard.)

Mackinnon, C.S. *The Imperial Fortresses in Canada: Halifax and Esquimalt, 1871-1906*, 2 v. (PhD thesis, Toronto, 1965; DA v. 27, p. 1018A).

(Mills, J.M.) *Preliminary List of Canadian Merchant Steamships (Coastal and Inland), 1809-1930* (World Ship Society, Toronto Branch), 1967.

AF – 2   New France

Gipson, L.H. *The British Empire before the American Revolution*. See Sect. Z-2, especially v. 3, 5-9.

Lunn, A.J.E. *Economic Development in New France, 1713-1760* (ms. PhD thesis, McGill, 1943).

Murray, J.E. *The Fur Trade in New France and New England prior to 1645* (ms. PhD thesis, Chicago, 1937). Brief 13-page summary, 1938.

Parkman, F. (Various portions of his famous and extensive writings.)

Reid, A.G. *The Growth and Importance of the City of Quebec, 1608-1760* (ms. PhD thesis, McGill, 1951).

Waller, G.M. *Samuel Vetch, Colonial Entrepreneur*, 1960 (PhD thesis, Columbia). Active in irregular trade with New France; promoted idea of attack on Canada and became first governor of Nova Scotia.

AF – 3   Maritime Provinces

*Brebner, J.B. *New England's Outpost: Acadia before the Conquest of Canada*, 1927 (PhD thesis, Columbia).
*————. *The Neutral Yankees of Nova Scotia: A Marginal Colony during the Revolutionary Years*, 1937, R1970.

Butler, G.F. *Commercial Relations of Nova Scotia with the United States, 1783-1830* (ms. MA thesis, Dalhousie, 1934). Like Chapman, MacDougall, and Mercer below, this deals with what was, geographically, an extension of the coasting trade. These masters' theses reflect the interest of Dalhousie and New Brunswick, like the University of Maine, in maritime history.

Campbell, R.C. *Simonds, Hazen and White: A Study of a New Brunswick Firm in the Commercial World of the Eighteenth Century* (ms. MA thesis, New Brunswick, 1970).

Chapman, J.K. *Relations of Maine and New Brunswick in the Era of Reciprocity, 1849-1867* (ms. MA thesis, New Brunswick, 1952).

Chard, D.F. *Pagans, Privateers and Propaganda: New England-Acadia Relations, 1680-1710* (ms. MA thesis, Dalhousie, 1967).

Evans, G.N.D. *Uncommon Obdurate. . . .* 1969. See Sect. P-2. J.F.W. DesBarres, Lieutenant Governor of Prince Edward Island.

Evans, R.A. *The Army and Navy at Halifax in Peace Time, 1783-1793* (ms. MA thesis, Dalhousie, 1970).

Ferguson, C.B., ed. *The Diary of Simon Perkins, 1790-1796* (Champlain Society), 1967. Connecticut native who played an important part in the development of Liverpool, N.S. Much valuable data on various aspects of the maritime trade. Five volumes projected.

Harrison, W. *The Maritime Bank of the Dominion of Canada, 1872-1887* (ms. MA thesis, New Brunswick, 1970).

Haynes, E.R. *The Development of Courtenay Bay, Saint John, New Brunswick, 1908-1918* (ms. MA thesis, New Brunswick, 1969).

MacDougall, I.L. *Commercial Relations Between Nova Scotia and the United States of America, 1830-1854* (ms. MA thesis, Dalhousie, 1961).

Mackinnon, C.S. *The Imperial Fortresses. . . .* See Sect. AF-1. Halifax.

MacNutt, W.S. *The Atlantic Provinces* (Canadian Centennial Series), 1968. Maritimes and Newfoundland.

Mercer, M.J. *Relations Between Nova Scotia and New England, 1815-1867* (ms. MA thesis, Dalhousie, 1938).

Morse, S.L. *Immigration into Nova Scotia, 1839-1851* (ms. MA thesis, Dalhousie, 1946).

Parker, J.P. *Cape Breton Ships and Men*, 1967.
*————. *Sails of the Maritimes: The Story of the Three- and Four-Masted Cargo Schooners of Atlantic Canada and Newfoundland, 1859-1929* (Maritime Museum of Canada), 1961.

Pincombe, C.A. *The History of Monckton Township* (ms. MA thesis, New Brunswick, 1969).

Raddall, T.H. *Halifax, Warden of the North*, 1948, R1965.

Spicer, S.T. *Masters of Sail*, 1969. The Maritimes in the 19th century, including shipbuilding.

*Wallace, F.W. *Wooden Ships and Iron Men: The Story of the Square-Rigged Merchant Marine of British North America*, 1924.
————. *In the Wake of the Wind Ships*, 1927.
————. *Record of Canadian Shipping*, 1938. In all three of these works, the emphasis is primarily on the Maritimes.

AF – 4   Newfoundland

Briffett, F.B. *A History of the French in Newfoundland Previous to 1714* (ms. MA thesis, Queens, 1927). Discusses fishing and furs, and the supplies from France, New England and Quebec. The material is included in the author's *Story of Newfoundland and Labrador*, 2nd ed. 1954.

Call, G.M. *The English in Newfoundland, 1577-1660* (ms. PhD thesis, Liverpool, 1964).

Forward, C.N. *The Shipping Trade of Newfoundland* (PhD thesis, Clark, 1958; DA v. 19, p. 1710).

Glerum-Laurentius, D. *Dutch Activity in the Newfoundland Fish Trade, 1590-1680* (ms. MA thesis, Memorial Univ., 1961).

Lounsbury, R.G. *The British Fishery at Newfoundland, 1634-1763*, 1934, R1969.

Matthews, K. *The West Country-Newfoundland Fisheries (Chiefly in the Seventeenth and Eighteenth Centuries)* (ms. DPhil thesis, Oxford, 1968).

Mowat, F. and de Visser, J. *The Rock in the Sea: A Heritage Lost*, 1969.

Parkinson, C.N., ed. *The Trade Winds*, 1948. Ch. 10, The Newfoundland Trade, 1793-1815.

Skelton, R.A., ed. *James Cook, Surveyor of Newfoundland. . . .* 1965. See Sect. P-2.

Thomas, A. *The Newfoundland Journal of Aaron Thomas, 1794*, ed. J.M. Murray, 1968. Able seaman on H.M.S. *Boston*.

AF – 5   Quebec – Ontario

Aitken, H.G.J. *The Welland Canal Company: A Study in Canadian Enterprise* (Studies in Entrepreneural History), 1954.

Leacock, S. *Montreal: Seaport and City* (Seaport Series), 1943. This final work of the economist-humorist is about 20 percent seaport and 80 percent city.

Muller, H.N. *The Commercial History of the Lake Champlain-Richelieu River*

Route, 1760-1815 (PhD thesis, Rochester, 1969; DA v. 30, p. 3616A).

Wilson, G.H. *The Application of Steam to St. Lawrence Valley Navigation, 1809-1840* (ms. MA thesis, McGill, 1961).

AF – 6   Hudson's Bay

*Rich, E.E. *The Hudson's Bay Company, 1670-1870* (Hudson's Bay Records Society), 2 v. 1958-61. Described as "most learned, readable and judicious." The author has long directed the publications of the Society. This pretty much supplants the earlier, shorter accounts by Beckles Wilson (2 v. 1900); George Bryce (1900); William Schooley (1920); R.E. Pinkerton (1931); and Douglas McKay (1936).

Stackpole, R.A. *American Whaling in Hudson Bay, 1861-1919*, P1969. See Sect. AM-1.

AF – 7   British Columbia

Allen, D.D. *The Effects of the Panama Canal on Western Canada* (ms. MA thesis, British Columbia, 1938).

Allen, G.A. *The Development of Canadian Trade with Latin America* (ms. MA thesis, British Columbia, 1927).

Arrowsmith, M.A. *The Pacific Ports of Canada* (ms. MA thesis, London, 1935).

Bancroft, H.H. *History of British Columbia, 1792-1887*, 1887. (*Works*, v. 32).

Constant, F.E. *Yankee Steamboats on the Fraser River, British Columbia*, P1965.

Francis, R.J. *An Analysis of British Columbia Lumber Shipments 1947-1957* (ms. MA thesis, British Columbia, 1961).

Howay, F.W. *British Columbia, the Making of a Province*, 1928.
————, et al. *British Columbia and the United States – The North Pacific from Fur Trade to Aviation*, 1942. Judge Howay, the dean of the region's historians, also produced numerous articles, lists of ships, etc.

Kerfoot, D.E. *Ports of British Columbia: Development and Trading Patterns*, 1966.

Mackinnon, C.S. *The Imperial Fortresses.* . . . See Sect. AF-1. Esquimalt.

Rothery, A.E. *The Ports of British Columbia* (Seaport Series), 1943. This account of Vancouver and Victoria has a somewhat higher salt water content than the rest of that series.

Wilson, D.A. *An Analysis of Lumber Exports from the Coast Region of British Columbia to the United Kingdom and United States, 1920-1952* (ms. PhD thesis, Berkeley, 1955). See also Francis above.

Kerr, W.B. *Bermuda and the American Revolution, 1760-1783*, 1969.

Wilkinson, H.C. *The Adventurers of Bermuda*, 1933.
——————. *Bermuda in the Old Empire . . . 1684-1789*, 1950.
——————. *Bermuda from Sail to Steam*, 1969.

Willock, R. *Bulwark of Empire: Bermuda's Fortified Naval Base, 1860-1920*, 1962.

AG   WEST INDIES

AG – 1   General

Burns, Sir A. *History of the British West Indies*, 1954, R1965. Covers in detail every British colony in or near the Caribbean from the beginning.

*Parry, J.H. and Sherlock, P.M. *A Short History of the West Indies*, 1956. A competent, readable account of the essentials.

*Ragatz, L.J. *Guide for the Study of British Caribbean History, 1763-1834*, 1932.
——————. *Statistics for the Study of British Caribbean Economic History*, 1927.

Williams, E. *From Columbus to Castro: The History of the Caribbean, 1492-1969*, 1970.

AG – 2   to 1783

Alberts, R.C. *The Golden Voyage: The Life and Times of William Bingham, 1752-1804*, 1969. American contraband agent in the West Indies during the American Revolution.

Bell, H.C. *Studies in the Trade Relations of the British West Indies and North America, 1763-1773 and 1783-1793*, 1917 (PhD thesis, Pennsylvania).

Clark, M.C. *The Coastwise and Caribbean Trade of Chesapeake Bay, 1696-1776* (PhD thesis, Georgetown, 1970; DA v. 31, p. 2297A).

*Crouse, N.M. *French Pioneers in the West Indies, 1624-1664*, 1940.
——————. *The French Struggle for the West Indies, 1665-1763*, R1966.

Fay, F.M. *English Trade between 1696 and 1700, with special reference to the West Indies* (ms. PhD thesis, Radcliffe, 1918).

Haring, C.H. *The Buccaneers in the West Indies in the XVII Century*, 1910, R1966, 1970.

Harlow, V.T. *A History of Barbados, 1625-85*, 1926.

Helwig, A.B. *The Early History of Barbados and Her Influence upon the Development of South Carolina* (ms. PhD thesis, Berkeley, 1931).

Hewitt, M.J. *The West Indies in the American Revolution* (ms. DPhil thesis, Oxford, 1938).

Higham, C.S.S. *The Development of the Leeward Islands under the Restoration, 1660-1688, a Study in the Foundation of the Old Colonial System*, 1921.

Horsfall, L.F. *The Free Port System in the British West Indies, 1766-1815* (ms. PhD thesis, London, 1939).

Huntley, F.C. *Trade of the Thirteen Colonies with the Foreign Caribbean Area* (ms. PhD thesis, Berkeley, 1949).

Makinson, D.H. *Barbados: A Study in North America-West Indian Relations, 1739-1789* (ms. PhD thesis, Iowa State, 1962). See also Helwig above.

Marx, R.F. *Pirate Port: The Story of the Sunken City of Port Royal*, 1967. Important Jamaican center, destroyed by earthquake.

*Mims, S.L. *Colbert's West India Policy*, 1912 (PhD thesis, Yale).

*Newton, A.P. *European Nations in the West Indies, 1493-1688*, 1933. Perhaps the best book to read first for orientation.

*Pares, R. *War and Trade in the West Indies, 1739-63*, 1936, R1966.
*————. *West-India Fortune*, 1950, R1968.
*————. *Yankees and Creoles: The Trade between North America and the West Indies before the American Revolution*, 1955, R1968.
————. *Merchants and Planters*, 1960. Together, these four volumes give by far the most adequate picture of the West Indian sugar economy in its maritime aspects. The first emphasized trade more than war, giving a clear picture of the concentration on "raising cane." The second is a valuable case history, mined from the papers of the Pinney family, sugar planters in Nevis, 1685-1808, and also later operating a sugar-factor business in Bristol. The third gives statistics as well as descriptions of the swapping of New England offerings for sugar, molasses and rum. The fourth, comprising lectures just before his death, compared the planter-trade relationship in the Chesapeake tobacco colonies with those in the British and French sugar islands.

Pitman, F.W. *The Development of the British West Indies, 1700-1763*, 1917, R1967.

Robertson, E.A. *The Spanish Town Papers. Some Sidelights on the American Revolution*, 1959. Jamaican documents of maritime interest.

Sheridan, R.B. *The Sugar Trade of the British West Indies from 1660 to 1756, with special reference to the Island of Antigua* (ms. PhD thesis, London, 1951).

Westergaard, W.C. *The Danish West Indies under Company Rule (1671-1754), with a Supplementary Chapter, 1755-1917*, 1917 (PhD thesis, Berkeley).

Willis, J.L. *Trade between North America and the Danish West Indies, 1756-1807, with special reference to St Croix* (ms. PhD thesis, Columbia, 1962).

Allen, G.W. *Our Navy and the West Indian Pirates*, 1929. See also Bradlee below, and articles by Admiral C.F. Goodrich, 1916-17, sometimes bound as a single volume.

Allen, H.M. *British Commercial Policy in the West Indies from 1783 to 1793* (ms. PhD thesis, London, 1928).

Benns, F.L. *The American Struggle for the British West India Carrying Trade, 1815-1830*, 1923 (PhD thesis, Clark), R1969.

Bradlee, F.B.C. *Piracy in the West Indies and Its Suppression*, 1921, R1970.

Brown, G. *The Illicit Slave Trade to Cuba and Other Islands of the Caribbean* (ms. PhD thesis, Ohio State, 1945).

Bunce, K.W.L. *American Interests in the Caribbean Islands, 1783-1830* (ms. PhD thesis, Ohio State, 1939).

Demas, W.G. *Trends in the West Indian Economy, 1870-1913* (ms. PhD thesis, Cambridge, 1956). This is one of numerous studies of the post-slavery slump in the sugar islands. Since the maritime content is far more tenuous than in earlier days, there is no need to note them all here.

Dowling, C. *The Convoy System in the West Indian Trade, 1803-1815* (ms. DPhil thesis, Oxford, 1965).

Eastman, S.E. and Marx, D. *Ships and Sugar: An Evaluation of Puerto Rican Offshore Shipping*, 1953.

Eisner, G. *Jamaica, 1830-1930; A Study in Economic Growth*, 1961 (PhD thesis, Manchester).

*Ely, R.T. *From Counting House to Cane Field: Moses Taylor and the Cuban Sugar Planter in the Reign of Isabella II, 1833-1868* (ms. PhD thesis, Harvard, 1959). Portions have been published in Spanish at Havana as *Commerciantes Cubanos del Sieglo XIX*, 1960, and at Caracas as *La Economia Cubana entre las dos Isabeles, 1492-1832*. Research based primarily on Moses Taylor papers at New York Public Library and on records of a leading Cuban sugar planter.

Gares, A.J. *Stephen Girard's West Indian Trade from 1789 to 1812* (ms. PhD thesis, Temple, 1947). Has a much richer "salt water content" than J.B. McMaster's life of Girard.

Hall, D. *Free Jamaica, 1838-1865: An Economic History*, 1959.

Huitt, H.C. *The British West Indies in Eclipse, 1838 to 1902* (ms. PhD thesis, Missouri, 1937).

Kneer, W.G. *Great Britain and the Caribbean, 1901-1913: A Study of Anglo-American Relations* (PhD thesis, Michigan State, 1966; DA v. 27, p. 7565).

Kohlmeier, A.L. *The Commercial Relations between the United States and the Netherlands and Dutch West Indies, 1783-1789* (ms. PhD thesis, Harvard, 1921).

Landry, H.E. *The Influence of the Caribbean in British Policy towards Spain, 1782-1793* (ms. PhD thesis, Alabama, 1963; DA v. 24, p. 4161).

Lawrence, K.O. *Immigration into Trinidad and British Guiana, 1834-1871* (ms. PhD thesis, Columbia, 1959). This was when the Indians first came to British Guiana where they have become a powerful political element. For Trinidad, see also Perry below.

McMaster, B.E. *The United States, Great Britain and the Suppression of the Cuban Slave Trade, 1835-1860* (PhD thesis, Georgetown, 1968; DA v. 29, p. 2645A).

Perry, J.A. *A History of the East Indian Indentured Plantation Workers in Trinidad, 1845-1917* (PhD thesis, Louisiana State, 1969; DA v. 30, p. 2949A). See also Lawrence above.

*Pratt, J.W. *Expansionists of 1898: The Acquisition of Hawaii and the Spanish Islands*, 1936, RP1964.

*Ragatz, L.J. *The Fall of the Planter Class in the British Caribbean*, 1928 (PhD thesis, Wisconsin), R1963. Effect of the breakdown of the old "triangular trade," the abolition of the slave trade and then slavery itself; and the loss of special market privileges for sugar in Britain.

Sanderson, M.W.B. *English Naval Strategy and Maritime Trade in the Caribbean, 1793-1802* (ms. PhD thesis, London, 1969).

Winks, R.W. *Canada-West Indies Union: A Forty-Year Minuet*, 1968.

Yates, R.C. *The Cost of Ocean Transport between England and Jamaica, 1784-1788* (PhD thesis, Univ. of Washington, 1969; DA v. 30, p. 5147A).

AH LATIN AMERICA

AH – 1 General

Allen, G.A. *The Development of Canadian Trade with Latin America* (ms. MA thesis, British Columbia, 1927).

Blair, C.P. *Fluctuations in United States Imports from Brazil, Colombia, Chile and Mexico, 1919-1956*, P1959.

Brading, D.A. *Miners and Merchants in Bourbon Mexico, 1763-1810* (Cambridge Latin American Studies), 1971.

Cushner, N.P. *Mexico, Manila, Andalusia: Consulado Rivalry and American Trade, 1704-34* (ms. PhD thesis, London, 1968).

Hannay, D. *The Sea Trader, His Friends and Enemies*, 1912. Ch. 8, 9.

*Haring, C.H. *The Spanish Empire in America*, 1947.

*Humphreys, R.A. *Latin American History, a Guide to the Literature in English*, 1958.

*Munro, D.G. *Intervention and Dollar Diplomacy in the Caribbean, 1900-1921*, 1964.

Potter, F.R. *The South American Trade of Baltimore*.

Pratt, E.J. *Anglo-American Rivalry in Mexico and South America* (ms. DPhil thesis, Oxford, 1929).

Reid, W.A. *Ports and Harbors of South America: A Brief Survey of Aspects, Facilities, Prospects*, 1934.

*Rippy, J.F. *British Investments in Latin America, 1822-1949: A Case Study in the Operations of Private Enterprise in Retarded Regions*, 1959, R1966.

Robertson, W.S. *Hispanic-American Relations with the United States*, 1923, R1969. Ch. 6.

Sperling, J.G. *The South Sea Company: An Historical Essay and Bibliographic Finding List* (Kress Library Pub. No. 17), 1962.

Tanner, E.C. *The Early Trade of Providence with Latin America* (ms. PhD thesis, Harvard, 1950).

AH – 2   Colonial Period – Spanish

Bensusan, H.G. *The Spanish Struggle against Foreign Encroachment in the Caribbean, 1675-1697* (PhD thesis, UCLA, 1970; DA v. 31, p. 1718A).

Bingham, H. *The Scots Darien Company* (ms. PhD thesis, Harvard, 1905).

Borah, W. *Early Colonial Trade Between Mexico and Peru*, 1954.

*Bourne, E.G. *Spain in America, 1450-1580*, P1962, R1968.

Cannon, R. *The Sea of Cortez*, 1966.

*Goodsell, J.N. *Cartegena de Indias: Entrepôt for a New World (1553-1597)* (ms. PhD thesis, Harvard, 1966).

*Haring, C.H. *Trade and Navigation between Spain and the Indies in the Time of the Hapsburgs*, 1918 (PhD thesis, Harvard), R1964. Analysis of the "flota" convoy system with the commercial controls, the movement of the convoys, the assembling of cargoes, etc. Findings summarized in his general work noted above, Sect. AH-1.

Humboldt, A. von and Bonpland, A. *Personal Narrative of Travels to the Equinoctial Regions of America*, tr. T. Ross, 3 v. 1907-08, R1969. The distinguished German scientist made detailed comments on various aspects of Latin America just before the revolutions.

Loosley, A.C. *The Isthmus of Panama in Spanish Colonial Commerce, a Study in Spanish American Economic History* (ms. PhD thesis, Berkeley, 1932).

Means, P.A. *The Spanish Main, Focus of Envy, 1492-1700*, 1935, R1965.

Mosk, S.A. *Spanish Voyages and Pearl Fisheries in the Gulf of California, a Study in Economic History* (ms. PhD thesis, Berkeley, 1932).

Neasham, V.A. *Emigration to the Spanish Indies, 1492-1592* (ms. PhD thesis, Berkeley, 1936).

*Parry, J.H. *The Spanish Seaborne Empire*, 1965.

Prebble, J. *The Darien Disaster: A Scots Colony in the New World, 1698-1700*, 1969. See Sect. T and Bingham above.

Sauer, C.O. *The Early Spanish Main*, 1966, RP1969. Critical of Columbus as a colonizer.

*Schurz, W.L. *The Manila Galleon*, 1939, RP1959. Fascinating scholarly account of the lonely annual transpacific run from Acapulco for 250 years. Not to be confused with F. Van W. Mason's semi-fictional account by the same name recounting Anson's grueling voyage during the War of Jenkins Ear. The broader aspects of the Manila-Acapulco run are discussed in P. Guzman-Rivas, *Reciprocal Geographical Influences of the Trans-Pacific Galleon Trade* (PhD thesis, Texas, 1960; DA v. 21, p. 1905); see also Walker below.

Tate, V. *The Founding of San Blas* (ms. PhD thesis, Berkeley, 1934). Naval base on Pacific coast of Mexico, south of Mazatlan. See also M.E. Thurman, Sect. AD-2.

Walker, G.J. *The Galeones and Flotas in Spain's American Trade, with special reference to the Period 1700-1733* (ms. PhD thesis, Cambridge, 1964).

Wood, W.G. *The Annual Ships of the South Sea Company, 1711-1736* (ms. PhD thesis, Illinois, 1939). See also Sperling, Sect. AH-1.

AH – 3 Colonial Period – Brazil

*Boxer, C.R. *The Dutch in Brazil, 1624-1654*, 1957.
* ————. *Salvador da Sa and the Struggle for Brazil and Angola, 1606-1686*, 1952.
————. *Portuguese Society in the Tropics: The Municipal Councils of Goa, Macao, Bahia and Luanda, 1500-1800*, 1965.
* ————. *The Golden Age of Brazil, 1695-1750: Growing Pains of a Colonial Society*, 1962, R1969.

*————. *The Portuguese Seaborne Empire*. See Sect. T. Having already, with his command of Portuguese and Dutch, given some of the best accounts in English of the exploits of those two peoples in the East, Boxer now proceeds to give the first adequate accounts in English of their connection with colonial Brazil.

Emert, M. *European Voyages to Brazil before 1532; A Chapter in International Rivalry in America* (ms. PhD thesis, Berkeley, 1944).

Verger, P. *Bahia and the West Coast Trade, 1549-1851*, 1964. West Africa, Angola in particular, was the main source of slaves for Brazil.

AH – 4 Wars of Independence

Baker, M.D., Jr. *The United States and Piracy during the Spanish-American Wars of Independence* (ms. PhD thesis, Duke, 1947).

*Billingsley, E.B. *In Defense of Neutral Rights: The United States Navy and the Wars of Independence in Chile and Peru*, 1967 (PhD thesis, North Carolina).

Bornholt, L.A. *Baltimore as a Port of Propaganda for South American Independence* (ms. PhD thesis, Yale, 1945).

*Graham, G.S. and Humphreys, R.A. *The Navy and South America . . . 1807-1823; Correspondence of the Commanders-in-Chief on the South American Station* (Navy Records Society, No. 104), 1962.

Hudson, J.E. *The United States and Latin American Independence, 1776-1812* (PhD thesis, Tulane, 1965; DA v. 27, p. 438A).

Jones, J.S. *Historical Study of Anglo-South American Trade, with special reference to the Period 1807-25* (ms. PhD thesis, London, 1934).

Keen, B. *David Curtis DeForest and the Revolution of Buenos Aires*, 1947 (PhD thesis, Yale). The DeForest firm of New York was long interested in South American trade.

Langnas, A.I. *The Relations between Great Britain and the Spanish Colonies, 1808-1812* (ms. PhD thesis, London, 1939). More concerned with diplomacy than the Jones thesis above.

Morgan, W.A. *Sea Power in the Gulf of Mexico and the Caribbean during the Mexican and Colombian Wars of Independence* (PhD thesis, Southern California, 1969; DA v. 30, p. 1507A).

*Rippy, J.F. *Rivalry of the United States and Great Britain over Latin America, 1808-1830*, 1964.

Street, J.C. *British Influence in the Independence of the River Plate Provinces, with special reference to the Period 1806 to 1816* (ms. PhD thesis, Columbia, 1951).

Walter, R.A., Jr. *Sir Home Popham; A Biography* (ms. PhD thesis, Harvard, 1945). Admiral Popham, nominally on his own authority, seized Buenos Aires in 1807.

*Whitaker, A.P. *The United States and the Independence of Latin America, 1800-1830*, 1964.

Worcester, D.E. *Sea Power and Chilean Independence*, 1963.

AH – 5   Post-1825

a. Mexico and Central America

Folkman, D.I., Jr. *Westward via Nicaragua: The United States and the Nicaragua Route, 1821-1869* (PhD thesis, Utah, 1966; DA v. 27, p. 1014A). For other works concerning the isthmian projects, see Sect. S.

Hammond, W.J. *The History of British Commercial Activity in Mexico, 1820-1830* (ms. PhD thesis, Berkeley, 1929). Subject continued in True below.

Naylor, R.A. *British Commercial Relations with Central America, 1821-1951* (ms. PhD thesis, Tulane, 1958).

True, C.A. *British Economic Interests and Activities in Mexico, 1830-1846* (ms. PhD thesis, Berkeley, 1933). See also Hammond above.

Williams, M.W. *Anglo-American Isthmian Diplomacy, 1815-1915*, 1916, R1965.

Wilson, C.M. *Empire in Green and Gold: The Story of the American Banana Trade*, 1947, R1968. Includes brief account of the United Fruit fleet.

b. South America – East Coast

Albion, R.G. *The Rise of New York Port, 1815-1860*, 1939, R1970. Ch. 9, The Caribbean and Latin America.

Bethell, L.M. *Great Britain and the Abolition of the Brazilian Slave Trade, 1830-52* (ms. PhD thesis, London, 1963).

Beyer, R.C. *The Colombian Coffee Industry: Origins and Major Trends, 1740-1940* (ms. PhD thesis, Minnesota, 1948).

Carl, G.E. *British Commercial Interest in Venezuela during the 19th Century* (PhD thesis, Tulane, 1968; DA v. 29, p. 1489A).

Carlson, D.A. *Great Britain and the Abolition of the Slave Trade to Latin America* (PhD thesis, Minnesota, 1964; DA v. 28, p. 583A). See also Bethell above.

Down, W.C. *The Occupation of the Falkland Islands* (ms. PhD thesis, Cambridge, 1927).

*Ferns, H.S. *Britain and Argentina in the Nineteenth Century*, 1960. Based on PhD thesis, Cambridge, 1951, *The Development of British Enterprise in Argentina, 1806-1895*.

Flickema, T.O. *The United States and Paraguay, 1845-1860: Misunderstanding, Miscalculation and Misconduct* (PhD thesis, Wayne State, 1966; DA v. 30, p. 232A).

Galloway, J.H. *Pernambuco, 1770-1920: An Historical Geography* (ms. PhD thesis, London, 1965).

*Graham, R. *Britain and the Onset of Modernisation in Brazil, 1850-1914* (Cambridge Latin American Studies, No. 4), 1968. Chapters on "The Export-Import Complex" and "Coffee and Rubber."

Grier, D.H. *Confederate Emigration to Brazil, 1865-1870* (PhD thesis, Michigan, 1968; DA v. 30, p. 245A).

Griffin, D.W. *The Normal Years: Brazilian-American Relations, 1930-1939* (ms. PhD thesis, Vanderbilt, 1962; DA v. 23, p. 3875). Considerable discussion of trade relations.

*Hanson, S.G. *Argentine Meat and the British Market; Chapters in the History of the Argentine Meat Industry*, 1938 (PhD thesis, Harvard).

Hilton, S.E. *Brazil and Great Power Trade Rivalry in South America* (PhD thesis, Texas, 1969; DA v. 30, p. 5382A).

Huck, E.R. *Colombian-United States Commercial Relations, 1821-1850* (ms. PhD thesis, Alabama, 1963; DA v. 24, p. 4160).

Humphreys, R.A., ed. *British Consular Reports on the Trade and Politics of Latin America, 1824-26* (Camden Soc., 3rd Series, v. 63), 1940.

Jacob, H.E. *Coffee: The Epic of a Commodity*, 1935.

*Kroeber, C.B. *Growth of the Shipping Industry in the Rio de la Plata Region, 1794-1860*, 1958 (PhD thesis, Berkeley).

*Manchester, A.K. *British Preeminence in Brazil, Its Rise and Decline, a Study in European Expansion*, 1933, R1964.

Melby, J.F. *Rubber River: Being an Account of the Rise and Collapse of the Amazon Boom* (ms. PhD thesis, Chicago, 1941). The flourishing trade at Manaos was suddenly cut short, around the time of World War I, by the cultivated rubber from Malaya and Indonesia. See also Tomlinson below.

Nichols, T.E. *The Caribbean Gateway to Colombia: Cartagena, Santa Marta and Barranquilla and Their Connections with the Interior, 1820-1940* (ms. PhD thesis, Berkeley, 1951).

Pryor, A.J. *Anglo-Brazilian Commercial Relations and the Evolution of Brazilian*

Tariff Policy, 1822-50 (ms. PhD thesis, Cambridge, 1965).

Safford, F. R. *Commerce and Enterprise in Central Colombia, 1821-1870* (PhD thesis, Columbia, 1965; DA v. 27, p. 170A).

Stevens, E.F. *One Hundred Years of Houlders: A Record of the History of Houlders Brothers & Co., Ltd., from 1849 to 1950,* 1950. Eventually very prominent in the refrigerated meat trade. See also Hanson above.

Swann, L.A., Jr. *John Roach, Maritime Entrepreneur. . . .* 1965 (PhD thesis, Harvard). Ch. 5 deals with Roach's persistent and frustrating efforts to develop American-flag steamship service to Brazil.

*Tomlinson, H.M. *The Sea and the Jungle,* 1912 ff. Story of a tramp voyage in 1909-10 from South Wales to Brazil and far up the Amazon just before the rubber boom collapsed.

Vazquez-Presedo, V. *The Role of Foreign Trade and Migration in the Development of the Argentine Economy, 1875-1914* (ms. DPhil thesis, Oxford, 1968).

Verger, P. See Sect. AH-3.

c. South America – West Coast

Deimel, H.L., Jr. *The Mexican Market for San Francisco's Exporters,* (ms. PhD thesis, Berkeley, 1923).

Duncan, R.E. *William Wheelwright, the Pioneer of Pacific Steam Navigation, 1825-1852* (ms. PhD thesis, Berkeley, 1960). Native of Newburyport, Mass. who founded Pacific Steam Navigation Co. See also A.C. Wardle, *Steam Conquers the Pacific* (1940) and Kinsbruner just below.

Kinsbruner, J. *The Business Activities of William Wheelwright in Chile, 1829-1860* (PhD thesis, New York Univ., 1964; DA v. 26, p. 328). See also Duncan, just above.

Lubbock, B. *The Nitrate Clippers,* 1934, R1966. See Sect. I.

Nolan, L.C. *The Diplomatic and Commercial Relations of the United States and Peru, 1826-1875* (ms. PhD thesis, Duke, 1935).

Peterson, D.W. *The Diplomatic and Commercial Relations between the United States and Peru from 1883 to 1918* (PhD thesis, Minnesota, 1969; DA v. 31, p. 533A).

AI   AFRICA AND THE SLAVE TRADE

The combination of political independence in Africa and the sudden demand for Negro studies in America has produced more new titles in this field than in any other. It is out of the question to cite more than the most pertinent here.

AI – 1   General

*Albion, R.G. *Seaports South of Sahara: The Achievements of an American Steam-ship Service*, 1959. This history of the Farrell Lines includes a survey of earlier maritime contacts with South, East and West Africa, together with detailed annual statistics of trade. See also Hoyle below.

*Bennett, N.R. and Brooks, G.E. *New England Merchants in Africa: A History through Documents 1802 to 1865* (Boston Univ. African Research Studies), 1966.

Clendenen, C.C. and Duignan, P. *Americans in Black Africa Up to 1865*, 1966.

Hatch, J. *The History of Britain in Africa: From the Fifteenth Century to the Present*, 1969.

Haywood, C.N. *American Whalers and Africa* (ms. PhD thesis, Boston Univ., 1967).

Howard, L.C. *American Involvement in Africa South of the Sahara, 1800-1860* (ms. PhD thesis, Harvard, 1956). See also Clendenen above.

Hoyle, B.S. and Hilling, D., eds. *Seaports and Development in Tropical Africa*, 1970. See also Albion above.

Rutherford, H.V. *Sir Joseph Banks and the Exploration of Africa, 1788 to 1820* (ms. PhD thesis, Berkeley, 1952). Banks, head of the Royal Society, stimulated this in addition to the South Seas voyages of Cook and Bligh.

AI – 2   North Africa

Fisher, Sir G. *Barbary Legend: War, Trade and Piracy in North Africa, 1415-1830*, 1958. Emphasizes commercial aspects of the Levant Company contacts, but is altogether too sympathetic with the pirates. See also the other Barbary Pirate accounts by E.H. Curry (1910); S. Lane-Poole (1890); and Sir B.L. Playfair (1884).

Irwin, R.W. *The Diplomatic Relations of the United States with the Barbary Powers, 1776-1816*, 1931 (PhD thesis, New York Univ).

(Pepys, S.) *The Tangier Papers of Samuel Pepys*, ed. W.E. Chappell (Navy Records Soc., Pub. 73), 1935. England occupied Tangier, 1662-84.

Savage, M.A. *American Diplomacy in North Africa, 1776-1817* (ms. PhD thesis, Georgetown, 1949). See also Irwin above.

*U.S. Office of Naval Records and Library, *Naval Documents Related to the United States War with the Barbary Powers*, 6 v. 1934-35. See Sect. BA-2.

Willan, T.S. *Studies in Elizabethan Foreign Trade*, 1959. Includes an account of the short-lived Barbary Company, formed for trade with Morocco.

Axelson, E. *Portugal and the Scramble for Africa, 1875-1891*, 1968.

Boxer, C.R. *Portuguese Society in the Tropics.* . . . 1965. See Sect. AH-3. Luanda.

*Brooks, G.E., Jr. *Yankee Traders, Old Coasters, and African Middlemen.* . . . (Boston Univ. African Research Center), 1970 (PhD thesis, Boston Univ.). See also Bennett, Sect. AI-1.

Buckingham, D. *The Portuguese Conquest of Angola*, 1965.
————. *Trade and Conflict in Angola: The Mhindi and Their Neighbors under the Influence of the Portuguese, 1483-1790* (Oxford Studies in African Affairs), 1966.

Campbell, P. *Maryland in Africa: The Maryland State Colonization Society, 1831-1857* (ms. PhD thesis, Ohio State, 1967). Influential in beginnings of Liberia.

Carson, P. *Materials for West African History in the Archives of Belgium and Holland*, 1962.

Collins, E.D. *"The Royal African Co.,"* A Study of the English Trade to Western Africa under Chartered Companies from 1585 to 1750 (PhD thesis, Yale, 1899; DA v. 28, p. 566).

Coombs, D. *The Gold Coast, Britain and the Netherlands, 1850-1874*, 1963.

Daaku, K.Y. *Trade and Politics on the Gold Coast, 1640-1720* (ms. PhD thesis, London, 1964).

Davidson, J. *Trade and Politics in the Sherbro Hinterland, 1849-1890* (PhD thesis, Wisconsin, 1969; DA v. 30, p. 242A). Sierra Leone.

Davies, P.N. *The British West African Trading Companies, 1910-50* (ms. PhD thesis, Liverpool, 1967). See also Leubescher, below.

Davis, R.W. *Historical Outline of the Kru Coast, Liberia, 1500 to the Present* (PhD thesis, Indiana, 1968; DA v. 29, p. 3944A).

Dike, K.O. *Trade and Politics in the Niger Delta, 1830-1885* (Oxford Studies in African Affairs), 1956 (PhD thesis, London). See also Newbury below.

Fox, E.L. *The American Colonization Society, 1817-1840*, 1919 (PhD thesis, Johns Hopkins). For founding of Liberia, see also Campbell above and Staudenraus below.

Getzel, C.J. *John Holt, a British Merchant in West Africa in the Era of "Imperialism"* (ms. DPhil thesis, Oxford, 1960).

Gosse, P. *St. Helena, 1502-1938*, 1938.

Hopkins, A.G. *An Economic History of Lagos, 1860-1914* (ms. PhD thesis, London, 1964).

Ifemesia, C.C. *British Enterprise in the Niger, 1830-1869* (ms. PhD thesis, London, 1959).

Ikime, O. *Merchant Prince of the Niger Delta: Rise and Fall of Nana Olumo, Last Governor of the Benin River*, 1969. One of the greatest traders of the 19th century.

*Lawrence, A.W. *Trade Castles and Forts of West Africa*, 1963. The author, an archaeologist like his brother, the late "Lawrence of Arabia," has directed for the governments of Gold Coast and then Ghana, the repair or restoration of eleven of these historic monuments, including the celebrated Elmina and Christenborg, and has surveyed four others. The volume is rich in illustrations, diagrams and history.

Leubescher, C. *The West African Shipping Trade, 1909-1959*, 1963. See also Davies above.

Metcalfe, G.E. *Maclean of the Gold Coast: The Life and Time of George Maclean, 1801-1847* (West African Hist. Studies), 1962. Throws light on the role of the merchants during the preimperialism period.

Morison, S.E. *"Old Bruin," Commodore Matthew C. Perry, 1794-1858*, 1967. Service on West African slave patrol.

Newbury, C.W. *The Western Slave Coast and Its Ruler; European Trade and Administration among the Yoruba and Adia-Speaking Peoples of South-Western Nigeria, Southern Dahomey, and Togo* (Oxford Studies in African Affairs), 1961. Companion work to Dike above.

Norregard, G., tr. S. Mammen. *Danish Settlements in West Africa, 1658-1850*, 1966.

*Perham, M. *Lugard*, 2 v. 1960. Vol. 1, *The Years of Adventure, 1853-98*; vol. 2, *The Years of Authority, 1898-1945*. The outstanding leader in Nigerian trade and empire.

Peterson, J.E. *Freetown: A Study of the Development of Liberated African Society, 1807-1870* (ms. PhD thesis, Northwestern, 1963).

Scotten, W.H. *International Rivalry in the Bights of Benin and Biafra, 1815-85* (ms. PhD thesis, Leeds, 1933).

Staudenraus, P.J. *The African Colonization Movement, 1816-1865*, 1961 (PhD thesis, Wisconsin; DA v. 21, p. 2696). See also Campbell and Fox above.

Stilliard, H.H. *The Rise and Development of Legitimate Trade in Palm Oil with West Africa* (ms. MA thesis, Birmingham, 1938).

Ugoh, S.E.U. *Nigerian International Trade, 1911-1960* (ms. PhD thesis, Harvard, 1965).

Verger, P. *Bahia and the West Coast Trade, 1549-1851,* 1964.

Wheeler, D.L. *The Portuguese in Angola, 1836-1891: A Study in Expansion and Administration* (ms. PhD thesis, Boston Univ., 1963). Includes commercial aspects.

Wolfson, F. *British Relations with the Gold Coast, 1843-1880* (ms. PhD thesis, London, 1950).

AI – 4   East Africa

Boxer, C.R. and Azevedo, C. de. *Fort Jesus and the Portuguese in Mombasa, 1593-1729,* 1960.

Brady, C.T., Jr. *Commerce and Conquest in East Africa, with particular reference to the Salem Trade with Zanzibar,* 1950.

*Coupland, Sir R. *East Africa and Its Invaders from the Earliest Times to . . .1856,* 1938.
*————. *The Exploitation of East Africa, 1856-1890; The Slave Trade and the Scramble,* 1939.

Duffy, J. *Portuguese Africa,* 1959.

Freeman-Grenville, G.S. *The French at Kilwa Island: An Episode in Eighteenth-Century East African History,* 1965.

Gray, R. and Birmingham, D. *Pre-Colonial African Trade: Essays on Trade in Central and Eastern Africa before 1900,* 1970.

Haight, M.J. *European Powers and South-East Africa: A Study of International Relations on the Southeast Coast of Africa, 1796-1856,* 1942, R1967.

Hoyle, B.S. *The Seaports of East Africa,* 1968. See also Sect. AI-1.

Ommanney, F.D. *Isle of Cloves: A View of Zanzibar,* 1955.

*Prins, A.H.J. *Sailing from Lamu: A Study of Maritime Culture in Islamic East Africa,* 1965. The work of a Dutch anthropologist who considered Lamu "a maritime area par excellence."

Smith, A.K. *The Struggle for Control of Southern Mozambique, 1720-1835* (PhD thesis, UCLA, 1970; DA v. 31, p. 5338A).

*Villiers, A.J. *Sons of Sinbad: An Account of Sailing with the Arabs in Their Dhows, in the Red Sea, around the Coasts of Arabia, and to Zanzibar and Tanganyika,* 1940, R1969.

AI – 5   South Africa

Burman, J.L. *Great Shipwrecks off the Coast of Southern Africa*, 1967.

*Duffy, J. *Shipwreck and Empire*. See Sect. AJ-4.

Horwood, O.P.F., ed. *The Port of Durban*, 1969.

Malherbe, J.A.N. *Port Natal; A Pioneer Story*, 1966.

*Murray, M. *Ships and South Africa: A Maritime Chronicle of the Cape, with particular reference to the Mail and Passenger Liners from the Earliest Days . . . (1825-1926)*, 1933.
————. *Union-Castle Chronicle, 1853-1953*, 1953. Includes much of the material from the earlier volume.

AI – 6   The Slave Trade

Bethell, L.M. *Great Britain and the Abolition of the Brazilian Slave Trade, 1830-52* (ms. PhD thesis, London, 1962).

Brown, G. *The Illicit Slave Trade to Cuba and the Other Islands of the Caribbean* (ms. PhD thesis, Ohio State, 1945).

Carlson, D.A. *Great Britain and the Abolition of the Slave Trade to Latin America* (PhD thesis, Minnesota, 1964; DA v. 28, p. 583A).

Constantine, J.R. *The African Slave Trade: A Study of Eighteenth Century Propaganda and Public Controversy* (PhD thesis, Indiana, 1953; DA v. 14, p. 97).

Cox, J.G. *Cox and the JuJu Coast*, 1968. Journal of an officer on HMS *Fly*, in attempting to suppress the slave trade, 1868-69.

*Curtin, P.D. *The Atlantic Slave Trade: A Census*, 1969. Effort to determine quantitative totals, by a foremost scholar in imperial history.

Davidson, B. *The African Slave Trade: Precolonial History, 1450-1850*, 1961, RP1965. British edition appeared under the title *Black Mother*. More concerned with the circumstances of gathering slaves in Africa than with their shipment to America.

Davies, K.G. *The Royal African Company*, 1957. Nominal monopoly, 1672-1752, to the English West Indian and American colonies.

*Donnan, E. *Documents Illustrative of the History of the Slave Trade to America*, 4 v. 1930-34; R1965. V. 1, 1440-1700; v. 2, 18th Century; v. 3, New England and Middle Colonies; v. 4, Border and Southern Colonies. By far the most useful collection of source material on the period of "legal" slaving to 1807.

Dow, G.F. *Slave Ships and Slaving*, 1927, R1969. A well-illustrated collection of excerpts from various sources.

DuBois, W.E.B. *The Suppression of the African Slave-Trade to the United States, 1638-1870*, 1896, R1970 (PhD thesis, Harvard). This study, by one of the foremost American Negro leaders, carries the story well past the "legal" period.

Duignan, P. and Clendenen, C.C. *The United States and the African Slave Trade, 1619-1862*, 1965.

Grant, D. *The Fortunate Slave: An Illustration of African Slavery in the Early Eighteenth Century*, 1968. A Gambian, sold into slavery, taken to Maryland, rescued by Oglethorpe, brought to London and sent back to Africa with presents.

*Howard, W.S. *American Slavers and the Federal Law, 1837-1862*, 1963 (PhD thesis, UCLA).

Knight, F.W. *Cuban Slave Society on the Eve of Abolition, 1838-1880* (PhD thesis, Wisconsin, 1969; DA v. 30, p. 1096A).

Lipscomb, P.C. *William Pitt and the Abolition of the Slave Trade* (PhD thesis, Texas, 1960; DA v. 20, p. 4642).

*Lloyd, C. *The Navy and the Slave Trade: The Suppression of the African Slave Trade in the Nineteenth Century*, 1949, R1968. Interesting and valuable. Part I covers the British abolition movement and the efforts of the Royal Navy on the Guinea Coast: part II deals primarily with Arab slavers operating from East Africa. Valuable data on the effects of the deadly climate. Part of the same subject is covered by Ward below. The less continued efforts of the United States Navy are recounted by two officers, Horatio Bridge (1845) and Andrew H. Foote (1854).

Mackenzie-Grieve, A. *The Last Years of the English Slave Trade: Liverpool, 1750-1807*, 1941.

Macmaster, B.E. *The United States, Great Britain and the Suppression of the Cuban Slave Trade, 1835-1860* (PhD thesis, Georgetown, 1968; DA v. 29, p. 2645A).

*Mannix, D.P. and Cowley, M. *Black Cargoes, A History of the Atlantic Slave Trade, 1518-1865*, 1962. The best book to read first for an authoritative, interesting general background, supplanting J.R. Spears' earlier "moralistic" account. Includes good, up-to-date critical bibliography.

Martin, C. *The* Amistad *Affair*, 1970. Mutiny of kidnapped free Nigerians, seizure by American authorities, and, after long legal arguments, acquittal by Supreme Court. Same subject covered in "quasi-novel" form in W.A. Owens, *Slave Mutiny: The Revolt on the Schooner* Amistad, 1953, R1968 as *Black Mutiny*.

Mathieson, W.L. *Great Britain and the Slave Trade, 1839-1865*, 1929.

*Mayer, B. *Captain Canot, or Twenty Years of an African Slaver*, 1854 ff. A long-popular lively case history. Entitled *Adventures of an African Slaver* in 1928 edition.

Owens, W.A. See Martin above.

Parkinson, C.N., ed. *The Trade Winds*, 1948. Ch. 11 on the slave trade in 1793-1815.

Polanyi, K. and Rotstein, A. *Dahomey and the Slave Trade: An Analysis of an Archaic Economy*, 1966. Concentrates on the internal rather than the seagoing aspects.

Pope-Hennessy, J. *Sins of the Fathers: A Study of the Atlantic Slave Traders, 1441-1807*, 1967.

Porter, D.H. *The Defense of the British Slave Trade, 1784-1807* (ms. PhD thesis, Oregon, 1967).

Postma, J. *The Dutch Participation in the African Slave Trade: Slavery on the Guinea Coast, 1675-1795* (PhD thesis, Michigan State, 1970; DA v. 31, p. 4068A).

Putney, M.S. *The Slave Trade in French Diplomacy, 1814-1865* (PhD thesis, Pennsylvania, 1955; DA v. 16, p. 110).

Soulsby, H. G. *The Right of Search and the Slave Trade in Anglo-American Relations, 1814-1862*, 1933 (PhD thesis, Johns Hopkins).

Spears, J.R. *The American Slave Trade. An Account of Its Organization, Growth and Development*, 1900, P1960. See Mannix above.

Tenkorang, S. *British Slave Trading Activities on the Gold and Slave Coasts in the Eighteenth Century and Their Effects on African Society* (ms. MA thesis, London, 1964).

Ward, W.E. *The Royal Navy and the Slavers. The Suppression of the Atlantic Slave Trade*, 1969. See also Lloyd above.

Wax, D.D. *The Negro Slave Trade in Colonial Pennsylvania* (ms. PhD thesis, Univ. of Washington, 1962; DA v. 24, p. 272).

Wells, T.H. *The Slave Ship* Wanderer, 1967.

Williams, E.E. *Capitalism and Slavery*, 1944, R1966. Based on his DPhil thesis, Oxford, *The Economic Aspect of the Abolition of the West Indian Slave Trade and Slavery*.

Williams, G. *History of the Liverpool Privateers and Letters of Marque, with an Account of the Liverpool Slave Trade*, 1897, R1966. Long the principal authority on the subject. See also Mackenzie-Grieve above.

Zook, G.F. *The Company of Royal Adventurers Trading into Africa*, 1919 (PhD thesis, Cornell). Short-lived predecessors, 1662-67, of the Royal African Company, described by Davies above.

AJ SOUTH AND SOUTHEAST ASIA

AJ – 1 General

*Bergsmark, D.R. *Economic Geography of Asia*, 1935.

Hakluyt Society Publications. See Sect. R.

Sherry, N. *Conrad's Eastern World*, 1966.

AJ – 2 Indian Ocean

*Anstey, V. *The Trade of the Indian Ocean*, 1929.

*Ballard, G.A. *Rulers of the Indian Ocean*, 1927. From the standpoint of strategy, Admiral Ballard analyzes the activity of the various European nations in eastern waters.

*Graham, G.S. *Great Britain in the Indian Ocean. A Study of Maritime Enterprise, 1810-1850*, 1967. Contains a wealth of pertinent new material, commercial and naval.

Hourani, G.F. *Arab Seafaring in the Indian Ocean in Ancient and Early Medieval Times*, 1951 (PhD thesis, Princeton).

Howell, B.M. *Mauritius, 1832-1849; A Study of a Sugar Colony* (ms. PhD thesis, London, 1951).

Thomas, A. *Forgotten Eden*, 1968. Seychelles Islands.

Toussaint, A. *Early American Trade with Mauritius*, 1954.
————. *A History of the Indian Ocean*, 1966.
————. *"Harvest of the Sea;" the Mauritius Story in Outline*, 1966.

*Villiers, ..J. *Sons of Sinbad; An Account of Sailing with the Arabs in Their Dhows, in the Red Sea, around the Coasts of Arabia, and to Zanzibar and Tanganyika*, 1940, R1969.
————. *Monsoon Seas: The Story of the Indian Ocean*, 1952.

AJ – 3 Red Sea to Persian Gulf

Albaharna, H.M. *The Legal Status of the Arabian Gulf States*. . . . 1969. Sheikhdom treaties with Great Britain.

Amin, A. *British Interests in the Persian Gulf, 1747-1778*, 1967 (PhD thesis, Maryland).

Anderson, J.R.L. *East of Suez*, 1968. History of the British Petroleum Co., from 1907.

Belgrave, Sir C. *The Pirate Coast*, 1966. Initial British efforts to curb piracy in the Persian Gulf; "desultory but attractive."

Busch, B.C. *Britain and the Persian Gulf, 1894-1914*, 1967 (PhD thesis, Berkeley). See also Daud below.

Daud, M.A. *British Relations with the Persian Gulf, 1890-1902* (ms. PhD thesis, London, 1957).

Ewart, E.A. (Boyd Cable, pseud.) *A Hundred Years of the P & O, Peninsular and Oriental Steam Navigation Company*, 1937.

Finnie, D.H. *Pioneers East. The Early American Experience in the Middle East* (Harvard Middle East Studies), 1967.

Gurney, J. *Sheba's Coast*, 1966.

Hakima, A.A. *The Rise and Development of Bahrain and Kuwait*, 1964.

*Hamilton, C.W. *Americans and Oil in the Middle East*, 1962.

*Hoskins, H.L. *British Routes to India*, 1928 (PhD thesis, Pennsylvania), R1966.

Kelly, J.B. *Britain and the Persian Gulf, 1795-1880*, 1968 (PhD thesis, London).

Landen, R.G. *Oman since 1856: Disruptive Modernization in a Traditional Arab Society*, 1967.

*Longrigg, S.H. *Oil in the Middle East: Its Discovery and Development*, 1953, R1961, 1967. "A classic in its field."

Mann, C. *Abu Dhabi: Birth of an Oil Sheikhdom*, 1964.

*Marlowe, J. *The Persian Gulf in the Twentieth Century*, 1963.

Marston, T.E. *Britain's Imperial Role in the Red Sea Area, 1800-1878*, 1961 (PhD thesis, Harvard).

Miles, S.B. *The Countries and Tribes of the Persian Gulf*, 2 v. 1966.

Moyse-Bartlett, H. *The Pirates of Trucial Oman*, 1966.

Paget, J. *Last Port: Aden 1964-67*, 1969.

Palmer, W.C. *The Activities of the English East India Company in Persia and the Persian Gulf, 1616-1657* (ms. PhD thesis, London, 1933).

*Schar, H.M. *The Emergence of the Middle East, 1914-1924*, 1969.

Serjeant, R.B. *The Portuguese off the South Arabian Coast*, 1963.

182

Wilson, Sir A.T. *The Persian Gulf: An Historical Sketch from the Earliest Times to the Beginning of the Twentieth Century*, 1928, 1954.

AJ – 4   India to 1756

Bhattachayya, A. *The East India Company and the Economy of Bengal, 1704-40* (ms. PhD thesis, London, 1953).

Bingham, H. *Elihu Yale: The American Nabob of Queen Square*, 1939, R1968. Good picture of Madras around 1690, when the original "Eli" was its president. He later won immortality by a gift to a struggling college in Connecticut.

Boxer, C.R. *Portuguese Society in the Tropics. . . .* 1965. Goa.

Brown, M.J. *Itinerant Ambassador: The Life of Sir Thomas Roe, 1580-1644*, 1970. Conducted mission for East India Co. to the court of the Great Mogul.

Cambridge History of the British Empire, v. 1; also ch. 3 of *Cambridge History of India*.

Chaudhuri, K.N. *The English East India Company. The Study of an Early Joint Stock Company, 1600-1640*, 1965 (PhD thesis, London).

Crowe, A.I.. *Sir Josiah Child and the East India Company* (ms. PhD thesis, London, 1956).

Dalgleish, W.H. *The Perpetual Company of the Indies in the Days of Dupleix; Its Administration and Organization for the Handling of Indian Commerce, 1722-1754*, 1933 (PhD thesis, Pennsylvania).

Danvers, F.C. *The Portuguese in India*, 2 v. 1894, R1966. An old standard work.

Das Gupta, A.R. *Malabar in Eastern Trade* (ms. PhD thesis, Cambridge, 1961).

*Duffy, J. *Shipwreck and Empire; Being an Account of Portuguese Maritime Disasters in a Century of Decline*, 1954 (PhD thesis, Harvard). The wrecks of overloaded carracks on the coast of Southwest Africa are also the subject of *Tragic History of the Seas* by Gomes de Brito, translated for Hakluyt Society by C.R. Boxer, 1959, with "Further Selections," 1969.

*Foster, Sir W. *The English Factories in India: A Calendar of Documents in the India Office, British Museum and Public Records Office, (1618-1669)*, 13 v. 1906-27. After his death, the series was continued by Sir C. Fawcett (1670-84), 4 v. 1936-

Hart, H.H. *Sea Road to the Indies. . . .* See Sect. Q-2.
————. *Luis de Camoens and the Epic of the Lusiads*, 1950.

*Hunter, Sir W.W. *History of British India*, 2 v. 1899-1900. Carries the story only to 1708, but is very good on that early period.

Insh, G.F. *Papers Relating to the Ships and Voyages of the Company of Scotland Trading to Africa and the Indies, 1696-1707* (Scottish Historical Society), 1924. Like the contemporary Scottish venture to Darien, it was a failure which made Scotland more ready for union.

Jayne, K.G. *Vasco da Gama and His Successors, 1460-1580*, 1910, R1970.

Krishna, B. *Commercial Relations between India and England, 1601-1757*, 1924.

*Linschoten, J.H. van. *The Voyage of John Huyghen van Linschoten to the East Indies*, ed. A.C. Burnell and P.A. Tiels (Hakluyt Soc. Pub. 1st Series, Nos. 70-71) 2 v. 1885, R1967. This book gives an excellent picture of the late, rotten days of the Portuguese empire around 1580 and it did much to stimulate the Dutch and English inroads shortly afterwards. See Parr below for Linschoten biography. Other Hakluyt Society publications give intimate pictures of the earlier days, especially the *Book of Duarte Barbosa* (1519), 2nd Series, Nos. 44, 49.

Maynard, G.E. *The Role of the East India Company in the Development of British Imperialism to 1688* (ms. PhD thesis, Ohio, 1950).

Mookerji, R.K. *Indian Shipping; A History of the Sea-Borne Trade and Maritime Activity of the Indians from the Earliest Times*, 1912, R1962.

Nambiar, O.K. *The Kunjalis: Admirals of Calicut*, 1963. Anti-Portuguese leaders in 16th-century India.

Nightingale, P. *Trade and Empire in Western India, 1784-1806*, 1970. Emphasizes the "country trade," especially the swapping of Indian raw cotton for Chinese tea.

*Parr, C.M. *Jan van Linschoten: The Dutch Marco Polo*, 1964. Fills a long-felt need for a biography in English. See Linschoten above.

*Prestage, E. *The Portuguese Pioneers*, 1930, R1967. Good general survey.

Raychaudri, T. *Jan Company in Coromandel, 1605-1690: A Study of the Interrelations of European Commerce and Traditional Economies*, 1962 (DPhil thesis, Oxford). "Jan Company" was the colloquial term for the Dutch East India Company, just as its English rival was "The Honourable John Company."

Samras, K.R. *Colbert and the Founding of the French East India Company* (ms. PhD thesis, Berkeley, 1934).

Stephens, H.M. *Albuquerque*, 1892. See also the later biography of the great empire builder by Elaine Sanceau. There is still need for a more adequate account.

Stevens, H.C., ed. *The Dawn of British Trade in the East Indies as Recorded in the Court Minutes of the East India Company, 1599-1603*, 1969.

Thomas, G.Z. *Richer than Spices*, 1965. Effect upon England of the new commodities from India.

184

Akhbar, S.M. *The Growth and Development of the Indian Tea Industry and Trade* (ms. PhD thesis, London, 1932).

Bernstein, H.T. *Steamboats on the Ganges, 1828-1840*, 1960.

Bever, V.M. *The Trade in East Indian Commodities to the American Colonies, 1690-1775* (ms. PhD thesis, Iowa, 1941).

Bhagat, C. *America's Commercial and Consular Relations with India, 1784-1860* (ms. PhD thesis, Yale, 1962).

Brown, H. *Parry's of Madras: A Story of British Enterprise in India*, 1954. History of "the oldest established firm in Southern India," founded in 1788.

Chaudhuri, K.N. *The Economic Development of India under the East India Company, 1814-1854*, 1971. Reprinted papers.

Coates, W.H. *The Old "Country Trade" of the East Indies*, 1911, R1969. Country trade defined by author as including "vessels owned by Englishmen resident in India as well as purely Indian ships."
————. *The Good Old Days of Shipping*, 1909, R1969. Also on Indian trade.

Cotton, Sir E. *East Indiamen. The East India Company's Maritime Service*, ed. Sir C. Fawcett, 1949.

Das Gupta, A. *Malabar in Asian Trade, 1740-1800* (Cambridge South Asian Studies), 1967.

Datta, K. *The Dutch in Bengal and Bihar, 1740-1825*, 1949, R1969.

Engles, D. *The Abolition of the East India Company's Monopoly, 1833* (ms. PhD thesis, Edinburgh, 1956).

Feldbark, D. *India Trade Under the Danish Flag, 1772-1808* (Scandinavian Institute of Asiatic Studies), 1969.

*Furber, H. *John Company at Work: A Study of European Expansion in India in the Late Eighteenth Century*, 1937 (PhD thesis, Harvard), R1970. A piece of excellent scholarship, utilizing the archives of the British, Dutch, French and Danish East India Companies, showing their interplay and intricate workings, c1783-93.
————. *Bombay Presidency in the Mid-Eighteenth Century*, 1965.

*Hoskins, H.L. *British Routes to India*, 1928 (PhD thesis, Pennsylvania), R1966.

Nightingale, P. *Trade and Empire in Western India, 1784-1806*, 1970.

*Parkinson, C.N. *Trade in the Eastern Seas, 1793-1813*, 1937 (PhD thesis, London), R1966. Like Furber above, an excellent analysis of all aspects of maritime and imperial activity. Its lucid chapters (by the future inventor of "Parkinson's Law"), in a topical arrangement, give a very clear account of "how things worked." Further material on the period is in his *War in the Eastern Seas, 1789-1815*, 1953.

Parshad, I.D. *Some Aspects of Indian Foreign Trade, 1757-1893*, 1932 (PhD thesis, London).

Philips, G.H. *The East India Interest and the British Government, 1784-1833*, 1940 (MA thesis, Liverpool; PhD thesis, London), R1961. Emphasizes the headquarters and high policy aspects.

Ranken, A. and Clay, N.I. and A.S., eds. *Shipmates*, 1967. Journal by Agnes Ranken (1784-1859) of a voyage from Portsmouth to Calcutta in an Indiaman in 1799.

Robinson, F.P. *The Trade of the East India Company, 1790-1813*, 1912.

Thomas, N.A. *Foreign Trade in the Economy of India* (ms. PhD thesis, Fordham, 1951).

*Thorner, D. *Investment in Empire: British Railway and Steam Shipping Enterprise in India, 1825-1849*, 1950 (PhD thesis, Pennsylvania).

Tripathi, A. *Trade and Finance in the Bengal Presidency, 1793-1833*, 1956 (PhD thesis, London).

*Wadia, R.A. *The Bombay Dockyard and the Wadia Master Builders*, 1957.

Wright, H.R.C. *East-Indian Economic Problems of the Age of Cornwallis and Raffles*, 1961. Essays "focused on four commodities: coffee, opium, cotton piece goods, and tin."

AJ – 6   Ceylon

Arasaratnam, S. *Dutch Power in Ceylon, 1658-1687*, 1958 (PhD thesis, London). Sequel to Goonewardena below.

Colgate, H.A. *Trincomalee and the East Indian Squadron, 1746 to 1844* (ms. MA thesis, London, 1859).

Forrest, D.M. *A Hundred Years of Ceylon Tea, 1867-1967*, 1967. Commissioned by the Ceylon Tea Propaganda Board.

Goonewardena, K.W. *The Foundations of Dutch Power in Ceylon, 1638-1658*, 1958 (PhD thesis, London).

Rasaputram, W. *Influence of Foreign Trade on the Level and Growth of National Income in Ceylon, 1926-57* (PhD thesis, Wisconsin, 1958; DA v. 20, p. 908).

Winius, G.D. *The Fall of Portuguese Ceylon, 1638-1656; Military, Diplomatic and Political Aspects in the Decline of an Empire* (ms. PhD thesis, Columbia; 1964; DA v. 25, p. 2936).

Barber, N. *Sinister Twilight: The Fall of Singapore*, 1942, R1968.

Bassett, D.K. *The Factory of the East India Company at Bantam, 1602-1682* (ms. PhD thesis, London, 1955). See also Bastin and Young below.

Bastin, J., ed. *The British in West Sumatra, 1685-1825*, 1965. Documents, chiefly from the East India Company's archives.

*Boxer, C.R. *The Dutch Seaborne Empire, 1600-1800*, 1965. Quickly became the "standard" work on the subject.

Cares, P.B. *The Dutch Conquest of the Malay Archipelago, Ceylon, Formosa, and the European Trade with Japan* (ms. PhD thesis, Michigan, 1941).

Chou, Y-M. *The Role of International Trade in the Economic Development of Southeast Asia, with particular reference to Malaya and Indonesia* (PhD thesis, Illinois, 1960; DA v. 20, p. 4564).

Day, C. *The Dutch in Java*, 1907, RP1966.

DeKlerck, E.S. *History of the Netherlands East Indies*, 1938.

Fraser, T.M. *The Fishermen of South Thailand: The Malay Villagers*, 1966.

Furnivall, J.S. *Netherlands India: A Study of Plural Economy*, 1939, R1967.

*Glamann, K. *Dutch-Asiatic Trade, 1620-1740*, tr. N. Haislund, 1958 (PhD thesis, Copenhagen). Statistical details which reverse some earlier opinions – cotton cloth overtook pepper in value, while other spices were never much in volume and the Dutch never established a real monopoly. Explains relation of East India Company to government, and its accounting methods.

Gould, W.J. *American Interests in Sumatra, 1784 to 1873* (ms. PhD thesis, Fletcher, 1955). Revises some of the earlier accounts about the early secrecy.

*Hahn, E. (Mrs. C.R. Boxer) *Raffles of Singapore, a Biography*, 1946. Sir Stamford Raffles, governor of Java during the British occupation 1811-16 and founder of Singapore. Unlike his earlier biographers – Lady Raffles, H.E. Egerton, D. E. Boulger, J.A.B. Cook, and Sir Reginald Coupland – this makes extensive use of Dutch sources.

Hyma, A. *The Dutch in the Far East: A History of the Dutch Commercial and Colonial Empire*, 1942. More rambling and less useful than Vlekke below.

Irwin, G.W. *British and Dutch Policy in Borneo, 1809-88* (ms. PhD thesis, Cambridge, 1953).

Kerr, W.L. *The Malayan Tin Industry to 1914*, 1965.

Makepeace, W., et al. *One Hundred Years of Singapore (1819-1919)*, 2 v. 1921.

*Masselman, G. *The Cradle of Colonialism*, 1964. Early Dutch policy in the East Indies, with particular emphasis on Jan Pieterzoon Coen.

Meilink-Roelofsz, M.A.P. *Asian Trade and European Influence.* . . . 1962.

Mills, L. *British Malaya, 1824-1867*, 1925, R1966.

*Morison, S.E. *The Maritime History of Massachusetts, 1783-1860*, 1921, RP1961. Ch. 7, The Salem East Indies.

Parkinson, C.N. *British Intervention in Malaya, 1867-1877*, 1960, RP1965.

*Parr, C.M. *The Voyages of David DeVries: Navigator and Adventurer.* . . . 1965. Played prominent role in early Dutch Java as well as in Dutch America.

Phillips, J.D. *Pepper and Pirates: Adventures in the Sumatra Pepper Trade of Salem*, 1949. See also a similar work by G.G. Putnam, 1922, Phillips' general works on Salem, and also Gould above.

Sandin, B. *The Sea Dyaks of Borneo before White Rajah Rule*, 1968.

Shein, M. *The Role of Transport and Foreign Trade in the Economic Development of Burma under British Rule (1885-1914)* (ms. PhD thesis, Cambridge, 1960).

Tarling, N. *Piracy and Politics in the Malay World: A Study of British Imperialism in Nineteenth-Century South-East Asia*, 1963.
————. *Anglo-Dutch Rivalry in the Malay World, 1780-1824*, 1962.

Tickner, F.J. *The Rise of the Dutch East India Company* (ms. DPhil thesis, Oxford, 1952).

Tomlinson, H.M. *Malay Waters: The Story of the Ships Coasting Out of Singapore and Penang in Peace and War*, 1950.

Tregonning, K.G. *Home Port Singapore: A History of Straits Steamship Co., Ltd., 1890-1965*, 1967.

*Vlekke, B.H.M. *The Story of the Dutch East Indies*, 1945. The most useful brief survey of the subject, a condensation of his *Nusantara, a History of the East Indian Archipelago*, 1943, omitting principally part of the passage on pre-Dutch culture.

Wolters, O.W. *Early Indonesian Commerce and the Origin of Srivilaya* (ms. PhD thesis, London, 1962).

Young, R.J. *The English East India Company's Trade on the West Coast of Sumatra, 1730-1760* (PhD thesis, Pennsylvania, 1970; DA v. 31, p. 2821A).

Zoal, A. *Trade Relations between the Netherlands East Indies and the United States of America* (ms. PhD thesis, Berkeley, 1925).

AK   EAST ASIA (FAR EAST)

AK – 1   General

Allen, G.C. and Donnithorne, A.G. *Western Enterprise in Far Eastern Development: China and Japan*, 1954.

Callahan, J.M. *American Relations in the Pacific and the Far East 1784-1900*, 1901, R1969.

*Fellner, F.V. *Communications in the Far East*, 1934. "Development of all forms in the last century." Good account of Japanese and Chinese shipping, as well as foreign lines to East Asia.

Field, F.V., ed. *Economic Handbook of the Pacific Area*, 1934. Includes China and Japan.

Kirker, J. *Adventurers to China. Americans in the Southern Oceans, 1792-1812*, 1970. Special emphasis on the killing of seals on South Pacific islands for the Canton market.

Paullin, C.O. *American Voyages to the Orient, 1690-1865*, 1971. Reprint of the five articles in U.S. Naval Institute *Proceedings*, 1910-11. Chiefly naval voyages.

Radius, W.A., Jr. *United States Shipping in Trans-Pacific Trade, 1922-1938*, 1944 (PhD thesis, Stanford).

Spence, J. *To Change China: Western Approaches to China, 1620-1960*, 1968.

Warburg, J.P. *Western Intruders: America's Role in the Far East*, 1967.

Woodcock, G. *The British in the Far East* (A Social History of the British Overseas), 1969.

Wright, P.G. *Trade and Trade Barriers in the Pacific*, 1935. Statistical.

AK – 2   China to 1839

*Boxer, C.R. *Fidalgos in the Far East, 1550-1770*, 1954, R1970. The Portuguese in Macao.
* —————. *The Great Ship from Amacon: Annals of Macao and the Old Japan Trade, 1555-1640*, 1962. Annual Portuguese voyages, similar to the Spanish Manila-Acapulco service, Macao-Japan, to avoid China's rigid Canton restrictions.

*Dulles, F.R. *The Old China Trade*, 1930, R1970. A very readable survey. Another is S. and M. Greenbie, *Gold of Ophir*, 1925.

Eang, C.W. *Some Aspects of British Trade and Finance in Canton, with special reference to the Role of Anglo-Spanish Trade in the Eastern Seas, 1784-1834* (ms. PhD thesis, London, 1963).

Greenberg, M. *British Trade and the Opening of China, 1800-1842*, 1951, R1969.

Hudson, G.F. *Europe and China: A Survey of Their Relations from the Earliest Times to 1800*, P1961.

*Latourette, K.S. *The History of the Early Relations between the United States and China, 1784-1844*, 1917 (PhD thesis, Yale), R1964.
————. *Voyages of American Shipping to China, 1784-1844*, 1927.

*Macartney, G.M. *An Embassy to China: Being the Journal Kept by Lord Macartney During his Embassy to the Emperor Ch'ien-lung, 1793-1794*, ed. J.L. Cranmer-Byng, 1962. A record of the frustrating efforts to overcome the polite but persistent Chinese evasions.

*Morse, H.B. *The Chronicle of the East India Company Trading to China, 1635-1834*, 5 v. 1926-29, R1965. The standard detailed work.

Owen, D.E. *British Opium Policy in China and India*, 1934 (PhD thesis, Yale), R1968.

Schantz, R.N. *The Image of China in the Age of Discovery* (PhD thesis, New York Univ., 1968; DA v. 29, p. 3962A).

*Scott, J.M. *The Great Tea Venture*, 1965. The whole story of the tea trade from the beginnings at Canton.

Snyder, J.W., Jr. *The Early American China Trade: A Maritime History of Its Establishment, 1783-1815* (ms. PhD thesis, N.Y. Univ., 1940). Bibliography published in *Americana*, v. 32, No. 4.

Stelle, C.C. *Americans and the China Opium Trade in the Nineteenth Century* (ms. PhD thesis, Chicago, 1939).

White, A.B. *The Hong Merchants of Canton* (PhD thesis, Pennsylvania, 1967; DA v. 29, p. 203A).

Wood, J.B. *The American Response to China, 1784-1844: Consensus Policy and the Origin of the East India Squadron* (PhD thesis, Duke, 1969; DA v. 31, p. 349A).

Yi-Yi, M. *English Trade in the South China Sea, 1670-1715* (ms. PhD thesis, London, 1958).

AK – 3   China since 1839

Boxer, B. *Ocean Shipping in the Evolution of Hong Kong*, P1961.

Chang, H-P. *Commissioner Lin and the Opium War* (Harvard East Asian Series), 1964.

Chiu, H.Y. *The Development of the Foreign Trade of China and Its Trade with the United Kingdom* (ms. PhD thesis, Birmingham, 1953).

Davis, S.G. *The Geographic Growth and Development of Hong Kong, 1841-1941* (ms. PhD thesis, London, 1947).

Dean, B. *Sino-British Relations, 1860-1864. The Implication of the Commercial Provisions of the Treaty of Tientsin during the Ministership of Frederick Bruce* (PhD thesis, Columbia, 1969; DA v. 30, p. 4367A).

Dernberger, R.F. *The Foreign Trade and Capital Movements of Communist China* (ms. PhD thesis, Harvard, 1965).

Endacott, G.B. and Hinton, A. *Fragrant Harbour: A Short History of Hong Kong,* 1962, RP1969.
*——————. *An Eastern Entrepôt,* 1965. A collection of documents concentrating on the commercial foundations of Hong Kong and the 19th-century outlook on the entrepôt function.

*Fairbank, J.K. *Trade and Diplomacy on the China Coast: The Opening of the Treaty Ports, 1842-1854,* 2 v. 1953, R1969. The main text is all in the first volume; the slender second volume consists of bibliography, notes, etc. Based in part on his DPhil thesis, Oxford.

Fox, G. *British Admirals and Chinese Pirates, 1832-1860,* 1960 (PhD thesis, Columbia).

Greenberg, M.M. *British Trade and the Opening of China, 1800-1842,* 1951 (PhD thesis, Cambridge). Based largely on the files of the important firm of Jardine, Matheson & Co.

*Griffin, E. *Clippers and Consuls: American Consular and Commercial Relations with Eastern Asia, 1845-1860,* 1938 (PhD thesis, Yale). Wealth of interesting case histories scarcely available elsewhere. Copies of a second typescript "extension volume" in 1954 were deposited in Harvard Business School and Berkeley. Extensive bibliography.

Hao, Y-P. *The Comprador in Nineteenth-Century China: Bridge Between East and West* (Harvard East Asia Studies), 1970.

Holt, E. *The Opium Wars in China,* 1964. Includes the second war, 1856-60 though it was not properly caused by opium. More proper term in next entry.

Hurd, D. *The Arrow War: An Anglo-Chinese Confusion, 1856-1860,* 1968.

Knight, B.L. *American Trade and Investment in China, 1890-1910* (PhD thesis, Michigan State, 1968; DA v. 30, p. 248A).

Kuo, C-Y. *British Trade in China, 1894-1914* (ms. PhD thesis, Wisconsin, 1948).

*Liu, K-C. *Anglo-American Steamship Rivalry in China, 1862-1874,* 1962 (PhD thesis, Harvard).

Lubbock, B. *The China Clippers,* 1914, R1954. The successors to the big American California clippers. See also MacGregor below.
——————. *The Opium Clippers.* See Sect. I.

*MacGregor, D.R. *The Tea Clippers: An Account of the China Tea Trade and Some of the British Ships Engaged in It from 1849 to 1869*, 1952. Written by an architect, it includes diagrams and analyses of design of some of the ships, including the celebrated *Cutty Sark, Ariel* and *Taiping*; also tables of passages and speed records.

————. *The China Bird*, 1961. More of the same, based on the records of Killoch, Martin Co., "tea importing and clipper owning firm."

McCormick, T.J. *China Market: America's Quest for an Informal Empire, 1893-1901*, 1967, R1970.

Murphey, R. *Shanghai, Key to Modern China*, 1953. Outgrowth of PhD thesis, Harvard, 1950: *The Economic Geography of Shanghai: The Role of Water Transport in the Growth of the City*.

*Pelcovits, N.A. *Old China Hands and the Foreign Office*, 1948 (PhD thesis, Columbia), R1969. Interplay of economic pressure groups with British diplomacy.

Selby, J. *The Paper Dragon: An Account of the China Wars, 1840-1900*, 1968.

Smith, W.J. *The Development of British Interests in China at Three Ports on the Yangtse River, 1860-1870* (ms. PhD thesis, Michigan, 1938).

*Swisher, E. *China's Management of the American Barbarians: A Study in Sino-American Relations, 1841-1861, with Documents*, 1954 (PhD thesis, Harvard). Includes translation of 544 Chinese documents.

Szczepanik, E.F. *The Economic Growth of Hong Kong*, 1960 (PhD thesis, London).

Willem, J.M. *The United States Trade Dollar: America's Only Unwanted, Unhonored Coin*, 1959. Counterpart of the popular Mexican dollar; coined for the China trade, 1873-78, 1887-91.

*Worcester, G.R.G. *Junks and Sampans of the Yangtse*, 2 v. 1948. The product of long research by a veteran official of the Chinese maritime customs.

AK – 4   Japan, General

Ballard, G.A. *The Influence of the Sea on the Political History of Japan*, 1921. By the same British admiral who analyzed the history of Indian Ocean strategy.

AK – 5   Japan to 1867

Beasley, W.G. *Great Britain and the Opening of Japan*, 1952 (PhD thesis, London).

*Boxer, C.R. *The Christian Century in Japan, 1549-1650*, 1951, R1969. Jesuit missionary work and Portuguese trade with Macao, finally brusquely terminated by the Tokugawas.

*——————. *The Great Ship from Amacon.* . . . 1962. See comments, Sect. AK-2.

*——————. *Jan Compagnie in Japan, 1600-1817; An Essay on the Artistic and Scientific Influences Exercised by the Hollanders in Japan from the Seventeenth Century to the Nineteenth Century,* 1936, R1969. Story of the Dutch trading concession at Deshima, the one leak in Japan's pre-Perry isolation.

Cole, A.B., ed. *Yankee Surveyors in the Shogun's Seas: Records of the U.S. Surveying Expedition to the North Pacific Ocean, 1853-1856,* 1947, R1969. The important Perry expedition itself is taken up later in the 1815-1860 section (BB-2) of naval activity.

Dulles, F.R. *Yankees and Samurai: America's Role in the Emergence of Modern Japan, 1791-1900,* 1965.

Eckel, P.E. *The Revival of European Economic Interest in Japan from 1800 to 1855* (ms. PhD thesis, Southern California, 1941).

Knauth, L.G. *Pacific Confrontation: Japan Encounters the Spanish Overseas Empire* (ms. PhD thesis, Harvard, 1970). Covers 1542-1630 period; see also Boxer above.

Lensen, G.A. *Russia's Japan Expedition of 1852 to 1855,* 1956 (PhD thesis, Columbia).
——————. *The Russian Push toward Japan,* 1959, R1970. Carries story to 1875.

McMaster, J. *British Trade and Traders in Japan, 1859-69* (ms. PhD thesis, London, 1962).

Rogers, P.G. *The First Englishman in Japan,* 1956. Will Adams, who arrived in 1600 as pilot for the Dutch and was active there for some time. His letters, 1611 to 1617, were published by the Hakluyt Society, Series 1, v. 8 as *Memorials of the Empire of Japan,* ed. T. Rundall, 1850.

Saris, J. *The Voyage of Captain John Saris to Japan in 1613* (Hakluyt Society, Series II, v. 5), 1900, 1967.

AK – 6   Japan since 1867

Borgstrom, G. *Japan's World Success in Fishing,* 1964. "Outlines the whole range of Japan's fishery enterprises, historically and commercially."

Boyer, S.P. *Naval Surgeon: The Diary of Dr. Samuel Pellman Boyer,* ed. E. and J.A. Barnes, 2 v. 1963. Vol. 2, Revolt in Japan, 1868-69.

Dulles, F.R. *Yankees and Samurai.* . . . See AK-5.

Haitani, K. *Japan's Export Trade: Its Structure and Problems* (ms. PhD thesis, Ohio State, 1965).

Hattori, Y. *The Foreign Commerce of Japan since the Restoration, 1869-1900,* 1904 (PhD thesis, Johns Hopkins).

*Hunsberger, W.S. *Japan and the United States in World Trade* (Council on Foreign Relations), 1964. "The volume's main value lies in the assembly of statistical data and institutional information about the postwar Japanese trade position."

Institute of Pacific Relations, *Trade and Trade Rivalry between the United States and Japan*, 1936.

Lensen, G.A., ed. *Trading Under Sail Off Japan, 1868 to 1889*, 1968. Memoirs of Captain John Baxter Will.

*Lockwood, W.W. *The Economic Development of Japan: Growth and Structural Change, 1868-1938*, 1954. Ch. 6-7, Foreign Trade and Economic Growth.

Neumann, W.L. *America Encounters Japan: From Perry to MacArthur*, 1963, RP1969. Analysis of American attitudes.

The Oriental Economist, *The Foreign Trade of Japan: A Statistical Summary*, 1935.

*Sheldon, C.S. *The Japanese Shipping Industry: An Analysis of Some Phases of the Industry in Relation to International Economic Rivalries* (ms. PhD thesis, Harvard, 1942).

U.S. State Department, *Japan's Shipping and Shipbuilding Position, 1928-36*, 1948.

AK – 7   Philippines

Guzman-Rivas, P. *Reciprocal Geographic Influences of the Trans-Pacific Galleon Trade* (PhD thesis, Texas, 1960; DA v. 21, p. 1905). See also Schurz below.

Irikara, J.K. *Trade and Diplomacy between the Philippines and Japan, 1585-1623* (ms. PhD thesis, Yale, 1958).

Lacebal, A. *International Trade and the Stability of a Dependent Economy: The Philippines, 1900-54* (ms. MEcon thesis, Sydney, 1957).

*Leebrick, K.C. *The English Expedition to Manila in 1762 and the Government of the Philippine Islands by the East India Company* (ms. PhD thesis, Berkeley, 1917).

Legarda, B.F., Jr. *The Philippine Economy*, 1958. Based on PhD thesis, Harvard, 1955, *Foreign Trade, Economic Change and Entrepreneurship in the Nineteenth Century Philippines*.

Palma, A. de L. *Economic History of the Philippines* (ms. PhD thesis, Berkeley, 1931).

Quiason, S.D. *English Trade Relations with the Philippines, 1644-1765* (PhD thesis, Pennsylvania, 1962; DA v. 23, p. 3339).

*Schurz, W.L. *The Manila Galleon*, 1939, RP1959. Ch. 1 is an excellent account of Manila's chief raison d'etre as an entrepôt between Mexican silver and China's silk and other exports. See further comments, Sect. AH-2.

AL THE PACIFIC AND AUSTRALASIA

AL – 1 General

Anderson, C.R. *Melville in the South Seas*, 1966.

Bassett, M. *Behind the Picture: H.M.S.* Rattlesnake's *Australia-New Guinea Cruise, 1846 to 1850*, 1966.

*Cambridge History of the British Empire, 8 v. 1929-40; v. 7, Australia-New Zealand. Ample bibliography.

Coulter, J.W. *The Pacific Dependencies of the United States*, 1957.

Davidson, J.W. *European Penetration of the South Pacific, 1779-1842* (ms. PhD thesis, Cambridge, 1942). See also Beaglehole, Sect. AL-2.

Docker, E.W. *The Blackbirders: The Recruiting of South Sea Labour for Queensland, 1863-1907*, 1971. See also Holthouse, Lubbock and Parnaby below.

**Dodge, E.S. *New England and the South Seas*, 1965. See also Wood below.

Field, F.V., ed. *Economic Handbook of the Pacific Area*, 1934.

Grattan, C.H. *The United States and the Southwest Pacific*, 1961.
**————. *The Southwest Pacific to 1900, a Modern History: Australia, New Zealand, the Islands, Antarctica*, 1963.
**————. *The Southwest Pacific since 1900*. . . . 1963. Excellent comprehensive coverage.

Holthouse, H. *Cannibal Cargoes*, 1969. "Blackbirding" of South Sea islanders for Queensland sugar plantations.

**Lewin, P.E. *The Pacific Region: A Bibliography of the Pacific and East Indian Islands, Exclusive of Japan*, 1944.
————. *Best Books on Australia and New Zealand: An Annotated Bibliography*, 1946.

Lubbock, B. *Bully Hayes, South Sea Pirate*, 1931. Another account of the same rascal, who ranged far and wide, is A.T. Saunders, *Bully Hayes, Barrator, Bigamist, Buccaneer, Blackbirder and Pirate*, 1915.

Martin, K.L.P. *Missionaries and Annexation in the Pacific*, 1925.

**Moorehead, A. *The Fatal Impact: An Account of the Invasion of the South Pacific, 1767-1840*, P1966. The effect of European contacts upon the natives, from the first visits to Tahiti to the annexation of New Zealand, with special attention to the Cook voyages.

**Morrell, W.P. *Britain in the Pacific Islands*, 1960.

Parnaby, O.W. *Britain and the Labor Trade in the Southwest Pacific*, 1966. Based on Oxford DPhil thesis, *The Policy of the Imperial Government towards the Recruitment and Use of Pacific Island Labour with special reference to Queensland, 1863-1901.* See also Docker and Holthouse above.

Purcell, D.C., Jr. *Japanese Expansion in the South Pacific, 1890-1935* (PhD thesis, Pennsylvania, 1967; DA v. 28, p. 4102A).

Radius, W.A. *United States Shipping in Trans-Pacific Trade, 1922-1938,* 1968.

Rhodes, F.C. *Pageant of the Pacific, Being the Maritime History of Australasia,* 2 v. 1937. A somewhat rambling account, by a sea captain, who brought together some interesting information.

Roe, M., ed. *The Journal and Letters of Captain Charles Bishop on the North-West Coast of America, in the Pacific, and in New South Wales, 1794-1799* (Hakluyt Society), 1967.

*Schurz, W.L. *The Manila Galleon.* See Sects. AH-2, AK-7.

Spoehr, A., ed. *Pacific Port Towns and Cities,* 1963.

Strauss, W.P. *Americans in Polynesia, 1783-1842,* 1963 (PhD thesis, Columbia).

*Wood, R.G., with introduction by E.S. Dodge, *American Activities in the Central Pacific, 1790-1870, A History, Geographical and Ethnographical, Pertaining to American Involvement and Americans in the Pacific, taken from Contemporary Newspapers, etc.,* 7 v. 1966-67, with atlas as part of v. 1. A well-indexed mine of information about men, ships and places.

Wright, P.G. *Trade and Trade Barriers in the Pacific,* 1935.

AL – 2   Pacific Exploration

Because of the large volume of works, these have all been assembled here rather than with the other "Major Regional Exploration" in Sect. Q-4.

Barbeau, M. *Pathfinders of the North Pacific,* 1958.

*Beaglehole, J.C. *The Exploration of the Pacific,* 1934, R1966. The most convenient approach to the subject; covers the 250 years from Magellan to Cook.
————. *The Discovery of New Zealand,* 1935, R1961. Disagrees with Sharp, below, on the original Polynesian voyages.
*————. ed. *The Journals of Captain James Cook on His Voyages of Discovery* (Hakluyt Society), 4 v. 1955-67. A monumental work.

Bougainville, L.A. de. *A Voyage Round the World,* 1967. The second European visit to the South Seas, in 1768.

Corney, P. *Early Voyages in the Northern Pacific, 1813-1818,* 1896, R1966.

Dale, P.W. *Seventy North to Fifty South: Captain Cook's Last Voyage,* 1969.

Day, A.G. *Explorers of the Pacific*, 1967.

*Dodge, E.S. *Beyond the Capes: Pacific Exploration from Captain Cook to the* Challenger, 1971.

*Dunmore, J. *French Explorers in the Pacific*, 2 v. 1965-69. Vol. 1, 18th century; vol. 2, 19th century.

Flinders, M. *A Voyage to Terra Australis*, 1966. Captain Flinders was the first to circumnavigate Australia.

*Friis, H.R., ed. *The Pacific Basin: A History of Its Geographical Exploration* (American Geog. Society, Special Publication, No. 38), 1967. A valuable comprehensive cooperative work.

*Golder, F.A. *Russian Expansion in the Pacific, 1641-1850, an Account of the Earliest and Later Expeditions Made by the Russians along the Pacific Coast of Asia and North America*, 1910 (PhD thesis, Harvard).
———. *Bering's Voyage: An Account of the Efforts of the Russians to Determine the Relation of Asia and America*, 2 v. 1922-25, R1968.

Gschaedler, A. *Mexico and the Pacific, 1540-1565: The Voyages of Villalobos and Legazpi and the Preparations Made for Them* (MA thesis, Melbourne, 1946; PhD thesis, Columbia, 1954; DA v. 14, p. 1372).

Heyerdahl, T. *Sea Routes to Polynesia*, 1967. Argument for two waves, one from South America and the other from Asia, by the *Kon Tiki* experimenter.

Jack-Hinton, C. *The Search for the Islands of Solomon, 1567-1838*, 1969. "Discovery, rediscovery and exploration of the Solomon Islands from Mendoza's expedition."

LaPerouse, I.F. *Voyages and Adventures*, tr. J.S. Gassner, 1969.

Lloyd, C. *William Dampier*, 1966.

Lubbock, A. *Owen Stanley, RN, 1811-1850: Captain of the* Rattlesnake, 1969. Devoted more than a quarter century to scientific exploration; discovered Inner Passage of Great Barrier Reef.

Mack, J.D. *Matthew Flinders, 1774-1814*, 1966.

Perry, T.M. and Simpson, D.H., eds. *Drawings by William Westall*. . . . See Sect. H-1.

Robertson, G. *The Discovery of Tahiti*. . . . See Sect. AL-6.

Sharp, A. *Ancient Voyagers in the Pacific*, P1958. Claims that the voyages of the Polynesians to New Zealand and Hawaii resulted from being accidentally blown off course on short runs, rather than deliberate migrations depending on skillful navigation. See also Heyerdahl above.
———. *The Discovery of the Pacific Islands*, 1960. Less controversial, this

has been called "the most accurate account of the sequence of European discovery."

*————. *The Voyages of Abel Janzsoon Tasman*, 1968. Discovered Australia, etc.

Skelton, R.A. *Captain James Cook, After Two Hundred Years*, 1969.

Williamson, J.A. *Cook and the Opening of the Pacific*, 1946.

Wood, G.A. *The Discovery of Australia*, 1922, R1969.

AL – 3   Australia

Abbott, G.N., et al. *Economic Growth of Australia, 1788-1821*, 1969.

Appleyard, R.T. *British Emigration to Australia*, 1964.

Bateson, C. *The Convict Ships, 1787-1888*, 1959, R1969. Transportation of prisoners from the British Isles to Australia.

*————. *Gold Fleet for California; Forty-Niners from Australia and New Zealand*, 1964.

Bird, J. *Seaport Gateways of Australia*, 1968.

Bowden, K.M. *Captain James Kelly of Hobart Town*, 1965. "The adventurous life of a tough Australian."

Britton, J.N.H. *The Ports of Victoria*, P1965.

Burley, K. *British Shipping and Australasia, 1920-1939*, 1967.

Clune, F. *Bound for Botany Bay: Narrative of a Voyage in 1798 Aboard the Death Ship* Hillsborough, 1965.

Cobley, J. *Sydney Cove, 1788*, 1962. A day-by-day account, based on the records, of the first year of the New South Wales convict settlement.

*Cumpston, J.S., comp. *Shipping Arrivals and Departures, Sydney, 1788-1825*, P1963.

Easty, J. *Transaction of a Voyage from England to Botany Bay, 1787-1793*, 1965. Diary of a marine private in the "First Fleet."

Eddy, J.J. *Britain and the Australian Colonies, 1818-1831*, 1969.

Fitzpatrick, B. *British Imperialism and Australia, 1783-1833, an Economic History of Australasia*, 1939.

*————. *The British Empire in Australia; An Economic History, 1834-1939*, 1941, R1970.

Gregory, D. *Australian Steamships, Past and Present*, 1928.

Lawson, W. *Bluegum Clippers and Whale Ships of Tasmania*, 1949.

Lubbock, B. *The Colonial Clippers*, 1921, R1968. See Sect. I.

Macknight, C.C. *The Farthest Coast*, 1969. Earliest voyages and attempts to settle the northern coast of Australia.

Mathieson, R.S. *The Commercial Fisheries of South-eastern Australia* (ms. PhD thesis, London, 1961).

Mitchell, J.W. *New South Wales, 1800-1900: A Case Study in the Staple Theory* (PhD thesis, Oregon, 1970; DA v. 31, p. 5011A).

Mudie, I. *Riverboats*, 1961. Australian inland navigation.

Phillip, A. *The Voyage of Governor Phillip to Botany Bay*, 1968.

Roughley, T.C. *Fish and Fisheries of Australia*, 1957, 4th ed. 1966.

Villiers, A.J. *Vanished Fleets; Ships and Men of Old Van Dieman's Land*, 1931. One of the first of his many books; he is a native of Tasmania, originally called Van Dieman's Land.
——————. *Convict Ships and Sailors*, 1936. See also Bateson above.
——————. *The Coral Sea*, 1949. History from the early Spanish contacts to the present.

Williams, P.J. and Serle, R. *Ships in Australian Waters: A Pictorial History from the Days of the Early Explorers to the Present Time*, 1968.

AL – 4   New Zealand

*Beaglehole, J.C. *New Zealand – A Short History*, 1936.

Brett, H. *White Wings: Fifty Years of Sail in the New Zealand Trade*, 1924.

Franklin, E.C. *A Century of Auckland Commerce, 1856-1956: A History of the Auckland Chamber of Commerce*, 1956.

Hawkins, C. *A Survey of the Commercial Sailing Craft Built in the Auckland Province and in Particular Those Sailing Out of Auckland*, 1960.

Kirk, A.A. *Express Steamers of Cook Strait*, 1968. Connecting North and South Islands. See Lambert below.

Lambert, M., et al. *The* Wahine *Disaster*, 1969. Cook Island ferry capsized with loss of 51 lives in 1968.

Ross, A. *New Zealand's Aspirations in the Pacific in the Nineteenth Century*, 1964. Expansion among the islands. (PhD thesis, Cambridge, 1949).

Ross, H. *A History of the Post Office in New Zealand*, 1964. Interesting account of communications methods.

Ross, J. *The White Ensign in New Zealand*, 1967. Naval involvement in expansion.

Stewart, I.G. *The Ships that Serve New Zealand*, v. 1, 1964.

Tapp, E.J. *Early New Zealand: A Dependency of New South Wales, 1788-1841*, 1958. Ch. 3, Trade and Commerce; appendix B, List of vessels visiting the Bay of Islands; appendix 9, Trade of New South Wales with New Zealand.

AL – 5   Hawaii

*Bradley, H.W. *The American Frontier in Hawaii: The Pioneers, 1789-1843*, 1942.

(Castle & Cook) *The First 100 Years: A Report on the Operations of Castle & Cook for the Years 1851-1951*, 1956.

Damon, E.M. *Sanford Ballard Dole and His Hawaii*, 1957.

Davis, G. *School of Time; A History of the Hawaiian Islands*, 1969.

Daws, A.G. *Honolulu – The First Century: Influences in the Development of the Town to 1876* (PhD thesis, Hawaii, 1966; DA v. 27, p. 1751A).

Gesler, C. *Tropic Landfall: The Port of Honolulu* (Seaport Series), 1942.

*Morgan, J.T. *Hawaii: A Century of Economic Change, 1778-1876*, 1948 (PhD thesis, Harvard).

Smith, B. *Yankees in Paradise: The New England Impact on Hawaii*, 1956.

Snowbarger, W.E. *The Development of Pearl Harbor* (ms. PhD thesis, Berkeley, 1951).

AL – 6   Other Pacific

Adams, H.B. *Memoirs of Arii Taimai of Tahiti*, 1968.

Akerblam, K. *Astronomy and Navigation in Polynesia and Micronesia*, 1968.

Brookes, J.I. *Anglo-French Rivalry in the Pacific Islands, 1815-1861* (ms. PhD thesis, Chicago, 1927).

Cockrum, E.E. *The Emergence of Modern Micronesia* (PhD thesis, Colorado, 1970; DA v. 31, p. 4665A).

Cumpston, J.S. *Macquarie Island*, 1968. Sealskins, sea elephants and penguins.

Legge, J.D. *Britain in Fiji, 1858-1880*, 1959.

Maude, H.E. *Of Islands and Men, Studies in Pacific History*, 1969. Collection of colorful South Sea episodes by a specialist in the life of the islands.

Meares, J. *Voyages made in the Years 1788 and 1789 from China to the North-West Coast of America*, 1790, R1967. Meares, who had been an officer under Cook, was a leader in the international rivalry for the sea otter region.

Nicolson, R.B. *The Pitcairners*, 1966. Descendants of the *Bounty* mutineers and Tahitian natives, living on into modern times.

*Nordhoff, C. and Hall, C.N. *Mutiny on the Bounty*. See Sect. O-1. Also G. Rawson, Pandora's *Last Voyage*.

Richard, D.E. *History of United States Naval Administration of the Trust Territory of the Pacific Islands* (Office of the Chief of Naval Operations), 3 v. 1957-63.

*Robertson, G. *The Discovery of Tahiti, a Journal of the 2nd Voyage of H.M.S. Dolphin Round the World, Under the Command of Captain Wallis, RN, in the Years 1766, 1767, and 1768, Written by Her Master*, ed. Hugh Carrington (Hakluyt Society Pub., 2nd Series, No. 98), 1948. Includes a play-by-play account of the first European contact with South Sea glamor at Tahiti in 1767, one year ahead of Bougainville, two years ahead of Cook, and twenty years ahead of the *Bounty* mutiny. The journal has also been privately published and is the basis of N.A. Rowe, *A Voyage to the Amorous Islands: The Discovery of Tahiti*, 1956. All are well illustrated with original drawings. See also Bougainville, Sect. AL-2.

Shineberg, D. *They Came for Sandalwood: A Study of the Sandalwood Trade in the South West Pacific*, 1968.

Stevenson, R.L. *In the South Seas: A Footnote to History*, 1896.

Thacker, J.W. *The Partition of Samoa* (PhD thesis, Univ. of So. Carolina, 1966; DA v. 28, p. 182A).

Wallis, M.D. *Life in Feejee, or Five Years among the Cannibals*, 1857, R1967.

Woodward, R.L., Jr. *Robinson Crusoe's Island: A History of the Juan Fernandez Islands*, 1969.

AM   WHALING AND FISHING

AM – 1   Whaling

Bennett, A.G. *Whaling in the Antarctic*, 1932.

Bock, P.G. *A Study in International Regulations: The Case of Whaling* (PhD thesis, New York Univ., 1966; DA v. 27, p. 2583A).

Bowden, K.M. *Captain James Kelly of Hobart Town*, 1965. See Sect. AL-3.

*Brewington, M.V. and D. *Kendall Whaling Museum Paintings*, 1966. See Sect. H-1.

Budker, P. *Whales and Whaling*, 1959. Modern.

Chase, O. *Narrative of the Most Extraordinary and Distressing Shipwreck of the Whaleship* Essex. . . . 1821, RP1963. Introduction by B.R. McElderry, Jr. Sunk by a whale.

Church, A.C. *Whaleships and Whaling*, 1938, R1960. "Picture book," with more than 200 photographs plus 40 pages of text.

Dow, G.F. *Whale Ships and Whaling*, 1925, R1967.

*Dulles, F.R. *Lowered Boats, a Chronicle of American Whaling*, 1933.

Edwards, E.J. and Rattray, J.E. *"Whale Off!" The Story of American Shore Whaling*, 2 v. 1932; R, 1 v. 1956.

Ely, B-E.S. *"There She Blows" A Narrative of a Whaling Voyage, in the Indian and South Atlantic Oceans*, 1971. Reprint by American Maritime Library of 1849 text, edited by C. Dahl, Ely's great-grandson.

Fonda, D.C., Jr. *Eighteenth Century Nantucket Whaling*, P1969.

*Garner, S., ed. *The Captain's Best Mate: The Journal of Mary Chipman Lawrence on the Whaler* Addison, *1856-1860*, 1966.

Haley, N.C. *Whale Hunt*, 1948, R1967.

*Hawes, C.B. *Whaling*, 1924.

Haywood, C.N. *American Whalers and Africa* (ms. PhD thesis, Boston Univ., 1967).

*Hegarty, R.B. and Puriton, P.F., comp. *Returns of Whaling Vessels Sailing from American Ports, 1876-1928; A Continuation of Alexander Starbuck's "History of the American Whale Fishery,"* 1959. Includes listing of Hawaiian whalers, 1832-1880. See also Starbuck below.
————. *Addendum to "Starbuck" and "Whaling Masters,"* 1964. See also U.S. Federal Writers Project, below.

*Hohman, E.P. *The American Whaleman: A Study of Life and Labor in the Whaling Industry*, 1928 (PhD thesis, Harvard), R1970.

*Jenkins, J.T. *A History of the Whale Fisheries*, 1921. Best general account for whaling of all nations and regions.

Lay, W. and Hussey, C.M. *Narrative of the Mutiny on Board the Ship* Globe, 1828, RP1963. Introduction by E.A. Stackpole.

Matthews, L.H., et al., eds. *The Whale*, 1968. Collection of source material, well illustrated.

Mielche, H. *There She Blows!*, 1954. Description of modern Norwegian whale ship.

Morgan, M. *Dixie Raider: The Saga of the CSS* Shenandoah, 1948. Includes destruction of American whaling fleet in Bering Sea after the Civil War had ended.

Munger, J.F. *Two Years in the Pacific.* . . . 1852, R1967. See Sect. O-5.

Murphy, R.C. *A Dead Whale or a Stove Boat*, 1967. See Sect. H-1.

Palmer, W.R. *The Whaling Port of Sag Harbor* (PhD thesis, Columbia, 1959; DA v. 20, p. 655).

Sawtell, C.C. *The Ship* Ann Alexander *of New Bedford, 1805-1851* (Marine Historical Assn., No. 40), 1962. Sunk by a whale.

Scamman, C.M. *The Marine Mammals of the Northwestern Coast.* . . . 1874, R1969.

Schultz, C.R. *Cost of Constructing and Outfitting the Ship* Charles W. Morgan, P1967.
————. *Statements of Profits and Losses for the Ship* Charles W. Morgan, *1863-1913*, P1967. Marine Historical Association Information Bulletins, 67-1, 67-2. The whaler *Morgan*, built in 1841, is still preserved at Mystic Seaport. See E.A. Stackpole below.

Scoresby, W.J. *An Account of the Arctic Regions, with a History and Description of the Northern Whale Fishery*, 2 v. 1820, R1969.

Sherman, S.C. *The Voice of the Whaleman, with an Account of the Nicholson Whaling Collection*, 1965. Guide to collection of 836 whaling logs, journals, and account books in the Providence Public Library.

*Stackpole, E.A. *The Sea Hunters*, 1953. The most comprehensive and authoritative account of early American whaling, by the former curator of Mystic Seaport and head of the Nantucket Historical Society. Carries the story through 1835 when the primacy was passing from Nantucket to New Bedford.
————. *The* Charles W. Morgan, *The Last Wooden Whaleship*, 1967. See also Schultz above.

*Stackpole, R.A. *American Whaling in Hudson Bay, 1861-1919* (Munson Institute of American Maritime History), P1969.

*Starbuck, A. *A History of the American Whaling Industry* . . . *to the Year 1876*, 1876; R, 2 v. 1964. The principal mine of information for details of particular ships and voyages, all of which are listed. Continued to 1928 by R.B. Hegarty, above.

*U.S. Federal Writers Project (WPB), *Whaling Masters, Voyages, 1731-1925*, 1938. Alphabetical list, with separate sailings, indicating year, ship, and port.

U.S. Survey of Federal Archives (WPB), *Ship Registers and Enrolments*, P1939-42. New Bedford, Mass., 3 v.

Venables, A. *Beleia, Beleia, Whale Hunters of the Azores,* 1968.

Whipple, A.B. *Yankee Whalers in the South Seas,* 1954. A series of colorful episodes which lose nothing in the telling.

AM – 2   Fisheries, General and Foreign

Allard, D.C. *Spencer Fullerton Baird and the U.S. Fish Commission: A Study in the History of American Science* (PhD thesis, George Washington, 1967; DA v. 28, p. 1750A).

Andrews, R.W. and Lassen, P.K. *Fish and Ships,* 1959.

Anson, P.F. *Scots Fisherfolk,* 1950.

Bartlett, N. *The Pearl Seekers,* 1954. History and description of pearl fishing on the Australian coast.

Blair, C.H., et al. *A Guide to Fishing Boats and Their Gear,* 1968.

Borgstrom, G. *Japan's World Success in Fishing,* 1964.
*————— and Heighway, A.J., eds. *Atlantic Ocean Fisheries,* 1961. "A complete picture of the fishing potential and practices of the Atlantic Oceans (North and South) with the Baltic and Mediterranean, followed by detailed descriptions of the fish catching, processing and marketing practices of all nations bordering on the Atlantic."

Brandt, A. von. *Fish Catching Methods of the World,* 1964.

Brody, J. *Fisheries By-Products Technology,* 1965.

Burgess, G.H.O., et al, eds. *Fish Handling and Processing,* 1967.

Christy, F.T., Jr. and Scott, A. *The Common Wealth in Ocean Fisheries,* 1965.

*Colman, J.S. *The Sea and Its Mysteries,* 1950. Ch. 9, Fish, Whales and their Migrations; ch. 11, Research and the Fisheries.

Craig, A.K. *Geography of Fishing in British Honduras and Adjacent Coastal Waters,* 1966.

Cushing, D.H. *The Arctic Cod,* 1966.

Eydal, A. *Some Geographical Aspects of the Fisheries of Iceland* (ms. PhD thesis, Univ. of Washington, 1964; DA v. 24, p. 1133).

Firth, R.W. *Malay Fishermen, Their Peasant Economy,* 1966. See also Fraser below.

Fishing News, *Mechanization of Small Fishing Craft,* 1965.

Fraser, T.M. *Fishermen of South Thailand: The Malay Villagers*, 1966.

Garcia-Amador, F.V. *The Exploration and Conservation of the Resources of the Sea* (ms. PhD thesis, Columbia, 1960).

Gillett, E. *A History of Grimsby*, 1970. Major fishing port on English East Coast.

Hardy, A.C. *Seafood Ships*, 1947.

Houk, R.J. *The Portuguese Maritime Fishing Industry* (ms. PhD thesis, Northwestern, 1951).

Howell, G.C. *Ocean Research and the Great Fisheries*, 1921.

International Labor Office (ILO), *Conditions of Work in the Fishing Industry*, 1952.

*Jenkins, J.T. *The Sea Fisheries*, 1920. Like his whaling volume above, this is an admirable comprehensive account.
*—————. *Herring and the Herring Fisheries*, 1927. See also Samuel below.

Kreuzer, R. *The Technology of Fish Utilization*, 1965.

Lounsbury, R.G. *The British Fishery at Newfoundland, 1643-1763*, 1969.

Maraini, F. *The Island of the Fisherwomen*, 1962. Contains many photographs of the girl divers on the western coast of Japan (*Hekura* in British edition).

*March, E.J. *Sailing Drifters. The Story of the Herring Luggers of England, Scotland and the Isle of Man*, 1953.
*—————. *Sailing Trawlers. The Story of Deep-Sea Fishing with Long Line and Trawl*, 1953.
—————. *Inshore Craft of Britain: In the Days of Sail and Oar*, 2 v. 1970.

Mathieson, R.R. *The Commercial Fisheries of South-eastern Australia* (ms. PhD thesis, London, 1961).

Matthews, K. *The West Country-Newfoundland Fisheries*. . . . See Sect. AF-4.

McManus, J.P. *Trade and Market in Fish in the London Area in the Early Sixteenth Century, 1485-1563* (ms. MA thesis, London, 1952).

Norbeck, E. *Takashima, a Japanese Fishing Village*, 1954 (PhD thesis, Michigan).

Ommanney, F.D. *The Ocean*, 1949, R1961. Ch. 8, Sea Fisheries; ch. 9, Whales and Whaling.
—————. *A Draught of Fishes*, 1966.

Roughley, T.C. *Fish and Fisheries of Australia*, 1957, 4th ed. 1966.

*Samuel, A.M. *The Herring: Its Effect on the History of Britain*, 1918. See also Jenkins above.

Sommers, L.M. *The Norwegian Fishing Industry, as Exemplified by More of Romsdal County* (ms. PhD thesis, Northwestern, 1951).

Syme, J.D. *Fish and Fish Inspection*, 1966.

Thomson, D.B. *The Seine Net*, 1969.

Traung, J-O., ed. *Fishing Boats of the World*, 1955. Seventy papers delivered at the International Fishing Boat Congress; Pt. 1, boat types; pt. 2, naval architecture; pt. 3, engineering; pt. 4, factory ships.

*Villiers, A.J. *The Quest of the Schooner* Argus: *A Voyage to the Banks and Greenland*, 1951. This prolific and tireless seagoing authority made a trip in a four-masted schooner in the Portuguese cod fleet in 1950.

Wilson, G. *Scottish Fishing Craft*, 1965.

Woolner, A.H. *A Comparative Geographical Study of the Exploitation of the Fishing Grounds of N.W. Europe by Britain and West Germany* (ms. PhD thesis, London, 1960).

The perennial troublesome question of fishing rights and territorial waters is considered in detail in the later section on "Fishery Rights and Territorial Waters" (Sect. BO-3).

AM – 3 Fisheries, North America, East Coast

Ackerman, E.A. *New England's Fishing Industry*, 1941.

Bartt, E.J., Jr. *An Economic Appraisal of the New England Fishing Industry* (ms. PhD thesis, Duke, 1950).

Bell, F.W. *The Economics of the New England Fishing Industry*, 1966.

Connolly, J.B. *The Port of Gloucester*, 1940.

DeGast, R. *The Oystermen of Chesapeake Bay*, 1970. See Sect. AC-2.

*Goode, G.B., et al. *The Fisheries and Fishing Industries of the United States* (U.S. Commission of Fish and Fisheries), 7 v. 1884-87. Extremely comprehensive survey, including two volumes of plates.

*Hawes, C.B. *Gloucester, by Land and Sea*, 1923, R1970.

*Innis, H.A. *The Cod Fisheries: The History of an International Economy*, 1940, R1954.

Liguori, V.A. *Stability and Change in the Structure of the Atlantic Coast Commercial Fisheries* (PhD thesis, Princeton, 1968; DA v. 29, p. 334A).

McFarland, R.A. *A History of the New England Fisheries*, 1911.

Miller, M.E. *The Delaware Oyster Industry: Past and Present* (ms. PhD thesis, Boston Univ., 1962).

Netboy, A. *The Atlantic Salmon: A Vanishing Species*, 1968.

Pierce, W.G. *Goin' Fishin'; The Story of the Deep-sea Fishermen of New England*, 1934. Good firsthand description of methods.

Quittmeyer, C.L. *The Seafood Industry of the Chesapeake Bay States of Maryland and Virginia: A Study in Private Management and Public Policy* (PhD thesis, Columbia, 1955; DA v. 16, p. 473).

Rothney, G.O. *British Policy in the North American Cod Fisheries, with special reference to Foreign Competition, 1776-1819* (ms. PhD thesis, London, 1939).

Strong, D. *Hail Columbia*. . . . See Sect. I.

*Thompson, E. *Draggerman's Haul: The Personal History of a Fishing Captain*, 1950. A full and frank account of successful activity afloat and ashore, by a New London, Connecticut fisherman; an unusually comprehensive and uninhibited case history.

*White, D.J. *The New England Fishing Industry: A Study in Price and Wage Setting*, 1954 (PhD thesis, Harvard). Analysis of conditions around Boston, Gloucester, New Bedford, Portland, and Rockland.

Wilson, R.P. *An Inquiry into the Use the English Inhabitants of Colonial Maine Made of the Fish and Game Resources of that Region* (ms. MA thesis, Maine, 1951).

AM – 4   Fisheries, North America, Gulf and Great Lakes

Howard, R.W., ed. *This is the South*, 1959. Ch. 23, Shrimp Fisheries.

Lassiter, R.L. *Utilization of U.S. Ottertrawl Shrimp Vessels in the Gulf Area, 1959-1961*, 1964.

Padgett, H.R. *The Marine Shell Fisheries of Louisiana* (PhD thesis, Louisiana State, 1908; DA v. 21, p. 588).

Saalfield, R.W. *Commercial Fish Production in the Great Lakes* (Great Lakes Fishery Commission, Technical Report No. 30.), 1962.

AM – 5   Fisheries, North America, West Coast

Cooley, R.A. *Decline of the Alaska Salmon, A Case Study in Conservation Policy* (PhD thesis, Michigan, 1962; DA v. 23, p. 686).

Crutchfield, J.A. *The Economics of the Pacific Coast Fresh Market Fish Industry* (ms. PhD thesis, Berkeley, 1955).

DeLoach, D.B. *The Salmon Canning Industry, with Particular Reference to Marketing* (ms. PhD thesis, Berkeley, 1915).

Dodds, G.B. *The Salmon King of Oregon: R.D. Hume and the Pacific Fisheries*, 1959, R1963.

Ingebritsen, H.R. *Roaming with Rita: Trolling with Salmon and Keeping Up with Affairs on Shore with Commercial Fishermen Working in Northwest Waters*, 1954. A delightful West Coast counterpart to the Ellery Thompson case history in Sect. AM-3.

*Johansen, D.O. and Gates, C.M. *Empire of the Columbia: A History of the Pacific Northwest*, 1957. Ch. 5, Harvests from the Sea.

Kelley, T.K. *The Commercial Fishery of Washington* (ms. PhD thesis, Univ. of Washington, 1947).

Peckham, E.T. *The Halibut Fishery of the Pacific Northwest* (ms. PhD thesis, Harvard, 1954).

Swygard, K.R. *The International Halibut and Sockeye Salmon Fisheries Commissions: A Study in International Control Administration* (ms. PhD thesis, Univ. of Washington, 1948).

*Walford, L.A. *Fishery Resources of the United States* (American Council on Public Affairs), 1947.

*Wick, C.I. *Ocean Harvest: The Story of Commercial Fishing in Pacific Coast Waters*, 1946.

AN   YACHTING AND SMALL BOAT VOYAGES

Baader, J., tr, J. and I. Moore, *The Sailing Yacht: How It Developed – How It Works*, 1965. Detailed discussion of all elements.

Barrault, J.M. *Great Moments of Yachting*, 1967.

Boswell, C. *The* America, 1967. A "biography"; interest was stimulated by the building of a replica.

Bradford, E. *The America's Cup*, 1964.

Burnell, R.D. *Races for the America's Cup*, 1965.

Burnett, C.B. *Let the Best Boat Win: The Story of America's Greatest Yacht Designer*, 1957. Biography of Nathanael Green Herreshoff. See also Herreshoff below.

Carrick, R.W., ed. *Defending the America's Cup*, 1969.

Chamier, J. *The Glory of Sail*, v. 1, 1897-1914, 1966. Narrower in scope than the title implies; emphasizes yachting events at Cowes. Large photographs of yachts.

Chichester, Sir F. Gipsy Moth *Circles the World*, 1968. The author was knighted for his solitary circumnavigation.

Crowninshield, F.B. *The Story of George Crowninshield's Yacht* Cleopatra's Barge *on a Voyage of Pleasure to the Western Islands and the Mediterranean, 1816-1817*, 1913.

Fox, U. *Sailing, Seamanship and Yacht Construction*, 1934. Pt. 1, Cruising; pt. 2, Racing, with details of individual yachts.
————. *Uffa Fox's Second Book*, 1935. Ch. 1, A Hundred Years of the Royal Yacht Squadron.

Heaton, P. *Yachting, a History*, 1956.

Heckstall-Smith, B. *Yachts and Yachting in Contemporary Art*, 1925.
————. *Sacred Cowes, or the Cream of Yachting Society*, 1955.

*Herreshoff, L.F. *An Introduction to Yachting*, 1962. A clear and well-illustrated account of the history of yachting.
————. *Captain Nat Herreshoff, the Wizard of Bristol*, 1953. See also Burnett above.

Heyerdahl, T. Kon Tiki, 1935, RP1953. Long Pacific voyage on a primitive balsa raft.

Jones, H.A., ed. *It's a Friendship*, 1965. Maine Friendship sloop. See Sect. I, including A. Roberts, ed., *Enduring Friendships*.

*Loomis, A.F. *Ocean Racing, 1866-1935*, 1967.

*Parkinson, J., Jr. *Nowhere is Too Far: The Annals of the Cruising Club of America*, 1960. Comprehensive coverage of ocean racing.
————. *The Bay and the Sound: Under Sail from Newport to Cape Cod*, 1968.

Philips-Birt, D. *Fore and Aft Sailing Craft and the Development of the Modern Yacht*, 1962.

Raymer, D.A. and Wykes, A. *The Great Yacht Race*, 1966. Transatlantic contest of three New York yachts in 1866.

*Slocum, J. *Sailing Alone Around the World*, 1900, R1967. The latest edition also includes his "The Voyage of the *"Liberdade."*

Stone, H.L. and Taylor, W.H. *The America's Cup Races*, 1958, R1970.

Watts, A. *Wind and Sailing Boats: The Structure and Behavior of the Wind as It Affects Sailing Craft*, 1967. British meteorologist explains the "secrets" of the winds in this "practical study of micro-meteorology."

VI NAVIES

The most adequate single study in English of the naval development of all major nations down through history is *E.B. Potter and C.W. Nimitz, eds., *Sea Power, A Naval History*, 1960. This cooperative work written by numerous members of the United States Naval Academy history faculty, blends American naval history into its world setting, tracing sea power down from ancient times, and showing the American experience as part of major world conflicts in the Napoleonic period and in the two World Wars, for instance. It shows an encouraging realization, rare in American naval history but long quite general in Britain, that there is much more to naval history than simply the occasional shooting. The book is an amplification and refinement of Potter's earlier volume, *The United States and World Sea Power*, 1955. The latter part of the new volume has also been published separately as *The Great Sea War*, 1960, covering the events and the aftermath of World War II. The new study supplants the earlier Annapolis texts of G.R. Clark, C.S. Alden, and W.O. Stevens and A.F. Westcott. A multi-volume comprehensive work, *War at Sea* by J.V.D. Southworth is under way: v. I, *The Ancient Fleets, The Story of Naval Warfare under Oars, 600 B.C.-1597 A.D.*, 1968; and v. 2, *The Age of Sails*, 1968. Also under way is a comprehensive history of sea power by C.G. Reynolds.

AO   SEA POWER AND NAVAL POLICY

Clark, J.J. and Barnes, D.H. *Sea Power and Its Meaning*, 1967.

*Colomb, P.H. *Naval Warfare: Its Ruling Principles and Practice Historically Treated*, 1891. A British approach similar to Mahan's at about the same time.

*Corbett, Sir J.S. *Some Principles of Maritime Strategy*, 1911. Corbett derived some interesting broad conclusions after having written distinguished works covering almost every period of England's naval activity.

Earle, E.M., et al., eds. *Makers of Modern Strategy*, 1943, Ch. 17, "Mahan, Evangelist of Sea Power" by M.T. Sprout.

*Eccles, H.E. *Military Concepts and Philosophy*, 1965. Like his earlier studies, *Operational Naval Logistics* and *Logistics in the National Defense*, this is an outgrowth of the author's lectures on strategy and logistics at the Naval War College, Newport.

Gilliam, B.M. *The World of Captain Mahan* (ms. PhD thesis, Princeton, 1961).

Hezlet, A. *The Submarine and Sea Power*, 1967.

Jeffries, W.W., ed. *Geography and National Power*, 4th ed., 1967.

Livezey, W.E. *Mahan on Sea Power*, 1947.

Mackinder, Sir J.H. *Britain and the British Seas*, 1902 ff.
———. *Democratic Ideals and Reality, a Study in the Policies of Reconstruction*, 1919 ff. Two chapters in this latter work, entitled "The Seaman's Point of View" and "The Landman's Point of View," suggests the emphasis of this British geographer upon land considerations which link him with the development of geopolitics.

*Mahan, A.T. *The Influence of Sea Power upon History, 1660-1783*, 1890 ff.
*———. *The Influence of Sea Power upon the French Revolution and Empire, 1793-1812*, 2 v. 1893.
*———. *Sea Power in Its Relations to the War of 1812*, 2 v., 1905.
*———. *Naval Strategy, Compared and Contrasted with the Principles of Military Operations on Land*, 1911.
The gist of the elements of "sea power," a phrase which Mahan coined, is in the first 89 pages of the first, and most celebrated, of these volumes. Thereafter, he went into a play-by-play analysis of the wars which gave England her naval supremacy, illustrating his strategical concepts by constant examples throughout the three great historical works. Later, he gathered these scattered ideas together, with more recent examples, in the single volume on *Naval Strategy*, which some consider his most useful work. Altogether, he wrote twenty books and some hundred articles by the time of his death in 1917. For later estimates consult Puleston, Livezey, West, Gilliam and Earle-Sprout, listed in this section.

Mahan on Naval Warfare; Selections from the Writings of Rear Admiral Alfred T. Mahan, ed. A. Westcott, 1918. A convenient collection of some of the most pertinent passages.

Martin, L.W. *The Sea in Modern Strategy*, 1967. Analyzes the role of sea power in modern diplomacy.

Mordel, J. *Twenty-five Centuries of Sea Warfare*, 1965.

Puleston, W.D. *Mahan: Life and Work of Capt. Alfred Thayer Mahan*, 1939. Incidentally, Mahan held the rank of captain at the time of his major writing and was promoted to rear admiral only after retirement.

*Sprout, H. and M., ed. *Foundations of National Power: Readings on World Politics and American Security*, 1945. Pertinent passages from varied works, with comments by the editors. Preparation was suggested by Secretary of the Navy Forrestal for use in college naval units.

West, R.S. *Admirals of American Empire*, 1948. Carries the career of Mahan, with three contemporary officers, from Annapolis through the Spanish-American War.

AP   NATIONAL NAVAL POLICY

Albion, R.G. *Makers of Naval Policy, 1798-1947*, ms. 1950. Prepared in the Office of Naval History, its copy was "lost," but microfilm copies are available at Harvard and Princeton. Analyzes interplay of Navy Department, White

House, Congress, and State Department in determining "internal policy" (what the Navy should *be*) and "external policy" (what it should *do*).

Andrade, E., Jr. *United States Naval Policy in the Disarmament Era, 1921-1937* (PhD thesis, Michigan State, 1966; DA v. 27, p. 2973A).

Bartlett, R. *Policy and Power; Two Centuries of American Foreign Relations,* 1967, P.

Baxter, C.F. *Admiralty Problems during the Second Palmerston Administration, 1859-1865* (PhD thesis, Georgia, 1965; DA v. 26, p. 6669).

Bennett, S. *The Price of Admiralty; An Indictment of the Royal Navy, 1825-1966,* 1968.

Bourne, K. *Britain and the Balance of Power in North America, 1815-1908,* 1967.

*Brodie, B. *A Guide to Naval Strategy,* 1944, R1965, originally *Layman's Guide to Naval Strategy,* 1943.
————. *Strategy in the Missile Age,* 1959.

Buhl, L.C. *The Smooth Water Navy: American Naval Policy and Politics, 1865-1876* (ms. PhD thesis, Harvard, 1969).

Crowe, W.J., Jr. *The Policy Roots of the Modern Royal Navy, 1949-1963* (PhD thesis, Princeton, 1965; DA v. 26, p. 7420).

*Davis, G.T. *A Navy Second to None: The Development of Modern American Policy,* 1940. See Sprout below.

Davis, V. (B.V., Jr.) *The Admirals' Lobby,* 1967. Based on Princeton PhD thesis, *Admirals, Politics and Postwar Defense Policy.*
————. *The Politics of Innovation: Patterns in Navy Cases,* 1967.

Divine, D. *The Blunted Sword,* 1964. Argument that for a century the British naval authorities were unwilling to appropriate adequate amounts for new improvements until war came. See also Bennett above.

*Gardiner, W.H. See Sect. BF.

Goldstein, W. *The Dilemma of British Defense,* 1967.

*Gordon, D.C. *The Dominion Partnership in Imperial Defense, 1870-1914,* 1965. Cooperation in naval and military affairs.

*Graham, G.S. *The Politics of Naval Supremacy: Studies in Maritime Ascendancy,* 1965.

Grenville, J.A.S. and Young, G.B. *Politics, Strategy and American Diplomacy: Studies in Foreign Policy, 1873-1917,* 1966.

Gretton, Sir P.W. *Maritime Strategy: A Study of British Defense Problems,* 1965.

Hammond, P.Y. *Super Carriers and B-36 Bombers*, 1963.

*Herrick, R.W. *Soviet Naval Strategy: Fifty Years of Theory and Practice*, 1968 (PhD thesis, Columbia). Author was formerly assistant naval attache at Moscow.

*Huntington, S.P. *The Soldier and the State: The Theory and Politics of Civil-Military Relations*, 1957. The American experience, 1789-1940.
————. *Changing Patterns of Military Politics*, 1962.

Kaufmann, W.W., ed. *Military Policy and National Security*, 1956.

Kelly, P.J. *The Naval Policy of Imperial Germany, 1900-1914* (PhD thesis, Georgetown, 1970).

*Langley, H.D. *Social Reforms in the United States Navy, 1798-1862*, 1967 (PhD thesis, Pennsylvania). Study of recruiting, corporal punishment, religious and temperance aspects.

Levy, M. *Alfred Thayer Mahan and United States Foreign Policy* (PhD thesis, New York Univ., 1965; DA v. 27, p. 1007A).

*Livermore, S.W. *American Naval Development, 1898-1914, with Special Reference to Foreign Affairs* (ms. PhD thesis, Harvard, 1944).

Lowe, C.J. *Salisbury and the Mediterranean, 1886-1896*, 1965. Politico-military problems, especially concerning the Italian fleet.

*Marder, A.J. *The Anatomy of British Sea Power*. . . . 1940, R1964. See Sect. BD-3.
*————. *From the Dreadnought to Scapa Flow*. . . . 5 v., 1961-1969. See Sect. BD-3.

Mayer, A.J. *Admirals and Foreign Policy, 1913-1919*, 1959 (PhD thesis, Yale).

Millis, W. *Arms and the State: Civil-Military Elements in National Policy* (Twentieth Century Fund), 1958. Covers period 1945-57.

Moll, D. *Decision Analysis of the British Naval Budget, 1865-1914* (PhD thesis, Stanford, 1968, DA v. 29, p. 4079A).

Peterson, C.W. *Anglo-Danish Naval Relations in the Age of Sail* (ms. PhD thesis, Maine, 1971).

*Preston, A. and Major, J. *Send a Gunboat! A Study of the Gunboat and Its Role in British Policy, 1854-1904*, 1967.

*Richmond, Sir H.W. *Statesmen and Sea Power*, 1946. Analysis of British naval policy from the time of Elizabeth through World War II.
*————. *The Navy as an Instrument of Policy, 1558-1727*, 1953. Posthumous volume in a study which the admiral-professor had intended to carry through 1918, analyzing the politico-military background of England's use of her navy. Omitting tactics and minor strategical details, it explains scores of ex-

peditions, including the unsuccessful and uneventful as well as the victorious.

*Ropp, T. *The Development of a Modern Navy: French Naval Policy, 1871-1914* (ms. PhD thesis, Harvard, 1937). The only adequate work in English on the French navy.
*——— . *War in the Modern World*, 1959, RP1962.

Rosecrance, R.S. *Defense of the Realm: British Strategy in the Nuclear Epoch*, 1968.

Schilling, W.R. *Admirals and Foreign Policy, 1913-1919* (PhD thesis, Yale, 1954; DA v. 26, p. 2306).

Schofield, B.B. *British Sea Power: Naval Policy in the Twentieth Century*, 1967.

*Schurman, D.M. *The Education of a Navy: The Development of British Naval Strategic Thought, 1867-1914*, 1965.

Sokol, A.E. *Sea Power in the Nuclear Age*, 1961.

Spector, R.H. *"Professors of War": The Naval War College and the Modern American Navy* (PhD thesis, Yale, 1967; DA v. 28, p. 4585A).

*Sprout, H. and M. *The Rise of American Naval Power, 1776-1918*, 1939, R1966.
——— . *Toward a New Order of Sea Power, American Naval Policy and the World Scene, 1918-1922*, 1940, R1969. These two works, together with G.T. Davis, above, give a very good analysis of American naval policy. Davis covers the period 1881-1939, thus overlapping the 1775-1922 span of the Sprouts.

Tuleja, T.V. *Statesmen and Admirals*, 1963. Criticism of American policy between the wars.

*Warner, Sir G., ed. *The Libelle of Englyshe Polycye: A Poem on the Use of Sea Power, 1436*, 1926. An early appreciation of the fundamentals.

Williamson, S.R. *The Politics of Grand Strategy: Britain and France Prepare for War, 1904-1914*, c1969.

Wood, J.B. *The American Response to China, 1784-1844 . . . the Origin of the East India Squadron*. See Sect. BB-2.

AQ   NAVAL ADMINISTRATION AND ORGANIZATION

AQ – 1   British

*Baugh, D.A. *British Naval Administration in the Age of Walpole*, 1965 (PhD thesis, Cambridge).

*Brassey, Earl (Thomas). *The British Navy: Its Strength, Resources and Administration*, 5 v. 1882-83. Brassey, son of a wealthy railway magnate, was a yachtsman, parliamentary reformer, and, at the time of this writing, a civilian member of the Admiralty. Useful descriptions and critical appraisal of other navies as well as the British. Vols. 1-3, shipbuilding methods and policy; 4, dockyards, reserves, training, pensions; 5, British seamen. Brassey started his celebrated *Naval Annual* shortly afterwards.

Briggs, Sir J.H. *Naval Administrations, 1827 to 1892, The Experience of 65 Years,* 1897. Briggs, Chief Clerk of the Admiralty, analyzes each of its successive administrations.

*Bryant, A. *Samuel Pepys,* 3 v. 1933-38. Pepys was virtual factotum of English naval administration during the Restoration; his famous diary is a mine of uncensored revelations of just how things worked.

Churchill, R.S. *Winston S. Churchill,* V. 2, *Young Politician, 1901-1914,* 1967. His services as First Lord of the Admiralty are described by his son.

Clayton, N. *Naval Administration Under James I* (ms. PhD thesis, Leeds, 1935).

Clowes, Sir W.L. *The Royal Navy,* 7 v. 1897-1903. See Sect. AU-1.

Doty, J.D. *The British Admiralty Board as a Factor in Colonial Administration, 1689-1763,* 1930 (PhD thesis, Pennsylvania).

*Ehrman, J. *The Navy in the War of William III, 1689-1697, Its State and Direction,* 1953. Able analysis, with comprehensive scope.

Fell, E.T. *Recent Problems in Admiralty Jurisdiction,* 1922 (PhD thesis, Johns Hopkins).

Gardiner, L. *The British Admiralty,* 1968. "A rather light-hearted approach to a serious and even complex historical subject." Another calls it "a disordered and anecdotal description."

Gretton, Sir P. *Winston Churchill and the Royal Navy,* 1968, R1969. By a British vice admiral. The first edition had the additional title "Former Naval Person," the whimsical phrase used by Churchill and Roosevelt in their correspondence.

Hamilton, Sir R.V. *Naval Administration – The Constitution, Character and Functions of the Admiralty and of the Civil Departments,* 1896.

*Hankey, Lord. *The Supreme Command, 1914-1918,* 2 v. 1961. Hankey, as Secretary of the Committee of Imperial Defense, of the Cabinet, the War Cabinet and Imperial War Cabinet, was in a unique position to observe the coordination of military and naval affairs with overall policy.

Hilbert, L.W. *The Role of Military and Naval Attaches in the British and German Service, with Particular Reference to Those in Berlin and London and Their Effect on Anglo-German Relations, 1871-1914* (ms. PhD thesis, Cambridge, 1955).

Irrmann, R.H. *Edward Russell, Earl of Orford (1653-1727) and the Administration of the Royal Navy to 1701* (ms. PhD thesis, Indiana, 1946).

*Johnson, F.A. *Defence by Committee: The British Committee of Imperial Defence, 1885-1959*, 1960. See also Hankey above.

*Kemp, P.K., ed. *The Papers of Sir John Fisher* (Navy Records Society, v. 102, 106), 2 v. 1960, 1964. Cover his period as First Sea Lord.

Kennedy, D.E. *Parliament and the Navy, 1642-1648: A Political History of the Navy during the Civil War* (ms. PhD thesis, Cambridge, 1959). See also J.A. Johnston, Sect. AX.

*Lewis, M.A. *The Navy of Britain, A Historical Portrait*, 1948. Pt. 5 is a lucid account of the evolution of the Admiralty, etc. See Sect. A.

*Lloyd, C. *Mr. Barrow of the Admiralty: A Life of Sir John Barrow, 1764-1848*, 1970. Barrow was Second Secretary of the Admiralty, 1804-1845. He was instrumental in many decisions, including the selection of St. Helena as the place for Napoleon.

McLachlan, D. *Room 39. A Study in Naval Intelligence*, 1968. British Intelligence Division in World War II.

Merriman, R.D., ed. *Queen Anne's Navy: Documents Concerning the Administration of the Navy of Queen Anne* (Navy Records Society, 103), 1963. Includes personal letters and other non-official material in addition to the official.

*Murray, Sir O.A.R. "The Admiralty," ten articles covering its historical development in the *Mariner's Mirror*, v. 33-35, 1937-39. These are the full equivalent of a book.

Navy Records Society Publications, v. 22, 23, 43, 45, 47, *The Naval Tracts of Sir William Monson*; v. 7, *Holland's Discourses of the Navy, 1638, 1658*; v. 89, *The Sergison Papers* (Sergison succeeded Pepys); v. 103, *Queen Anne's Navy*; v. 69, 71, 75, 78, *The Private Papers of John, Earl of Sandwich*; v. 32, 38, 39, *Letters and Papers of Charles, Lord Barham* (Sir John Middleton); v. 46, 48, 58, 59, *The Private Papers of George, second Earl Spencer*; v. 55, 61, *The Letters of Lord St. Vincent, 1801-1804*. (The last four were First Lords of the Admiralty between 1771 and 1805.)

*Oppenheim, M. *A History of the Administration of the Royal Navy and of Merchant Shipping in Relation to the Navy (1509-1660)*, 1896, R1961. He carried this valuable work into later periods but never published it; the manuscript was destroyed at Southampton during a bombing raid in World War II.

Pollitt, R.L. *The Elizabethan Navy Board: A Study in Administrative Evolution* (PhD thesis, Northwestern, 1968; DA v. 29, p. 2192A).

Richmond, C.F. *Royal Administration and the Keeping of the Seas, 1422-85* (ms. DPhil thesis, Oxford, 1963).

Robinson, C.N. *The British Fleet*, 1894. Pt. 2, Naval Administration, pt. 3, Naval Material.

Roskill, S.W., ed. *Documents Relating to the Naval Air Service*, v. 1 (Navy Records Society, 113), 1969. Administration and organization rather than operational.

Usher, R.G., Jr. *The Civil Administration of the British Navy During the American Revolution* (ms. PhD thesis, Michigan, 1943). Other unpublished theses on the Sandwich regime include those of C.A. Morrison, Ohio State, 1950; M.B. Wickwire, Yale, 1962; and M.J. Williams, Oxford, 1962. See Sect. AY-3.

Wilcox, L.A. *Mr. Pepys' Navy*, 1966. Topical arrangement, based on his diary.

AQ – 2   American

*Albion, R.G. *Makers of Naval Policy*. . . . ms. 1950. See Sect. AP.
*——————and Connery, R.H. *Forrestal and the Navy*, 1962. Broad background for the Forrestal 1940-47 period in Ch. 3, "Tradition and Prejudices."
——————and Reed, S.H.P. *The Navy at Sea and Ashore, an Informal Account of the Organization and Workings of the Naval Establishment of the United States Today, with Some Historical Notes on Its Development*, 1947. Prepared at the request of Secretary Forrestal.

Baldwin, H.W. *What the Citizen Should Know About the Navy*, 1941.

Borklund, C.W. *Men of the Pentagon: From Forrestal to MacNamara*, 1966.

Caraley, D. *The Politics of Military Unification: A Study of Conflict and the Policy Process*, 1966.

Carrigg, J.J. *Benjamin Stoddert and the Foundation of the American Navy* (ms. PhD thesis, Georgetown, 1953). See also Smelser below.

Cowling, B.F. *Benjamin Franklin Tracy: Lawyer, Soldier, Secretary of the Navy* (PhD thesis, Pennsylvania, 1969; DA v. 30 p. 4363A). See also Herrick, below.

Daniels, J. *The Cabinet Diaries of Josephus Daniels, 1913-1921*, ed. E.D. Cronon, 1963.

*Eberstadt, F. *Report to James Forrestal, Secretary of the Navy, on Unification of the War and Navy Departments and Postwar Organization of National Security*, 1945. This report by a New York financier is important both for its contents and its effect. It changed the original Army-Air Force drive for a tight military "merger" into the broader form of the 1947 act with the National Security Council and other devices for more effective policy determination. The appendix contains valuable studies by his temporary staff: 1, Foreign and military policies; 2, Military conduct of war – the Joint Chiefs of Staff; 3, Mobilization of national resources; 4, Procurement and logistics; 5, Personnel; 6, Science and the armed services; 7, Intelligence; 8, Education and training; 9, Communications; 10, Pearl Harbor and unification; 11, Proposals for unification; 12, Organizational trends within the Navy Department; 14, History of military air power.

Eckert, E.K. *William Jones and the Role of the Secretary of the Navy in the War of 1812* (PhD thesis, Florida, 1969; DA v. 31, p. 337A).

Enders, C.W. *The Vinson Navy* (PhD thesis, Michigan State, 1970; DA v. 31, p. 2301A). The long-term Georgia congressman, for many years the powerful chairman of House Naval Affairs, was a prime mover in the legislation which led to rapid naval growth before and during World War II.

Farrell, H.C., Jr. *Claude A. Swanson of Virginia* (ms. PhD thesis, Virginia, 1964). Secretary of the Navy, 1933-39.

*Fiske, B.A. *The Navy as a Fighting Machine*, 1916. Admiral Fiske writes vigorously of his efforts to coordinate military control in the Navy Department.

Furer, J.A. *Administration of the Navy Department in World War II*, 1960. This 1,047-page tome, compiled by a retired naval constructor in the Naval History Division, falls far short in critical qualities of the administrative studies produced by professional scholars in the Army's comprehensive program.

Gurney, G. *The Pentagon*, 1964. See also Borklund above and Raymond below.

Hall, C.H. *Abel Parker Upshur: Conservative Virginian*, 1963 (PhD thesis, Virginia). Upshur, Secretary of the Navy, 1841-43, was Secretary of State when killed in the gun explosion on the *Princeton*. See also Miller below.

Hammeth, H.B. *Hilary Abner Herbert: A Southerner Returns to the Union* (PhD thesis, Virginia, 1969; DA v. 31, p. 325A). Chairman of House Naval Affairs Committee and then, 1893-97, Secretary of the Navy.

Hammond, P.Y. *The Secretaryships of War and Navy: A Study in Civilian Control of the Military* (ms. PhD thesis, Harvard, 1953). Carries story back to 1903.

Haugen, R.N.B. *The Setting of Internal Administrative Communication in the United States Naval Establishment, 1775-1920* (ms. PhD thesis, Harvard, 1953). "Communication" is used in the public administration sense of contacts, rather than transmission of messages.

Herrick, W.R., Jr. *The American Naval Revolution*, 1965. Originally Virginia PhD thesis: *General Tracy's Navy: A Study of the Development of American Naval Power*. Tracy, as Secretary of the Navy, 1889-93, sponsored the Navy's shift to battleships instead of cruisers alone.

Jenkins, I.L. *Josephus Daniels in the Navy Department, 1913-16; A Study in Military Administration* (PhD thesis, Maryland, 1960; DA v. 22, p. 1963). Daniels, one of the most controversial Secretaries of the Navy, also told his own story in *The Wilson Era.*

*King, E.J. and Whitehill, W.M. *Fleet Admiral King: A Naval Record,* 1952. Useful primarily for details of King's earlier career, including service as bureau chief; less valuable for the period of his top wartime command. See Sect. BD-5.

Kittredge, T.B. *Naval Lessons of the Great War,* 1921. A pro-Sims account of the Sims-Daniels fight over naval administration.

Lobdell, G.H. *A Biography of Frank Knox* (PhD thesis, Illinois, 1954; DA v. 14, p. 2049). Knox was Secretary of the Navy, 1940-44.

Long, J.D. *The New American Navy,* 2 v. 1903. Long was Secretary of the Navy, 1897-1902.

Miller, R.E. *Abel Parker Upshur: A Study in Ante-Bellum Social and Political Philosophy* (PhD thesis, Princeton, 1952; DA v. 12, p. 379). See also Hall above.

Mollenhoff, C.R. *The Pentagon,* 1967. Violent disapproval of civilian administration.

*Morison, E.E. *Admiral Sims and the Modern American Navy,* 1942, R1968. This biography by his son-in-law is a penetrating analysis of naval administration in the early 20th century.
*————. *The War of Ideas: The United States Navy, 1870-1890,* P1969.

Morrison, J.L. *Josephus Daniels; The Small-d Democrat,* 1966. See also Jenkins above.

*Paullin, C.O. *The Navy of the American Revolution: Its Policy and Administration,* 1906 (PhD thesis, Chicago).
*————. *Paullin's History of Naval Administration, 1775-1911,* 1968. The United States Naval Institute has brought out as a bound volume the series of articles covering Naval Administration chronologically from 1775 to 1911. They appeared originally in the Institute's *Proceedings,* v. 20-40, 1906-14 and have long been utilized as the only comprehensive American account.

Peck, M.J. and Scherer, F.M. *The Weapons Acquisition Process, An Economic Analysis,* 1962.

*Rappaport, A. *The Navy League of the United States,* 1962. A valuable critical appraisal of its motives, methods and influence.

Rogow, A.A. *James Forrestal: A Study of Personality, Politics and Policy,* 1963. Includes psychological analysis of sorts.

*Smelser, M. *The Congress Founds the Navy, 1787-1798,* 1959. See also Carrigg above.

Stillson, A.C. *The Development and Maintenance of the Naval Establishment* (PhD thesis, Columbia, 1959; DA v. 20, p. 3813).

Thomas, F.P. *Career of John Grimes Walker, USN, 1835-1907*, 1959. Coming into the Navy Department in 1881 as Chief of the Bureau of Navigation at the beginning of the New Navy movement, Walker did much to coordinate and strengthen naval line influence in that office.

Turnbull, A.D. and Lord, C.L. *History of United States Naval Aviation*, 1949. Particular emphasis upon the administrative aspects.

*Welles, G. *The Diary of Gideon Welles, Secretary of the Navy under Lincoln and Johnson*, 3 v., ed. J.T. Morse, 1911, R1960. The revised edition, ed. H.K. Beale, shows changes from the original draft. See also West below.

Wells, T.H. *The Confederate Navy: A Study in Organization* (ms. PhD thesis, Emory, 1963; DA v. 25, p. 1884).

West, R.S. *Gideon Welles, Lincoln's Navy Department*, 1943.

*White, L.D. *The Federalists: A Study in Administrative History, 1789-1801*, 1948; Ch. 13, The Navy Department. Continued in *The Jeffersonians . . . 1801-1829*, 1951, ch. 19, 20; *The Jacksonians . . . 1829-1861*, 1954, ch. 11, 12; *The Republican Era, 1869-1901*, 1958.

AR   PROCUREMENT AND LOGISTICS

Albion, R.G. and Connery, R.H. *Forrestal and the Navy*, 1962. Ch. 4, 5 and 6 summarize Forrestal's important work with material procurement as Under Secretary, 1940-44, given in more detail in Connery's book below. Extensive bibliography.

Ballantine, D.S. *U.S. Naval Logistics in the Second World War*, 1947 (PhD thesis, Harvard). Emphasizes the Washington planning in Naval Operations. For the distribution, see Carter below.

Bolton, R.E. *Defense Purchases and Regional Growth in the United States* (ms. PhD thesis, Harvard, 1966).

Brewer, M.C. *Science and Defense; Military Research and Development in tne United States* (ms. PhD thesis, Harvard, 1956).

Carter, W.R. *Beans, Bullets and Black Oil: The Story of Fleet Logistics in the Pacific in World War II*, 1953.
————— and E.E. Duvall. *Ships, Salvage and Sinews of War: The Story of Fleet Logistics in the Atlantic and Mediterranean During World War II*, 1954.

Condon, M.E.A. *Transport Service . . . 1793-1802*. See Sect. AZ-2.

*Connery, R.H. *The Navy and the Industrial Mobilization in World War II*, 1951. Another product of the Administrative History program. The various aspects of the procurement process were prepared in collaboration with a group of officers. Summarized in Albion and Connery above.

Davies, C.S.L. *Supply Services of the English Armed Forces, 1509-50* (ms. DPhil thesis, Oxford, 1963).

*Dyer, G.C. *Naval Logistics*, 1960, R1962. The most comprehensive and authoritative coverage of all aspects, by an admiral prominently associated with logistics.

*Eberstadt, F. *Report to James Forrestal.* . . . 1945. See Sect. AQ-2. Appendix 4, Procurement and Logistics.

*Eccles, H.E. *Logistics in the National Defense*, 1959. Like Dyer, Admiral Eccles was a prominent practitioner in the logistics field, and taught the subject at the Naval War College.

Esso International Bunker Guide, 1953. See U.S. War Industries below.

Keller, H.B. *Forecasting the Logistic Impact of Operational Decisions* (PhD thesis, George Washington, 1968; DA v. 29, p. 3747A).

*Leighton, R.G. and Coakley, R.W. *Global Logistics in World War II* (USA-WW II), 1955.

*McLellan, W.C. *A History of American Military Sea Transportation* (ms. PhD thesis, American, 1953). Traces the separate Army and Navy transport services from 1898 up to their merger in "M.S.T.S." in 1949. See also U.S. Naval History Division, *History of the Naval Overseas Transportation Service in World War I*, 1969.

Peck, M.J. and Scherer, F.M. *The Weapons Acquisition Process*, 1962.

*Pool, B. *Navy Board Contracts, 1600-1832; Contract Administration Under the Navy Board*, 1966.

Robinson, C.N. *The British Fleet*, 1896. Pt. 3, Naval Material.

Ruppenthal, R.G. *The Logistical Support of the Armies* (USA-WW II), 2 v. 1954-
————. See also Leighton above.

Sargent, D.A. *Shipping and the American War.* . . . See Sect. AY-2.

Schreiber, C. *The Armed Services Procurement Act of 1947: An Administrative Study* (PhD thesis, American, 1964; DA v. 25, p. 4246).

*Sherman, R.U. *The Formation of Military Requirements for Munitions and Raw Materials* (ms. PhD thesis, Harvard, 1953).

Sigwart, E.E. *Royal Fleet Auxiliary: Its Ancestry and Affiliations*, 1969. The Royal Navy's "train" and its history.

Smith, G. *Britain's Clandestine Submarines, 1914-1915*, 1964. Because of the objection of the neutral United States furnishing warships to a belligerent, sections of ten submarines from Bethlehem Steel were nominally cancelled but actually shipped to Canadian Vickers for assembly.

Syrett, D. *Maritime Logistics . . . 1775-83*. See Sect. AY-2.

U.S. War Industries Board, General Bureau of Planning and Statistics, *The World's Steamship Fuel Stations*, 1918. Excellent logistical study of the coal and oil bunkerage situations and policies of the major countries of Europe and America. See also Esso International above.

Watson, P.K. *The Commission for Victualling the Navy . . . and the Commission for Transport, 1702-1714* (ms. PhD thesis, London, 1965).

AS NAVAL BASES, YARDS, AND FORTIFICATIONS

Albion, R.G. *The Development of the Naval Districts, 1903-1945*, P1945.

Andrews, A. *Proud Fortress: The Fighting Story of Gibraltar*, 1959.

Attiwill, K. *Fortress: The Story of the Siege and Fall of Singapore*, 1960.

Bee, B.M.C. *The Leasing of Kiaochow: A Study in Diplomacy and Imperialism* (ms. PhD thesis, Harvard, 1935).

Belote, J.H. and W.M. *Corregidor: The Saga of a Fortress*, 1967.

Blackburne, K. *The Romance of English Harbour*, 1969. "Nelson's Dockyard," Antigua.

Blouet, B. *A Short History of Malta*, 1967.

*Braisted, W.R. *The United States Navy in the Pacific, 1897-1909*, 1958.

Colgate, H.A. *Trincomalee and the East Indian Squadron, 1746 to 1844* (ms. MA thesis, London, 1950). Shows strategic importance of this Ceylon base.

Cousins, G. *The Story of Scapa Flow*, 1966.

Decker, G. *A Short History of Devonport Royal Dockyard*, P1969. The major base at Plymouth.

Downey, F. *Louisbourg, Key to a Continent*, 1965.

Evans, R.A. *The Army and Navy at Halifax in Peace Time, 1783-1793* (ms. MA thesis, Dalhousie, 1970).

Gray, J.A.C. *Amerika Samoa: A History of American Samoa and its United States Naval Administration*, 1960.

Grenfell, R. *The Art of the Admiral*, 1937. Ch. 7, Bases.
————————. *Main Fleet to Singapore*, 1931. Includes background of the building of the great base.

Hammer, D.H. *Lion Six*, 1947. Building of great base at Guam in World War II.

Jury, E.M. *The Establishment of Penstanguishene, Bastion of the North, 1814-1856* (Univ. of Western Ontario), P1956.

Kauffman, J.L. *Philadelphia's Navy Yards (1801-1948)* (Newcomen Society), P1948. The yard was moved to a new site at League Island at the close of the Civil War.

*Lewis, E.R. *Seacoast Fortifications of the United States: An Introductory History* (Smithsonian Institution), 1970. Development of design and ordnance from the beginning.

*Livermore, S.W. *American Naval Development, 1898-1914* (ms. PhD thesis, Harvard, 1944). Stresses the vigorous quest for coaling stations by W.H. Brownson, Chief of the Bureau of Equipment. See also Braisted above.

Long, R.E. *A Study of the Naval Base, with particular reference to the Pacific Islands* (ms. PhD thesis, Yale, 1942).

Longstaff, F.V. *Esquimalt Naval Base: A History of the Work and Its Defenses*, 1941. Canada's principal Pacific base, on Vancouver Island. See also Mackinnon below.

*Lott, A.S. *A Long Line of Ships: Mare Island's Centenary of Naval Activity in California*, 1954. For many years, the Mare Island Navy Yard was the Navy's only Pacific base.

Mackinnon, C.S. *The Imperial Fortresses in Canada: Halifax and Esquimalt, 1871-1906*, 2 v. (PhD thesis, Toronto, 1965; DA v. 27, p. 1018A). These remained under British imperial control after the withdrawal of British troops from the rest of Canada. See also Longstaff above.

Makepeace, W., et al. *One Hundred Years of Singapore (1818-1919)*, 2 v. 1921.

*Mariners Museum, *Catalog of Marine Photographs*, 5 v. 1964. Sect. PNa, U.S. Government Establishments.

McGuffie, T.H. *The Siege of Gibraltar, 1779-1783*, 1964.

McKee, L.A.M. See Sect. BA-3, Boston Navy Yard.

Miller, E.H. *Strategy at Singapore*, 1942. Based on his Clark PhD thesis, *The Singapore Naval Base*.

Peck, T. *Round Shot to Rockets, A History of the Washington Navy Yard and the U.S. Naval Gun Factory*, 1949.

Pomeroy, E.S. *Pacific Outpost: American Strategy in Guam and Micronesia*, 1951.

Randall, T.R. *Halifax, Warden of the North*, 1948. Founded in 1748 to serve as a base for the British Navy in northern waters.

Richard, D.E. *History of the United States Naval Administration of the Trust Territory of the Pacific Islands* (Office of the Chief of Naval Operations), 3 v. 1957-63.

Russell, J. *Gibraltar Besieged, 1779-1783*, 1965.

Snowbarger, W.E. *The Development of Pearl Harbor* (ms. PhD thesis, Berkeley, 1951).

*Stephens, A.E. *Plymouth Dock: A Survey of the Development of the Royal Dockyard in Hamoaze during the Sailing Ship Era* (ms. PhD thesis, London, 1940). See also Decker above and Sillick Sect. Y-4f.

Stewart, J.D. *Gibraltar, the Keystone*, 1967.

Strahan, J.B. *American Colonial Administration in the Western Pacific: A Study in Civil Military Relations* (ms. PhD thesis, Ohio State, 1951).

Thomas, F.N.C. *Portsmouth and Gosport: A Study in the Historical Geography of a Naval Port* (ms. MSc thesis, London, 1961).

Thurman, M.E. *The Naval Development of San Blas: New Spain's Bastion for Alta California and Nootka, 1767 to 1798*, 1967.

Tucker, G.N. *The Naval Service of Canada*, v. 2, *Activities on Shore*, 1952.

*U.S. Bureau of Yards and Docks, *Building the Navy's Bases in World War II: History of the Bureau of Yards and Docks and the Civil Engineer Corps, 1940-1946*, 2 v. 1947.

Wadia, R.A. *The Bombay Dockyard and the Wadia Master Builders*, 1957. The Royal Navy began to build some warships at Bombay during the home oak shortage in the Napoleonic Wars.

Warner, O. *Portsmouth and the Royal Navy*, P1965. An illustrated booklet.

Wiens, H.J. *Pacific Island Bastions of the United States*, P1962.

*Willock, R. *Bulwark of Empire: Bermuda's Fortified Naval Base, 1860-1920*, 1962. One of the most thoroughgoing analyses of the development and functions of an overseas base, by a colonel of the United States Marine Corps.

AT NAVAL TACTICS, ETC.

Broome, J.E. *Make a Signal*, 1955. See Sect. N-2.

Buker, G.E. *Riverine Warfare . . . Second Seminole War*. See Sect. BB-2.

Clark, Sir J. *An Essay on Naval Tactics, Systematical and Historical*, 1790 ff. Influential work of an Edinburgh banker, "Clark of Eldon," who never went to sea.

Corbett, Sir J.S., ed. *Fighting Instructions, 1530-1816* (Navy Records Society, 29), 1895. These include the Duke of York's instructions which had such a cramping effect on 18th century tactics.
——————— . *Signals and Instructions, 1776-1794* (ibid. m 35) 1908.

Creswell, J. *Naval Warfare*, 1937.
——————— . *Generals and Admirals, the Story of Amphibious Command*, 1952. Case histories over three centuries, analyzing the relationships between the army and navy commanders.

Custance, Sir R. *The Ship of the Line in Battle*, 1913. Includes modern capital ships.

Featherstone, D.F. *Naval War Games*, 1965.

Falls, C. *The Art of War from the Age of Napoleon to the Present Day*, 1961.

*Grenfell, R. *The Art of the Admiral*, 1937. Ch. 1, Nature of Strategy; 2, Overseas Expeditions; 3-4, Trade Warfare; 5, Convoy Question in War; 6, Command and Cover; 7, Bases; 8, Moral Factor; 9, Attitudes of Mind; 10, Technique of Victory; 11, Influences of the Air; 12, Composition of the Fleet.

*Isely, J.A. and Crowl, P.A. *The U.S. Marines and Amphibious War: Its Theory and Practice in the Pacific*, 1951.

Jackson, Sir T.S., ed. *Logs of the Great Sea Fights, 1794-1805* (Navy Records Soc. 16, 18), 2 v. 1899-1900.

*Lewis, M.A. *The Navy of Britain*, 1948. Pt. 6 is the best brief account of the development of naval tactics, in 215 pages to Admiral Robison's 936. See Sect. AU-1.

Robison, S.S. *History of Naval Tactics from 1530 to 1930: The Evolution of Tactical Maxims*, 1942. Rambling and lacking in emphasis, by a former American commander-in-chief of the fleet.

Russell, Sir H. *Sea Shepherds: Wardens of Our Food Flocks*, 1941. A history of convoying from Elizabethan times.

Rutter, O. *Red Ensign, a History of Convoy*, 1942.

Stokesbury, J.C. *British Concepts and Practices of Amphibious Warfare, 1867-1916* (ms. PhD thesis, Duke, 1967).

Vagts, A. *Landing Operations: Strategy, Psychology, Tactics, from Antiquity to 1945*, 1946.

Waldron, T.J. and Gleeson, J.J. *The Frogmen*, 1966.

Warner, O. *Great Sea Battles*, 1964. 26 engagements, Lepanto to Leyte Gulf.

Whitehouse, A. *Amphibious Operations*, 1963. "From the Roman invasion of Britain to World War II."

Wilson, H.W. *Battleships in Action*, 2 v. 1926, R1968. Carries story further than his original *Ironclads in Action.*

AU GENERAL NATIONAL NAVAL HISTORY

AU – 1 British

*Callender, Sir G.A.R. *The Naval Side of British History*, 1924, R1963.

Capper, D.P. *Moat Defense, A History of the Waters of the Nore Command, 55 B.C. to 1961*, 1963. Headquarters for the defense of London and the whole southeast coast.

*Clowes, Sir W.L., ed. *The Royal Navy: A History from the Earliest Times to the Present*, 7 v. 1897-1903. Useful cooperative work, with contributors including Theodore Roosevelt and A.T. Mahan. Text uneven in quality but invaluable for reference for full detailed coverage of operations and "civil history" in each volume.

Gordon, L.L. *British Battles and Medals*, 1950, R1962. "Every campaign medal and bar awarded since the Armada, with the reason for the award and the names of all the ships, regiments and squadrons whose personnel are entitled to them." Useful for identifying the little "brush fire wars" in Africa, Asia and the South Seas.

Hannay, D. *A Short History of the Royal Navy (1217-1815)*, 2 v. 1897-1909.

Hargreaves, R. *The Narrow Seas: A History of the English Channel, Its Approaches and Its Immediate Shores*, 1959. See also Capper above and Williamson below.

*Lewis, M.A. *The Navy of Britain, A Historical Portrait*, 1948. Following the example of Robinson's earlier work, adopts a topical rather than chronological treatment, carrying various subjects down through the centuries. The six parts are 1, Origins; 2, Ships; 3, Officers; 4, Men; 5, Management (Direction and Administration); 6, In Action (Weapons, Tactics and Fights). The Lewis treatment, scholarly and sophisticated but breezy and informal, is about the best of its kind for each topic.
————. *History of the British Navy*, 1959, RP. A conventional narrative treatment, in contrast to the topical arrangement above.

*Lloyd, C. *The Nation and the Navy*, 1954, R1964. Like Clowes, Hannay, Callender, Lewis and Tunstall, this is one of the best chronological histories of the Royal Navy. In length, they grow progressively shorter, from about 4,000 pages through 1,000 to 300 or less. They show the trend toward a broader interpretation than the old blow-by-blow emphasis alone.

Mahan, A.T. *Types of Naval Officers, Drawn from the History of the British Navy*, 1901. Studies of Hawke, Rodney, Howe, Jervis, Saumarez and Pellew.

*Marcus, G.J. *A Naval History of England*, 4 v. 1961-   . V. 1, *The Formative Centuries* (to 1783); v. 2, *The Age of Nelson*. A projected multi-volume work, treating various aspects afloat and ashore.

*Richmond, Sir H.W. *Statesmen and Sea Power*, 1946. Analysis of British naval policy from the time of Elizabeth through World War II.
———— . *The Navy as an Instrument of Policy, 1558-1727*, 1953.

Robinson, C.N. *The British Fleet: The Growth, Achievements, and Duties of the Navy of the Empire*, 1894. Pt. 1, Naval Power; pt. 2, Naval Administration; pt. 3, Naval Material; pt. 4, Personnel.

*Roskill, S.W. *The Strategy of Sea Power: Its Development and Application*, 1962. A series of lectures at Cambridge; traces the broad development of British sea power from the earliest times.

Tunstall, B. *Realities of Naval History*, 1936. See Lloyd, above.

Williamson, J.A. *The English Channel: A History*, 1959. See Hargreaves, above.

AU – 2   American

*Albion, R.G. and Pope, J.B. *Sea Lanes in Wartime: The American Experience, 1775-1945*, 2nd ed. 1968. A study of the relative control of the seas during the various wars as it affected the coming and going of American ships and cargoes.

Cooney, D.M. *A Chronology of the United States Navy, 1775-1965*, 1965.

*Davis, G.T. *A Navy Second to None: The Development of Modern American Policy*, 1940.

Heinl, R.D. *Soldiers of the Sea: A Definitive History of the United States Marine Corps, 1775-1962*, 1962. The most comprehensive and critical history of the Corps, supplanting the older history by C.H. Metcalf (1939). See also Pierce and Hough below.

Knox, D.W. *A History of the United States Navy*, 1936, R1948. Meticulous operational detail.

Miller, W.M., et al. *A Chronology of the United States Marine Corps, 1775-1934*, P1964, P1965. Continued by C.A. Tyson for 1965-66.

Mitchell, D.W. *History of the Modern American Navy from 1883 through Pearl Harbor*, 1946 (PhD thesis, So. California). Marred by scores of careless errors.

*Neeser, R.W. *A Statistical and Chronological History of the United States Navy, 1755-1907*, 2 v. 1909. Useful reference work. Vol. 1 is a very comprehensive but uncritical bibliography. Vol. 2 consists of three sets of chronological tables in minute detail: 1, major events and dates; 2, "engagements, expeditions, and captures of vessels of war;" 3, captures of merchantmen. Well indexed.

Pierce, P.N. and Hough, F.O. *Compact History of the United States Marine Corps*, 1961, R1964. See also Heinl, above.

*Potter, E.B. and Nimitz, C.W., eds. *Sea Power: A Naval History*, 1960. See remarks at head of this section. Full coverage of American as well as foreign naval history. This supplants not only the previous Annapolis text, E.B. Potter, ed. *The United States and World Sea Power*, 1955, but also the general histories by J.Fenimore Cooper (2 v. 1840), J.R. Spears (4 v. 1897), E.S. Maclay, (3 v. 1894-1907) and D.W. Knox, above.

Pratt, F. *The Navy, A History: The Story of a Navy in Action*, 1938; new edition, with H.E. Howe, *Compact History of the United States Navy*, 1957. Emphasis on the "shooting" side.

Roscoe, T., et al. *Picture History of the U.S. Navy from the old Navy to the New*, 1957. Covers period 1776-1897.

*Sprout, H. and M. *The Rise of American Naval Power, 1776-1918*, 1939, R1943.

Van Alstyne, R.W. *American Diplomacy in Action*, 1947. Ch. 28-30, Protection of the Flag and Trade Routes; 42-45, Expansion in Eastern Asia and the Pacific; 49-51, Impressment and the Right of Search; 52-54, Neutrality and the Belligerent Control of Commerce.

AU – 3   Other Navies

The most useful continuing accounts of foreign navies will be found in *Brassey's Naval Annual*, 1886-1950, continued in *Brassey's Annual: The Armed Forces Yearbook*; the U.S. Naval Institute's new *The Naval Review*, starting with the 1962-63 issue; and *Jane's Fighting Ships*, since 1898. The jubilee edition of *Jane's* in 1948 gives a particularly good picture of the preceding half century.

Anderson, R.C. *Naval Wars in the Baltic during the Sailing Ship Epoch, 1522-1850*, 1910. Useful for Russian and Scandinavian navies.
————. ed. *Lists of Men-of-War. 1650-1700*. 5 parts, 1935-38. Pt. 1, English; 2, French; 3, Swedish; 4, Danish-Norwegian; 5, German.

Ballard, G.A. *The Influence of Sea Power on the History of Japan*, 1921.

Clark, G.S.C. *Russia's Sea Power, Past and Present*, 1898.

*Falk, E.A. *Tojo and the Rise of Japanese Sea Power*, 1936.

Feakes, H.J. *White Ensign – Southern Cross: A Story of the King's Ships of Australia*, 1952.

Gebhard, L.A., Jr. *The Development of the Austro-Hungarian Navy, 1897-1914: A*

Study in the Operation of Dualism (PhD thesis, Rutgers, 1965; DA v. 26, p. 5993).

Golovko, A.G. *With the Red Fleet*, 1965, tr. P. Broomfield. Memoirs of long career including wartime command of Russia's northern fleet.

Hucul, W.G. *The Evolution of Russian and Soviet Sea Power 1853-1963* (ms. PhD thesis, Berkeley, 1954).

*Laughton, Sir J.K. *Studies in Naval History*, 1887. Consists chiefly of chapters on men prominent in French naval history: Jean de Vienne, Colbert, Duquesne, Suffren, Jean Bart, Duguay Trouin, Thurot, Surcouf. See also C.B. Norman, *The Corsairs of France*.

Low, C.R. *History of the Indian Navy, 1613-1863*, 2 v. 1877. This outfit was quite distinct from the Royal Navy serving on the East Indian station.

Macandie, G.L. *The Genesis of the Royal Australian Navy*, 1949.

McGuire, F.M. *The Royal Australian Navy. Its Origin, Development and Organisation*, 1949. See also Macandie above.

McLachlan, J.O. *Trade and Peace with Old Spain*, 1940.

*Perry, J.C. *Great Britain and the Imperial Japanese Navy, 1858-1905*, 1905 (PhD thesis, Harvard).

*Ropp, T. *The Development of a Modern Navy: French Naval Policy, 1871-1914*, 1937 (PhD thesis, Harvard).

Saunders, M.G., ed. *The Soviet Navy*, 1958.

Shepard, A.M. *Sea Power in Ancient History: The Story of the Navies of Classic Greece and Rome*, 1924. See also the numerous works on ancient navies in the next section.

Steve, F.K. *The Rise of Soviet Naval Power in the Nuclear Age*. See Sect. BI-1.

Taylor, T.D. *New Zealand's Naval Story*, 1948.

NAVAL HISTORY BY CHRONOLOGICAL PERIODS

AV   ANCIENT AND MEDIEVAL

*Anderson, R.C. *Oared Fighting Ships: From Classical Times to the Coming of Steam*, 1962.

Armstrong, J.I. *The Trierarchy and the Tribal Organization of the Athenian Navy* (PhD thesis, Princeton, 1929; DA v. 15, p. 397).

Brooke, F.W. *The English Naval Forces, 1199-1272*, 1932.

Carter, J.M. *The Battle of Actium: The Rise and Triumph of Augustus Caesar,* 1970.

*Casson, L. *The Ancient Mariners: Seafarers and Sea-Fighters of the Mediterranean in Ancient Times,* 1959, RP1967. See Sect. W-1.

Clark, F.W. *The Influence of Sea Power on the History of the Roman Republic,* 1915 (PhD thesis, Chicago).

El Adawi, I.A. *Egyptian Maritime Power in the Early Middle Ages* (ms. PhD thesis, Liverpool, 1948).

Fahmy, A.M. *Muslim Sea Power in the Eastern Mediterranean from the Seventh to the Tenth Century: Studies in Naval Organization,* 1950 (PhD thesis, London).

Green, P. *Xerxes at Salamis, 480-479 B.C.,* 1970.

Hourani, G.F. *Arab Seafaring in the Indian Ocean in Ancient and Early Medieval Times,* 1951 (PhD thesis, Princeton), R1963.

Hyde, W.W. *Ancient Greek Mariners,* 1947.

Jordan, B. *The Administration and Military Organization of the Athenian Navy in the Fifth and Fourth Centuries, B.C.* (PhD thesis, Berkeley, 1968; DA v. 30, p. 1099A).

Laing, D.R. *A New Interpretation of the Athenian Naval Catalogue IG II, 1951* (PhD thesis, Cincinnati, 1965; DA v. 26, p. 3889).

*Lane, F.C. *Venetian Ships and Shipbuilding of the Renaissance,* 1934 (PhD thesis, Harvard).
————. *Venice and History.* . . . 1966. See Sect. W-2.

*Lewis, A.R. *Naval Power and Trade in the Mediterranean, A.D. 500-1100,* 1951. Analyzes the interplay of the Byzantine, Arab and Western elements.
* ————. *The Northern Seas: Shipping and Commerce in Northern Europe, A.D. 300-1100,* 1958. Includes the fighting and informal raiding of the Vikings and others.

Lo, F-J. *China as a Sea-Power, 1127-1368* (ms. PhD thesis, Berkeley, 1957).

Merker, I.L. *Studies in Sea-Power in the Eastern Mediterranean in the Century following the Death of Alexander* (PhD thesis, Princeton, 1958; DA v. 20, p. 2765).

*Morrison, J.S. and Williams, R.T. *Greek Oared Ships, 900-322 B.C.,* 1968.

Moscati, S. *The World of the Phoenicians,* 1968. See Sect. W-1.

Oppenheim, M., ed. *Naval Accounts and Inventories in the Reign of Henry VII* (Navy Records Society, 8), 1896.

Richmond, C.F. *Royal Administration and the Keeping of the Seas, 1422-85* (ms. DPhil thesis, Oxford, 1963).

Robertson, F.W. *The Rise of a Scottish Navy, 1460-1513* (ms. PhD thesis, Edinburgh, 1934).

*Rodgers, W.L. *Greek and Roman Naval Warfare*, 1937, 1970.
*————. *Naval Warfare under Oars*, 1939, 1970. These two studies by an admiral, one of America's most distinguished naval dynasty, carry the whole story of the Mediterranean galley fighting through the battle of Lepanto in 1571.

Rose, J.H. *The Mediterranean in the Ancient World*, 1934.

Sawyer, P.H. *The Age of the Vikings*, 1967. Ch. 4, the Ships; ch. 6, The Raids. See also T.D. Kendrick, *A History of the Vikings*, 1930, R1968.

Shepard, A.M. *Seapower in Ancient History.* . . . 1924. See Sect. AU-3.

Southworth, J.V. *The War at Sea*, V. 1, *The Ancient Fleets*, 1967.

Starr, C.G. *The Roman Imperial Navy*, 31 B.C.-A.D. 324, 1941, R1960.

Tarn, W.W. *Hellenistic Military and Naval Developments*, 1930, R1966.

Thiel, J.H. *Studies in the History of Roman Sea-Power in Republican Times*, 1946.
————. *A History of Roman Sea-Power before the Second Punic War*, 1954.

Torr, C. *Ancient Ships*, 1894, R1964.

Weil, A. *The Navy of Venice*, 1910.

Welch, G.P. *Britannia: The Roman Conquest and Occupation of Britain*, 1963.

Yehya, L. *Military and Naval Administration in Athens in the Fourth Century, B.C., Including Finance* (ms. PhD thesis, London, 1953).

AW   1500-1650

See also Section Q-3 on Elizabethan Seafaring.

AW – 1   General

American Heritage, *The Spanish Armada*, 1966.

Anderson, R.C. *Naval Wars in the Baltic in the Sailing-Ship Epoch, 1522-1850*, 1910, R1970.
*————. *Naval Wars in the Levant, 1559-1853*, 1951.
————. *Oared Fighting Ships*, 1962. Ch. 6-11 deal with vessels of this period both in southern and northern waters.

Andrews, K.R. *Elizabethan Privateering: English Privateering during the Spanish War, 1585-1603,* 1964 (PhD thesis, London).
——————. *English Privateering Voyages to the West Indies, 1588-1595* (Hakluyt Soc. 2nd series, 111), 1959.

*Ballard, G.A. *Rulers of the Indian Ocean,* 1927. From the advent of the Portuguese to the 20th century.

Bradford, E. *The Great Siege: Malta, 1565,* 1961.

Brockman, E. *The Two Sieges of Rhodes, 1480-1522,* 1969.

*Corbett, Sir J.S. *Drake and the Tudor Navy, with a History of the Rise of England as a Maritime Power,* 2 v. 1898, 1965.
——————. *The Successors of Drake (1589-1603),* 1900, 1970.
*——————. *England in the Mediterranean: A Study of the Rise and Influence of British Power within the Straits, 1603-1713,* 2 v. 1904.

Curry, E.H. *Sea Wolves of the Mediterranean: The Grand Period of the Modern Corsairs,* 1910. See also S. Lane-Poole, *The Story of the Barbary Corsairs* (1890) and Sir B.L. Playfair, *The Scourge of Christendom* (1884). See also Fisher, below.

Davies, C.S.L. *The Supply Services of the English Armed Forces, 1509-50* (ms. DPhil thesis, Oxford, 1963).

Fisher, Sir G. *Barbary Legend: War, Trade and Piracy in North Africa, 1415-1830,* 1958. See Sect. AI-2.

Hardy, E. *Survivors of the Armada,* 1966.

Hoffman, P.E. *The Defence of the Indies 1535-1576: A Study of the Modernization of the Spanish State* (PhD thesis, Florida, 1969; DA v. 31, p. 1195A).

Kennedy, D.E. *Parliament and the Navy, 1642-1648: A Political History of the Navy during the Civil War* (ms. PhD thesis, Cambridge, 1959).

Lawetz, G., ed. *Correspondence between Philip II of Spain and the Duke of Medina Sidonia,* 1965.

Lewis, M.A. *The Spanish Armada* (British Battles Series), 1959.
*——————. *The Armada Guns,* 1961. Reprint of eight separate articles from the *Mariner's Mirror,* 1942-43; important conclusions.

Marx, R.F. *The Battle of Lepanto, 1571,* 1966. See also Petrie below.

*Mattingly, G. *The Armada,* 1959. Important best-seller; only half the book has a "salt-water content;" the rest reflects the author's long-standing interest in the politico-religious influences at that time.

Navy Records Society Publications, 1, 2, *State Papers relating to the Defeat of the Spanish Armada;* 11, *Papers relating to the Spanish War, 1585-87;* 10, *Letters and Papers relating to the War with France, 1512-13; 29, Fighting Instructions, 1530-1816; 49, Documents relating to Law and Custom of the Sea (1205-1648); 105, Documents relating to the English Civil War (see also the biographical section).*

*Oppenheim, M. See Sect. AQ-1.

Penn, C.D. *The Navy under the Early Stuarts, and Its Influence on English History*, 1913.

Powell, J.R. *The Navy in the English Civil War*, 1962.

*Richmond, Sir H.W. *The Navy as an Instrument of Government, 1558-1727*, 1953. See also the appropriate parts of his *Statesmen and Sea Power*, 1946.

Stearns, S.J. *The Caroline Military System, 1625-1627: The Expedition to Cadiz* (PhD thesis, Berkeley, 1967; DA v. 21, p. 1218).

Uden, G. *Drake at Cadiz*, 1969.

Unwin, R. *The Defeat of John Hawkins; A Biography of his Third Slaving Voyage*, 1960, RP1961.

*Wernham, R.B. *Before the Armada*, 1967. The formative stage of English sea power, 1485-1588.

AW – 2   Biography and Memoirs (1500-1650)

Bradford, E. *The Sultan's Admiral: The Life of Barbarossa*, 1968.

Kenny, R.W. *Elizabeth's Admiral: The Political Career of Charles Howard, Earl of Nottingham, 1536-1624*, c1969. In the Armada period he was known as "Lord Howard of Effingham."

Lease, O.C. *Lord Admiral Thomas Seymour* (ms. PhD thesis, Pennsylvania, 1951). He devoted far less time to being a flag officer afloat than to the more hazardous occupation of being a Seymour ashore.

Lewis, M.A. *The Hawkins Dynasty: Three Generations of a Tudor Family*, 1970.

Lloyd, C. *Sir Francis Drake*, 1957.

Mason, A.E.W. *Life of Francis Drake*, 1941.

McGowan, A.P. *The Royal Navy under the 1st Duke of Buckingham, Lord High Admiral, 1618-28* (ms. PhD thesis, London, 1967).

Navy Records Society Publications, 7, *Hollond's Discourses of the Navy, 1638 and 1658*; 22, 23, 43, 45, 47, *The Naval Tracts of Sir William Monson*.

*Petrie, Sir C. *Don John of Austria*, 1967. Chapter on Lepanto, and discussion of warfare conditions and techniques.

Rowse, A.L. *Sir Richard Grenville of the* Revenge: *An Elizabethan Hero*, 1937, R1962.

*Williamson, J.A. *Sir John Hawkins, the Time and the Man*, 1927. A shorter, more popular, version in 1949 had the title *Hawkins of Plymouth*. See also Lewis above.

*————. *The Age of Drake*, 1938, R1961, P1962 with title *Sir Francis Drake*.

AX   1650-1763

From preceding: Anderson, Ballard, Corbett (Mediterranean), Curry, Fisher, Richmond.

AX – 1   General

*Albion, R.G. *Forests and Sea Power: The Timber Problem of the Royal Navy, 1652-1862* (Harvard Economic Studies, 29), 1926, (PhD thesis, Harvard), R1965. Discusses the manifold problems arising from Britain's complete lack of native masts and an inadequate supply of native oak, a situation causing the maritime powers to turn to the to the Baltic and America. See also Bamford.

Asher, E.L. *The Resistance to the Maritime Classes: The Survival of Feudalism in the France of Colbert*, 1960. A form of conscription.

*Bamford, P.W. *Forests and French Sea Power, 1660-1789*, 1956 (PhD thesis, Columbia). A companion work to Albion, above.

Battick, J.F. *Cromwell's Navy and the Foreign Policy of the Protectorate, 1653-1658* (PhD thesis, Boston Univ., 1968; DA v. 28, p. 1752A).

Baugh, D.A. *British Naval Administration in the Age of Walpole*, 1965 (PhD thesis, Cambridge).

*Boxer, C.R. *The Dutch Seaborne Empire, 1600-1800*, 1965.

Clark, G.N. *The Seventeenth Century*, 1929, R1947, P1961. Ch. 8, Navies; ch. 13, colonies.

*Ehrman, J. *The Navy in the War of William III, 1689-1697, Its State and Direction*, 1953. One of the most ambitious post-Oppenheim studies of overall British naval administration.

Irrmann, R.H. *Edward Russell, Earl of Oxford.* . . . 1946. See Sect. AQ-1.

Johnston, J.A. *Parliament and the Navy, 1688-1714* (ms. PhD thesis, Sheffield, 1968).

*Lydon, J.G. *The Role of New York in Privateering down to 1763* (PhD thesis, Columbia, 1956; DA v. 16, p. 1436).

234

*Mahan, A.T. *The Influence of Sea Power upon History, 1660-1783*, 1890 ff, RP1962. After the initial 89-page statement of principles, gives play-by-play analysis of major operations.

Merriman, R.D., ed. *Queen Anne's Navy*. . . . 1963. See Sect. AQ-1.

Monk, W.F. *Britain in the Western Mediterranean*, 1950. Covers the period c1688-1900.

Morris, R. *Island Treasure*, 1969. Removal of wreck of Sir Cloudsley Shovell's flagship *Asia* off the Scillies.

Murray, J.J. *George I, the Baltic and the Whig Split of 1717, A Study in Diplomacy and Propaganda*, 1970.

Natharius, E.W. *The Maritime Powers and Sweden, 1698-1702* (PhD thesis, Indiana, 1959; DA v. 20, p. 1344).

Navy Records Society Publications, 13, 17, 20, 37, 41, 56, *Papers relating to the First Dutch War*, 1652-54; 15, *History of the Russian Fleet during the Reign of Peter the Great. By a contemporary Englishman*; 34, 76, *Third Dutch War*; 42, *Papers relating to the loss of Minorca in 1756*; 44, *The Old Scots Navy, 1689-1710*; 50, *Papers relating to the Law and Custom of the Sea*, II (1649-1767); 67, 68, 70, *The Byng Papers*; 73, *The Tangier Papers of Samuel Pepys*; 94, *The Walker Expedition to Quebec*, 1711. (See also biographical section.)

Ogg, D. *England in the Reign of James II and William III*, 1955. Ch. 12, The War at Sea, 1689-92; ch. 13, The War on Land and Sea, 1692-95.

Powley, E.B. *The English Navy in the Revolution of 1688*, 1928. Interesting conclusions, based on hydrography.
————. *The Naval Side of King William's War*, 1970. See also Ehrman, above.

*Richmond, Sir H.W. *The Navy in the War of 1739-1748*, 3 v. 1920.

Rose, J.H. *Man and the Sea: Stages in Maritime and Human Progress*, 1936.

Wilcox, L.A. *Mr. Pepys' Navy*, 1966. Extracts from his diary.

AX – 2   Anglo-Dutch Wars

Deen, L.D. *Anglo-Dutch Relations from 1660 to 1668* (ms. PhD thesis, Radcliffe, 1936).

DeVries, H. *The Anglo-Dutch War, 1672-1674* (ms. PhD thesis, Michigan, 1939).

Hansen, H.A. *The Sound Trade and Anglo-Dutch Conflicts, 1640-1654* (ms. PhD thesis, UCLA, 1947).

National Maritime Museum, *The Second Dutch War, Described in Pictures and Manuscripts of the Time*, 1967.

Rogers, P.G. *The Dutch in the Medway*, 1970.

*Tedder, A.W. *The Navy of the Restoration, from the Death of Cromwell to the Treaty of Breda and Its Work, Growth and Influence*, 1916.

Wilcox, L. *Mr. Pepys' Navy*, 1966. See Sect AX-2.

Wilson, C.H. *Holland and Britain*, 1946.
*————. *Profit and Power: A Study of England and the Dutch Wars*, 1957.

AX – 3   Anglo-French "Second Hundred Years War"

Bourne, R. *Queen Anne's Navy in the West Indies*, 1939.

Chard, D.F. *Pagans, Privateers and Propagandists: New England-Acadian Relations, 1690-1710* (ms. MA thesis, Dalhousie, 1967).

Clark, C.E. *The Eastern Frontier: The Settlement of Northern New England, 1610-1763*, 1970. Details of French and Indian Wars.

*Clark, G.N. *The Dutch Alliance and the War against French Trade, 1688-97*, 1923. See also the naval section of his general Seventeenth Century volume, already noted.

*Corbett, Sir J.S. *England in the Seven Years War: A Study in Combined Strategy*, 2 v. 1907.

Devine, J.A., Jr. *The British North American Colonies in the War of 1739-1748* (PhD thesis, Virginia, 1968; DA v. 30, p. 243A).

Downey, F. *Louisbourg, Key to a Continent*, 1965.

Gibson, J.S. *Ships of the '45; The Rescue of the Young Pretender*, 1968. French vessels and British blockaders and transports.

*Gipson, L.A. *The British Empire before the American Revolution*. See Sect. Z-2, 12 v., especially volumes on King George's War (Austrian Succession) and "The Great War for the Empire" (Seven Years War).

*Graham, G.S. *Empire of the North Atlantic: The Maritime Struggle for America*, 1950, 1958. A brilliant discussion of the maritime conditions affecting the Anglo-French rivalry for control of North America.

Hackmann, W.K. *English Military Expeditions to the Coast of France, 1757-1761* (PhD thesis, Michigan, 1969; DA v. 30, p. 384A).

Lawson, J.A. *Naval Strategy during the War of the League of Augsburg* (ms. PhD thesis, Leeds, 1952).

Lloyd, C. *The Capture of Quebec* (British Battles Series), 1959. One of the crop of works stimulated by the 200th anniversary. Like Stacey below, this tends to

236

downgrade the estimate of Wolfe's generalship as given in Parkman's classic *Montcalm and Wolfe*, 1892 ff, and, as a corollary, to upgrade the naval contribution under Saunders.

*Marcus, G.J. *Quiberon Bay: The Campaign in Home Waters, 1759* (British Battles Series), 1960. Valuable account of the somewhat neglected Eastern Atlantic aspects of the "annus mirabilis."

Norman, C.B. *The Corsairs of France*, 1887. Jean Bart and Duguay Trouin were at their most effective after the smashing of the regular French naval forces at La-Hogue in 1692.

Ogelsby, J.C.M. *War at Sea in the West Indies, 1739-1748* (PhD thesis, Univ. of Washington, 1963; DA v. 24, p. 2881). See also Pares below.

Owen, J.H. *The War at Sea under Queen Anne, 1702-1708*, 1938. See also Bourne above.

*Pares, R. *War and Trade in the West Indies, 1739-63*, 1936, 1963.
* —————. *Colonial Blockade and Neutral Rights, 1739-63*, 1938.

Peckham, H.H. *The Colonial Wars, 1689-1762*, 1964, RP1965.

Pope, D. *At 12 Mr. Byng was Shot*, 1962. The inexcusable execution of Admiral Byng as a scapegoat for the loss of Minorca in 1756. See also the biography by Brian Tunstall (1928) and *Papers Relating to the Loss of Minorca*, ed. H.W. Richmond (Navy Records Society, 42).

Powley, E.B. *The Naval Side of "King William's War" – Opening Phase 16/26 November 1689 to 31 December 1689* (ms. DPhil thesis, Oxford, 1962).

Smelser, M.T. *The Campaign for the Sugar Islands, 1759; A Study of Amphibious Warfare*, 1955 (PhD thesis, Harvard).

*Stacey, C.P. *Quebec, 1759; The Siege and the Battle*, 1959. See also Lloyd above.

AX – 4   Spanish, Portuguese, Etc.

Bensusan, H.G. *The Spanish Struggle against Encroachment . . . 1675-1690*. See Sect. AH-2.

*Boxer, C.R. *The Dutch in Brazil, 1624-1652*, 1957.
* —————. *Salvador da Sa and the Struggle for Brazil and Angola, 1602-1686*, 1953. The expulsion of the Dutch led to the very important introduction of sugar in the English and French West Indies.

Exquemelin, A.O. (Esquemling, J.) *The Buccaneers of America. . . .* 1684 ff. See Sect. BP.

Leebrick, K.C. *The English Expedition to Manila in 1762 and the Government of the Philippines by the East India Company* (ms. PhD thesis, Berkeley, 1917).

*MacLeish, F. and Krieger, M.L. *The Privateers, a Raiding Voyage in the Great South Sea*, 1962 (*Fabulous Voyage* in British edition). Raiding voyage of Woodes Rogers, Edward Cooke and William Dampier during the War of the Spanish Succession, 1708 ff, raiding the west coast of South America, rescuing Selkirk ("Robinson Crusoe") and capturing a Manila galleon. See also B. Little, *Crusoe's Captain* (1960) and J.C. Shipman, *William Dampier, Seaman-Scientist* (P1962).

Wilcox, L.A. *Anson's Voyage*, 1969.

AX – 5   Biography and Memoirs (1650-1763)

Abrahams, D.C. and Sherrin, N. *Benbow Was His Name*, 1967.

Beadon, R. *Robert Blake*, 1935.

Coxere, E. *The Adventures by Sea of Edward Coxere*, ed. E.H.W. Morgenstern, 1945.

Hakluyt Society, 1967. *Bryon's Journal of His Circumnavigation; Carteret's Voyage Round the World.*

Hartmann, C.H. *The Angry Admiral: The Later Career of Edward Vernon*, 1953.

*Hervey, A.J. *Augustus Hervey's Journal: Being the Intimate Account of the Life of a Captain in the Royal Navy Ashore and Afloat*, ed. D. Erskine, 1953. Covers the years 1746-59, including details of the loss of Minorca and the battle of Quiberon Bay. Gives vivid tactical details of the "wife in every port" aspect of naval life. Hervey became Earl of Bristol.

Laughton, Sir J.K. *From Howard to Nelson: Twelve Sailors*, 1899. Biographical sketches by various authors, including Blake, Rooke, Anson, Hawke, Boscawen and Rodney for this period.

Mackay, R.F. *Admiral Hawke*, 1965.

Navy Records Society Publications, 5, *Life of Captain Stephen Martin, 1666-1740*; 9, *Journal of Sir George Rooke*; 51, *Autobiography of Phineas Pett*; 52-53, *The Life of Admiral Sir John Leake*; 60, *Samuel Pepys's Naval Minutes*; 64, *The Journal of the First Earl of Sandwich* (not to be confused with the fourth earl); 65, *Boteler's Dialogue*; 76, *The Letters of Robert Blake*; 79, 80, *The Journals of Sir Thomas Allin, 1660-1678*; 88, *Pattee Byng's Journal* (2nd Viscount Torrington, c. 1718-20); 89, *The Sergison Papers* (successor to Pepys); 99, *The Vernon Papers.*

Ollard, R.L. *Man of War: Sir Robert Holmes and the Restoration Navy*, 1969. Holmes captured New Amsterdam from the Dutch in 1664.

*Pepys, S. *The Diary of Samuel Pepys*, 11 v. V. 1-3, 1969. "In a new and complete transcription edited by Robert Latham and William Matthews." Will supplant the standard Wheatley edition when completed.

Rogers, W. *Life Aboard a British Privateer in the Time of Queen Anne: The Journal of Captain Woodes Rogers, Master Mariner,* 1889, R1970. See also MacLeish, Sect. AX-4.

Simpson, R.F. *The Naval Career of Admiral Sir George Pocock, KB, 1743-1763* (ms. PhD thesis, Indiana, 1951).

AY   1764-1792

From preceding – Anderson, Ballard, Graham, Mahan.

AY – 1   General

*Albion, R.G. *Forests and Sea Power.* . . . 1926, R1965. Ch. 7, Masts and American Independence.
───────── and Pope, J.B. *Sea Lanes in Wartime: The American Experience, 1775-1945,* 1942, R1968. A study of wartime shipping conditions. Ch. 2, Gunrunning in the Revolution.

*Allen, G.W. *A Naval History of the American Revolution,* 2 v. 1913, R1962. Best for the little American Navy.
───────── . *Massachusetts Privateers of the Revolution,* 1927.

*Anderson, T.S. *The Command of the Howe Brothers during the American Revolution,* 1936 (DPhil thesis, Oxford).

Begnaud, A.E. *British Operations in the Caribbean and the American Revolution* (PhD thesis, Tulane, 1966; DA v. 27, p. 3390A).

Brebner, J.B. *The Neutral Yankees of Nova Scotia: A Marginal Colony During the Revolutionary Years,* 1937.

*Clark, W.B., ed. *Naval Documents of the American Revolution,* c15 v. 1964-
This ambitious series is being prepared under the direction of the Naval History Division. The selection of material is on a very broad basis, not limited to purely naval matters. The arrangement is chronological, on the basis of the arrival of overseas material. Dr. Clark died after the completion of the fourth volume; his successor as editor is Dr. W.L. Morgan of the Naval History Division staff.

Coakley, R.W. *Virginia Commerce During the American Revolution* (ms. PhD thesis, Virginia, 1949).

Coggins, J. *Ships and Seamen of the American Revolution: Vessels, Crews, Weapons, Gear, Naval Tactics and Actions of the War for Independence,* 1969.

*East, R.A. *Business Enterprise in the American Revolutionary Era,* 1938, R1965. Extensive bibliography.

239

*Gipson, L.A. *The British Empire Before the American Revolution.* See Sect. Z-2. V. 11, *The Rumbling of the Coming Storm, 1766-1770,* 1965; v. 12, *Britain Sails into the Storm, 1770-1776,* 1965.

Gruber, I.D. *Admiral Lord Howe and the War for American Independence* (PhD thesis, Duke, 1961; DA v. 26, p. 3901). See also Anderson above.

*(Hamond, A.S.) *The Hamond Naval Papers, 1766-1825,* 1967. Three rolls of microfilm and a printed guide. Includes papers of Capt. Andrew Snape Hamond, RN, Lt. Governor of Nova Scotia and active frigate captain. Microfilmed by Univ. of Virginia Library. See also G.E. Hamond, Sect. AZ-3.

Hewitt, M.J. *The West Indies in the American Revolution* (ms. DPhil thesis, Oxford, 1938).

*James, Sir W.M. *The British Navy in Adversity: A Study of the War of American Independence,* 1926, 1970. By a British admiral.

*Mackesy, P. *The War for America, 1775-1783,* 1966. "A study in British strategy and leadership . . . . There are few references to tactics and barely any to individual engagements. This is the war as North and the King, as Germain and Sandwich saw it; a war for America that after Saratoga was fought almost everywhere else."

Maclay, E.S. *History of the American Privateers,* 1899. Part I.

*Mahan, A.T. *Major Operations of the Navies in the War of American Independence,* 1915, R1969. Practically the same as the section he contributed to W.L. Clowes' cooperative *The Royal Navy.* He treats the subject more briefly in his initial volume, *The Influence of Sea Power upon History, 1660-1783,* 1890 ff.

Morse, S.G. *New England Privateering in the American Revolution* (ms. PhD thesis, Harvard, 1941).

Naval History Society, 1, *The Logs of the* Serapis . . . . 4, *Out-Letters of the Continental Marine Committee and Board of Admiralty, August 1776-September 1780.* This American counterpart of the Navy Records Society published a number of useful volumes during its relatively brief career.

*Nettels, C.P. *The Emergence of a National Economy, 1775-1815,* 1962.

*Paullin, C.O. *The Navy of the American Revolution: Its Policy and Its Administration,* 1906 (PhD thesis, Chicago), R1970.

Powers, S.T. *The Decline and Extinction of American Naval Power, 1781-1787* (PhD thesis, Notre Dame, 1965; DA v. 26, p. 2169).

Stout, N.R. *The Royal Navy in American Waters, 1760-1775* (ms. PhD thesis, Wisconsin, 1961).

AY – 2   Individual Operations and Aspects

Ahlin, J.H. *New England Rubicon: A Study of Eastern Maine during the American Revolution* (ms. PhD thesis, Boston Univ., 1961).

Andrews, A. *Proud Fortress: The Fighting Story of Gibraltar*, 1959. Ch. 6, The Great Siege. See also McGuffie and Russell below.

Augur, H. *The Secret War of Independence: French, Dutch and Spanish Connivance at the Furnishing of Supplies to the Americans*, 1955.

Clark, W.B. *Ben Franklin's Privateers*, 1956. Fitted out in France.
————. *George Washington's Navy: Being an Account of His Excellency's Fleet in New England Waters*, 1960. Small force organized to capture British supplies.

Davies, J.A. *An Inquiry into Faction among British Naval Officers during the War of the American Revolution* (ms. MA thesis, Liverpool, 1964).

Evans, R.A. *The Army and Navy at Halifax in Peace Time, 1783-1793* (ms. MA thesis, Dalhousie, 1970).

*Fleming, T. *Beat the Last Drum: The Siege of Yorktown, 1781*, 1963. See also Larrabee below.

Glasscock, M.B. *New Spain and the War for America, 1779-1782* (PhD thesis, Louisiana State, 1969; DA v. 30, p. 2039A). Silver, etc., from Mexico in support of anti-British war effort. Based on archives at Mexico City and Madrid.

Johnson, R.F. *The* Royal George, 1971. Capsizing of huge flagship at Spithead, 1778, with heavy loss of life.

Kerr, W.B. *Bermuda and the American Revolution, 1760-1783*, 1969.

Larrabee, H.A. *Decision at the Chesapeake*, 1964. Yorktown; see also Fleming above.

Lemisch, L.J. *Jack Tar vs. John Bull: The Role of New York's Seamen in Precipitating the Revolution* (ms. PhD thesis, Yale, 1962).

Lundeberg, P.K. *The Continental Gunboat* Philadelphia, P1966. Part of Benedict Arnold's little lake flotilla.

McGowan, G.S., Jr. *The British Occupation of Charles Town, 1780-1782* (ms. PhD thesis, Emory, 1965).

McGuffie, T.H. *The Siege of Gibraltar, 1779-1783* (British Battles Series), 1964. See also Andrews above and Russell below.

McLarty, R.N. *The Expedition of Major General John Vaughn to the Lesser Antilles, 1779-1781* (PhD thesis, Michigan, 1951; DA v. 11, p. 660).

Middlebrook, L.F. *History of Maritime Connecticut during the American Revolution*, 2 v. 1925.

*Patterson, A.T. *The Other Armada: The Franco-Spanish Attempt to Invade Britain in 1779*, 1960. One of England's narrowest escapes; despite helplessness of outnumbered British fleet, the Allies were kept from utilizing their unique opportunity by a combination of faulty supplies, sickness, storms and dissension.

Rawson, G. *Pandora's Last Voyage*, 1964. Follow-up of *Bounty* mutiny; see comments, Sect. O-1.

*Richmond, Sir H.W. *The Navy in India, 1763-1783*, 1931. Analysis of the campaigning of Suffren and Hughes.

Russell, J. *Gibraltar Besieged, 1779-1783*, 1965.

*Sargent, D. *Shipping and the American War 1775-1783: A Study of the Board of Trade Transport Organization*, 1970. See also Syrett below.

Stewart, R.A. *The History of Virginia's Navy of the Revolution*, 1933.

Syrett, D. *The Navy Board Administration of the Maritime Logistics of the British Forces during the American War, 1775-83* (ms. PhD thesis, London, 1966). See also Sargent above.

Van Dusen, A.E. *The Trade of Revolutionary Connecticut* (ms. PhD thesis, Pennsylvania, 1948).

Wells, D.F. *The Trial of Admiral Keppel, 1779; A Study of Political Opposition to the North Ministry* (ms. PhD thesis, Kentucky, 1957).

AY – 3   Biography, Memoirs and Papers, 1764-1792

Alberts, R.C. *The Golden Voyage: The Life and Times of William Bingham, 1752-1804*, 1969. During the Revolution, Bingham was American contraband agent in the West Indies.

Anderson, B. . . . *Captain George Vancouver*, 1960, R1967. See Sect. Q-4.

*Billias, G.A., ed. *George Washington's Opponents: British Generals and Admirals in the American Revolution*, 1969. Cooperative biographies.

Clark, W.B. *Lambert Wickes, Sea Raider and Diplomat*, 1932.
————. *Gallant John Barry, 1745-1803*, 1938.
————. *Captain Dauntless*, the *Story of Nicholas Biddle*. . . . 1949.

Field, E. *Esek Hopkins, Commander-in-Chief of the Continental Navy*, 1898.

Footner, H. *Sailor of Fortune* . . . *Commodore Barney, USN*, 1940.

Greenwood, I.J. *Captain John Manley* . . . *1775-1783*, 1915.

Jones, C.H. *Captain Gustavus Conyngham*, 1903.

Lewis, C.L. *Admiral DeGrasse and American Independence*, 1945.

Lorenz, L. *The Admiral and the Empress: John Paul Jones and Catherine the Great*, 1954. Also wrote one of the better biographies of Jones, 1943.

*Macintyre, D. *Admiral Rodney*, 1963. See also Spinney below.

Martelli, G. *Jemmy Twitcher. A Life of the Fourth Earl of Sandwich, 1718-1792*. The first formal biography of the highly controversial First Lord of the Admiralty during the Revolution. See also the several theses on his administration by R. G. Usher (1943), G.A. Morrison (1950), M.J. Williams (1962), and M.B. Wickwire (1962) below. Also the volume of *Private Papers of John, Earl of Sandwich* (Navy Records Society, 77, 81).

Morgan, W.J. *Captains to the Northward: The New England Captains in the Continental Navy*, 1959 (PhD thesis, So. California).

*Morison, S.E. *John Paul Jones: A Sailor's Biography*, 1959. The best of the many lives of Jones, bringing out his strong and less admirable qualities. The best of the other accounts are by A.F. DeKoven (2 v. 1913) and L. Lorenz (1943). The worst, embodying many errors, was by A.C. Buell, 2 v. 1900.

Morrison, G.A. *The Earl of Sandwich and British Naval Administration in the War of the American Revolution* (ms. PhD thesis, Ohio State, 1950).

Naval History Society, 2, *Fanning's Narrative. . . 1778-1783*; 6, *Letters and Papers Relating to the Cruise of Gustavus Conyngham*; 7, *The Graves Papers*.

Navy Records Society Publications, 3, *Letters of Lord Hood, 1781-82*; 32, *Letters and Papers of Charles, Lord Barham* (at this period he was Sir Charles Middleton, Controller of the Navy); 69, 71, 75, 78, *The Private Papers of John, Earl of Sandwich*; 77, 81, *Letters and Papers of Admiral the Hon. Samuel Barrington*; 101, *A Memoir of James Trevenen* (on Cook's third voyage and then in Russian navy).

*Spinney, D. *Rodney*, 1969. The definitive biography.

Usher, R.G., Jr. *The Civil Administration of the British Navy during the American Revolution* (ms. PhD thesis, Michigan, 1943).

Vancouver, G. *Voyage of Discovery to the North Pacific Ocean and Round the World*, 3 v. 1788, R1966. See also Anderson above.

Wickwire, F.B. and M.B. *Cornwallis, the American Adventure*, 1970.

Wickwire, M.B. *Lord Sandwich and the King's Ships. British Naval Administration, 1771-1782* (ms. PhD thesis, Yale, 1962). Sympathetic.

Williams, M.J. *The Naval Administration of the Fourth Earl of Sandwich, 1771-1782* (ms. DPhil thesis, Oxford, 1962). See Martelli above.

AZ – 1 General

Arthur, C.B. *The Revolution of British Naval Strategy, 1800-1801* (ms. PhD thesis, Harvard, 1964).

Gwynne-Timothy, J.R.W. *Anglo-French Colonial Rivalry, 1783-1815* (ms. DPhil thesis, Oxford, 1943).

*Heckscher, E.F. *The Continental System, an Economic Interpretation,* 1922.

*James, W. *Naval History of Great Britain* (1793-1820), 6 v. 1860 ff. Useful for its minutely detailed play-by-play account, but has strongly pro-British slant. Index was published by the Navy Records Society, No. 6, 1895 but it does not fit all editions.

*Lewis, M.A. *The Social History of the Royal Navy, 1793-1815,* 1961. Aside from discussion of origins, recruitment and professional aspects of the naval personnel, Part 6, "The Price of Admiralty: Action, Accidents and Disease" brings out a surprising contrast between the British and their enemies. The British lost 101 major vessels by shipwreck, etc., but only 10 by enemy action. The enemy lost 24 by shipwreck, etc., and 377 to the British. The same proportion held for deaths by sickness, etc., and by enemy action.

*Mahan, A.T. *The Influence of Sea Power upon the French Revolution and Empire, 1793-1812,* 2 v. 1893 ff. A valuable work, much more so than his *The Life of Nelson, the Embodiment of the Sea Power of Great Britain,* 2 v., 1897.

Melvin, F.E. *Napoleon's Navigation System: A Study of Trade Control during the Continental Blockade,* 1919 (PhD thesis, Pennsylvania).

Navy Records Society Publications, 16, 18, *Logs of the Great Sea Fights, 1794-1805.*

Rose, J.H. *The Indecisiveness of Modern Naval War,* 1927, R1968. A collection of separate studies, including Ch. 3, Plans of Invasion of the British Isles; 4, The Struggle for the Mediterranean in the Eighteenth Century; 5, The Influence of Sea Power on Indian History (1746-1813); 6, Napoleon and Sea Power; 8, The State of Nelson's Fleet before Trafalgar; 9, The British Title to Malta; 10, Admiral Duckworth's Failure at Constantinople in 1807; 11, Chivalry at Sea.

AZ – 2 Individual Operations and Aspects

*Albion, R.G. *Forests and Sea Power. . . .* 1926 (PhD thesis, Harvard), R1965. Ch. 8, Timber Trust and Continental System; ch. 9, Searching the World for Timber; ch. 10, Trafalgar and Dry Rot.

Austen, H.C.M. *Sea Fights and Corsairs of the Indian Ocean: Being the Naval History of Mauritius from 1715 to 1810*, 1935.

Bond, G.C. *The British Expedition to the Scheldt, 1809* (PhD thesis, Florida, 1966; DA v. 30, p. 5369A).

Carrillo, E.A. *The British Occupation of Corsica, 1794-1796, a Study in Mediterranean Politics* (ms. PhD thesis, Fordham, 1953).

Condon, M.E.A. *The Administration of the Transport Service during the War against Revolutionary France, 1793-1802* (ms. PhD thesis, London, 1968).

*Corbett, Sir J.S. *The Campaign of Trafalgar*, 1910. Later studies, in addition to the Nelson biographies, have been written by E. Desbriere (1933), R. Maine (1957), O. Warner (1959), D. Pope (1960), D. Howarth (1969), R.H. Mackenzie (1969).

Desbriere, E. *The Naval Campaign of 1805 – Trafalgar*, 2 v. 1933. Originally drawn up as part of research for war plans for an invasion of England at the time of the Fashoda crisis in 1898.

*Dugan, J. *The Great Mutiny*, 1965. The Spithead and Nore mutinies of 1797 with an account of their political background.

Howarth, D. *Trafalgar: The Nelson Touch*, 1969. Very well illustrated.

Kennedy, W.B. *French Projects for the Invasion of Ireland, 1796-1798* (PhD thesis, Georgia, 1966; DA v. 27, p. 3399A).

Legg, S., ed. *Trafalgar, An Eye Witness' Account*, 1966. "Told here almost entirely in the words of the men, British, French and Spanish."

*Lloyd, C. *Battles of St. Vincent and Camperdown* (British Battles Series), 1964.

Longridge, G.N. *The Anatomy of Nelson's Ships*, 1953. Of particular interest to model-makers.

Mackenzie, R.H. *The Trafalgar Roll*, 1969.

*Mackesy, P. *War in the Mediterranean, 1803-1810*, 1958 (DPhil thesis, Oxford). Offsets the tendency to neglect major strategic considerations after Trafalgar.

Nasatir, A.P. *Spanish War Vessels in the Mississippi, 1792-1799*, 1967.

Navy Records Society Publications, 14, 21, *Papers Relating to the Blockade of Brest, 1803-1805*.

Norway, A.H. *History of the Post-Office Packet Service during the Years 1793-1815*, 1895.

Olson, M.L., Jr. *The Economics of Wartime Shortage: A History of British Food Supplies in the Napoleonic Wars and in World War I and World War II*, 1963.

*Parkinson, C.N. *War in the Eastern Seas, 1793-1815*, 1953, R1965. A companion work to his *Trade in the Eastern Seas, 1793-1813*. Ably analyzes the operations of the British and French fleets around the Indian Ocean.

Pengelly, C. *The First* Bellerophon: *The Life of a Famous Ship*, 1966. Among other things, Napoleon took refuge on her after Waterloo.

Richardson, F. *Nelson's Navy*, 1967.

Rodgers, A.B. *The War of the Second Coalition, 1798 to 1801*, 1965. Includes considerable detail on the Egyptian operations.

Roselli, J. *Lord William Bentinck and the British Occupation of Sicily, 1811-1814*, 1957 (PhD thesis, Cambridge).

Sanderson, M.W.B. *Naval Strategy and Maritime Trade in the Caribbean*. See Sect. AG-3.

Saul, N.E. *Russia and the Mediterranean, 1797-1807* (PhD thesis, Columbia, 1965; DA v. 26, p. 7286).

Warner, O. *The Battle of the Nile*, 1960.
————. *The Glorious First of June*, 1961. These, with his *Trafalgar*, 1959, were written for the British Battles Series.

AZ – 3   Biography, Memoirs and Papers, 1793-1815 – European

Arnold-Forster, D. *At War with the Smugglers*. . . . See Sect. BJ-2.

Berckman, E. *Nelson's Dear Lord: A Portrait of St. Vincent*, 1965. See also James below.

Gardiner, J.A. *Above and Under Hatches, Being Naval Recollections in Shreds and Patches*, ed. C. Lloyd, 1955. For this and various other memoirs of this period see Sect. O-6.

(Hamond, G.E.) *The Hamond Naval Papers, 1766-1825*, 1967. See comments under A.S. Hamond, Sect. AY-1.

Hardwick, M. *Emma, Lady Hamilton*, 1969.

James, Sir W. *Old Oak, the Life of John Jervis, Earl of St. Vincent*, 1950.

*Kennedy, L.H.C. *Nelson's Captains*, 1951. The British edition appeared under the title *The Band of Brothers*.

*Mahan, A.T. *Types of Naval Officers*, 1893. Examples drawn chiefly from the British Navy in this period.

Navy Records Society Publications, 28, *The Correspondence of Admiral John*

Markham, 1801-07; 46, 48, 58, 59, *The Private Papers of George, Second Earl Spencer* (First Lord of the Admiralty); 55, 61, *The Letters of Lord St. Vincent whilst First Lord of the Admiralty, 1801-1804*; 62, 90, 96, *Letters and Papers of Admiral Viscount Keith*; 100, *Nelson's Letters to His Wife and Other Documents*; 110, *The Saumarez Papers, 1808-1812*.

*Oman, C. *Nelson, a Biography*, 1954. Probably the best of the many biographies; other good ones include A.T. Mahan (2 v. 1897) and O. Warner (1958). The earliest was by the poet Robert Southey.

(Richardson, W.) *A Mariner of England: An Account of William Richardson from Cabin Boy in the Merchant Service to Warrant Officer in the Royal Navy (1780 to 1819), as told by himself*, ed. S. Childers, 1908, R1970.

Russell, Lord. *Knight of the Sword: The Life and Letters of Admiral William Sidney Smith*, 1965.

Waite, R.A., Jr. *Sir Home Riggs Popham, a Biography* (ms. PhD thesis, Harvard, 1945). British admiral who took the Cape of Good Hope and the Plata in 1806.

Warner, O. *Nelson's Battles* (British Battles Series), 1965. See Sect. AZ-2.

BA 1793-1815 AMERICAN

BA – 1 General

*Adams, H. *History of the United States* (1801-1817), 9 v. 1889-91. Long the best account of the whole maritime-naval situation.

Albion, R.G. and Pope, J.B. *Sea Lane in Wartime*, 1942. Ch. 3, 4.

Brant, I. *James Madison*, 6 v. 1941-61. V. 4, *Secretary of State*, 1800-09; v. 2, *Commander-in-Chif*, 1812-15. Also P1968.

Hyneman, C.S. *Neutrality During the European Wars of 1792-1815*, 1930 (PhD thesis, Illinois).

*Mahan, A.T. *Sea Power in Its Relation to the War of 1812*, 2 v. 1905, R1968. V. 1, includes an analysis of the prewar maritime conditions; in v. 2, Mahan emphasizes the effectiveness of the British blockade and minimizes the usefulness of privateers.

*Nettels, C.P. *The Emergence of a National Economy, 1775-1815*, 1962, RP1969.

Porter, K.W. *John Jacob Astor, Business Man*, 2 v. 1931 (PhD thesis, Harvard), R1966. Ch. 9-11.

White, P.T. *Anglo-American Relations from 1803 to 1815* (PhD thesis, Minnesota, 1954; DA v. 15, p. 2523).

*Allen, G.W. *Our Naval War with France*, 1909, 1967.
*————. *Our Navy and the Barbary Corsairs*, 1905, R1965.

Barnaby, H.C. *The Prisoners of Algiers: An Account of the Forgotten American-Algerian War, 1785-1797*, 1966.

*Bemis, S.F. *Jay's Treaty: A Study in Commerce and Diplomacy*, 1923 (PhD thesis, Harvard), RP1962. See also Perkins below.
*————. *Pinckney's Treaty: America's Advantage from Europe's Distress, 1783-1800*, 1926, RP1960.

Carrigg, J.J. *Benjamin Stoddert and the Foundation of the American Navy* (ms. PhD thesis, Georgetown, 1953). See also Smelser below.

*Clauder, A.C. *American Commerce as Affected by the Wars of the French Revolution and Napoleon, 1793-1812*, 1932 (PhD thesis, Pennsylvania).

Crosby, A.W., Jr. *America, Russia, Hemp and Napoleon: A Study of the Trade Between the United States and Russia, 1783-1814*, 1965 (PhD thesis, Boston Univ.).

DeConde, A. *The Quasi-War, The Politics and Diplomacy of the Undeclared War with France, 1797-1801*, 1967.

Elkins, W.H. *British Policy in Its Relation to the Commerce and Navigation of the United States of America from 1794 to 1807* (ms. DPhil thesis, Oxford, 1936).

Emmerson, J.C., Jr. *The Chesapeake Affair of 1807*, 1954.

Jackson, M.H. *Privateers in Charleston, 1793-1796: An Account of the French Palatinate in South Carolina* (Smithsonian Institution), 1969 (PhD thesis, Harvard).

Jennings, W.W. *The American Embargo, 1807-1809, with particular reference to Its effect on Industry*, 1921.

Jessup, P.C., et al. *Neutrality: Its History, Economics and Law*, 4 v. 1935-36. V. 2, *The Napoleonic Period*.

Lester, M. *Anglo-American Diplomatic Problems Arising from British Naval Operations in American Waters, 1793-1802* (ms. PhD thesis, Virginia, 1954).

Luke, M.H. *The Port of New York, 1800-1810: The Foreign Trade and Business Community*, 1953 (PhD thesis, New York Univ.).

Nash, H.P. *The Forgotten Wars*, 1968. The Quasi-War and Tripolitan War.

*Perkins, B. *First Rapprochement: England and the United States, 1795-1805*, 1955.
*————. *Prologue to War: England and the Unitea States, 1805-1812*, 1961.
————. *Causes of the War of 1812*, P1962.

Polich, J.L. *Foreign Maritime Intervention on Spain's Pacific Coast 1786-1810* (PhD thesis, New Mexico, 1968; DA v. 30, p. 665A).

Richmond, A.A., III. *The United States in the Armed Neutrality of 1800* (ms. PhD thesis, Yale, 1951).

Rubin, I.I. *New York State and the Long Embargo* (PhD thesis, New York Univ., 1961; DA v. 23, p. 612).

Savage, C. *The Policy of the United States toward Maritime Commerce in War* (U.S. Dept. of State), 2 v. 1934-36.

Sears, L.M. *Jefferson and the Embargo*, 1967.

*Smelser, M. *The Congress Founds the Navy, 1787-1798*, 1959. See also Carrigg above.

Stephen, J. *War in Disguise, or the Frauds of the Neutral Flags*, 1805. This Briton's criticism, at a time when Napoleon was threatening invasion, led to a curtailment of American profits in transshipping cargoes between France and her West Indian colonies.

*U.S. Office of Naval Records and Library, *Naval Documents Related to the Quasi-War between the United States and France, Naval Operations, from February 1797 to May 1800*, 7 v. 1935-38.
*————. *Naval Documents Related to the United States Wars with the Barbary Powers*, 6 v. 1934-35. The *Register of Officer Personnel and Ships' Data*, 1945, is essentially a seventh volume. These two admirable collections of a wide variety of source material, arranged chronologically in "calendar" form, are a rich mine of information for many varied subjects. They were conceived and directed by Commodore D.W. Knox. At long last, after a period of inactivity, the Naval History Division is undertaking a very ambitious collection of the records of the American Revolution under W.B. Clark (see Sect. AY-1).

Wright, L.B. and Macleod, J.H. *First Americans in North Africa: William Eaton's Struggle for a Vigorous Policy Against the Barbary Pirates, 1799-1805*, 1945.

Zimmerman, J.F. *Impressment of American Seamen*, 1925 (PhD thesis, Columbia).

BA – 3   The War of 1812

Bierne, E.F. *The War of 1812*, 1949, R1965.

Brooks, C.B. *The Siege of New Orleans*, 1961. Like next item, emphasizes the amphibious aspects.

Brown, W.S. *The Amphibious Campaign for West Florida and Louisiana, 1814-1815. A Critical Review of Strategy and Tactics at New Orleans*, 1969.

Eckert, E.K. *William Jones . . . in the War of 1812*. See Sect. AQ-2.

Handren, B.E. *The Anglo-American Competition in Wartime, 1812-15* (ms. PhD thesis, Edinburgh, 1961).

Horgan, T.P. *Old Ironsides, the Story of the USS* Constitution, 1963.

Horsman, R. *Causes of the War of 1812*, 1969.

Jacobs, J.R. and Tucker, G. *The War of 1812, a Compact History*, 1969.

*James, W. *An Inquiry into the Merits of the Principal Naval Actions between Great Britain and the United States, comprising an account of all British and American Ships of War, reciprocally captured and destroyed since the 18th of June, 1812*, 1816. A vigorous presentation of the British point of view.

Johnes, B.J. *The War of 1812; The British Navy, New England, and the Maritime Provinces* (ms. MA thesis, Maine, 1971).

Maclay, E.S. *History of the American Privateers*, 1899. Part II.

*Mahan, A.T. *Sea Power in Its Relation to the War of 1812*, 2 v., 1905, R1968.

McKee, L.A.M. *Captain Isaac Hull and the Boston Navy Yard, 1813-1815* (PhD thesis, St. Louis, 1968; DA v. 29, p. 1620A).

Muller, C.G. *The Proudest Day: MacDonough on Lake Champlain*, 1966. "Although he knows enough to have produced a sound historical treatise, he has succumbed to the temptation to fictionalize."
—————. *The Darkest Day, 1814. The Washington-Baltimore Campaign* (Great Battles), 1964.

*Napier, H.E. *New England Blockaded in 1814: The Journal of Henry Edward Napier, Lieutenant in H.M.S.* Nymph, ed. W.M. Whitehill. Graphic details of the thoroughness of the blockade, even against Cape Ann fishing boats.

Padfield, P. *Broke and the* Shannon, 1968. See also Poolman and Pullen below.

*Picking, S. *Sea Fight Off Monhegan:* Enterprise *and* Boxer, 1941. Excellent account by a naval officer, including surprising details of clandestine trading with the enemy.

*Poolman, K. *Guns Off Cape Ann*, 1961. Competent British account of the defeat of the *Chesapeake* by the *Shannon*.

Pullen, H.F. *The* Shannon *and the* Chesapeake, 1970. The third account in ten years of Britain's favorite frigate action.

Roosevelt, T. *The Naval War of 1812*, 1882, R1968. The first literary effort of the future president. He also contributed a section on this war to Clowes, *The Navy*.

Rosenberg, M. *The Building of Perry's Fleet on Lake Erie, 1812-1813*, 1950, P1968. The same subject is treated in fictional form in C.D. Lane, *The Fleet in the Forest*; 1943.

Snider, C.H.J. *Under the Red Jack: Privateers of the Maritime Provinces of Canada in the War of 1812*, 1928.

—————. *In the Wake of the Eighteen-Twelvers*, 1928.

Tucker, G. *Poltroons and Patriots, A Popular Account of the War of 1812*, 2 v. 1954.

BA – 4   Biography, Memoirs and Papers, American 1789-1815

Allen, G.W., ed. *Commodore Hull, Papers of Isaac Hull, Commodore U.S.N.* 1929. Although Hull captured the *Guerriere*, he had to wait a longer time than most before he commanded more than one ship so as to rate the title of Commodore. See also L.A.M. McKee, Sect. BA-3.

Cobb, E. *Elijah Cobb, 1768-1848, a Cape Cod Skipper*, ed. R.D. Paine, 1925, R1970.

*Coggeshall, G. *Voyages to Various Parts of the World*, 1851 ff, R1970. Like the more compact reminiscences of Cobb, above, full of excellent "case histories" of trading adventures during the period.

Evans, A.A. *Journal Kept on Board the Frigate* Constitution, *1812*, 1967.

Ferguson, E.S. *Truxtun of the* Constellation: *The Life of Commodore Thomas Truxtun, U.S. Navy, 1755-1822*, 1956.

Gares, A.J. *Stephen Girard's West Indian Trade from 1789 to 1812* (ms. PhD thesis, Temple, 1947).

Grenfell, R. *Nelson the Sailor*, 1949. Second edition, 1968, retitled *Horatio Nelson, A Short Biography*.

*Guttridge, L.F. *The Commodores: The U.S. Navy in the Age of Sail*, 1969. See also Pratt below.

*Pratt, F. *Preble's Boys: Commodore Preble and the Birth of American Sea Power*, 1950. Brief biographical sketches of 15 naval commanders of the War of 1812 who had received rigid indoctrination under Preble; Hull, Jacob Jones, Decatur, Bainbridge, Lawrence, Chauncey, Porter, Burrowes, Blakely, Warrington, Biddle, Stewart, Macdonough, Cassin, and Patterson. Other biographies of that group include those of Bainbridge by J. Barnes (1897) and H.A.S. Dearborn (1816, R1931); Decatur by I. Anthony (1931) and C.L. Lewis (1937); Hull by B. Grant (1947) and G.W. Allen, noted above (1929); Macdonough by R. Macdonough (1909) and Porter by A.D. Turnbull (1929). Not in that group, Rodgers by *C.O. Paullin (1910, R1968) and James Barron by W.O. Stevens (1969).

Reindehl, J.B. *The Impact of the French Revolution and Napoleon Upon the United States As Revealed by the Fortunes of the Crowninshield Family of Salem* (PhD thesis, Michigan State, 1953; DA v. 14, p. 794).

BB – 1   Foreign

*Bartlett, C.J. *Great Britain and Sea Power, 1815-1853*, 1963. The author "attempts a synthesis, not of all naval history of the period, but of the main forces determining British naval policy." Chapters: 1, Peace, Parsimony and the Post-War Navy; 2, Sea Power and Foreign Policy, 1815-1835; 3, Sea Power and International Rivalry, 1836-41; 4, Steamers and the First Invasion Scare; 5, Steam Power and National Defence; 6, British Naval Policy, 1848-53; 7, Portrait of the Pre-Crimean Navy; 8, British Sea Power in 1853. See also Lewis below.

Bassett, M. *Behind the Picture: HMS* Rattlesnake's *Australia-New Guinea Cruise, 1846 to 1850*, 1966. See also Lubbock, *Owen Stanley*, Sect. AL-3.

Baxter, C.F. *Admiralty Problems During the Second Palmerston Administration, 1859-1865* (PhD thesis, Georgia, 1965; DA v. 26, p. 6669).

*Baxter, J.P. *The Introduction of the Ironclad Warship*, 1933 (PhD thesis, Harvard), R1968.

Bealer, L.W. *The Privateers of Buenos Aires, 1815-1821: Their Activities in the Hispano-American Wars of Independence* (PhD thesis, Berkeley, 1935). Published in Spanish as *Los Corsarios de Buenos Aires*, 1937.

Fox, G.E. *British Admirals and Chinese Pirates, 1832-1860*, 1940 (PhD thesis, Columbia).

*Graham, G.S. *The Politics of Naval Supremacy: Studies in British Maritime Ascendancy*, 1965.
*————. *Great Britain and the Indian Ocean: A Study of Maritime Enterprise, 1810-1850*, 1967.
*———— ed. *The Navy and South America, 1807-1823* (Navy Records Society, 104), 1960. Despatches from admirals on that station.

Holt, E. *The Opium Wars in China*, 1964. Emphasis on the military and naval aspects. See also Hurd and Navy Records Society, below, and Sect. AK-3.

Hurd, D. *The Arrow War: An Anglo-Chinese Confusion, 1856-60*, 1968.

Lensen, G.A. *The Russia Push toward Japan*, 1959. Development of PhD thesis, Columbia, 1956: *Russia's Japan Expedition of 1852 to 1855*. This, of course, was exactly the period of Perry's expedition.

*Lewis, M.A. *The Navy in Transition, 1814-1864, A Social History*, 1965. Sequel to his valuable *Social History of the Navy, 1793-1815*, with different emphasis from the Bartlett volume on the same period.

*Lloyd, C. *The Navy and the Slave Trade....* See Sect. AI-6.

McCleary, J.W. *Anglo-French Naval Rivalry, 1815-1848* (ms. PhD thesis, Johns Hopkins, 1947). See also Swain below.

McKnight, J.L. *Admiral Ushakov and the Ionian Republic: The Genesis of Russia's First Balkan Satellite* (PhD thesis, Wisconsin, 1965; DA v. 26, p. 1615).

Moorehead, A. *Darwin and the* Beagle, 1969. The scientific voyage on British cruiser, on which he got start for his *Origin of Species*. See Mellersh biography of Capt. Fitzroy, Sect. BB-3.

Navy Records Society Publications, 72, *Piracy in the Levant, 1827-8*; 83-85, *Russian War . . . Official Correspondence*; 87, *The Naval Brigade in the Indian Mutiny*; 95, *The Second China War, 1856-60*; 104, *The Navy and South America, 1807-1823*.

Selby, J. *The Paper Dragon: An Account of the Chinese Wars, 1840-1900*, 1968.

Soulsby, H.G. *The Right of Search and the Slave Trade in Anglo-American Relations, 1814-1862*, 1933 (PhD thesis, Johns Hopkins).

Swain, J.E. *The Struggle for the Control of the Mediterranean prior to 1848: A Study in Anglo-French Relations*, 1933 (PhD thesis, Pennsylvania).

Wallin, F.W. *The French Navy During the Second Empire: A Study of Technological Development on French Government Policy* (ms. PhD thesis, Berkeley, 1954).

Ward, W.E. *The Royal Navy and the Slavers. . . .* See Sect. AI-6.

*Woodhouse, C.M. *The Battle of Navarino* (British Battles Series), 1965.

Worcester, D.E. *Sea Power and Chilean Independence*, 1962.

Consult also, for further naval items the sections on the Slave Trade, AI-6 and Pacific Exploration, Q-4.

BB – 2   American

Allen, G.W. *Our Navy and the West Indian Pirates*, 1929.

Baker, M.D., Jr. *The United States and Piracy during the Spanish-American Wars of Independence* (ms. PhD thesis, Duke, 1947).

*Bauer, K.J. *Surfboats and Horse Marines: United States Naval Operations in the Mexican War, 1846-48*, 1969 (PhD thesis, Indiana). See also Betts and Manno below.

Betts, J.L. *The United States Navy and the Mexican War* (ms. PhD thesis, Chicago, 1955).

Bidwell, R.L. *The First Mexican Navy, 1821-30* (PhD thesis, Virginia, 1960; DA v. 21 p. 170).

*Billingsley, E.B. *In Defense of Neutral Rights: The United States Navy and the*

Wars of Independence in Chile and Peru, 1967 (PhD thesis, North Carolina, 1965).

*Bradlee, F.B.C. *Piracy in the West Indies and Its Suppression*, 1923, 1970. See also articles by C.F. Goodrich in U.S. Naval Institute *Proceedings*, sometimes bound as a book.

Buker, G.E. *Riverine Warfare: Naval Combat in the Second Seminole War, 1835-1847* (PhD thesis, Florida, 1961; DA v. 31, p. 1181A). "A specialized form of amphibious combat, neither naval nor military but a combination of the two."

Callahan, J.M. *The Neutrality of the American Lakes and Anglo-American Relations*, 1898 (PhD thesis, Johns Hopkins).

Downey, J.T. *The Cruise of the* Portsmouth, *1845-1847*, 1958.

*Guttridge, L.F. *The Commodores: the U.S. Navy in the Age of Sail*, 1969. Useful survey of the Old Navy. See Sect. BA-4.

*Haskell, D.C., ed. *The United States Exploring Expedition, 1838-1842, and Its Publications, 1844-1874, a Bibliography*, 1942, 1968. See also Tyler and Wilkes below and Henderson, Sect. BB-3.

Hayford, H. *The* Somers *Mutiny Affair*, P1956. See also F.F. Van de Water, *The Captain Called It Mutiny*, 1954.

Henson, C.T., Jr. *The United States Navy and China, 1839-1861* (PhD thesis, Tulane 1965; DA v. 26, p. 2162).

*Howard, W.S. *American Slavers and the Federal Law, 1837-1862*, 1963 (PhD thesis, UCLA).

Klay, A. *Daring Diplomacy: The Case of the First American Ultimatum*, 1957. Delivered by Commander Duncan H. Ingraham of the *St. Louis* and the American consul at Smyrna in securing the release of the Hungarian Martin Kosta from an Austrian warship in 1853.

Langley, H.D. *Social Reform in the United States Navy*. See Sect. N-1.

Manno, F.J. *History of United States Naval Operations, 1846-1848* (ms. PhD thesis, Georgetown, 1954). See also Bauer and Betts above. These three theses on the same subject were produced almost simultaneously at three widely separated universities.

Morgan, W.A. *Sea Power in the Gulf of Mexico and the Caribbean during the Mexican and Colombian Wars of Independence* (PhD thesis, So. California, 1969; DA v. 30, p. 1507A).

Naval Historical Foundation, *General Orders, USS* Independence, *1815*, P1969.

Neumann, W.L. *The Role of the United States in the Chilean Wars of Independence* (ms. PhD thesis, Michigan, 1948).

O'Neil, D.J. *The United States Navy in California, 1840-1850* (PhD thesis, So. California, 1969; DA v. 29, p. 4436).

*Paullin, C.O. *Diplomatic Negotiations of American Naval Officers, 1778-1883*, 1912, R1967.
———. *American Voyages to the Orient*, 1971. See Sect. AK.

Price, G.W. *The Origins of the War with Mexico: The Polk-Stockton Intrigue* (PhD thesis, So. California, 1966 DA v. 27, p. 428A). Role of Commodore Robert F. Stockton, commanding Gulf squadron in 1845.

Stewart, C.S. *A Visit to the South Seas in the U.S. Ship* Vincennes *during the Years 1829 and 1830; with Scenes in Brazil, Peru, Manila, the Cape of Good Hope and St. Helena*, 1831, R1970.

Towle, E.L. *Science, Commerce and the Navy on the Seagoing Frontier (1842-1861)* (ms. PhD thesis, Rochester, 1966).

*Tyler, D.B. *The Wilkes Expedition: The First United States Exploring Expedition (1838-1842), (Memoirs of the American Philosophical Society* v. 73), 1968. See also Haskell above.

U.S. Naval History Division, *The Texas Navy*, P1968. A 40-page pamphlet.

*Walworth, A.C. *Black Ships Off Japan: The Story of Commodore Perry's Expedition*, 1946, 1966. See also Barrows, McCauley, Morison and Preble in biographical section (BB-3) below.

Wells, T.H. *Commodore Moore and the Texas Navy*, 1960. See also J.D. Hill, *The Texas Navy*. . . . 1937, RP1962, and Naval History Division above.

Wheeler, R. *In Pirate Waters: Captain David Porter, USN, and America's War on Piracy in the West Indies*, 1969.

*Wilkes, C. *Narrative of the United States Exploring Expedition During the Years 1838-1842*, 6 v. 1845, R 5 v. 1970.

Wood, J.B. *The American Response to China, 1784-1844: Consensus Policy and the Origin of the East India Squadron* (ms. PhD thesis, Duke, 1969; DA v. 31, p. 349A).

BB – 3   Biography, Memoirs and Papers, 1815-1860

Alden, C.S. *Lawrence Kearney, Sailor Diplomat*, 1936. In command on the Asiatic (East Indian) station, Kearney paved the way for American expansion in Chinese trade after the Opium War.

Barrows, E.M. *The Great Commodore: The Exploits of Matthew Galbraith Perry*, 1935. The best, until Morison wrote.

Bradley, U.T. *The Contentious Commodore, Thomas apCatesby Jones of the Old*

Navy (ms. PhD thesis, Cornell, 1933). Jones, commanding the Pacific station, "jumped the gun" by seizing Monterey in 1842.

Duvall, M. *Navy Surgeon in California, 1846-1847*, 1957.

Fitzpatrick, D. and Sapphire, S. *Navy Maverick*, 1963. Uriah P. Levy, (1792-1862), America's first high-ranking Jewish naval officer; court-martialled six times, dismissed three times, and later reinstated.

Henderson, D. *The Hidden Coasts: A Biography of Admiral Charles Wilkes*, 1953.

*Johnson, R.E. *Rear Admiral John Rodgers, 1812-1882*, 1967. One of the outstanding Union naval commanders; son of Commodore John Rodgers, 1773-1839 and one of America's foremost naval dynasty.

Lloyd, C. *Lord Cochrane: Seaman-Radical-Liberator: A Life of Thomas Lord Cochrane, 10th Earl of Dundonald*, 1947. Brilliant British naval officer who also commanded the Chilean, Brazilian and Greek navies. See also J.P.W. Lallalieu, *Extraordinary Seaman*, 1957.
———. *Captain Marryatt and the Old Navy*, 1939, R1953. Before writing *Mr. Midshipman Easy*, etc. Marryatt served under Cochrane and pioneered in steam. See also O. Warner, *Captain Marryatt, a Rediscovery*, 1953.

Lubbock, A. *Owen Stanley, RN, 1811-1850. Captain of the* Rattlesnake, 1969. See also Bassett, Sect. BB-1.

McCauley, E.Y. *With Perry in Japan: Diary of Edward York McCauley*, ed. A.B. Cole, 1947.

Mellersh, H.F.L. *Fitzroy of the* Beagle, 1968. In addition to commanding the famous Darwin expedition, served as a member of Parliament and governor of New Zealand and continued his scientific activity. See also Moorehead, Sect. BB-1.

Meyers, W.H. *Journal of a Cruise to California and the Sandwich Islands in the United States Sloop-of-War* Cyane, *1841-1844*, ed. J.H. Kemble, 1955.

*Morison, S.E. *"Old Bruin," Commodore Matthew C. Perry, 1794-1958. The American Naval Officer who Helped to Found Liberia, Hunted Pirates in the West Indies, Practiced Diplomacy with the Sultan of Turkey and the King of the Two Sicilies, Commanded the Gulf Squadron in the Mexican War, Promoted the Steam Navy and the Shell Gun, and Conducted the Naval Expedition which Opened Japan*, 1967.

Naval History Society, 8, *The Papers of Francis Gregory Dallas, United States Navy, Correspondence and Journal, 1857-1859*.

Navy Records Society Publications, 12, 19, 24, *Journals of Admiral of the Fleet Sir Thomas Byam Martin, 1773-1854*; 82, *Captain Boteler's Recollections (1808 to 1830)*; 93, 97, *Sir William Dillon's Narrative of Professional Adventures (1790-1839)*.

Perry, M.C. *The Japan Expedition, 1852-54; The Personal Journal of Commodore Matthew C. Perry*, ed. R. Pineau, 1968.

Preble, G.H. *The Opening of Japan: A Diary of Discovery in the Far East, 1853-1856*, ed. B. Szczesniak, 1962.

Rogers, F.B. *Montgomery and the* Portsmouth, 1858. Mexican War in the Pacific, especially the seizure of the San Francisco Bay region in 1856.

Sproston, J.G. *A Private Journal of John Glendy Sproston, USN*, ed. S. Sakanishi, 1969. Officer on *Macedonian* in Perry expedition.

Summersell, C.G. *The Career of Raphael Semmes prior to the Cruise of the* Alabama (ms. PhD thesis, Vanderbilt, 1940).

Taylor, N.M. *The Journal of Ensign Best, 1837-1843*, 1966.

Wickman, J.E. *Political Aspects of Charles Wilkes's Work and Testimony, 1842-1849* (PhD thesis, Indiana, 1964; DA v. 26, p. 1012). Aftermath of Exploring Expedition.

BC 1861-65 AMERICAN CIVIL WAR

BC – 1 General

*Anderson, B. *By Sea and by River: The Naval History of the Civil War*, 1962. With its emphasis on strategic aspects, this is one of the very best general naval histories of the war. The author was a rear admiral with a PhD in naval-maritime history.

Bigelow, J. *France and the Confederate Navy (1862-1868): An International Episode*, 1868, R1968. Author was U.S. consul and then minister at Paris.

Boynton, C.B. *History of the Navy during the Rebellion*, 2 v. 1867. This officially-inspired work, like Scharf's, was long almost the only overall naval account.

Carrison, D.J. *The Navy from Wood to Steel, 1860-1890*, 1965.

Coulemanche, R.A. *Vice-Admiral Sir Alexander Milne, KCB, and the North America and West Indies Station, 1860-64* (ms. PhD thesis, London, 1967).

*Dalzell, G.W. *The Flight from the Flag: The Continuing Effect of the Civil War upon the American Carrying Trade*, 1940. Discusses the effect of transferring American vessels to foreign registry to avoid high war risk insurance charges, in addition to the history of each raider.

Edwards, F.T. *The United States Consular Service in the Bahamas during the American Civil War: A Study of the Friction within Naval and Diplomatic Content* (PhD thesis, Catholic Univ., 1968; DA v. 29, p. 3933A).

Gilbert, B.F. *Naval Operations in the Pacific, 1861-1866* (ms. PhD thesis, Berkeley, 1951).

Goldberg, M.S. *A History of United States Naval Operations during 1861* (PhD thesis, New Mexico, 1970; DA v. 31, p. 5967A).

Jones, V.C. *The Civil War at Sea*, 3 v. 1961-62. Readable account, with strictly chronological arrangement of episodes; less critical than Anderson or West; some inaccuracies in first volume.

Lott, A.S. *Most Dangerous Sea, A History of Mine Warfare*, 1959. Appendix includes long list of vessels sunk or damaged by mines during the Civil War.

Merli, F.J. *Great Britain and the Confederate Navy*, 1970 (PhD thesis, Indiana).

Photographic History of the Civil War, ed. F.T. Mikler and J. Barnes, 10 v. 1911. V. 6, original naval photographs. The more recent vogue of "picture books" has produced various other collections, including D. Donald, *Divided We Fought: A Pictorial History of the War, 1861-1865*, 1953, ch. 3, 10; and P.V. Stein, *The Confederate Navy: A Pictorial History*, 1962.

Robinson, R.H. *The Boston Economy During the Civil War* (ms. PhD thesis, Harvard, 1958).

Scharf, J.T. *History of the Confederate States Navy*, 1887. See Boynton above.

Sim, E.J. (John, E. pseud.) *Atlantic Impact, 1861*, 1952. The *Trent* affair as viewed by contemporary Englishmen and Americans.

Thompson, S.B. *Confederate Purchasing Operations Abroad*, 1935 (PhD thesis, Vanderbilt). See also Bulloch, Sect. BC-6, and Todd, Sect. BC-2.

*U.S. Office of Naval War Records, *Official Records of the Union and Confederate Navies in the War of the Rebellion*, 30 v. 1894-1922. A companion work to the far more extensive series of Army records, this set an example for the later Navy Dept. series for the Quasi-War, the Barbary Wars, and, still in progress, the Revolution. Very well indexed.

U.S. Naval History Division, *Civil War Chronology, 1861-1865*, 5 v. 1962-65.
————. *Civil War Naval Ordnance*, P1969.

Wells, T.H. *The Confederate Navy: A Study in Organization* (ms. PhD thesis, Emory, 1963; DA v. 25, p. 1884).

BC – 2   Ships

American Heritage, *Ironclads of the Civil War*, 1964.

*Baxter, J.P. *The Introduction of the Ironclad Warship*, 1933, 1968.

*Bennett, F.M. *The Steam Navy of the United States*, 2 v. 1896. Ample detail on the different kinds of vessels.

Jones, W.D. *The Confederate Rams at Birkenhead,* P1961. See also Thompson above; Todd and Bulloch below.

McBride, R. *Civil War Ironclads: The Dawn of Naval Armor,* 1962. Good introduction to the subject; clear descriptions and useful sketches.

Perry, M.F. *Infernal Machines: The Story of the Confederate Submarine and Mine Warfare,* 1965. See also Lott above.

Still, W.J., Jr. *Confederate Shipbuilding,* 1969. Based on his PhD thesis, Alabama, *The Construction and Fitting Out of Ironclad Vessels-of-War within the Confederacy.*

Switzer, D.C. *Maritime Maine and the Union Naval Construction Effort, 1861-1865* (ms. PhD thesis, Connecticut, 1970).

Todd, H.H. *The Building of the Confederate States Navy in Europe,* P1941. A 30-page summary of this PhD thesis, Vanderbilt, 1940.

*U.S. Office of Naval War Records, *Official Records.* . . . See Sect. BC-1. An extensive and fairly accurate list of all vessels in the rival navies with data on each is in Series II, v. 1.

White, W.C. and R. *Tin Can on a Shingle,* 1967. Includes details on the construction of the *Monitor.*

BC – 3   The Blockade and Coastal Actions

Ammen, D. *The Atlantic Coast,* 1883. This, with J.R. Soley's *The Blockade and the Cruisers,* and A.T. Mahan's first book, *The Gulf and Inland Waters,* comprised Scribner's series, "The Navy in the Civil War," the last general operational coverage until the mid-20th century.

*Bernath, S. *Squall across the Atlantic: American Civil War Prize Cases and Diplomacy,* 1970 (PhD thesis, Univ. Cal. - Santa Barbara). See also Robinton below.

Bradlee, F.B.C. *Blockade Running during the Civil War and the Effect on Land and Water Transportation in the Confederacy,* 1925.

Bright, S.R. *Confederate Coast Defense* (PhD thesis, Duke, 1961; DA v. 25, p. 2940).

Carse, R. *Blockade: The Civil War at Sea,* 1958.

Cochrane, H. *Blockade Runners of the Confederacy,* 1958. Readable, like Carse above, but neither volume has added much to the knowledge of the subject.

*Daly, R.W. *How the* Merrimac *Won: The Strategic Story of the CSS* Virginia, 1957. Discussion of her effect on McClellan's Peninsula Campaign in 1862.

Dufour, C.L. *The Night the War Was Lost*, 1960. Farragut's passing of the forts below New Orleans. Good account despite the extravagant title.

Hendricks, G. *Union Army Occupation of the Southern Seaboard* (ms. PhD thesis, Columbia, 1952).

Hobart-Hampden, A.C. *Never Caught*, 1967. Captain's account of twelve trips through the Union blockade.

Horner, O. *The Blockade Runners*, 1968. Location of the remaining sunken blockade runners, in connection with scuba diving.

Irby, J.A. *Line of the Rio Grande: War and Trade on the Confederate Frontier, 1861-1865* (PhD thesis, Georgia, 1969; DA v. 30, p. 5360A).

Merrill, J.M. *The Rebel Shore: The Story of Union Sea Power in the Civil War*, 1957. Developed from his PhD thesis, Berkeley, 1954: *Naval Operations along the South Atlantic Coast.*

*Robinton, M.R. *An Introduction to the Papers of the New York Prize Court*, 1945 (PhD thesis, Columbia).

Tolbert, F.X. *The Battle of Sabine Pass*, 1962. A scratch Confederate force beats off Union attack on Texas.

Vandiver, F.E., ed. *Confederate Blockade Running through Bermuda, 1861-1865*, 1947.

BC – 4   The Western Waters

Bearss, E.C. *Hardluck Ironclad: The Sinking and Salvage of the* Cairo, 1966. Sunk by Confederate mines in the Yazoo River and raised in 1964.

Cunningham, E. *The Port Hudson Campaign, 1862-1863*, 1963.

Elliott, J.W. *Transport to Disaster*, 1962. "The greatest marine disaster in all peacetime history," just after close of war. Boiler explosion and fire on the Mississippi river packet *Sultana*, overloaded with freed northern prisoners, took more than 1,500 lives.

*Gosnell, H.P. *Guns on the Western Waters: The Story of the River Gunboats in the Civil War*, 1949.

Hamilton, J.J. *The Battle of Fort Donelson*, 1968. Colorful but technically fiction because it includes imaginary conversations.

Hoehling, A.A. *Vicksburg: 47 Days of Siege, May 18-July 4, 1863*, 1969.

*Johnson, L.H. *Red River Campaign: Politics and Cotton in the Civil War*, 1958 (PhD thesis, Johns Hopkins). Farcical Army-Navy venture, with gunboats barely escaping Confederate cavalry when river grew low.

Milligan, J.D. *Gunboats down the Mississippi*, 1965. Based on PhD thesis, Michigan, 1961, *The Federal Freshwater Navy and the Opening of the Mississippi: Its Origin, Design, Construction and Operation through the Fall of Vicksburg.*

Parker, T.R. *The Federal Gunboat Flotilla on the Western Rivers during Its Administration by the War Department* (ms. PhD thesis, Pittsburgh, 1939).

*Pratt, F. *The Civil War on Western Waters*, 1956.

BC – 5   Cruiser Warfare

Balch, T.W. *The* Alabama *Arbitration*, 1900. Consult also the voluminous official records connected with the *Alabama* claims, giving details about the construction and commissioning of the raiders and the record of their numerous victims, including cargoes.

Boykin, E.C. *Ghost Ship of the Confederacy: The Story of the* Alabama *and her Captain, Raphael Semmes*, 1957. Like W. Armstrong, *Cruise of a Corsair*, 1963, this is based primarily on Semmes' memoirs, cited below.
—————. *Sea Devil of the Confederacy*, 1959. Captain John N. Maffitt of the *Florida.*

Cranwell, J.P. *Spoilers of the Sea: Wartime Raiders in the Age of Steam*, 1941. Civil War through World War I.

Khan, N.H. *The* Alabama *Arbitration* (PhD thesis, Virginia, 1962; DA v. 23, p. 2586). See also Balch above.

Morgan, M. *Dixie Raider; The Saga of the CSS* Shenandoah, 1948.

Owsley, F.L., Jr. *The CSS* Florida: *Her Building and Operations*, 1965. See also Boykin above.

Robinson, W.M. *The Confederate Privateers*, 1928. These "last of all privateers" were small and ineffectual compared with the commissioned raiders like the *Alabama* and *Florida.*

Summersell, C.G. *The Cruise of the CSS* Sumter, 1965. This was Semmes' first command before he shifted to the *Alabama.*

Warren, G.H. *The* Trent *Affair, 1861-1862* (PhD thesis, Indiana, 1969; DA v. 30, p. 4929A). See also Sim, Sect. BC-1.

BC – 6   Biography, Memoirs and Papers, 1861-65

Boyer, S.P. *Navy Surgeon: The Diary of Dr. Samuel Pelman Boyer*, ed. E. and J.A. Barnes, 2 v. 1963. V. 1, *Blockading the South, 1862-66.*

Browne, H.R. and S.E. *From the Fresh Water Navy, 1861-64: The Letters of Act-*

ing Master Mate Henry R. Browne and Acting Ensign Symmes E. Browne, ed. J.D. Milligan, 1971. Experiences in the "western waters."

Bulloch, J.D. *The Secret Service of the Confederate States in Europe, or How the Confederate Cruisers Were Equipped*, 2 v. 1883, R1959. The new edition has an introduction by P. Van Doren. Bulloch, who headed this important mission was a father-in-law of Theodore Roosevelt.

*DuPont, S.F. *Samuel Francis DuPont: A Selection from his Civil War Letters*, ed. J.D. Hayes, 3 v. 1969. V. 1, The Mission, 1860-62; 2, The Blockade, 1862-63; 3, The Repulse, 1863-65.

*Durkin, J.T. *Stephen R. Mallory: Confederate Navy Chief*, 1954. Biography of the only Confederate Secretary of the Navy, previously chairman of the Senate Naval Affairs Committee at Washington.

Graves, H.L. *A Confederate Marine*, 1963.

*Hill, J.D. *Sea Dogs of the Sixties: Farragut and Seven Contemporaries*, 1935, R1963, P1964. Sketches of Farragut, Bulloch, Wilkes, Wilkinson, John Rodgers II, Read, Winslow, and Waddell.

Hoole, W.S. *Four Years in the Confederate Navy: The Career of Captain John Low in the CSS* Fingal, Florida, Alabama, Tuscaloosa *and* Ajax, 1964. Able Scottish mariner who served in several responsible positions.

Jeffries, W.W. *The Civil War Career of Charles Wilkes* (ms. PhD thesis, Vanderbilt, 1941).

Keeler, W.F. *Aboard the USS* Monitor, *1862; The Letters of Acting Paymaster William Frederick Keeler, U.S. Navy, to his Wife, Anna*, ed. R. W. Daly, 1964. This is the first in the U.S. Naval Institute's series of naval memoirs.

*Lewis, C.L. *David Glasgow Farragut*, 2 v. 1941-43. The first volume covers the period before the Civil War.
————. *Admiral Franklin Buchanan, Fearless Man of Action*, 1929.

McCartney, C.E.N. *Mr. Lincoln's Admirals*, 1956.

*Naval History Society, V. 9-10, *Confidential Correspondence of Gustavus Vasa Fox, Assistant Secretary of the Navy, 1861-1865*, 2 v. 1918-20.

Roske, R.J. and Van Doren, C. *Lincoln's Commando: The Biography of Commodore W.B. Cushing, USN*, 1957, P1958. Cushing torpedoed the Confederate ram *Albemarle*.

*Semmes, R. *Memoirs of Service Afloat during the War between the States*, 1869, R1962. Commanding the *Sumter* and then the *Alabama*, Semmes was the most spectacular and articulate of the Confederate sea raiders. It is said that the German admiral, Graf Spee, studied this book in preparation for his own raiding in 1914. The *Alabama* section was reissued in 1962, edited by P.V. Stern.

*Sloan, E.W., III. *Benjamin Franklin Isherwood, Naval Engineer; The Years as Engineer-in-Chief, 1861-1869*, 1966 (PhD thesis, Harvard).

Waddell, J.I. *CSS* Shenandoah*: The Memoirs of Lieutenant Commanding James I. Waddell*, ed. J.D. Horan, 1961. See also Morgan, Sect. BC-5.

*Welles, G. *The Diary of Gideon Welles, Secretary of the Navy Under Lincoln and Johnson*, 3 v., ed. J.T. Morse, 1911. Revised ed. showing the changes from the original draft, ed. H.K. Beale, 1960.

West, R.S. *Gideon Welles, Lincoln's Navy Department*, 1943.
————. *The Second Admiral: A Life of David Dixon Porter, 1813-1891*, 1937. Porter was a superlative fighter afloat and a shameless intriguer ashore.
*————. *Admirals of American Empire. The Combined Story of George Dewey, Alfred Thayer Mahan, Winfield Scott Schley, and William Thomas Sampson*, 1948. An ingenious arrangement, carrying the four men, period by period, from the Civil War through the "Dark Ages" to the Spanish-American War. It gives a very good idea of the varied aspects of a naval career.

BD   1865-1913

BD – 1   General

Brassey's Naval Annual, since 1886. As stated earlier, this is the chief source of information in English about navies other than British and American. It includes able analyses of all the wars of the period, great and small, as well as analyzing all the significant developments.

Earle, E.M., et al., eds. *Makers of Modern Strategy*, 1943. Ch. 18, "Continental Doctrines of Sea Power" by T. Ropp.

Halpern, P.G. *The Mediterranean Naval Situation, 1912-1914* (ms. PhD thesis, Harvard, 1966).

Kneer, W.G. *Great Britain and the Caribbean 1901-1913: A Study in Anglo-American Relations* (PhD thesis, Michigan State, 1966; DA 67, p. 7565).

Nish, I.H. *The Anglo-Japanese Alliance: The Diplomacy of Two Island Empires, 1894-1907* (Univ. of London Hist. Studies), 1966.

Sterling, E.W. *Imperial Rivalries and the Strategy of the British Empire, 1878-1904* (ms. PhD thesis, Iowa, 1941).

Wells, S.F. *Anglo-American Friendship. 1904-1914: The Strategic Aspect* (ms PhD thesis, Harvard, 1967).

*Wilson, H.W. *Battleships in Action*, 2 v. 1926. Contains some of the best accounts of the "shooting" in the various South American wars, the Sino-Japanese War (1894-95), the Spanish-American War (1898), the Russo-Japanese War (1904-05) and the Italo-Turkish War (1912-13). Much of the earlier material was included in his *Ironclads in Action*, 2 v. 1896. When steel supplanted iron for armor in the 1880s, the name "ironclad" gave way to "battleship."

Azoy, A.C.M. *Signal 250! The Sea Fight off Santiago Bay*, 1964.

Beale, H.K. *Theodore Roosevelt and the Rise of America to World Power*, 1957. See also Dulles below.

Beers, H.P. *American Naval Occupation and Government of Guam, 1898-1902* (Navy Dept. Administrative Reference Service Report No. 6), P1944. This and several other titles in the series were prepared as case studies for the Navy's military government school.

Benton, E.J. *International Law and Diplomacy of the Spanish-American War*, 1968.

*Braisted, W.R. *The United States Navy in the Pacific, 1897-1909*, 1958 (PhD thesis, Chicago), R1971.

Buhl, L.C. *The Smooth Water Navy: American Naval Policy and Politics, 1865-1876* (ms. PhD thesis, Harvard, 1969).

Carrison, D.J. *The Navy from Wood to Steel, 1860-1890*, 1965.

*Chadwick, F.E. *Relations of the United States and Spain: The Spanish-American War*, 2 v. 1911, 1968. Written by a prominent participant, this is still regarded as the best account of the actual operations.

Dalzell, G.W. *The Flight from the Flag*. . . . See Sect. BC-1.

Donahue, W.J. *The United States Newspaper Press Reaction to the* Maine *Incident, 1898* (PhD thesis, Colorado, 1970; DA v. 31, p. 4656A).

Drake, F.C. *"The Empire of the Seas"*. . . . See Sect. BD-5.

Dulles, F.R. *The Imperial Years: The History of America's Brief Moment of Imperial Fervor*, 1957. See also Beale above.

*Freidel, F.B. *The Splendid Little War*, 1958. A generously illustrated and readable account of the Spanish-American War.

Hart, R.A. *The Great White Fleet: Its Voyage around the World, 1907-1909*, 1965 (PhD thesis, Indiana).

Herrick, W.R., Jr. *The American Naval Revolution*, 1965. Outgrowth of his Virginia PhD thesis, *General Tracy's Navy*. Chiefly on decade before the Spanish-American War; Tracy, Secretary of the Navy, 1889-93, led the shift to battleships.

Hoyt, E.P. *The Typhoon that Stopped a War*, 1968. American and German squadrons wrecked at Apia, Samoa, 1889.

Lindsell, H. *The Chilean-American Controversy of 1891-1892* (ms. PhD thesis, New York Univ., 1942).

*Livermore, S.W. *American Naval Development, 1898-1914, with special reference to Foreign Affairs* (ms. PhD thesis, Harvard, 1944). See comments, Sect. AS.

Long, J.D. *The New American Navy*, 2 v. 1903. Long was Secretary of the Navy, 1897-1902.

*McClellan, W.C. *A History of American Military Sea Transportation* (ms. PhD thesis, American, 1953). See comments, Sect. AR.

McPherson, G. and Watts, M. *Fixing Wages and Salaries of Navy Civilian Employees in Shore Establishments, 1862-1945* (Administrative Reference Service Report, No. 9), P1945.

*Millis, W. *The Martial Spirit, a Study of Our War with Spain*, 1931. Millis catches the spirit of the occasion in delightful fashion; see also Chadwick and Freidel for treatment from other angles.

*Morison, E.E. *Admiral Sims and the Modern American Navy*, 1942, R1968. Sims, father-in-law of the author, able and contentious, helped to reform naval gunnery; strove to reform naval administration and headed the American naval forces in Europe in World War I. The book gives a valuable picture of the Navy as a whole.

Potter, D. *Sailing the Sulu Seas*, 1940. Lively episodes recounted by a Paymaster General of the Navy. See also Sawyer below.

Read, G.H. *The Last Cruise of the* Saginaw, 1912. Wrecked near Midway in 1870. Of five men who set out in gig for relief, only one reached Hawaii alive.

Reisner, R.L. *Twelve Against Empire: The Anti-Imperialists, 1898-1900*, 1968.

Sargent, N. *Admiral Dewey and the Manila Campaign*, 1947.

Sawyer, F.L. *Sons of Gunboats*, 1946. Anecdotes of service in the Philippines at the turn of the century. See also Potter above.

Van Deurs, G. *Wings of the Fleet: A Narrative of Naval Aviation's Early Development, 1910-1916*, 1967.

Weems, J.E. *The Fate of the* Maine, 1958, P. "From the laying of her keel in 1888 to her final burial at sea in 1912."

Zeus, M.D. *United States Naval Government and Administration of Guam* (ms. PhD thesis, Iowa, 1950). See also Beers above.

BD – 3 Britain and Germany

Bee, B.M.C. *The Leasing of Kiaochow: A Study in Diplomacy and Imperialism* (ms. PhD thesis, Harvard, 1935).

Chamberlain, W. *The German Naval Law of 1912* (ms. PhD thesis, Stanford, 1939).

*Graham, G.S. *The Politics of Naval Supremacy: Studies in British Maritime Ascendancy*, 1965.

Grimm, H.G. *German Naval Legislation, 1898-1914* (ms. PhD thesis, Ohio, 1948).

Halpern, P.C. *The Mediterranean Naval Situation, 1912-1914* (ms. PhD thesis, Harvard, 1966).

Hough, R.A. *Admirals in Collision*, 1959, RP1961. Sinking of HMS *Victoria* by HMS *Camperdown* with loss of 358 lives in 1893, as a result of faulty order given by Admiral Tryon. "It is a good story, but has no new information to offer." See also H.W. Baldwin, *Sea Fights and Shipwrecks*, 1955, ch. 7.

Hurd, Sir A.S. and Castle, H. *German Sea Power: Its Rise, Progress and Economic Basis*, 1913.

*Johnson, F.A. *Defense by Committee: The British Committee of Imperial Defence, 1885-1959*, 1960 (PhD thesis, Harvard).

Kelly, P.J. *The Naval Policy of Imperial Germany, 1900-1914* (ms. PhD thesis, Georgetown, 1970).

*Marder, A.J. *The Anatomy of British Sea Power: A History of Naval Policy in the Pre-Dreadnought Era, 1880-1905*, 1940, R1964.
*————. *From the Dreadnought to Scapa Flow: The Royal Navy in the Fisher Era, 1904-1919*, 4 v. 1961-69. V. 1, *The Road to War, 1904-1914*, 1961. These are some of the most important contributions to naval history; for a full appreciation of their significance, see Sect. BE-1. These two prewar volumes give an admirable analysis of conditions and policy-making which produced the timely adjustments to meet the threats of German rivalry. See also, below, Marder's editing of Fisher correspondence and his life of Richmond.

*Preston, A. and Major, J. *Send a Gunboat! A Study of the Gunboat and Its Role in British Policy, 1854-1904*, 1967.

Ranft, B.M. *The Naval Defence of British Sea-borne Trade, 1860-1905* (ms. DPhil thesis, Oxford, 1967).

Schurman, D.M. *Imperial Defence, 1868-1887. . . .* (ms. PhD thesis, Cambridge, 1956).

Spry, W.J. *The Cruise of HMS* Challenger, 1877. Five-year cruise which inaugurated scientific oceanography.

*Steinberg, J. *Yesterday's Deterrent: The Story of Tirpitz and the Birth of the German Battle Fleet*, 1965, R1968. In the second edition, the "Yesterday's Deterrent" was moved to the end of the title.

Sutton, J.E. *The Imperial German Navy, 1910-1914*, 1915.

*Willock, R. *Bulwark of Empire: Bermuda's Fortified Naval Base, 1860-1920*, 1962. The most thoroughgoing study of any overseas naval base.

266

*Williamson, S.R., Jr. *The Politics of Grand Strategy: Britain and France Prepare for War, 1904-1914*, 1969 (PhD thesis, Harvard).

*Woodward, E.L. *Great Britain and the German Navy*, 1935, R1964.

BD – 4   Japan, Russia and Others

Atkins, E.H. *General Charles Legendre and the Japanese Expedition to Formosa, 1874* (ms. PhD thesis, Florida, 1954).

Busch, N.F. *The Emperor's Sword*, 1969. Tsushima.

Clinard, O.J. *Japan's Influence on American Naval Power, 1897-1917*, 1947. Pushes his thesis a bit hard.

Dotson, L.O. *The Sino-Japanese War of 1894-1895* (ms. PhD thesis, Yale, 1951).

Eisenstein, S. Potemkin, 1968. See also Hough below.

*Falk, E.A. *Tojo and the Rise of Japanese Sea Power*, 1936.
*————. *From Perry to Pearl Harbor: The Struggle for the Supremacy of the Pacific*, 1943.

Gebhard, L.A., Jr. *The Development of the Austro-Hungarian Navy, 1897-1914; A Study in the Operation of Dualism* (PhD thesis, Rutgers, 1965; DA v. 26, p. 5993).

*Great Britain, Committee of Imperial Defense, Historical Section, *Official History of the Russo-Japanese War*, 3 v. 1910-20. Because of the new instruments of war being used on land and sea, most of the powers sent official observers. This British account, well-equipped with maps, is perhaps the best of the reports.

Hargreaves, R. *The Red Sun Rising: The Siege of Port Arthur* (Great Battles), 1962.

Hough, R. *The* Potemkin *Mutiny*, 1960. Mutiny aboard Russian battleship in the Black Sea at the time of the 1905 revolution. One reviewer called the book "superficial and inaccurate." See also Eisenstein above.
————. *The Fleet that Had to Die*, 1958, P. The tragic odyssey of Rozhestvensky's Baltic force, culminating at Tsushima. Ran serially in the *New Yorker*. See also Novikov-Priboi, Klado and Westwood.

Hucul, W. C. *The Evolution of Russian and Soviet Sea Power, 1853-1953* (ms. PhD thesis, Berkeley, 1954).

Klado, N. *The Russian Navy in the Russo-Japanese War*, 1905.
————. *The Battle of the Sea of Japan*, 1906. Tsushima.

Neu, C. *Sea Power and American-Japanese Relations* (ms. PhD thesis, Harvard, 1963).

*Novikov-Priboi, A.S. *Tsushima*, tr. E. and C. Paul, 1937. Vivid account, by a Russian petty officer, of the progressive demoralization aboard the Baltic squadron, with graphic detail of its smashing by the Japanese.

*Perry, J.C. *Great Britain and the Imperial Japanese Navy, 1858-1905* (ms. PhD thesis, Harvard, 1962). The first full account of the British naval missions in advising and training the Japanese.

Purcell, E.C., Jr. *Japanese Expansion*. . . . See Sect. BF-1.

*Ropp, T. *The Development of a modern Navy: French Naval Policy, 1871-1914* (ms. PhD thesis, Harvard, 1937).

Ward, J.G.S. *The Activities of Spain on the Pacific Coast of South America, and Her War with the "Confederation of the Andes," 1860-1886* (ms. PhD thesis, London, 1939).

Westwood, J.N. *Witnesses of Tsushima*, 1970.

BD – 5   Biographies, Memoirs and Papers, 1865-1913

Ammen, D. *The Old Navy and the New* (1891). This was the earliest of numerous autobiographies of varying merit by American admirals of the period. In addition to the few cited separately below, these include A.S. Barker (1928), C.E. Clark (1917), R.E. Coontz (1930), G. Dewey (1913), R.D. Evans (1902, 1910), R. Franklin (1898), R.S. Rodman (1928), B.F. Sands (1899), W.F. Schley (1904), S. Schroeder (1922), T.O. Selfridge (1924), Y. Sterling (1929).

Biographies include J.A. Dahlgren by M.V. Dahlgren; G.H. Perkins by C.S. Alden; and William Radford by S.R. DeMeissner.

Bacon, Sir R.H. *Life of Lord Fisher of Kilverstone, Admiral of the Fleet*, 2 v. 1929.

Beresford, Lord C. *Memoirs of Lord Charles Beresford*, 2 v. 1914. States that these were "written by himself," in contrast to the increasingly common "ghosting" of naval memoirs. Beresford was Fisher's most bitter opponent.

Bigelow, D.N. *William Conant Church and the Army & Navy Journal*, 1952 (PhD thesis, Columbia).

Blond, G. *Admiral Tojo*, tr. E. Hyams, 1960. Not nearly as adequate as the Falk volume cited, Sect. BD-4.

Churchill, R.S. *Winston S. Churchill*; vol. 2, *Young Politician, 1901-1914*, 1967. See Sect. AQ-1.

Cummins, D.E. *Admiral Richard Wainwright and the United States Fleet*, 1962. Wainwright served in the Navy from 1864 to 1911, and was prominent at the turn of the century.

*Cunningham, A.B. *Sailor's Odyssey, the Autobiography of Admiral of the Fleet, Viscount Cunningham of Hyndhope*, 1951. Like the King volume below, this recounts the long, distinguished career leading to top command in World War II.

Drake, F.C. *"The Empire of the Seas." A Biography of Robert Wilson Shufeldt, USN* (ms. PhD thesis, Cornell, 1970; DA v. 31, p. 3370). The "foremost exponent of American expansion in the United States Navy between M.C. Perry and Mahan. . . . Insight into American diplomacy in the Caribbean, Africa, Asia and the Pacific," 1850-1880.

*Fisher, J.A. *The Papers of Admiral Sir John Fisher*, ed. P.K. Kemp (Navy Records Society, v. 102, 106), 2 v. 1960, 1964.
——————. *Memories and Records*, 2 v. 1920. See also Marder below.

*Fiske, B.A. *From Midshipman to Rear Admiral*, 1919. A brilliant inventor and reformer in naval administration, Fiske in his memoirs devotes more space to events ashore than do most of the other admiral-autobiographers.

Gleaves, A. *Life and Letters of Stephen B. Luce, U.S. Navy: Founder of the Naval War College*, 1925.

Gretton, Sir P. *Winston Churchill and the Royal Navy, 1911-1939*, 1968, R1969. See Sect. AQ-1.

Hammeth, H.B. *Hilary Abner Herbert*. See Sect. AQ-2.

Hatch, A. *The Mountbattens: The Last Royal Success Story*, 1965. See Sect. BH-12.

Hough, R. *First Sea Lord: An Authorized Biography of Admiral Lord Fisher*, 1969.

*King, E.J. and Whitehill, W.M. *Fleet Admiral King, a Naval Record*, 1952. Useful for the details of King's varied career before his top command in World War II. This included duty on a fleet staff, with submarines, in naval aviation, and as a bureau chief. Less valuable for the period after 1941, when King from his unique vantage point as "CominCh-CNO" and a member of the Joint Chiefs of Staff might have taken his readers behind the scenes far more than he does in this "semi-autobiography." But, with his "silent service" attitude, many were surprised that he told as much as he did.

Manning, F. *The Life of Sir William White*, 1923. Director of Naval Construction, 1885-1901.

*Marder, A.J. *Fear God and Dread Nought: The Correspondence of Admiral of the Fleet Lord Fisher of Kilverstone*, 3 v. 1957-59. Full of pungent, quotable passages; see also Fisher above.
*——————. *Portrait of an Admiral: The Life and Papers of Admiral Herbert Richmond*, 1951. Richmond was one of the Royal Navy's most brilliant planners; he also wrote several volumes of first-rate naval history.

*Morison, E.E. *Admiral Sims and the Modern American Navy*. See Sect. BD-5.

Ogasawara, N. *The Life of Admiral Tojo*, 1934.

Scott, Sir P. *Fifty Years in the Royal Navy*, 1919. Scott, like Sims, was active in the improvement of naval gunnery early in the century.

*Swann, L.A., Jr. *John Roach, Maritime Entrepreneur*, 1965 (PhD thesis, Harvard). Roach built the first four steel ships for the "New Navy" at his Delaware River yard and went into bankruptcy thereby.

*Tirpitz, A.P.E., von. *My Memoirs*, 2 v. 1919, 1970. Tirpitz and Fisher were the tough, able rival protagonists of the Anglo-German naval race starting in 1900. See also Steinberg, Sect. BD-3.

*West, R.S. *Admirals of American Empire*, 1948. Continues the careers of Dewey, Sampson, Schley and Mahan to their climax in the Spanish-American War.
——————. *The Second Admiral: A Life of David Dixon Porter*, 1937. Porter's postwar role might have been criticized more sharply.

BE   WORLD WAR I, 1914-1918

BE – 1   General

Baldwin, H.W. *World War I: An Outline History*, 1962.

Barnett, C. *The Swordbearers: Supreme Command in the First World War*, 1964, P1965. Includes controversial estimate of Jellicoe along with several generals.

Bennett, G. *Naval Battles of the First World War* (British Battles Series), 1968.

*Churchill, W.S. *World Crisis*, 4 v. 1923-27. Churchill not only made history in the grand manner, but he also wrote it in a style that is the envy of professional historians. The first two volumes deal with his years as First Lord of the Admiralty from 1911 until after Gallipoli in 1915. His *Aftermath*, 1929, is sometimes reckoned as a fifth volume.

*Corbett, Sir J.S. and Newbolt, Sir H. *Naval Operations* (Official History), 5 v. 1920-31; R1928-40. Part of the excellent British "History of the Great War" based on official documents. Corbett, who had written outstanding naval histories all the way from Drake to Trafalgar, died before the projected work was completed. Long a standard account, it has now been overshadowed by Marder, except in specific operational details.

*Frothingham, T.G. *The Naval History of the World War*, 3 v. 1924-27. Comprehensive survey by an American.

Guinn, P. *British Strategy and Politics, 1914 to 1918*, 1965.

Hankey, Lord *The Supreme Command, 1914-1918*, 2 v. 1961.

Hoehling, A.A. *The Great War at Sea*, 1965.

Kittredge, T.B. *Naval Lessons of the Great War*, 1921.

*Marder, A.J. *From the Dreadnought to Scapa Flow: The Royal Navy in the Fisher Era, 1904-1919*, 5 v. 1961-70. Vol. I, *The Road to War* (1904-1914); 2, *The War Years: To the Eve of Jutland* (1914-1916); 3, *Jutland and After* (May 1916-Dec. 1916); 4, *1917: Year of Crisis*; 5, *Victory and Aftermath* (Jan. 1918-June 1919). Of this magnificent work, one prominent English historian has written "From Professor Marder we can never have enough. His naval history has a unique function. To unveiled history of sources he adds a gift for simple narrative. . . . This book, like its predecessors is a model of humane learning."

*May, E.R. *The World War and American Isolation, 1914-1917*, 1959.

Millis, W. *The Road to War: America 1914-1917*, 1935. The American approach.

*Tuchman, B. *The Guns of August*, 1962. Able analysis of the not-so-able leadership in the first weeks of the war; see especially ch. 10, "Goeben . . . An Enemy then Flying," and ch. 11, "Blue Water, Blockade, and the Great Neutral." Some of the background of these men in command is given in her *The Proud Tower* analyzing the two previous decades in several countries.

BE – 2   Battle Fleets, North Sea

Bennett, G. *The Battle of Jutland* (British Battles Series), 1964.

Bowman, G. *The Man Who Bought a Navy*, 1965. Salvage of German warships scuttled at Scapa Flow.

Frost, H.H. *The Battle of Jutland*, 1936, R1970. Detailed tactical analysis by an American naval officer.

Gibson, L. and Harper, J.E.T. *The Riddle of Jutland*, 1934. Gibson, an American journalist, presented in lively form the pro-Jellicoe findings of a board headed by Admiral Harper. The whole controversy has since been well-summed up by Marder.

Irving, J.J.C. *The Smoke Screen of Jutland*, 1966.

*Jellicoe, J.R., Earl. *The Grand Fleet, 1914-1916, Its Creation, Development and Work*, 1919.
————. *The Crisis of the Naval War*, 1921. Jellicoe was Commander-in-Chief until after Jutland and then First Sea Lord during the submarine crisis.

Legg, S., ed. *Jutland: An Eyewitness Account of the Great Battle*, 1967. "A compilation of personal letters, ships' logs, etc. by officers and men of both sides."

Macintyre, D. *Jutland*, 1958.

Scheer, R.U. *Germany's High Sea Fleet in the World War*, 1920. Scheer was Jellicoe's opposite number at Jutland.

Schubert, P. and Gibson, L. *Death of a Fleet, 1917-1919*, 1932. The post-Jutland story of the German High Seas Fleet to its scuttling at Scapa Flow.

BE – 3   Cruisers and Raiders

Alexander, R. *The Cruise of the Raider* Wolf, 1939.

*Bennett, G. *Coronel and the Falklands* (British Battles Series), 1962.

Cranwell, J.P. *Spoilers of the Sea: Wartime Raiders in the Age of Steam*, 1941.

Hoehling, A.A. *Lonely Command: The Epic Story of the* Emden, 1957. Successful raiding, for a while, in the Indian Ocean.

Hough, R. *The Pursuit of Admiral von Spee*, 1968. Alternative title, *The Long Pursuit. A Gallant Enemy Meets the Royal Navy at the End of a Classic Sea Chase*, 1969. See also Bennett above.

Hoyt, E.P. *Count Von Luckner, Knight of the Sea*, 1969. See also Thomas below.

Hoyt, E.P., Jr. *The Germans Who Never Lost; The Story of the* Konigsberg, 1968. Ran up an East African river and joined in the German land defense.
———. *The Elusive Seagull*, 1970. Adventures of the German minelayer *Moewe*.

Thomas, L. *Count Luckner, the Sea Devil*, 1927. Raiding under sail.

BE – 4   Dardanelles – Gallipoli

Naval history has generally applied the name Dardanelles – the strait separating Asia from Europe – to the huge joint operation of 1915; the army historians have preferred the name Gallipoli, the peninsula on the European side of that strait.

Aspinall-Oglander, C.F. *Military Operations, Gallipoli* (Official History), 2 v. 1929-32.
*———. *Roger Keyes, Being the Biography of Admiral of the Fleet Lord Keyes of Zeebrugge and Dover*, 1951. Keyes was the naval chief of staff, urging successive admirals to play a more positive role. This, and his bitter memoirs, are valuable for the naval side of the story.

Hargrave, J. *The Suvla Bay Landings*, 1964.

Higgins, T. *Winston Churchill and the Dardanelles: A Dialogue of Ena and Means*, 1963.

James, R.R. *Gallipoli*, 1965.

*Moorehead, A. *Gallipoli*, 1956, P. This seems far and away the best brief book on the whole operations.

272

Puleston, W.D. *The Dardanelles Expedition*, 1927. By an American Director of Naval Intelligence. Also useful are the accounts of the rival commanders ashore, Sir Ian Hamilton and General Liman von Sanders.

Webster-Wemyss, Lord. *The Navy in the Dardanelles Campaign*, 1924. He was one of the successive admirals in command.

BE – 5   Submarine Warfare

*Albion, R.G. and Pope, J.B. *Sea Lanes in Wartime*, 1942, R1968. Includes table of monthly sinkings and war risk insurance fluctuations on the various routes.

Belknap, R.R. *Yankee Mining Squadron, or Laying the North Sea Mine Barrage*, 1920. Ambitious American naval effort to catch German submarines entering or leaving the North Sea.

Birnbaum, K.E. *Peace Moves and U-Boat Warfare: A Study of Imperial Germany's Policy towards the United States, April 8, 1916-Jan. 9, 1917*, 1958, R1970.

Grant, R.M. *U-Boats Destroyed: The Effect of Anti-Submarine Warfare, 1914-1918*, 1964.
————. *U-Boat Intelligence, 1914-1918*, 1969.

Hoehling, A.A. and M. *The Last Voyage of the* Lusitania, 1956, RP1961.

Jellicoe, J.R. Earl. *The Submarine Peril in 1917*, 1934.

Shankland, P. and Hunter, A. *Dardanelles Patrol*, 1964. Exploits of a British submarine in Turkish waters.

Sims, W.S. *The Victory at Sea*, 1920. Sims was instrumental in inaugurating convoy and other effective anti-submarine measures. See also his biography by E.E. Morison.

Smith, G. *Britain's Clandestine Submarines, 1914-1915*, 1964. See comments, Sect. AR.

BE – 6   Merchant Shipping and Transport

Bailey, T.A. *The Policy of the United States toward Neutrals, 1817-1918*, 1964.

Beers, H.P. *U.S. Naval Port Officers in the Bordeaux Region, 1917-1919* (Administrative Reference Service Report, No. 3), P1943, with accompanying reprint of U.S. Naval Port Regulations, Port of Bordeaux.

*Bentinck-Smith, J. *The Forcing Period: A Study of the American Merchant Marine, 1914-1917* (ms. PhD thesis, Radcliffe, 1958).

Crowell, B. and Wilson, R.F. *The Road to France . . . The Transportation of Troops and Military Supplies*, 2 v. 1921. Crowell was Assistant Secretary of War and this was one of his several volumes on the American war effort.

Elderton, W.P. *Shipping Problems, 1916-1921*, 1928.

*Fayle, C.E. *Seaborne Trade* (Official History), 3 v. 1920-24.
——————. *The War and the Shipping Industry*, 1927.

*Gleaves, A.L. *A History of the Transport Service: Adventures and Experiences of U.S. Transports and Cruisers in the World War*, 1921. Gleaves commanded the Transport Service, the principal contribution of the United States Navy to the war effort. It delivered more than two million men safely in Europe, with vast quantities of supplies.

Hurd, Sir A.S. *The Merchant Navy* (Official History), 3 v. 1921-29. This concentrated on ships and men, whereas the Fayle study above was primarily concerned with cargoes and regulations.

*Mattox, W.C. *Building the Emergency Fleet: A Historical Narrative of the Problems and Achievements of the United States Shipping Board Emergency Fleet Corporation*, 1920, R1970. See also E.N. Hurley, *The New Merchant Marine*, 1920.

McClellan, W.C. *A History of American Military Sea Transportation* (ms. PhD thesis, American, 1953). See Sect. AR.

Mitchell, W.H. and Sawyer, T.A. *British Standard Ships of World War I*, 1968.

*Salter, Sir A. *Allied Shipping Control, an Experiment in International Administration*, 1921. Salter was the principal British shipping representative in Washington in both World Wars.

BE – 7   Blockade

*Bell, A. *A History of the Blockade of Germany and the Countries Associated with Her in the Great War . . . 1914-1918*, 1937.
——————. *The Economic Blockade, 1914-1919*, 1961. This, like the Davis volume below, was printed as a staff monograph in 1920 but was not released for public sale by H.M. Stationery Office for more than 40 years.

*Davis, H.W.V. *History of the Blockade* (1920), 1961. See Bell above.

Guichard, L. *The Naval Blockade, 1914-1918*, 1930.

Ritchie, H. *The "Navicert" System during the World War*, 1937. Certificates by consuls or other British officials at the port of clearance concerning the non-contraband status of cargoes.

*Siney, M.C. *The Allied Blockade of Germany, 1914-1916*, 1957.

Beach, E.L. *The Wreck of the* Memphis, 1966. The armored cruiser, ex-*Tennessee*, commanded by the author's father, was wrecked by a tremendous tidal wave at Santo Domingo in August 1916.

Carpenter, A.F.B. *The Blocking of Zeebrugge,* 1924. See also Pitt below and the Keyes memoirs on this daring April 1918 raid.

Horn, D., ed. and trans. *War, Mutiny and Revolution in the German Navy,* 1967. From diary of Seaman Richard Stumpf. Also published as *The German Naval Mutinies of World I,* 1969. These mutinies, of course, sparked the revolution which transformed the Hohenzollern monarchy into a republic.

Ironsides, E. *Archangel, 1918-1919.* By British general in command of allied Arctic attempt to offset Red spread. See Strakhovsky below.

Lever, A.W. *The British Empire and the German Colonies, 1914-1919* (PhD thesis, Wisconsin, 1963; DA v. 24, p. 2446).

Longmaid, K. *The Approaches Are Mined,* 1965.

Pitt, B. *Zeebrugge,* 1958, P1959.

Riste, O. *The Neutral Ally: Norway's Relation with Belligerent Powers in the First World War,* P1965.

Shankland, P. *The Phantom Flotilla,* 1968.

Strakhovsky, L.I. *Intervention at Archangel,* 1944.

Sweetman, J. *Landing at Veracruz: 1914,* 1968. American attack and occupation of Mexican port.

BE – 9   Biography, Memoirs and Papers, 1914-1918

Aspinall-Oglander, C.F. *Roger Keyes.* See Sect. BE-4.

Bacon, Sir R.H. *The Life of Lord Fisher of Kilverstone,* 2 v. 1929.
——————. *The Life of John Rushworth, Earl of Jellicoe,* 1926.

Blackford, C.M. *Torpedoboat Sailor,* 1967. Destroyer convoy duty.

Chalmers, W.S. *The Life and Letters of David, Earl Beatty, Admiral of the Fleet,* 1951.
——————. *Full Cycle: The Biography of Sir Bertram Home Ramsey,* 1959.

Coady, J.W. *F.D.R.'s Early Washington Years (1913-1920)* (PhD thesis, St. John's, 1968; DA v. 30, p. 1103A). Assistant Secretary of the Navy. See also Freidel below.

Daniels, Jonathan. *The End of Innocence,* 1954. A study of the Wilson era, with much to say about the author's father, Josephus Daniels, as Secretary of the Navy.

Daniels, Josephus. *The Wilson Era*, 2 v. 1944-45. Includes much of the material in his *Our Navy at War*, 1922, with similar inaccuracies.
——————. *Cabinet Diaries of Secretary of the Navy Josephus Daniels, 1913-1921*, ed. E.D. Cronon, 1963.

*Freidel, F. *Franklin D. Roosevelt*, 3 v. 1952 ff. Vols. 1 and 2; a wealth of detail on his administrative experience as Assistant Secretary of the Navy, 1913-20.

Gretton, Sir P. *Winston Churchill and the Royal Navy, 1911-1939*. 1968, R1969. See Sect. AQ-1.

*Horn, D. See Sect. BE-8.

Hoyt, E.P. *Count von Luckner, Knight of the Sea*, 1969. See also L. Thomas, Sect. BE-3.

*Jameson, Sir W.S. *The Fleet that Jack Built*, 1962. Nine detailed biographical sketches of British naval leaders in World War I: Keppel, Wilson, Fisher, Beresford, Scott, Jellicoe, Beatty, Tyrwhitt, and Keyes. "Jack," of course, refers to Fisher.

Jellicoe, J.R., Earl. *The Jellicoe Papers*, ed. A. T. Patterson (Navy Records Soc., v. 108, 111), 2 v. 1966-68.

Jenkins, I.L. *Josephus Daniels and the Navy Department, 1913-16; A Study in Military Administration* (PhD thesis, Maryland, 1962; DA v. 22, p. 1963).

Morrison, J.L. *Josephus Daniels, the Small-d Democrat*, 1966. See Sect. AQ-2.

Müller, G.A., von. *The Kaiser and His Court: The Diaries, Note Books and Letters of Admiral George Alerad von Müller, Chief of the Naval Cabinet, 1914-1918*, 1961.

Patterson, A.T. *Jellicoe: A Biography*, 1969.

Young, D. *Rutland of Jutland*, 1963. "A shocking revelation of a travesty of justice."

See also the various naval memoirs previously noted for officers whose careers extended into this period.

BF   1919-1939

BF – 1   General

Beard, C.A. *The Navy: Defense or Portent?*, 1939. Negative views on "navalism."

Belote, J.H. *The Development of German Naval Policy, 1933-1939* (ms. PhD thesis, Berkeley, 1954).

*Borg, D. *The United States and the Far Eastern Crisis of 1933-38: From the Manchurian Incident through the Initial Stage of the Undeclared Sino-Japanese War* (Harvard East Asian Study, No. 14), 1964.

Bywater, H.C. *Sea Power in the Pacific: A Study of the American-Japanese Naval Power*, 1921, 1970.
————. *A Searchlight on the Navy*, 1934. British, critical.

Costell, D.J. *Planning for War: A History of the General Board of the Navy, 1900-1914* (ms. PhD thesis, Tufts, 1968).

Ellinger, W.B. and Rosinski, H. *Sea Power in the Pacific, a Selected Bibliography (1936-1941)*, 1942.

Fagan, G.V. *Anglo-American Naval Relations, 1927-1937* (ms. PhD thesis, Pennsylvania, 1954).

*Gardiner, W.H. (Writings on sea power and naval policy, 1920-32). A large number of articles, the equivalent of a book and bound as such at Harvard, written by a onetime president of the Navy League who was an unofficial adviser to the State and Navy Departments and exercised considerable influence on official and public thinking on the subject. Particularly significant were his "Insular America," *Yale Review*, April 1925, and "Elements and Outlook of American Sea Power," U.S. Naval Institute *Proceedings*, October 1928.

Higham, R.D.S. *Armed forces in Peacetime: Britain 1918-1940, a Case Study*, 1963.

Hinsley, F.H. *Command of the Sea: The Naval Side of British History from 1918 to the End of the Second World War*, 1950. Continuation of Sir Geoffrey Callendar's *The Naval Side of British History*.

Leutze, J.R. *If Britain Should Fail: Roosevelt and Churchill and British-American Naval Relations, 1938-1940* (PhD thesis, Duke, 1970; DA v. 31, p. 5325A).

Lewis, W.L. *The Survival of the German Navy, 1917-1920: Officers, Sailors, Politics* (PhD thesis, Iowa, 1969; DA v. 30, p. 680A).

*Morison, S.E. *History of United States Naval Operations in World War II*, v. 3, *The Rising Sun in the Pacific, 1931-1942*, 1948. Opening chapter reviews the decade before Pearl Harbor. V. 1, *The Battle of the Atlantic, 1939-1943* has a less objective foreword by D.W. Knox.

Oyos, L.E. *The Navy and United States Far Eastern Policy, 1930-1939* (PhD thesis, Nebraska, 1958; DA v. 19, p. 1356).

Purcell, E.C., Jr. *Japanese Expansion in the South Pacific, 1890-1935* (PhD thesis, Pennsylvania, 1967; DA v. 28, p. 4102A).

*Rappaport, A. *The Navy League of the United States*, 1962. See also Gardiner above.

*Roskill, S.W. *Naval Policy between the Wars*, 2 v. in 1, 1968.

Tuleja, T.V. *Statesmen and Admirals*, 1963. "The best military and naval resources of a nation break down when that nation's foreign policy lacks clarity and realism."

*Wheeler, G.E. *Prelude to Pearl Harbor: The United States Navy and the Far East, 1921-1931*, 1963, 1968 and P. See Sect. BF-3.

BF – 2   Disarmament

Andrade, E., Jr. *U.S. Naval Policy in the Disarmament Era, 1921-1937* (PhD thesis, Michigan State, 1966; DA v. 27, p. 2973A).

Atkinson, J.D. *The London Naval Conference of 1930* (ms. PhD thesis, Georgetown, 1949).

Berg, M.W. *The United States and the Breakdown of Naval Limitation, 1934-1939* (PhD thesis, Tulane, 1966; DA v. 27, p. 3390A).

Birn, D.S. *Britain and France at the Washington Conference, 1921-1922* (PhD thesis, Columbia, 1964; DA v. 26, p. 2156).

Bright, C.C. *Britain's Search for Security, 1930-1936: The Diplomacy of Naval Disarmament and Imperial Defence* (PhD thesis, Yale, 1970; DA v. 31, p. 6509A).

Buckley, T.H. *The United States and the Washington Conference, 1921-1922* (PhD thesis, Indiana, 1961; DA v. 22, p. 1595).

Buell, R.L. *The Washington Conference*, 1922 (PhD thesis, Princeton), 1970.

DeBoe, D.C. *The United States and the Geneva Disarmament Conference, 1932-1934* (PhD thesis, Tulane, 1969; DA v. 30, p. 4367A).

Douglas, L.H. *Submarine Disarmament, 1919-1938* (PhD thesis, Syracuse, 1970; DA v. 31, p. 2840A). "The history of the international efforts to abolish or limit the submarine was fraught with frustration and failure."

Forbes, H.W. *The Strategy of Disarmament*, 1962.

Fry, M.G. *Anglo-American-Canadian Relations with special reference to Far Eastern and Naval Issues, 1918-22* (ms. PhD thesis, London, 1964).

Groeling, D.T. *Submarines, Disarmament and Modern Warfare* (ms. PhD thesis, Columbia, 1950).

Hercher, W.H. *Great Britain and Naval Disarmament* (ms. PhD thesis, New York Univ., 1939).

Kitchans, J.B., Jr. *The Shearer Scandal and the Origins of Big Navy Politics and Diplomacy in the 1920s* (PhD thesis, Georgia, 1968; DA v. 29, p. 4428A).

Klachko, M. *Anglo-American Naval Competition, 1918-1922* (ms. PhD thesis, Columbia, 1962; DA v. 23, p. 4737).

Knox, D.W. *The Eclipse of American Sea Power*, 1922.

Meyer-Oakes, F.F. *Prince Saionji and the London Naval Conference, Being Part of Volume One of the Memoirs of Harada Kunaio . . . translated into English with annotation* (ms. PhD thesis, Chicago, 1955).

O'Connor, R.G. *Perilous Equilibrium. The United States and the London Naval Conference of 1930*, 1962 (PhD thesis, Stanford).

Oliver, J.B. *Japan's Role in the Origin of the London Naval Treaty of 1930; A Study in Diplomatic History* (PhD thesis, Duke, 1954).

Rattan, S. *The Four Party Treaty of 1921 and the American National Interest* (PhD thesis, American Univ., 1967; DA v. 28, p. 1377A).

Rudoff, R.M. *The Influence of the German Navy on the British Search for Arms Control, 1928-1935* (PhD thesis, Tulane, 1964; DA v. 25, p. 4113).

Shaw, R. *The London Naval Conference of 1930; A Study in Naval and Political Relations among.the Western Powers* (ms. PhD thesis, Fordham, 1946).

*Sprout, H. and M. *Toward a New Order of Sea Power: American Naval Policy and the World Scene, 1918-1922*, 1940, 1946. Includes a long account of the Washington Naval Conference of 1921-22.

Stephen, E.P. *The Race to Pearl Harbor: The Failure of the Second London Conference and the Coming of World War II* (ms. PhD thesis, Harvard, 1971).

BF – 3   Special Subjects

Agar, A.W.S. *Baltic Episode*, 1963. Adventures in 1919 in which the Royal Navy "carried out its task with a traditional mixture of diplomatic skill and fighting initiative."

Avrich, P. *Kronstadt, 1921*, 1970. Uprising of sailors at Kronstadt Naval Base, leading to a 16-day struggle crushed by the Soviet troops.

Bates, J.L. *The Origins of Teapot Dome: Progressives, Parties and Petroleum, 1909-1921*, 1963. See also Noggle below.

Beers, H.P. *U.S. Naval Detachment in Turkish Waters, 1919-1924* (Navy Dept. Administrative Reference Service Report, No. 2), P1953.

Cooper, L. *The* Royal Oak *Affair*, 1969. Confrontation on the Mediterranean flagship involving various characters from the Admiral to a bandmaster. See also Gardiner below.

Davidonis, A.S. *The American Naval Mission in the Adriatic, 1918-1921*, P1943.

Davis, B. *The Billy Mitchell Affair,* 1967. Violent attack on the Navy and naval aviation by a senior Army aviator.

Divine, D. *Mutiny at Invergorden,* 1970. See Sect. O-1.

Frank, W.C., Jr. *Sea Power and Politics, and the Onset of the Spanish War,* 1936 (PhD thesis, Pittsburgh, 1969; DA v. 30, p. 3397).

Gardiner, L. *The* Royal Oak *Courts Martial,* 1965. See also Cooper above.

Glenn, B. *Demobilization of Civilian Personnel by the U.S. Navy after the First World War* (Navy Dept. Administrative Reference Service, No. 8), P1945.

Koginos, E.T. *The* Panay *Incident: Prelude to War* (PhD thesis, American Univ., 1966; DA v. 26, p. 6675). Japanese attack on U.S. gunboat in China, Dec. 12, 1937. Better on general background than the "highly journalistic" Perry volume, below.

Lincoln, A. *The United States Navy and Air Force: A History of Naval Aviation, 1920-1934* (ms. PhD thesis, Berkeley, 1966).

Lockwood, C.A. and Adamson, H.C. *Tragedy at Honda,* 1960. Grounding of seven U.S. destroyers within five minutes through faulty navigation, near Santa Barbara, September 1923.

McCrocklin, J.H., ed. *Garde D'Haiti, 1915-1934: Twenty Years of Organization and Training by the United States Marine Corps,* 1956 (PhD thesis, Texas). Virtually the only time Haiti was ever subjected to such efficiency and regularity.

Miller, E.H. *Strategy at Singapore,* 1942. Based on Clark Univ. PhD thesis, *The Singapore Naval Base.*

Moseley, H.W. *The "Cash and Carry" Section of the 1937 Neutrality Act* (ms. PhD thesis, Harvard, 1939).

Noggle, B. *Teapot Dome: Oil and Politics in the 1920s,* 1962, P1965. See also Bates above.

Perry, H.D. *The* Panay *Incident: Prelude to Pearl Harbor,* 1969. See also Koginos, above.

Rapp, N.G. *The Anglo-German Naval Agreement of 1935* (PhD thesis, Connecticut, 1968; DA v. 30, p. 2948).

Smith, R.K. *The Airships* Akron *and* Macon: *Flying Aircraft Carriers of the United States Navy,* 1965 (PhD thesis, Chicago). Rigid airships during the period 1919-40.

Snowbarger, W.E. *The Development of Pearl Harbor* (ms. PhD thesis, Berkeley, 1951).

Wheeler, G.E. *Prelude to Pearl Harbor*. . . . 1963. Analysis of politico-military considerations influencing Japanese-American policy, 1921-31.

Wieand, H.T. *A History of the Development of the United States Naval Reserve, 1889-1941* (ms. PhD thesis, Pittsburgh, 1953).

BF – 4   Biography and Memoirs, 1919-1939

Arpee, E. *From Frigates to Flat Tops*, 1953. Biography of Rear Admiral W.A. Moffett, first Chief of the Bureau of Aeronautics, with some account of early naval aviation.

Bennett, G.M. *Cowman's War: The Story of British Naval Operations in the Baltic, 1918-20*, 1964. See also Agar, Sect. BF-3.

*Bowen, H.G. *Ships, Machinery and Mossbacks: The Autobiography of a Naval Engineer*, 1954. See Sect. L-5.

Ferrell, H.C., Jr. *Claude A. Swanson of Virginia* (ms. PhD thesis, Virginia, 1964), Secretary of the Navy, 1933-39.

Pound, R. *Evans of the* Broke: *A Biography of Admiral Lord Mountevans*, 1964. Life of E.R.G.R. Evans, RN (1881-1957), later Lord Mountevans. Commanded destroyer *Broke* in World War I and later explored the Antarctic.

BG   WORLD WAR II – GENERAL

BG – 1   Official Programs

The British and Americans covered much of their war efforts, military and civil, in official history programs, varying widely in scope and content. Much of this material has superseded in value many of the earlier unofficial accounts which consequently no longer call for citation here. The most comprehensive coverage was by the British, who produced dozens of volumes of high uniform quality, under able professional supervision, in their "History of the Second World War," (hereafter abbreviated "Hist. 2nd WW"), with a "United Kingdom Civil Series" and "United Kingdom Military Series." In scope and quality, it followed the general British program of World War I. In the Military Series, it produced a few overall analytical volumes and then more detailed studies of operations in particular areas, combining all three services. On this side of the Atlantic, the most effective coverage came in the Army's series, "The United States Army in World War II" hereafter abbreviated "USA-WWII," which produced more than a hundred volumes in uniform format, under the direct supervision of Dr. Kent R. Greenfield of Johns Hopkins, later of Dr. Stetson Conn of Amherst. These included very ample coverage of administrative and other "non-shooting" aspects. There were doubtless some things which the United States Navy could do better than the Army, but official history was not one of them. In 1944, it set up an Office of Naval History, later Naval History Division with operational aspects headed by S.E. Morison, who concentrated on the 15-volume program bearing his name, and the administrative by R.G. Albion, also of Harvard, which produced some 200 volumes of typescript analyses of shore-based activities at Washington and elsewhere, some of which were published under separate auspices. The Navy also supported several other projects, mostly journalistic, including Karig's comprehensive operational history with its "human interest" emphasis, and Roscoe's detailed coverage of destroyer and submarine activity. The United States Marine Corps provided effective coverage, first in a series of monographs on particular operations, then in a five-volume summary. The U.S. Air Historical Group, under Dr. L.W.F. Craven and J.L. Cate, covered army air activity in seven volumes. Under the impetus of the Bureau of the Budget, various civilian agencies including the Maritime Commission prepared histories of their wartime activities. In the British Commonwealth, Canada, Australia, and New Zealand each had an historical series including one or more naval volumes.

BG – 2   Comprehensive Accounts

Albion, R.G. and Pope, J.B. *Sea Lanes in Wartime, The American Experience, 1775-1945*, 1942, R1968. The revised edition carries an additional chapter on the second half of World War II.

*Auphan, P. and Mordal, J., tr. A.C. Sabalot. *The French Navy in World War II*, 1959. Like Bragadin, Ruge and the one-volume Roskill, this was one of a series, written by professional officers of the navies concerned, promoted and published by the U.S. Naval Institute and covering the war experience of the different navies.

Berenbrok, H.O. (C.O. Bekker, pseud.) *Swastika at Sea: The Struggle and Eventual Destruction of the German Navy, 1939-1945*, 1953, R1955, P1956 (*Defeat at Sea* in American edition).

Bragadin, M.A. *The Italian Navy in World War II*, 1957. See Auphan above.

Butow, R.J.C. *Tojo and the Coming of the War*, 1961, 1969 and P.
————. *Japan's Decision to Surrender*, 1962, 1967 and P.

*Churchill, Sir W.S. *The Second World War*, 6 v. 1948-53, P1961-62 Vol. 1, *The Gathering Storm*; 2, *Their Finest Hour*; 3, *The Grand Alliance*; 4, *The Hinge of Fate*; 5, *Closing the Ring*; 6, *Triumph and Tragedy*.
*————. *Memoirs of the Second World War*, 1959. A one-volume compression of the above, with "a meaty epilogue on the postwar years." With his unique vantage point as Prime Minister, he still retained his keen interest in naval affairs and gives constantly readable, though rather subjective, accounts, reproducing many of his state papers.

Creswell, J. *Sea Warfare, 1939-1945*, 1937, rev. ed. 1967. See Sect. AT.

*Davis, K.S. *Experience of War: The United States in World War II* (Mainstream of America), 1965.

Gill, G.H. *Royal Australian Navy, 1939-1945* (Australia in the War of 1939-45), 2 v. 1957, 1969.

Isakov, I.S. *The Red Fleet in the Second World War*, 1947.

*Itō, M. and Pineau, R. *The End of the Imperial Japanese Navy*, 1962. Broad coverage of the entire war.

Karig, W., et al. *Battle Report . . . prepared from Official Sources*, 5 v. 1944-49. An officially sponsored account of the Navy's war activities, prepared under the Navy's Office of Public Relations, with emphasis on the "human interest" aspects.

LeMasson, H. *The French Navy*, 2 v. 1969. Details of all ships in the French Navy in 1939, with an introductory analysis of French naval policy during the war.

Maass, W.B. *The Netherlands at War, 1940-1945*, 1970.

*Morison, S.E. *History of United States Naval Operations in World War II*, 15 v. 1947-62, with frequent corrected revisions.
 V. 1. *The Battle of the Atlantic, September 1939-May 1943.*
 2. *Operations in North African Waters, October 1942-June 1943.*
 3. *The Rising Sun in the Pacific, 1931-April 1942.*
 4. *The Coral Sea, Midway and Submarine Actions, May 1942-August 1942.*
 5. *The Struggle for Guadalcanal, August 1942-February 1943.*
 6. *Breaking the Bismarck's Barrier, 22 July 1942-1 May 1944.*
 7. *Aleutians, Gilberts and Marshalls, June 1942-April 1944.*
 8. *New Guinea and the Marianas, March 1944-August 1944.*
 9. *Sicily-Salerno-Anzio, January 1943-June 1944.*
 10. *The Atlantic Battle Won, May 1943-May 1945.*
 11. *The Invasion of France and Germany, 1944-1945.*
 12. *Leyte, June 1944-January 1945.*
 13. *The Liberation of the Philippines, 1944-1945.*
 14. *Victory in the Pacific.*
 15. *Supplement and General Index.*
This ambitious 20-year project, with its wealth of tactical detail, was carried out under the direction of Morison who went on leave from Harvard in 1942 with a reserve commission, finally retiring as rear admiral. It received very generous support from the Navy Department, and by the 1950s became the almost sole concern of the Director of Naval History. Morison's collaborators, who participated in the research and the preparation of the first drafts, included Rear Admirals Bern Anderson and James Shaw, in addition to Roger Pineau, Henry Salomon, Philip K. Lundeberg, K. Jack Bauer, Donald R. Martin and others.
*————. *The Two-Ocean War: A Short History of the U.S. Navy in the Second World War*, 1963. A convenient single-volume summary of the high points, somewhat more critical in its estimates than the original series.

O'Connor, R., ed. *The Japanese Navy in World War II*, 1971. Anthology of articles from the U.S. Naval Institute *Proceedings*.

*Potter, E.B. and Nimitz, C.W., eds. *The Great Sea War: The Story of Naval Action in World War II*, 1960. The second half of their comprehensive, cooperative Annapolis volume on *Sea Power*, this covers the operations of all the navies. In a further reduction, the Pacific portion of World War II was issued as a paperback, *Triumph in the Pacific*, 1963.

Richard, D.E. *United States Naval Chronology, World War II* (ms. PhD thesis, Georgetown, 1949). After revision, this was published by the Naval History Division in 1956.

*Roskill, S.W. *The War at Sea* (Hist. 2nd WW, United Kingdom Military Series), 3 v. in 4, 1956-61. Considered by many the outstanding work of World War II naval history, this analyzes the major strategy of the various navies, leaving the tactical details to the official histories of the different areas. Captain Roskill was allowed to express his critical estimates with a freedom rather unique in official histories.
————. *White Ensign: The British Navy at War, 1939-1945*, 1960. Deals mainly with the British experience.

*Ruge, F. *Der Seekrieg, The German Navy's Story, 1939-1945*, 1957. See Auphan above.

Schull, J. *The Far Distant Ships: An Official Account of Canadian Naval Operations in the Second World War*, 1950.

Smith, S.E., ed. *The United States Navy in World War II*, 1966, P1967. A 1,049-page anthology of first-hand accounts.

Tucker, G.N. *The Naval Service of Canada*: v. 2, *Activities on Shore*, 1952. See also Schull above.

Tuleja, T.V. *Twilight of the Sea Gods*, 1958. The German Navy in World War II.

U.S. Air Historical Group, *The Army Air Forces in World War II*, ed. W.F. Craven and J.L. Cate, 7 v. 1948-58. Especially v. 5-6 dealing with the Pacific War.

U.S. Marine Corps Historical Unit. Monographs of Individual Operations, 1947 ff: R.D. Heinl, *The Defense of Wake*, 1947; *Marines at Midway*, 1948; J.R. Stockman, *The Battle for Tarawa*, 1947; J.N. Rentz, *Bougainville and the Northern Solomons*, 1948; *Marines in the Central Solomons*, 1952; J.L. Zimmerman, *The Guadalcanal Campaign*, 1949; C.W. Hoffman, *Saipan*, 1950; *The Siezure of Tinian*, 1951; F.O. Hough, *The Assault on Peleliu*, 1950; F.O. Hough and J.A. Crown, *Campaign on New Britain*, 1952; O.R. Lodge, *The Recapture of Guam*, 1953; W.S. Bartley, *Iwo Jima, Amphibious Epic*, 1954.
*————. *History of Marine Corps Operations in World War II*, 4 v. 1959-68.

*Von der Porten, E.P. *The German Navy in World War II*, 1969. Analysis of important policy decisions.

Willoughby, M.F. *The United States Coast Guard in World War II*, 1957.

BG – 3 Strategy and High Policy

*Butler, J.R.M., ed. *Grand Strategy* (Hist. 2nd WW, United Kingdom Military Series), 6 v. 1957-66.

*Greenfield, K.R., et al., eds. *Command Decisions* (USA-WWII), 1959.

Howard, M. *The Mediterranean Strategy in the Second World War*, 1968.

*Johnson, F.A. *Defence by Committee: The British Committee of Imperial Defence, 1885-1959*, 1960.

*Martienssen, A.K. *Hitler and His Admirals*, 1949. This valuable study of German policy-making combines the evidence in the Nuremburg war-guilt trials with the material in the so-called "Fuhrer Conferences" on naval affairs which the author edited and which appear in *Brassey's Naval Annual* for 1948.

Matloff, M. and Snell, E.M. *Strategic Planning for Coalition Warfare* (USA-WW II), 2 v. 1953-59.

Morison, S.E. *Strategy and Compromise*, 1958, RP1966.

*Morton, L. *Strategy and Command: The First Two Years* (USA-WWII), 1963. The Pacific war through 1943.

Pogue, F.C. *The Supreme Command, European Theatre of Operations* (USA-WWII), 1954.

BG – 4   Administration

*Albion, R.G. and Connery, R.H. *Forrestal and the Navy*, 1962. Covers his experience as Under Secretary and Secretary from 1940 until he became first Secretary of Defense in 1947.

Furer, J.A. *Administration of the Navy Department in World War II*, 1959. See comments, Sect. AQ-2.

James, Sir W. *The Code Breaker of Room Forty: The Story of Sir William Hall, Genius of British Counter-Intelligence*, 1956 (*The Eyes of the Navy* in British edition).

McLachlan, D. *Room 39: Wherein Took Place the Exciting Story of British Naval Intelligence in World War II*, 1968.

Rowland, B. and Boyd, W.B. *U.S. Navy Bureau of Ordnance in World War II*, 1953. Each chapter deals with a different specialty of "BuOrd," including a frank account of the shortcomings of torpedo production.

U.S. Bureau of Medicine and Surgery, Navy Dept. *History of the Medical Department of the United States Navy in World War II*, 2 v. 1953-54.

U.S. Bureau of Ships, Navy Dept. *An Administrative History of the Bureau of Ships during World War II*, 4 v. 1952. A processed edition of the Bureau's "first narrative."

U.S. Bureau of Yards and Docks, Navy Dept. *Building the Navy's Bases in World*

War II: History of the Bureau of Yards and Docks and the Civil Engineer Corps, 1940-1946, 2 v. 1947. See also E.L. Castillo, *The Seabees of World War II*, 1963.

*U.S. Office of Naval History *First Draft Narratives of U.S. Naval Administration in World War II*, c 200 ms. volumes, 1944-46. These typescript studies were the principal concern of the Administrative History Program which, until 1946, was devoted to service within the Navy rather than publication. These studies analyze the wartime experience of the various bureaus and offices of the Navy Dept., the major fleet commands, naval operating bases, sea frontiers, naval districts, and shore stations, for the Navy's future use. The nonclassified volumes were deposited in the Office of Naval History (later Naval History Division, Op-29), with duplicate copies in the individual commands and units.

BG – 5   Supply, Logistics, and Blockade

Ballantine, D.S. *U.S. Naval Logistics in the Second World War*, 1947 (PhD thesis, Harvard). Emphasizes the headquarters planning in Naval Operations. See also the later logistical studies of Admirals Dyer and Eccles.

*Behrens, C.B.A. *Merchant Shipping and the Demands of War* (Hist. 2nd WW, United Kingdom Civil Series), 1955. Roughly the counterpart of the Fayle and Salter volumes in the British official series of World War I.

Carter, W.B. *Beans, Bullets and Black Oil: The Story of Fleet Logistics Afloat in the Pacific during World War II* (Naval History Division), 1953.
——————and Duvall, E.E. *Ships, Salvage and Sinews of War: Story of Fleet Logistics Afloat in Atlantic and Mediterranean Waters during World War II* (Naval History Division), 1954.

Coakley, R.W. and Leighton, R.M. *Global Logistics and Strategy, 1943-1945* (USA-WWII, The War Dept.), 1968. See Leighton and Coakley below.

Connery, R.H. *The Navy and the Industrial Mobilization in World War II*, 1951. Findings summarized in Albion and Connery, *Forrestal and the Navy*, above.

Easton, A. *50 North: An Atlantic Battleground*, 1963. Blockade.

Hall, H.D. *North American Supply* (Hist. 2nd WW, United Kingdom Civil Series), 1955. American-Canadian-British cooperation in meeting British needs.

Leighton, R.C. and Coakley, R.W. *Global Logistics in World War II* (1939-1942) (USA-WWII, The War Dept.), 1955. For continuation, see Coakley and Leighton above.

*Medlicott, W.N. *The Economic Blockade* (Hist. 2nd WW, United Kingdom Civil Series), 2 v. 1952.

Olson, M., Jr. *The Economics of Wartime Shortage: A History of British Food Supplies in the Napoleonic Wars and World Wars I and II*, 1963.

Owens, C.H., Jr. *The Logistical Support of the Army in the Central Pacific, 1941-1944* (ms. PhD thesis, Georgetown, 1954).

Ruppenthal, R.G. *The Logistical Support of the Armies* (USA-WWII), 2 v. 1954-58.

BG – 6   Merchant Shipping

*Behrens, C.B.A. See Sect. BG-5.

Bushell, T.H. *Eight Bells: Royal Mail Lines War Story, 1939-1945*, 1950.

Carse, R. *The Long Haul: The United States Merchant Service in World War II*, 1965.

Hodson, J.J. *British Merchantmen at War: The Official Story of the Merchant Navy, 1934-44*, 1945. More meager than most of the official studies.

Kerr, G.F. *Business in Great Waters: The War History of the P & O, 1939-1945*, 1951. Peninsular and Oriental.

*Lane, F.C., et al. *Ships for Victory: A History of Shipbuilding under the U.S. Maritime Commission in World War II* (Historical Reports on War Administration, U.S. Maritime Commission), 1951.

McCoy, S.D. *Nor Death Dismay*, 1948. Wartime experiences of the American Export Lines.

Mitchell, W.H. and Sawyer, L.A. *Empire Ships of World War II*, 1965. See comments, Sect. J-3.

Riesenberg, F., Jr. *Sea War: The Story of the U.S. Merchant Marine in World War II*, 1956. This, and Carse above, still leave room for a much more adequate account.

Roskill, S.W. *A Merchant Fleet in War: Alfred Holt & Co., 1939-1945*, 1962. The "Blue Funnel" fleet to the East; much detail on the Malta convoys.

Savage, C.I. *Inland Transport* (Hist. 2nd WW, United Kingdom Civil Series), 1957. Includes British coastal shipping.

Savage, L.A. and Mitchell, W.H. *The Liberty Ship*. . . . See Sect. J-3.

Sawyer, L.H., et al. *The Liberty Ship*, 1970.

Schofield, B.B. *Russian Convoys*, 1964. For further actual experiences, see Sect. BH-6.

Shaw, A. *Victory Ships and Maritime Commission "C" Classes*, P1963.

Standard Oil Company of New Jersey, *Ships of the Esso Fleet in World War II*, 1946.

Blundell, W.D.G. *Ships of the Modern Royal Navy*, 1967.

Enders, C.W. *The Vinson Navy*. See Sect. AQ-2.

Fraccaroli, A. *Italian Warships of World War II*, 1968.

LeMasson, H. *The French Navy*, 2 v. 1969. See Sect. BG-2.

Lenton, H.T. *British and Dominion Warships of World War II*, 1968.
————. *American Battleships, Carriers and Cruisers*, 1968.
————. *German Surface Vessels*, 1967.
————. *The Royal Netherlands Navy*, 1968.

Taylor, J.C. *German Warships of World War II*, 1968, with companion volume
  for World War I, 1969.

Watts, A.J. *Japanese Warships of World War II*, 1969.

BH   WORLD WAR II – SPECIFIC TYPES, AREAS, OPERATIONS

BH – 1   Submarine Warfare

*Beach, E.L. *Submarine!* 1952. Case histories of numerous American submarines, by
  an outstanding sub commander who later led first submerged atomic circumnavigation. To appreciate emotionally both the offensive and defensive aspects of submarine warfare, this might be read in company with Nicholas
  Monsarrat's fictional *The Cruel Sea*, 1951, RP1963.

Doenitz, K. *Memoirs*. . . . 1959. German admiral, at first in command of submarines and then commander-in-chief.

Everitt, D. *K-Boats: A Dramatic First Report on the Navy's Most Calamitous
  Submarines*, 1964. British; see Sect. K-7.

Farago, L. *The Tenth Fleet*, 1963. Staff set up at American headquarters to coordinate operations against German submarines; describes the "Battle of the
  Atlantic" from the American and German command viewpoint.

Frank, W. *Enemy Submarine: The Story of Gunther Prien, Captain of U-47*,
  1954. See also Prien below. He sank the British battleship *Royal Oak* at anchor in Scapa Flow.

Gallery, D.V. *Twenty Million Tons Under the Sea: The Submarine War in the
  Atlantic and the Daring Capture of the U-505*, 1957 (*We Captured a U-Boat*
  in British edition). By a very vocal naval aviator, active in "hunter-killer"
  operations.

*Hashimoto, M. *Sunk! The Story of the Japanese Submarine Fleet, 1942-1945*,
  1954, P. Unlike the Americans and Germans, the Japanese failed to use their
  subs effectively for commerce destruction.

Hezlet, A.R. *The Submarine and Sea Power*, 1967.

*Irving, D. *The Destruction of Convoy PQ 17*, 1969. Deadly German attack on inadequately protected convoy on the Murmansk run; only 11 of the 35 ships reached port. This has been called "one of the best books yet to appear about a single operation of the war."

Lockwood, C.A. *Sink 'em All: Submarine Warfare in the Pacific*, 1951.
————. *Down to the Sea in Subs*, 1967.
———— and Adamson, H.C. *Through Hell and Deep Water. The Stirring Story of the Navy's Deadly Submarine, the USS* Harder. . . . 1956.
————. *Hell at 50 Fathoms*, 1962.
————. *Hellcats of the Sea*, 1955.
Though submarines have been called the "silent service," Admiral Lockwood, overall commander of the "SubsPac" (Submarines Pacific Fleet) has been one of the most effectively prolific regular USN officers.

*Lundeberg, P.K. *American Anti-Submarine Operations in the Atlantic* (ms. PhD thesis, Harvard, 1954). Prepared as the first draft for vol. 10 of the Morison history.

*Macintyre, D. *The Battle of the Atlantic* (British Battles Series), 1961. Captain Macintyre, also author of several other books on wartime naval subjects, was one of the most successful ASW (anti-submarine warfare) leaders.

Peillard, L. *The* Laconia *Affair*, 1963. Cunarder, with 3,000 passengers and 1,800 prisoners of war, sunk by U-156 which undertook rescue operations until attacked by allied aircraft, whereupon Doenitz forbade all submarine commanders to rescue survivors.

Prien, G. *I Sank the* Royal Oak, 1954. See also Frank above.

Roscoe, T. *United States Submarine Operations in World War II*, 1949. One of the various projects backed by the Navy Dept. outside its regular history program. Abridged edition published as *Pig Boats: The True Story of the Fighting Submarines of World War II.*

U.S. Naval History Division, *U.S. Submarine Losses, World War II*, 6th printing. Includes all submarine losses 1939-45.

Werner, H. *Iron Coffins: A Personal Account of the German U-Boat Battles in World War II*, 1969. By a grim statistical coincidence, the 30,000 lives lost in U-boat crews was about equal to the number lost on the allied merchant ships they sank.

Yokota, Y. *Suicide Submarine*, 1968. Equivalent of the aerial kamikazes.

BH – 2   Other Techniques and Ship Types

Best, H. *The Webfoot Warriors*, 1962. Underwater demolition.

Bulkley, R.J. *At Close Quarters: PT Boats in the United States Navy* (Naval History Division), 1962. After the early interest in his *They Were Expendable*, the subject lay dormant until revived by interest in President Kennedy's wartime PT experience. See also Granville below.

Cameron, I. *Wings of the Morning: The Story of the Fleet Air Arm in the Second World War*, 1962.

Castillo, E.L. *The Seabees of World War II*, 1963. The name was a contraction of "Construction Battalions."

Cowie, J.S. *Mines, Minelayers and Minelaying*, 1949. See also Lott below.

Goodhart, P. *Fifty Ships that Saved the World*, 1965. The over-age American destroyers transferred to the Royal Navy in the 1940 "Destroyer-Base" deal.

Granville, W. and Kelly, R.A. *Inshore Heroes: The Story of the Little Ships*, 1961. British motor torpedo boats, etc.

*Inoguchi, R., et al. *The Divine Wind, Japan's Kamikaze Force in World War II*, 1958, P1960, R1968. The same subject is treated in Y. Kuwahara, et al. *Kamikaze*, P1958.

*Isely, J.A. and Crowl, P.A. *The U.S. Marines and Amphibious War: Its Theory and Practice in the Pacific*, 1951. Prepared in the Princeton History Dept. under contract with the Marine Corps.

*Lott, A.S. *Most Dangerous Sea: A History of Mine Warfare and an Account of U.S. Navy Mine Warfare Operations in World War II and Korea*, 1959, P (abridged). See also Cowie above.

McLachlan, D. *Room 39*. . . . See Sect. BG-4.

Postan, M.M., et al. *Design and Development of Weapons*, 1964. See Sect. K-9.

*Reynolds, C.G. *The Fast Carriers: The Forging of an Air Navy*, 1968. Based on his Duke PhD thesis, *History and Development of the Fast Carrier Task Force, 1943-1945*.

Roscoe, T. *United States Destroyer Operations in World War II*, 1953. Like his above-mentioned companion work on submarines, organized on a ship-by-ship basis. Abridged as *Tin Cans*, P1960.

*Roskill, S.W. *H.M.S.* Warspite: *The Story of a Famous Battleship*, 1958. Excellent case study of a highly successful class (with the *Queen Elizabeth, Barham, Malaya* and *Valiant*) which served with distinction in both World Wars.

Rutter, O. *The British Navy's Air Arm, The Official Story of the British Navy's Air Operations*, 1944.

Sherman, F.C. *Combat Command: The American Aircraft Carriers in the Pacific War*, 1950. Like Adm. F.P. Sherman, later CNO, the author was a carrier commander.

U.S. Office of Naval Operations, *The Navy's Air War*, 1946.
——————. *U.S. Naval Aviation in the Pacific*, 1947. These were produced by the Naval Aviation History Unit under H.M. Dater.

U.S. Strategic Bombing Survey (Pacific), *Summary Report*, 1946.
*——————. *Interrogation of Japanese Officials*, 2 v. 1946.
*——————. *War Against Japanese Transportation*, 1946.

Woodward, D. *The Secret Raiders: The Story of the German Armed Merchant Raiders of the Second World War*, 1955, RP1958.

BH – 3   Individual Ship Histories

Some of these will also be noted in connection with the particular operations in which they were involved.

Bradford, E.D.S. *The Mighty* Hood: *The Life and Death of Britain's Proudest Warship*, 1960, P. Huge battle cruiser, largest warship between the wars, sunk in action with the *Bismarck*.

Brennecke, H.J. *Cruise of the Raider HK-33*, 1955 (*Ghost Cruiser HK-33* in British edition). The *Pinguin*, which operated successfully in the Indian Ocean.
——————. *The* Tirpitz, 1963. Powerful sister ship of the *Bismarck*.

Bryan, J. *Aircraft Carrier*, 1954, P. The *Yorktown*.

Busch, F.O. *Holocaust at Sea: The Drama of the* Scharnhorst, 1955 (First part of title omitted in British edition). See also Watts below.
——————. *The Story of the* Prince Eugen, tr. E. Brocket, 1960. Germany's "most modern heavy cruiser."

Detmers, Y. *The Raider* Kormoran, 1959. By her captain.

Donovan, R.J. *PT-109. John F. Kennedy in World War II*, 1961, RP1962.

Forester, C.S. *The Last Nine Days of the* Bismarck, 1959, P1959 ff. *Sink the* Bismarck in later edition; *Hunting the* Bismarck in British edition. Fictionalized, with imaginary dialogue. Less satisfactory than Grenfell below.

Frank, W. and Rogge, B. *German Raider* Atlantis, tr. R.B. Long, P1956. Reissued as *Under Ten Flags*.

*Grenfell, R. *The* Bismarck *Episode*, 1948, P1962; R1967. See also Forester above, D. Berthold, *Sinking the* Bismarck and the Bradford and Busch accounts above, of the *Hood* and the *Prince Eugen*.

Helm, T. *Ordeal by Sea: The Tragedy of the USS* Indianapolis, 1963. Sunk by Japanese submarine in Pacific, in last days of war, after delivering first atomic bombs; inexcusable delay in rescue caused heavy loss of life. See also Newcomb below.

Hoehling, M. *The* Lexington *Goes Down, the Last Seven Hours of a Fighting Lady*, 1971. See also Johnston below.

*Jameson, Sir W.S. Ark Royal, *1939-1941*, 1957. British aircraft carrier.

Johnston, S. *Queen of the Flat Tops: The USS* Lexington *and the Coral Sea Battle*, 1942, P1943, R1968, P1970.

Landsborough, G. *The Battle of the River Plate*, 1956, P. Action of "pocket battleship" *Graf Spee* with British cruiser squadron, 1939. Other accounts by D. Pope, M. Powell below, and Sir E. Millington-Drake, Sect. BH-12.

*Lott, A.S. *Brave Ship, Brave Men*, 1965. Graphic man-by-man and blow-by-blow account of the destroyer *Aaron Ward* under deadly kamikaze attack on picket duty off Okinawa.

McKee, A. *Black Saturday: The Tragedy of the* Royal Oak, 1959. Daring torpedoing of British dreadnought at Scapa Flow, by German U-47, Oct. 14, 1939. See also Frank and Prien, Sect. BH-1.

Newcomb, R.F. *Abandon Ship! Death of the USS* Indianapolis, 1958. See also Helm above.

Newell, G. and Smith, A.L. *Mighty Mo: The USS* Missouri, *a Biography of the Last Battleship*, 1969. Primarily a "picture book."

*Roskill, S.W. *HMS* Warspite. . . . See comments, Sect. BH-2.

Schaeffer, H. *U-boat 977*, 1953. Escape of schnorkel submarine to Argentina at close of war.

Stafford, E.P. *The Big E*, 1962. The *Enterprise*, often called the most celebrated American carrier.

Watts, A.J. *The Loss of the* Scharnhorst, 1971. See also Busch above.

BH – 4   Atlantic – General

See Macintyre, Sect. BH-1; Bradford, Brennecke, Busch, Grenfell, Landsborough, Sect. BH-3.

Anglin, D.G. *The St. Pierre and Miquelon Affaire of 1941*, 1966. DeGaulle seizure of little French islands off Newfoundland.

Conn, S. and Fairchild, B. *The Framework of Hemisphere Defense* (USA-WWII).
* ————, et al. *Guarding the United States and Its Outposts*, 1964. Post-Pearl Harbor defense, including Caribbean, Canal Zone, Greenland and Iceland, in addition to Alaska and Hawaii.

Creighton, K. *Convoy Commodore*, 2nd ed., 1956.

Gretton, Sir P. *Convoy Escort Commander*, 1964.

Heckstall-Smith, A. *The Fleet that Faced Both Ways*, 1963. In this account of the French Navy, divided between Vichy and Free France, the author is more favorable to Vichy than to Churchill.

Schofield, B.B., et al. *The Rescue Ships*, 1968.

Schofield, W.G. *Eastward the Convoys*, 1965.

BH – 5   English Channel, North Sea, British Waters

Ansel, W. *Hitler Confronts England*, 1960. A study of "Operation Sea Lion," analyzing German policy concerning the possible invasion of Britain in 1940, by an American admiral. See also Fleming and Wheatley below.

Brownlowe, L.C. *The Mulberry Project*, 1957. Creation of an artificial harbor for the Normandy landings in 1944.

*Chalmers, W.S. *Max Horton and the Western Approaches*, 1954. See Sect. BH-13.

Collier, R. *The Sands of Dunkirk*, 1961, P1962. The "miracle" rescuing of trapped British forces. See also Divine below.

Divine, D. *The Nine Days of Dunkirk*, 1959.

Ellis, L.F., et al. *The Battle of Normandy* (Hist. 2nd WW, United Kingdom Military Series), 1963.

*Fergusson, Sir B. *The Watery Maze: The Story of Combined Operations*, 1961. Story of the Combined Operational Headquarters for amphibious operations.

*Fleming, P. *Operation Sea Lion: The Projected Invasion of England in 1940; An Account of the German Preparation and the British Countermeasures*, 1957. *Invasion, 1940* in British edition. The most readable approach to the subject; see also Ansel and Wheatley.

Harrison, M. *Mulberry: The Return to Europe*, 1965. Normandy landings. See also Haupt, Howarth and Ryan.

Haupt, W. and Feist, U. *Invasion D-Day, June 6, 1944*, 1968. Also Normandy.

Howarth, D. *D-Day, the Sixth of June, 1944*, 1959. The first day of the Normandy landings.

McKee, A. *Black Saturday*. . . . See Sect. BH-3.

Reynolds, Q. *Dress Rehearsal: The Story of Dieppe*, 1943. For this costly "hit-and-run" raid, see also T. Robertson, *The Shame and Glory of Dieppe*, 1962, and C.P. Stacey, *The Canadian Army, 1939-1945*.

Robertson, T. *Channel Dash: The Fantastic Story of the German Battle Fleet's Escape through the English Channel in Broad Daylight*, 1958, P1959.

*Ryan, C. *The Longest Day*, 1959, RP1962. The D-Day Normandy landings. See also Harrison, et al., above.

*Scott, P.M. *The Battle of the Narrow Seas: A History of the Light Coastal Forces in the Channel and North Sea, 1939-1945*, 1946.

Wheatley, R.H. *Operation Sea Lion: German Plans for the Invasion of England, 1939-42*, 1958. See also Ansel and Fleming above.

BH – 6   Northern European Waters

Ash, B. *Norway, 1940*, 1964.

Brookes, E. *Prologue to a War: The Navy's Part in the Narvik Campaign*, 1966.

Busch, F.O. *Holocaust at Sea.* . . . See Sect. BH-3.

*Campbell, Sir I. and Macintyre, D. *The Kola Run: A Record of Arctic Convoys, 1941-1945*, 1958.

Derry, T.K. *The Campaign in Norway* (Hist. 2nd WW United Kingdom Military Series), 1952.

*Irving, D. *The Destruction of Convoy PQ-17.* See Sect. BH-1.

Macintyre, D. *Narvik*, 1960. See also Ash and S.R. Roskill, *HMS* Warspite. . . . Sect. BH-2.

Moulton, J.L. *The Norwegian Campaign of 1940. A Study of Warfare in Three Dimensions*, 1966.

Ogden, M. *The Battle of the North Cape*, 1962.

Poolman, K. *The Battle of Sixty North*, 1958.

Pope, D. *73 North: The Defeat of Hitler's Navy*, 1958.

*Schofield, B.B. *Russian Convoys*, 1964.

BH – 7   The Mediterranean and North Africa

*Auphan, P. and Mordal, J. (pseud.). *The French Navy in World War II*, 1959.

Blumenson, M. *Anzio: The Gamble that Failed* (Great Battles), 1963.

*Bragadin, M.A. *The Italian Navy in World War II*, 1957.

Cameron, I. (pseud.). *Red Duster, White Ensign: The Story of Malta and the Malta Convoys*, 1960. See also S.S. Roskill, *A Merchant Fleet in War*, 1962.

Cocchia, A. *The Hunters and the Hunted: Adventures of Italian Naval Forces*, 1958. Not to be confused with H.J. Brennecke's book of the same title, dealing with U-boat warfare.

*Cunningham, A.B., Lord. *Sailor's Odyssey*, 1951. See Sect. BH-12.

deBelot, R. *The Struggle for the Mediterranean, 1939-1945*, 1951. Analysis by a French admiral.

Garland, A.N. and Smith, H.M. *Sicily*, 1965.

*Macintyre, D. *The Battle for the Mediterranean* (British Battles Series), 1964.

Pack, S.W.C. *The Battle of Matapan* (British Battles Series), 1961.

*Playfair, I.S., et al. *The Mediterranean and the Middle East* (Hist. 2nd WW United Kingdom Military Series), 6 v. 1960-

Robertson, T. *Ship with Two Captains*, 1957, P. Clandestine adventures of submarine with two Anglo-American top negotiators seeking French cooperation before North African landings, 1941.

Robichon, J. *The Second D-Day*, 1969. Landings in Southern France, Aug. 1944.

Stewart, I.M.G. *The Struggle for Crete*, 1967.

Wingate, J. *Never So Proud*, 1966. Like Stewart above, deals with the German airborne seizures of Crete, resulting in very heavy British military and naval losses.

BH – 8   Pacific – General

*Feis, H. *The Road to Pearl Harbor: The Coming of War between the United States and Japan*, 1950, RP1962. One of the best-balanced accounts of the politico-military aspects of the situation; followed by successive studies of succeeding periods, culminating in *Japan Subdued*, 1961.

Leckie, R. *Strong Men Armed: The United States Marines against Japan*, 1962, P1969.

*Macintyre, D. *The Battle for the Pacific*, 1961, R1966.

Smith, C.P. *Task Force 57*, 1969. The British Pacific force, whose services were treated in rather cavalier fashion by the Americans. Same subject covered in J. Winston, *The Forgotten Fleet*, 1969.

Toland, J. *But Not in Shame*, 1961. Account of the first six months of the United States war with Japan.

BH – 9   The Pearl Harbor Attack

Brownlow, D.G. *The Accused. The Ordeal of Rear Admiral Husband Edward Kimmel, U.S. Navy,* 1968.

Kimmel, H.E. *Admiral Kimmel's Story,* 1954. Apologia by the naval commander at Pearl Harbor.

Lord, W. *Day of Infamy,* 1957, P. A play-by-play "mosaic" of the attack.

*Morton, L. "Pearl Harbor in Perspective: A Bibliographical Survey," in U.S. Naval Institute *Proceedings,* April 1955. A competent analysis of the literature to date, by one of the leading Army historians.

Theobald, R.A. *The Final Secret of Pearl Harbor: The Washington Contribution to the Japanese Attack,* 1954. Fatuous argument by an American admiral that President Roosevelt and his advisers deliberately paved the way for the attack, to get the United States involved in the war.

*U.S. Congress, Joint Committee in the Investigation of the Pearl Harbor Attacks, 79th Congress, 1st Session, *Hearings* and *Report,* 30 parts, 1946. Valuable because they made public a wealth of pertinent data which would probably otherwise have long remained unavailable in highly classified categories.

*Wohlstetter, R. *Pearl Harbor: Warning and Decision,* 1962. Generally regarded as the outstanding analysis of the situation, emphasizing the lack of adequate coordination between the services and with the government.

BH – 10   Individual Pacific Operations and Aspects

Adamson, H.C. and Kosco, G.F. *Halsey's Typhoons: A First Hand Account of How Two Typhoons, More Powerful than the Japanese, Dealt Death and Destruction to Admiral Halsey's Third Fleet,* 1967. December 1944 and June 1945.

Barbey, D.E. *MacArthur's Amphibious Navy,* 1969. Author commanded 7th Amphibious Force.

Cook, C. *The Battle of Cape Esperance,* 1968. Off Guadalcanal, Oct. 11, 1942.

Crowl, P.A. *Campaign in the Marianas* (USA-WWII), 1960.
——— and Love, E.C. *Seizure of the Gilberts and Marshalls* (USA-WWII), 1955.

Devereux, J. P.S. *The Story of Wake Island,* 1947, P.

Donovan, R.J. *PT 109.* See Sect. BH-3.

Falk, S.L. *Decision at Leyte,* 1966.

*Field, J.A., Jr. *The Japanese at Leyte Gulf: The Sho Operation*, 1947 (PhD thesis, Harvard). See also Falk above and Macintyre and Woodward below.

Frank, P. and Harrington, J.D. *Rendezvous at Midway: USS* Yorktown *and the Japanese Carrier Fleet*, 1967. See also Fuchida and Lord below.

*Fuchida, M., et al. *Midway: The Battle that Doomed Japan: The Japanese Navy's Story*, 1955, P, R1968.

Griffith, S.B.H. *The Battle for Guadalcanal* (Great Battles), 1963.

Hara, T., et al. *Japanese Destroyer Captain*, P1961, 1967.

Leckie, R. *Challenge for the Pacific – The Turning Point of the War* (Crossroads of World History), 1965.

Lockwood, C.A. and Adamson, H.C. *Battles of the Philippine Sea* 1967.

Lord, W. *Incredible Victory*, 1967. An account of Midway in his unique "mosaic" style.

Macintyre, D. *Leyte Gulf*, 1970.

Miles, M.E. *A Different Kind of War*, 1967. American naval activities in China, headed by the author, "to train and equip guerrilla troops and develop a combined Chinese and American staff for operations against the Japanese forces in China."

Murray, M. *Hunted: A Coast Watcher's Story*, 1967. Behind Japanese lines in New Guinea. See also Feldt, E.A., *The Coast Watchers*, 1967.

Newcomb, R.F. *Savo: The Incredible Naval Debacle off Guadalcanal*, 1961. Quick sinking of three American cruisers and one Australian by the Japanese.
————. *Iwo Jima.* 1965.

Shaw, H.I. and Kane, O.T. *The Isolation of Rabaul* (History of Marine Corps Operations in World War II, v. 2), 1964.

Smith, R.R. *Approach to the Philippines* (USA-WWII), 1953.
————. *Triumph in the Philippines* (USA-WWII), 1963.

Thomas, D.A. *The Battle of the Java Sea*, 1969.

*Turner, G.B. *The Amphibious Complex: A Study of Operations at Saipan* (ms. PhD thesis, Princeton, 1950).

U.S. Marine Corps, Historical Unit. See list of monographs of individual operations, Sect. BG-2.

Underbrinton, R.L. *Destination Corregidor*, 1971. Account of the "gallant though futile efforts to relieve the garrison at the doomed outpost" near Manila.

Valcher, W.H., Jr. *Combat Propaganda Against the Japanese in the Central Pacific* (ms. PhD thesis, Stanford, 1950).

Woodward, C.V. *The Battle for Leyte Gulf*, 1947, P1965. See also Field, et al., above.

BH – 11   South and Southeast Asia

Ash, B. *Someone Had Blundered*, 1961. Account of the loss of the *Prince of Wales* and *Repulse* and the fall of Singapore. See also Attiwill and Grenfell below.

Attiwill, K. *Fortress: The Story of the Siege and Fall of Singapore*, 1960.

Barber, N. *A Sinister Twilight: The Fall and Rise Again of Singapore*, 1960.

Ennis, J. *The Great Bombay Explosion*, 1959. Disastrous results from explosion on munitions ship, similar to Halifax affair of 1917.

Grenfell, R. *Main Fleet to Singapore*, 1951.

Tsuji, M. *Singapore, The Japanese Version*, 1961.

BH – 12   Biography, Memoirs and Papers

*Albion, R.G. and Connery, R.H. *Forrestal and the Navy*, 1962.

Boyle, A. *Trenchard*, 1963. The aggressive British Chief Air Marshal who affected the history of the Royal Navy's Air Service.

*Chalmers, W.S. *Max Horton and the Western Approaches: A Biography of Admiral Sir Max Kennedy Horton*, 1954.
————. *Full Cycle: The Biography of Admiral Sir Bertram Home Ramsey*, 1959.

Clark, J.J. and Reynolds, C.G. *Carrier Admiral*, 1967. A semi-autobiography of Admiral "Jocko" Clark.

*Cunningham, A.B. *Sailor's Odyssey, the Autobiography of Admiral of the Fleet, Viscount Cunningham of Hyndhope*, 1951.

*Doenitz, K., tr. T.H. Stevens. *Memoirs: 10 Years and 20 Days*, 1959.

Enders, C.W. *The Vinson Navy*. See Sect. AQ-2.

Fahey, J.J. *Pacific War Diary, 1942-45*, 1963. By a seaman on a cruiser; "World war as it appeared to nine out of ten Americans in naval uniform."

*Forrestel, E.P. *Admiral Raymond Spruance: A Study in Command*, 1966.

Frank, W. *Enemy Submarine: The Story of Gunther Prien, Captain of U-47*. See Sect. BH-1, Frank and Prien.

Gallery, D.V. *Now Hear This!* 1965.
————. *Eight Bells and All's Well,* 1965.

Halsey, W.F. and Bryan, J. *Admiral Halsey's Story,* 1947. More atmosphere than analysis.

Hatch, A. *The Mountbattens: The Last Royal Success Story,* 1965. Prince Louis of Battenberg (later Mountbatten), First Sea Lord until 1914; his son, Lord Louis Mountbatten, and his nephew Prince Philip, consort of Queen Elizabeth II. Lord Louis had some destroyers sunk under him, directed some amphibious operations, headed the Southeast Asia Command during the war, and gave India back to the Indians. See Sect. BD-5.

*Hoyt, E.P. *How They Won the War in the Pacific: Nimitz and His Admirals,* 1970.

James, Sir W. *The Code Breaker of Room Forty*. See Sect. BG-4.

King, E.J. and Whitehill, W.M. *Fleet Admiral King*. See comments Sect. BD-5.

Leahy, W.D. *I Was There: The Personal Story of the Chief of Staff to Presidents Roosevelt and Truman, Based on His Notes and Diaries Made at the Time,* 1950. Rather carelessly ghosted.

Macintyre, D. *Fighting Admiral: The Life and Battles of Admiral of the Fleet Sir James Somervell,* 1961. Commanded in Western Mediterranean and then Indian Ocean.

*Raeder, E., tr. E. Fitzgerald *My Life,* 1959. (*Struggle for the Sea* in British edition). Memoirs of the supreme commander of the German navy since 1928.

Rogow, A.A. *James Forrestal, A Study of Personality, Politics and Policy,* 1963. More psychological than administrative; see also Albion and Connery above.

Smith, H.M. and Finch, B. *Coral and Brass,* 1949, P. Marine general commanding in Pacific actions, nicknamed "Howling Mad."

Strauss, L.L. *Men and Decisions,* 1962. Prominent financier, serving as reserve officer, ultimately rear admiral, was one of Secretary Forrestal's closest advisers.

Taylor, T. *The Magnificent Mitscher,* 1954. Biography of the admiral who did much to develop and utilize the fast carrier task force.

Terraine, J. *The Life and Times of Lord Mountbatten,* 1968. See also Hatch above.

Vandegrift, A.A. *Once a Marine: The Memoirs of General A.A. Vandegrift, USMC, as told to Robert B. Asprey,* 1964.

Warner, O. *Admiral of the Fleet, Cunningham of Hyndhope,* 1967.

BI SINCE 1945

For studies of some of the major postwar politico-military policy problems see Sect. AP.

BI – 1 General

Albion, R.G. *The National Shipping Authority*. See Sect. J-6.
*———— and Connery, R.H. *Forrestal and the Navy*, 1962. Ch. 11, "The Road to the Pentagon" is a play-by-play account of the unification movement, leading to the National Security Act of 1947.

*Baldwin, H.W. *The New Navy*, 1964.

*Breyer, S., tr. M.W. Henley. *Guide to the Soviet Navy*, 1970. "Includes profiles of every known ship type and class . . . naval aircraft, guns, and missiles, shipyards, ports, bases, naval training programs."

Center for Strategic and International Studies, *Soviet Sea Power*, 1969.

Davis, V. *Postwar Defense Policy and the U.S. Navy, 1943-1946*, 1966.

*Eberstadt, F. *Report to James Forrestal, Secretary of the Navy. . . .* ("Eberstadt Report"), 1945. See Sect. AQ-2.

Howard, J.L. *Our Modern Navy*, 1961.

Lowenstein, H., et al. *NATO and the Defense of the West*, 1963. Especially good on the men who make up the NATO commands.

Millis, W. *An End to Arms*, 1965.

Schilling, W.R., et al. *Strategy, Policy and Defense Budgets*, 1962. Analysis of the 1948-55 situation.

Steve, F.K. *The Rise of Soviet Naval Power in the Nuclear Age* (ms. PhD thesis, Harvard, 1971).

Uhlig, F., Jr., ed. *Naval Annual*, 1964-65. Articles on many current subjects.

BI – 2 Technical Developments

Barr, J. and Howard, W.I. *Polaris!*, 1961.

Kuenne, R.E. *The Attack Submarine: A Study in Strategy*, 1965.
————. *The Polaris Missile Strike. . . .* 1967.

Moulton, H.B. *American Strategic Power: Two Decades of Nuclear Strategy and Weapons Systems, 1945-1965* (PhD thesis, Minnesota, 1969; DA v. 30, p. 5392A).

Parson, N.A., Jr. *Missiles and The Revolution in Warfare*, 1960. An amplification of his earlier missile volume. Includes naval aspects.

Polmar, N. *Atomic Submarines*, 1963. Account of development and novel operations.

*Rees, E. *The Sea and the Subs*, 1951. Excellent account of the Navy's important developments, particularly the work of Rickover with atomic propulsion and Raborn with Polaris missiles.

BI – 3   Operations

Anderson, W.R. and Blair, C., Jr. *Nautilus 90 North*, 1959, P. Anderson commanded the first atomic submarine.

Armbrister, T. *A Matter of Accountability: The True Story of the* Pueblo *Affair*, 1970. The *Pueblo*, on an intelligence reconnaissance mission, was seized by the North Koreans, who imprisoned her crew. See Brandt, Bucher, Gallery below.

Beach, E.L. *Around the World Submerged*, 1962. The author commanded the submarine *Triton* on an underwater circumnavigation in 1960.

Beaufre, A. *The Suez Expedition, 1956*, 1968, 1970.

Blanchard, C.H. *Korean War Bibliography and Maps of Korea*, 1965.

Brandt, E., ed. *The Last Voyage of the USS* Pueblo, 1969.

Bucher, L.M. and Rascovich, M. *Bucher, My Story*, 1970. The story of the *Pueblo's* commander who surrendered, perhaps wisely, without a fight. See Armbrister above and Brandt.

*Cagle, M.W. and Manson, F.A. *The Sea War in Korea*, 1957.

Calvert, J. *Surface at the Pole*, 1960. By the commander of the atomic submarine *Skate*.

Ferenback, T.R. *This Kind of War*, 1963. Korean War.

*Field, J.A. *U.S. Naval Operations, Korea* (Naval History Division), 1962. The official Army and Marine Corps histories also contain some account of naval operations.

Fuller, J. *Our Navy Explores Antarctica*, 1966.

Gallery, D.V. *The* Pueblo *Incident*, 1969.

Heinl, R.D. *Victory at High Tide* (Great Battles), 1968. Inchon. See also Sheldon below.

Johnson, H. *The Bay of Pigs*, 1965. The American amphibious fiasco in Cuba.

Kennedy, R.F. *Thirteen Days*, 1968, P1970. The Cuban missile crisis.

Koliphkis, I.A. *Submarines in Arctic Waters*, 1966. Russian.

Kydis, S.G. *American Naval Visits to Greece and the Eastern Mediterranean in 1946* (ms. PhD thesis, Columbia).

Leckie, R. *Conflict: The History of the Korean War*, 1962.

Lewis, F. *One of Our H-Bombs is Missing*, 1967. Air Force loss and Navy recovery of H-bomb off Palomares, Spain, 1966. See also Szulc below.

Moeser, R.O. *U.S. Navy, Vietnam*, 1969. 192 photographs.

Montross, L., et al. *U.S. Marine Operations in Korea, 1950-1953*, 3 v. 1969.

Phillips, C.S. *Escape of the* Amethyst, 1956. Harrowing experience of little British frigate attacked by Communists on the Yangtse.

Polmar, N. *Death of the* Thresher, 1964. Nuclear submarine lost with all hands off New England coast, April 1963.

Sheldon, W. *Hell or High Water: MacArthur's Landing at Inchon*, 1968.

Szulc, T. *The Bombs of Palomares*, 1967. See Lewis above.

Thorgrimsson, T. and Russell, E.C. *Canadian Naval Operations in Korean Waters, 1950-1953*, 1966.

U.S. Naval History Division, *Riverine Warfare – The U.S. Navy's Operations on Inland Waters*, 1969.

VII SPECIAL TOPICS

BJ AUXILIARY SERVICES

BJ – 1 General

*Blake, G. *Lloyd's Register of Shipping, 1760-1960*, 1960. An account of the famous classification society, not to be confused with the insurance organization noted elsewhere. Copies of the early *Register* itself have recently been made available.

Grosvenor, J. *Trinity House*, 1959. See also Mead below.

*Mead, H.P. *The Trinity House: Its Unique Record from the Days of Henry VIII*, 1947. This ancient and prestigious organization still has cognizance of lighthouses, pilotage, etc.

Moir, D.R. *The Birth and History of Trinity House, Newcastle-upon-Tyne*, 1958.

Schmeckebeier, L.F. and Weber, G.A. *The Bureau of Foreign and Domestic Commerce: Its History, Activities and Organization*, 1924.
————. *The Public Health Service: Its History, Activities and Organization*, 1923.

Short, L.M. *The Bureau of Navigation: Its History, Activities and Organizations*, 1923. Not to be confused with the Navy Dept. bureau of the same name (later Naval Personnel). This was in the Treasury Dept., 1884-1903; Commerce and Labor, 1903-13; and thereafter in Commerce.

*Staff, G. *The Transatlantic Mail*, 1957. Postal history, beginning with the British government mail brigs and then New York sailing packets before the advent of steam.

Storey, A. *Trinity House of Kingston-upon-Hull*, 1967.

*Williams, R.C. *The United States Public Health Service, 1798-1950*, 1951. Ch. 1, Marine Hospitals; 2, Quarantine; 10-11, Wars.

BJ – 2 Customs, Coast Guard and Smuggling

Andros, R.S., ed. *The United States Customs Guide*, 1859.

Appleton, T.E. *Usque ad Mare: A History of Canadian Coast Guard and Marine Service*, 1967.

Arnold-Forster, D. *At War with the Smugglers: Career of Dr. Arnold's Father*, 1936, R1970. Collector of Customs at Cowes, Isle of Wight, 1777-1801. His son, Dr. Thomas Arnold, was headmaster of Rugby School, one of England's celebrated educators.

*Atton, H. and Holland, H.H. *The King's Customs: An Account of Maritime Revenue and Contraband Traffic in England*, 2 v. 1908-10, R1968. Vol. 1 to 1800; vol. 2, 1801-55.

Baker, R.L. *The English Customs Service, 1307-1343; A Study of Medieval Administration*, 1961 (PhD thesis, Princeton).

*Barrow, T.C. *Trade and Empire: The British Customs Service in Colonial America, 1660-1775*, 1967 (PhD thesis, Princeton).

Bixby, W. *The Track of the* Bear, *1875-1963*, 1965. See Sect. AD-4.

Bloomfield, H.V. *The Compact History of the United States Coast Guard*, 1966.

Bowen, F.C. *H.M. Coastguard: The Story of This Important Naval Service from the Earliest Times to the Present Day*, 1928.

Capron, W.C. *The United States Coast Guard*, 1965.

Carse, R. *Rum Row*, 1959. There is still need for an adequate account of rumrunning during the Prohibition era.

Chatterton, E.K. *King's Cutters and Smugglers, 1700-1855*, 1912. Like Bowen, above, well illustrated.

Colby, C.B. *Coast Guard Academy*, 1965.

Corbett, S. and Zora, M. *The Sea Fox: The Adventures of Cape Cod's Most Colorful Rumrunner*, 1956. Includes dialogue.

*Evans, S.H. *The United States Coast Guard, 1790-1915, a Definitive History*, 1949. The U.S. Coast Guard was established in 1915 by merging the Revenue Cutter Service (originally Revenue Marine, 1790) and the Life-saving Service, 1878. The Lighthouse Service was later absorbed in 1939. The Service was usually absorbed into the Navy in time of war.

Fribourg, M.G. *Ports of Entry, USA*, 1962. "Stories of the expert, dangerous work of the men and women of the Customs Service."

Harper, C.G. *The Smugglers: Picturesque Chapters in the Story of an Ancient Craft*, 1909.

*Hoon, E.E. *The Organization of the English Customs System, 1696-1786*, 1938 (PhD thesis, London), 1968.

Murphy, J.F. *Cutter Captain: Life and Times of John C. Cantwell* (ms. PhD thesis, Connecticut, 1968). Career in Revenue Cutter Service-Coast Guard, 1882-1920, especially in Alaskan waters.

Paxton, G. *The Coast Guard: From Civilian to Coast Guardsman*, 1962.

Schmeckebeier, L.F. *The Customs Service: Its History, Activities, Organization,* 1924.

Smith, D.H. and Powell, F.W. *The Coast Guard: Its History, Activities and Organization,* 1929. Like the Schmeckebeier and Short studies, this is in a series of Service Monographs of the Institute of Government Research. Each has a good bibliography.

Smith, H.D. *Early History of the United States Revenue Marine Service, 1789-1849,* 1931. See also Evans above. There are also several "atmosphere" books on the Coast Guard.

Teignmouth, Lord (H.N. Shore). *Smuggling Days and Smuggling Ways, or the Story of a Lost Art . . . with an Account of the Rise and Development of the Coastguard,* 2nd ed. 1892.

Van de Water, F.F. *The Real McCoy,* 1931. That phrase, denoting supreme quality, reflected the activity of McCoy, "the founder of Rum Row of New York and the trade's most daring and successful exponent," who "actually furnished 700,000 cases to slake America's thirst."

Verrill, A.H. *Smugglers and Smuggling,* 1924.

*Williams, N. *Contraband Cargoes: Seven Centuries of Smuggling,* 1959, R1961. "Admirable historical study."

*Willoughby, M.F. *Rum War at Sea,* 1964. A Government Printing Office publication dealing with the Coast Guard's efforts to enforce Prohibition, 1920-34.

BJ – 3 Lighthouses and Lightships

Adams, W.H.D. *Lighthouses and Lightships: A Descriptive and Historical Account of Their Mode of Construction and Organization,* 1870.

Adamson, H.C. *Keepers of the Lights,* 1955.

Gibbs, J.A. *Sentinels of the North Pacific: The Story of Pacific Coast Lights and Lightships,* 1955.

Hardy, W.J. *Lighthouses: Their History and Romance,* 1895.

Jerome, E.G. *Lighthouses, Lightships and Buoys,* 1966.

Magdalany, F. *The Red Rocks of Eddystone,* 1959. History of the four successive lights since 1696, including Smeaton's which lasted 120 years.

Mariner's Museum, *Lighthouses and Other Aids to the Mariner*, 1946.

*Putnam, G.R. *Lighthouses and Lightships of the United States*, 1933, R1970.

Snow, E.R. *Famous Lighthouses of New England*, 1945. Like many of his other works, this is an informal "atmosphere" book, useful in bringing together a type of material not always found in the more formal works. His emphasis is on lighthouses, shipwrecks and other aspects of New England coastal "romance."

*Stevenson, D.A. *The World's Lighthouses before 1820*, 1959.

*Theiss, L.E. *Keepers of the Sea: The Story of the United States Lighthouse Service*, 1927.

U.S. Coast Guard, *The Significance of Aids to Marine Navigation*, 1943.
——————. *Historically Famous Lighthouses*, 1951.

Weiss, G. *The Lighthouse Service: Its History, Activities and Organization*, 1926.

Willoughby, M.F. *Lighthouses of New England*, 1929.

BK PORTS AND PORT FUNCTIONS

BK – 1 General

*Barney, W.J. *Selected Bibliography of Ports and Harbours and Their Administration, Laws, Finance, Equipment and Engineering*, 1916. A similar bibliography, with more American emphasis was later issued by the Association of Port Authorities.

Bird, J. *The Major Seaports of the United Kingdom*, 1963.

*Brown, A.H.J. *Port Operation and Administration*, 2nd ed., 1961. This is one of the very useful volumes on current practical maritime subjects published by the Cornell Maritime Press.

Campbell, F.S. *Port Dues, Charges, and Accommodations*, 1967.

Carse, R. *Great American Harbors*, 1963. Rather thin chapters on eight ports, with illustrations.

Cunningham, B. *Port Administration and Operation: A Review of Systems in Vogue in Various Countries*, 1925.
*——————. *Port Studies with special reference to the Western Ports of the North Atlantic*, 1929. New York, Philadelphia, Baltimore, Boston, Montreal, Quebec.

*Fair, M.L. *Port Administration in the United States*, 1954.

*Hawkes, F.A., ed. *Lloyd's Maritime Atlas, Including a Comprehensive List of*

Ports and Shipping Places of the World, 3rd ed., 1958. By the shipping editor of Lloyd's.

Hurd, Sir A. *Ports of the World*, 1946 ff. Details for all world ports, of import and export commodities, port authorities, accommodations, charges, pilotage rates, officials, etc.

*Mariners Museum, *Catalog of Marine Photographs*, 5 v. 1964. Sect. PH, Harbors and Towns, Files arranged by name of place, all countries; then U.S. harbors arranged by state, followed by foreign harbors arranged by country.

Murphy, J.S. *Docks and Harbours*, 1966.

National Ports Council, *Port Development*, 2 v. 1965.

*Pellett, M.E. *Water Transportation: A Bibliography, Guide and Union Catalogue*, 2 v. 1931. Vol. 1, Harbors, Ports and Terminals.

Rennie, Sir J. *The Theory, Formation and Construction of British and Foreign Harbours*, 2 v. 1854. Contains 123 engraved plates.

*Sargent, A.J. *Seaports and Hinterlands*, 1938.

Shoup, D.S. *Port Operations and Economic Development* (ms. PhD thesis, Harvard, 1967).

Swann, D. *English Docks and Harbours, 1660-1830* (ms. PhD thesis, Leeds, 1960).

*U.S. Board of Engineers for Rivers and Harbors and U.S. Shipping Board (later Maritime Commission, etc.), *Port Series*, 1921 ff. Detailed studies of individual major U.S. ports. 1st series, 1921 ff; 2nd series, 1931 ff; 3rd series, 1940 ff, etc. Particular concern with volume of traffic, local and coastal as well as foreign, in its relation to harbor improvements. Ports of the Great Lakes are in the separate Lakes Series.
————. *Shore Control and Port Administration: Investigation of the Status of National, State and Municipal Authority over Port Affairs*, 1923.
————. *Port and Terminal Charges at U.S. Ports*, 1929 ff.

U.S. Office of Naval Intelligence, *Port Directory of the Principal Foreign Ports*, 1911 ff.

BK – 2 Individual Ports

Consult also the general port histories included in the regional sections, especially the British and American.

Axelrod, D. *Government Covers the Waterfront – An Administrative Study of the Background, Organization, Development and Effectiveness of the Bi-state Waterfront Commission of New York Harbor, 1953-1966* (PhD thesis, Syracuse, 1967; DA v. 29, p. 2513).

*Chinitz, B. *Freight and the Metropolis: The Impact of the Transport Revolution in the New York Region* (New York Metropolitan Region Studies), 1960. See also Griffin below.

Griffin, J.I. *The Port of New York* (Institute of New York Area Studies), 1959. Description of various port functions and statistical data on trade, etc.

Johnson, T. *The Waterfront Commission of New York Harbor: A Case Study of a Bi-state Regulating Agency* (PhD thesis, Columbia; DA v. 24, p. 2553).

*Kemble, J.H. *San Francisco Bay: A Pictorial Maritime History*, 1957. The chapters on the waterfront, the Bay region, and local craft include material of a sort not available elsewhere.

Landon, C.E. *The North Carolina State Ports Authority*, 1963.

LeBreton, P.P. *The Organization and Post-war Administrative Policies of the Port of New Orleans* (ms. PhD thesis, Illinois, 1953).

Masterson, T. *The Milwaukee Board of Harbor Commissioners: A Study in Public Port Administration* (ms. PhD thesis, Chicago, 1957).

Mitchell, J. *The Bottom of the Harbor*, 1959. "Little-known scenes of waterfront life" in New York.

Page, R.A.H. *The London Dock Companies, 1796-1864* (ms. MA thesis, Sheffield, 1959).

Reid, W.A. *Ports and Harbors of South America. A Brief Survey of Aspects, Facilities, Prospects*, 1935.

Schneider, R.I. *The Port of Hamburg*, 1930 (U.S. Dept. of Commerce and U.S. Shipping Board, Foreign Ports Series, Vol. 1).

Voget, L.M. *The Waterfront of San Francisco, 1863-1930: A History of Administration by the State of California* (ms. PhD thesis, Berkeley, 1943).

A wide variety of brochures, sometimes containing a little history in addition to description and promotion, are issued hopefully by local port authorities, chambers of commerce, etc.

BK – 3   Docks, Wharves and Cargo Handling

*Cunningham, B. *Cargo-Handling at Ports: A Survey of the Various Systems in Vogue, with a Consideration of Their Relative Merits*, 1925. The author also wrote two highly technical volumes, *Dock Engineering* and *Harbour Engineering*.

Du Platt-Taylor, F.M. *The Design, Construction and Maintenance of Docks, Wharves and Piers*, 1928.

Ford, A.G. *Handling and Stowing of Cargo*, 1911.

Greene, C. *Wharves and Piers, Their Design, Construction and Equipment*, 1917.

Hardy, A.C., ed. *Progress in Cargo Handling*, 1965.

*LaDage, J.R., et al. *Merchant Ships: A Pictorial Study*, 1955, R1968. Ch. 4, The Handling and Storage of Cargo.

Lovell, J.C. *Stevedores and Dockers: A Study of Trade Unionism in the Port of London, 1870-1914*, 1969 (PhD thesis, London).

*McElwee, R.S. and Taylor, T.R. *Wharf Management, Stevedoring, and Storage*, 1921.

Minikin, R.R. *Winds, Waves and Maritime Structures*, 2nd ed., 1963.

Oram, R.B. *Cargo Handling at a Modern Port*, 1965.

Quinn, A.D. *Design and Construction of Ports and Marine Structures*, 1961.

Redal, T.T. *Pacific Coast Marine Cargo Handling: Analysis and Potential*, P1962.

Sauerbier, C.I.. *Marine Cargo Operations*, 1956.

Swanstrom, E.E. *The Waterfront Labor Problem; A Study in Decasualization and Unemployment Insurance*, 1958 (PhD thesis, Fordham). For the thorny long-shoremen labor situation, see Section M-2, especially the works of Larrowe, Liebes, Palmer, Schneider, Stern and Wiseman.

BK – 4   Special Port Topics

Armitage, W.F. *Tugs and Towing Operations*, 1962.

Bowen, F.C. *A Hundred Years of Towage: History of Messrs. William Watkins, Ltd., 1833-1933*, 1933.

Brady, E.M. *Tugs, Towboats and Towing*, 1967. "A basic, how-to-do-it general reference manual."

Braynard, F.O. *A Tugman's Sketchbook*, 1965. 125 drawings of tugs, ships, and the New York waterfront.

Eastman, R.M. *Pilots and Pilot Boats of Boston Harbor*, 1958.

Harbeson, R.W. *The North Atlantic Port Differentials: A Problem in Railway Rates* (ms. PhD thesis, Harvard, 1931).

Harlan, G. and Fisher, C. *On Walking Beams and Paddle Wheels: A Chronicle of San Francisco Bay Ferryboats*, 1951. See also Perry below.

Hughes, J.Q. *Seaport Architecture and Townscape in Liverpool*, 1967.

Lowrey, W.M. *Navigational Problems at the Mouth of the Mississippi River, 1698-1880* (PhD thesis, Vanderbilt, 1956; DA v. 16, p. 1436). For the approach to New Orleans, the silted mud of the "passes" was finally modified by the Eads jetties.

Marvil, J.E. *Pilots of the Bay and River Delaware. . . .* 1965.

Moran, E.F. and Reed, L. *Tugboat: The Moran Story*, 1957.

Perry, J. *American Ferryboats*, 1957.

*Pross, E.L. *A History of Rivers and Harbors Appropriation Bills, 1866-1933* (ms. PhD thesis, Ohio State, 1938). Analysis of "pork barrel" pressures, legitimate and otherwise.

Ramberg, J. *Unsafe Ports and Berths*, 1968.

Thoman, R.S. *Free Ports and Foreign Trade Zones*, 1956, 1970.

BL   BUSINESS METHODS AND MARITIME ECONOMY

BL – 1   General

*Goss, R.O. *Studies in Maritime Economics*, 1968.

*Gras, N.S.B. and Larson, H.M. *Casebook in American Business History*, 1939. The most valuable single work for this purpose; specific cases of "how things worked," all the way from the Virginia Company to the International Mercantile Marine. Gras, who long taught at Harvard Business School, was a pioneer in stimulating the study of business history. See also Larson below.

Kaunitz, R.D. *The British Trading Estate: A Study in Commercial, Local and Central Government Enterprise* (ms. PhD thesis, Radcliffe, 1951).

*Larson, H.M. *Guide to Business History: Materials for the Study of American Business History and Suggestions for Their Use* (Harvard Studies in Business History), 1948, R1964. Its 1,207 pages include a critical bibliography of some 5,000 items; particularly helpful in connection with commercial or shipping houses.

O'Loughlin, C. *The Economics of Sea Transport*, 1967.

BL – 2   Early Methods

Albion, R.G. *The Rise of New York Port, 1815-1860*, 1939, R1970. Ch. 12, Merchant Princes; 13, Within the Counting House.

Baxter, W.T. *The House of Hancock: Business in Boston, 1724-1775* (Harvard

Studies in Business History), 1945. See Sect. AA-2 and AB-2 for other studies of individual merchants and houses, especially the works of Bruchey, Fairchild, Gregory, Harrington, Hedges, Larsen, Marriner and Porter.

*Blunt, J. *The Shipmaster's Assistant and Commercial Digest*, 1837 ff, R1970. See "Manuals," Sect. B-4, for breakdown by chapters and also entries on Pope and Street.

*Buck, N.S. *The Development of the Organization of Anglo-American Trade, 1800-1850*, 1925 (PhD thesis, Yale), R1969.

Cohen, I. *The Auction System in the Port of New York, 1817-1837* (PhD thesis, N.Y. Univ., 1969; DA v. 31, p. 1183A).

Dubois, A.B. *The English Business Company after the Bubble Act, 1720-1800*, 1938.

East, R.A. *Business Enterprise in the American Revolutionary Era*, 1938, R1965.

*Furber, H. *John Company at Work: A Study of European Expansion in India* . . . . See comments, Sect. AJ-5: also H. Brown, *Parry's of Madras*, 1954.

Greenberg, M.M. *British Trade and the Opening of China, 1800-1842*, 1951 (PhD thesis, Cambridge), 1969. Based largely on the files of the great house of Jardine, Mathieson & Co.

Hannay, D. *The Great Chartered Companies*, 1926.

Haskins, R.W. *The Cotton Factor, 1800-1860: A Study in Southern Economic and Social History* (ms. PhD thesis, Berkeley, 1950).

Horlick, A.S. *Countinghouses and Clerks: The Social Control of Young Men in New York, 1840-1860* (PhD thesis, Wisconsin, 1969; DA v. 31, p. 708A).

Johnson, H.A. *The Law Merchant and Negotiable Instruments in Colonial New York, 1664 to 1730*, 1963.

Lillywhite, B. *London Coffee Houses*, 1964. Includes maritime centers such as the Baltic, Coal Exchange, and Jamaica, in addition to Lloyd's.

Lipson, E. *Economic History of England*, 3 v. 1915-38, R1961-62. Vol. 2, ch. 2 contains an excellent account of the early trading companies, with very full bibliographical references in the footnotes.

*Lopez, R.S. and Raymond, I.W. *Medieval Trade in the Mediterranean World: Illustrative Documents translated with Introduction and Notes*, 1955. Includes some 200 original documents, about three-quarters of Italian origin; valuable on business methods. See also Origo below.

*Marriner, S. *The Rathbones of Liverpool, 1845-73*, 1961. Essays in business history. Importers of American cotton and breadstuffs, Brazilian coffee and China tea.

Mason, F.N., ed. *John Norton & Sons, Merchants of London and Virginia*, 1968. Based on Rosenblatt PhD thesis, Rutgers, 1960; DA v. 21, p. 2525, *The House of John Norton & Sons. A Study of the Consignment Method of Marketing Tobacco from Virginia to England.*

Origo, I. *The Merchant of Prato: Francesco di Marco Datini, 1355-1410*, 1957, RP1963. Detailed account of a big businessman of Tuscany, with chapters on the cloth trade, other trade, trading companies, and money.

*Parkinson, C.N. *Trade in the Eastern Seas, 1793-1813*, 1937, R1966. See comments, Sect. AJ-5.

*Scott, R.R. *Constitution and Finance of English, Scottish and Irish Joint Stock Companies to 1820*, 3 v. 1900-12.

Sperling, J.G. *The South Sea Company: An Historical Essay and Bibliographical Finding List* (Harvard Business School, Kress Library Pub. No. 17), 1962.

*Stevens, M. *Merchant Campbell, 1769-1846; A Study of Colonial Trade*, 1965. Australian pioneer. See comments, Sect. AL-3.

Sutherland, L.S. *A London Merchant, 1695-1774*, 1963. William Braund, engaged in Portuguese ventures, East Indies shipping, and marine insurance.

*White, P.L. *The Beekmans of New York in Politics and Commerce, 1647-1877*, 1956.
*————. ed. *The Beekman Mercantile Papers, 1746-1799*, 3 v. 1957.

BL – 3   20th-Century Methods

a. General

Bennathan, E. and Walters, A.A. *The Economics of Ocean Freight Rates*, 1969.

*Bes, J. *Chartering and Shipping Terms*, 7th ed., 1970; also *Chartering Practice*, 1961; *Tanker Chartering*, 1957; *Liner and Tramp Shipping*, 1966.

Bonavia, M.R. *The Economics of Transport*, 1960.

*Bonwick, G.J., et al. *Ship's Business*, 5th ed., 1964.

Branch, A.E. *The Elements of Shipping*, 1964. "Designed mainly for students preparing for shipping examinations." British.

Bridges, R.H. *Freight Conferences and Rebate Terms, a Guide to Freight Conferences*, 1969. British.

Bross, S.R. *Ocean Shipping*, 1956.

Calvin, H.C. and Stuart, E.G. *The Merchant Shipping Industry*, 1925.

Carver, T.G. *Carriage by Sea*, 11th ed., 1969.

Clapp, B.W. *John Owens: Manchester Merchant*, 1965. Textile exporter.

Davis, R. See Sect. Y-3.

Dover, V. *The Shipping Industry: Its Constitution and Practice*, 1952.

Eldridge, F.R., et al. *Export and Import Practice*, 1952.

Hopkins, F.N. *Business and Law for the Shipmaster*, 1966. A modern counterpart of the old Blunt work. See also Martin below.

Huebner, G.G. *Ocean Steamship Traffic Management*, 1920.

*Hyde, F.E., ed. *Shipping Enterprise and Management, 1830-1939; Harrisons of Liverpool*, 1967.

Jauch, H. *American Foreign Trade and Domestic Industrial Organization* (ms. PhD thesis, Columbia, 1955).

Johnson, E.R. and Huebner, G.G. *Principles of Ocean Transportation*, 1919.

*Kirkaldy, A.W. *British Shipping: Its History, Organization and Importance*, 1914, R1970. Pt. 2, The Ownership, Management and Regulation of Shipping. See also Thornton below for more recent treatment.

Kurz, C., II. *Oil Tanker Chartering. An Economic and Historical Analysis*, 1969.

Laroch, K.J. *Vessel Voyage Data Analysis*, 1966.

Martin, B. *Shipmaster's Handbook on Ship's Business*, 1969. See also Hopkins above.

*McDowell, C.E. and Gibbs, H.M. *Ocean Transportation*, 1954. "Shipping industry techniques, practices and problems from the ship owners' and operators' point of view." See Sect. B-4 for breakdown by parts.

Owen, Sir D. *Ocean Trade and Shipping*, 1914.

Payne, P.F. *British Commercial Institutions*, 2nd ed., 1964.

Rosenthal, M.S. *Techniques of International Trade*, 1954. "Export . . . from the start of its interior journey to overseas shipment, with special attention to transportation." See Sect. B-4 for breakdown by chapters.

Smith, J.R. *The Organization of Ocean Commerce*, 1905 (PhD thesis, Pennsylvania).

Stanton, L.F.H. *The Law and Practice of Sea Transport*, 1938, R1964.

Stevens, E.F. *Shipping Practice*, rev. ed., 1967. Legal aspects.

Thorburn, T. *Supply and Demand of Water Transport* (Stockholm School of Economics), 1960.

*Thornton, R.H. *British Shipping*, 1939, 2nd ed., 1959. See especially the chapters on "The Office," "Competition and Combination," and "The Business of Shipbuilding."

Todd, J.A. *The Shipping World, Afloat and Ashore*, 1929. See especially Ch. 7, The Ship Broker; 9, Shipping Office Organization; and 10, Trade Organization. Like many of the other works in this section, this was designed primarily as a text for schools of commerce.

b. Special Aspects

Abersold, J.R. *Commercial Arbitration in Pennsylvania*, 1933 (PhD thesis, Pennsylvania).

*Allen, G.C. and Donnithorne, A.G. *Western Enterprise in Far Eastern Economic Development: China and Japan*, 1954. Part I, China: 2, The Western Merchant in China; 3-4, The Organization of Import Trade; 7, Western Shipping in Chinese Waters. Part II, Japan: 12, The Western Merchant in Japan; 13, Banking and Communication.

Breyer, R.F. *Agents and Contracts in Export Trade: A Study of Foreign Agents and Foreign Agency Contracts in the Export Trade of American Manufactures*, 1925 (PhD thesis, Pennsylvania).

Chinitz, B. *Rate Discrimination in Ocean Transportation* (ms. PhD thesis, Harvard, 1956).

Cufley, C.F. *Ocean Freights and Chartering*, 1962.

Dixon, R.C. *Freight Forwarders and Their Position in the Field of Transportation* (PhD thesis, Princeton, 1942; DA v. 12, p. 259).

(Funch, Edye & Co.) *A Century of Ship Agency and Brokerage: The Story of Funch, Edye & Co., Inc., 1847-1947*, 1947.

Geisert, W.F. *Transportation Costs in the Theory of International Trade* (ms. PhD thesis, Northwestern, 1951).

Ito, J. *North Atlantic Transportation: Its Organization and Management*, 1911 (PhD thesis, Pennsylvania). Printed in Japanese as a textbook, with a 10-page English abstract.

James, F.C. *Cyclical Fluctuations in the Shipping and Shipbuilding Industries*, 1927 (PhD thesis, Pennsylvania).

Johnson, E.R. and Huebner, G.G. *Ocean Rates and Terminal Charges*, 1919.

Kramer, R.L. *The History of Export and Import Railroad Rates and Their Effect upon the Foreign Trade of the United States*, 1923 (PhD thesis, Pennsylvania).

Macmurray, C.D. and Cree, M.M. *Introduction to Shipbrokering: The Elements of the Subject*, 1922, R1925.

*Marx, D. *International Shipping Cartels, a Study of Industrial Self-Regulation by Shipping Conferences*, 1952, R1969.

McLachlan, D.L. *Pricing in Ocean Transportation: A Study of the Liner Conference System* (ms. PhD thesis, Leeds, 1939).

Parkinson, J.R. *The Economics of Shipbuilding in the United Kingdom*, 1960.

Sanderson, A.E. *Control of Ocean Freight Rates in Foreign Trade, a World Survey*, 1938. Like Eldridge above, this appeared in the Trade Promotion Series of the Bureau of Foreign and Domestic Commerce, Dept. of Commerce.

Ullman, G.H. *The Ocean Freight Forwarder: The Exporter and the Law*, 1967.

BL – 4   Marine Insurance

Arnauld, J. *The Law of Marine Insurance and Average*, 15th ed., 1966.

Brown, H.R. *Marine Insurance*, 2 v. 1968.

Buglass, L.J. *Marine Insurance Claims – American Law and Practice*, 1963.

*Chubb, T.C. *If There Were No Losses: The Story of Chubb & Son from Its Founding in 1882 until 1957*, 1957. The title comes from the saying, "If there were no losses, there would be no premiums."

Gibbs, D.E.W. *Lloyd's of London: A Study in Individualism*, 1957. Emphasis on the outstanding leaders in its history.

Gillingham, H.R. *Marine Insurance in Philadelphia, 1721-1800*, 1933.

Golding, C.E. and King-Page, D. *Lloyd's*, 1952. Emphasis on present organization.

Huebner, S.S. *Marine Insurance*, 1920 (PhD thesis, Pennsylvania).

(Johnson & Higgins), *The First Hundred Years of an American Institution: The Story of Johnson & Higgins, Insurance Brokers and Average Adjustors from 1845 to 1945*, 1945.

*Mitchell, C.B. *A Premium on Progress: An Outline History of the American Marine Insurance Market, 1820 to 1870* (Newcomen Society), P1970.
————. *Touching the Adventures and Perils: A Semi-Centennial History* (The American Hull Insurance Syndicate, 1920-1970), 1970.

Parkinson, C.N., ed. *The Trade Winds. . . .* 1948. Ch. 1, Shipowning and Marine Insurance, for 1789-1815 period.

Prentice, O. *Travails and Travels of a Marine Underwriter*, 1947.

Raynes, H.E. *The History of British Insurance*, 1948, 2nd ed., 1964.

Telley, E. *Marine Cargo Claims*, 1965.

Templeman, F. and Greenacre, C.T. *Marine Insurance*, 1968.

Winter, W.D. *Marine Insurance: Its Principles and Practice*, 1929, 3rd ed., 1952.

Worsley, F. and Griffith, G. *The Romance of Lloyd's; From Coffee House to Palace*, 1932.

*Wright, C. and Fayle, C.E. *A History of Lloyd's from the Foundation of Lloyd's Coffee House to the Present Day*, 1928. A wealth of pertinent information on the development of underwriting. A leading English economist called this "one of the very few first-rate specialized commercial histories in existence."

BL – 5   Finance in Its Relation to Maritime Activity

*Condliffe, J.B. *The Commerce of Nations*, 1950. Excellent account of the development and importance of the London money market as the nexus of world trade, and the consequences of its decline after World War I.

*Feis, H. *Europe, the World's Banker, 1870-1914*, 1930.

*Hidy, R.W. *The House of Baring in American Trade and Finance* (Harvard Studies in Business History), 1949 (PhD thesis, Harvard).

Hoffman, R.J.S. *Great Britain and the German Trade Rivalry, 1875-1914*, 1933 (PhD thesis, Pennsylvania). Includes passages on ingenious German financial competition.

*Jenks, L.H. *The Migration of British Capital to 1875*, 1927 (PhD thesis, Columbia).

King, W.T.C. *History of the London Discount Market*, 1936.

*Rabb, T.K. *Enterprise and Empire*. . . . 1967. See Sect. Q-3.

Towers, G. *Financing Foreign Trade*, 2nd ed., 1927.

BM   COMMODITIES OF COMMERCE

BM – 1   General

Bergsmark, D.R. *Economic Geography of Asia*, 1935.

*Chisholm, G.G. *Handbook of Commercial Geography*, various editions since 1889. One of the most useful works of this sort for this particualr subject, with full treatment of particular commodities.

Emeny, B. *The Strategy of Raw Materials: A Study of America in Peace and War*, 1934. A pioneer study, in the days when the nation was still relatively self-sufficient.

Field, F.V., ed. *Economic Handbook of the Pacific Area*, 1934.

*Garoche, P. *Dictionary of Commodities Carried by Ship*, 1952.

Hardy, A.C. *Seaways and Sea Trade*, 1941. Sea lanes have naturally taken form from the commodities available at either end.

Highsmith, R.M. and Jensen, J.G. *Geography of Commodity Production*, 1963.

Newton, A.P., ed. *The Staples of Empire*, 1918. Oils and fats, sugar, cotton, metals, wheat, wool.

Olson, M., Jr. *The Economics of Wartime Shortage: A History of British Food Supplies in the Napoleonic War and World Wars I and II*, 1963.

*Poole, B. *The Commerce of Liverpool*, 1854. Each of its 24 chapters is devoted to a particular commodity-trade.

*Postlethwayt, M. *Universal Dictionary of Trade and Commerce*, 4th ed., 2 v. 1774. See Sect. B-3.

Sherman, R.U. *Formation of Military Requirements for Munitions and Raw Materials* (ms. PhD thesis, Harvard, 1953).

Staley, E. *Raw Materials in Peace and War*, 1937.

Taylor, H.C.D. *World Trade in Agricultural Products*, 1943.

Tressler, D.R. and Lemon, J.M. *Marine Products of Commerce*, 1951.

Vanstone, J.H. *The Commodities of Commerce, Vegetable, Animal, Mineral and Synthetic*, 1934.

U.S. Bureau of Foreign and Domestic Commerce, *Trade Promotion Series*. Numerous studies of general and specific commodities.

BM – 2   Cotton, Wool, and Textiles

*Albion, R.G. *The Rise of New York Port, 1815-1860*, 1939, R1970. Ch. 4, Dry Goods, Hardware and Wet Goods; 6, The Cotton Triangle.
————. *Square-Riggers on Schedule*, 1938, R1965. Ch. 3, Enslaving the Cotton Ports.

Barnard, A. *The Development of the Australian Wool Market, 1840-1900* (ms. PhD thesis, Australian National University, 1957).

Boulnois, J. *The Silk Road*, 1966. See Sect. W-1.

Bowden, P.J. *The Wool Trade in Tudor and Stuart England*, 1962.

*Bruchey, S., ed. *Cotton and the Growth of the American Economy, 1790-1860, Sources and Readings*, 1967.

*Buck, N.S. *The Development of the Organization of Anglo-American Trade, 1800-1850*, 1925 (PhD thesis, Yale), R1969.

Crawford, M.D.C. *The Heritage of Cotton: The Fibre of Two Worlds and Many Ages*, 1924.

*Edwards, M.M. *The Growth of the British Cotton Trade, 1780-1815*, 1966. Includes a discussion of the effects of the French and American wars and an examination of the foreign markets.

*Ellison, T. *The Cotton Trade of Great Britain, Including a History of the Liverpool Cotton Market and the Liverpool Cotton Brokers Association*, 1886.
———. *A Hand-Book of the Cotton Trade, or a Glance at the Past History, Present Condition, and Future Prospects of the Cotton Commerce of the World*, 1858.

Haskins, R.W. *The Cotton Factor, 1800-1860; A Study in Southern Economic and Social History* (ms. PhD thesis, Berkeley, 1950).

*Heaton, H. *The Yorkshire Woolen and Worsted Industries*, 1920, R1965.

Henderson, W.O. *The Lancashire Cotton Famine, 1861-1865*, 1934, 2nd ed., 1969. Ch. 2, Commercial Aspects; 3, Cotton Supply. See also Silver below.

*Hole, E. *The Boston Wool Market* (ms. PhD thesis, Harvard, 1938).

Martin, T.P. *The Influence of Trade in Cotton and Wheat on Anglo-American Relations from 1829 to 1846* (ms. PhD thesis, Harvard, 1922).

Mitchell, J.W. *New South Wales . . . Staple Theory*. See Sect. AL-3.

Owen, E.R.J. *Cotton and the Egyptian Economy, 1820-1914*, 1969.

Ponting, K.G. *Wool Marketing, Past and Present*, 1966.

*Redford, A., et al. *Manchester Merchants and Foreign Trade*, 2 v. 1934-36, 1969. Vol. I, 1794-1858; II, 1850-1939.

*Scherer, J.A.B. *Cotton as a World Power; A Study in the Economic Interpretation of History*, 1916.

Schultze-Gaevernitz, G. *The Cotton Trade in England and the Continent*, 1895.

Silver, A.W. *British Efforts to Secure an Empire Cotton Supply, 1850 to 1872* (ms. PhD thesis, Harvard, 1946). See also Henderson and Owen above.

Wadsworth, A. and Mann, J.D. *The Cotton Trade and Industrial Lancashire, 1600-1780*, 1931, R1968.

Warden, A.J. *The Linen Trade: Ancient and Modern*, 1867, R1967.

White, B.S. *American Cotton in Foreign Markets* (ms. PhD thesis, Harvard, 1937).

Wright, G. *The Economy of Cotton in the Antebellum South.* . . . See Sect. AC-1.

Wright, H.R.C. *East-Indian Economic Problems of the Age of Cornwallis and Raffles*, 1961. Essays focused on four commodities: coffee, opium, cotton piece goods, and tin.

BM – 3   Spices

*Glamann, K. *Dutch-Asiatic Trade, 1620-1740*, 1958. See comments, Sect. AJ-7.

Howe, S.E. *In Quest of Spices*, 1948.

Miller, J.I. *The Spice Trade under the Roman Empire* (ms. DPhil thesis, Oxford, 1964).

Ommanney, F.D. *Isle of Cloves: A View of Zanzibar*, 1957.

Parry, J.W. *The Story of Spices*, 1953.

Phillips, J.D. *Pepper and Pirates: Adventures in the History of the Pepper Trade with the Island of Sumatra*, 1949. See similar work by G.G. Putnam, 1922, and comments on W.J. Gould, Sect. AJ-7.

Verrill, A.H. *Perfumes and Spices, Including an Account of Soaps and Cosmetics: The Story of the History, Source, Preparation and the Use of Spices, Perfumes, Soaps, and Cosmetics which Are in Every-day Use*, 1940.

BM – 4   Sugar

*Aykroyd, W.R. *The Story of Sugar*, 1967. Excellent summary of all aspects.

Beachey, R.W. *The British West Indian Sugar Industry in the Late Nineteenth Century*, 1957 (PhD thesis, Edinburgh).

*Deerr, N. *The History of Sugar*, 2 v. 1949-50. Comprehensive, with much statistical data.

Eastman, S.E. and Marx, D. *Ships and Sugar: An Evaluation of Puerto Rican Offshore Shipping*, 1953.

Howell, B.M. *Mauritius, 1831-1849; A Study of a Sugar Colony* (ms. PhD thesis, London, 1952).

Lowndes, A.G., ed. *South Pacific Enterprise: The Colonial Sugar Refining Company, Ltd.*, 1956. Australian company established in 1855; includes account of recruiting island labor.

McAvoy, M.G. *Boston Sugar Merchants before the Civil War* (PhD thesis, Boston Univ., 1967; DA v. 28, p. 1768A).

*Pares, R. *War and Trade in the West Indies, 1739-63*, 1936.
*——————. *A West Indian Fortune*, 1950.
*——————. *Yankees and Creoles*, 1955, R1968.
*——————. *Merchants and Planters*, 1960. See Sect. AG-2 for comments on these important works. Other material will also be found in that same West Indian section.

Strong, L.A.G. *The Story of Sugar*, 1954.

Surface, G.T. *The Story of Sugar*, 1910.

Swerling, B.C. *The International Control of Sugar, 1918-41*, 1949 (PhD thesis, Harvard). See also Timoshen below.

Taylor, W.H. *The Hawaiian Sugar Industry* (ms. PhD thesis, Berkeley, 1935).

Timoshen, V.P. and Swerling, B.C. *World's Sugar: Progress and Policy*, 1957.

Vogt, P.L. *The Sugar Refining Industry in the United States: Its Development and Present Condition*, 1908.

BM – 5   Coffee and Tea

Akhbar, S.M. *The Growth and Development of the Indian Tea Industry and Trade* (ms. PhD thesis, London, 1932).

Beyer, R.C. *The Colombian Coffee Industry: Origins and Major Trends, 1740-1940* (ms. PhD thesis, Minnesota, 1948).

Forrest, D.M. *A Hundred Years of Ceylon Tea*, 1967. See Sect. AJ-6.

Glamann, K. *Dutch-Asiatic Trade, 1620-1740*, 1958. See Sect. AJ-7.

*Jacob, H.E. *Coffee: The Epic of a Commodity*, 1945. An outstanding history of a commodity, showing what can be done with such a subject.

*Labaree, B.W. *The Boston Tea Party*, 1964. See Sect. V-2b.

*Scott, J.M. *The Great Tea Venture*, 1965. Roughly equivalent to Aykroyd or Deer for sugar or Jacob for coffee. See Sect. AK-2.

Tsou, S.S. *The World Tea Industry and China* (ms. PhD thesis, Harvard, 1947). For the early important tea trade with China see the various general accounts in Sect. AK.

Wright, H.R.C. *East-Indian Economic Problems in the Age of Cornwallis and Raffles*, 1961. Includes section on coffee. See Sect. BM-2.

BM – 6 Tobacco

Arnold, B.W. *History of the Tobacco Industry in Virginia from 1860 to 1894*, 1897 (PhD thesis, Johns Hopkins).

MacInnes, C.M. *The Early English Tobacco Trade*, 1926.

Nichol, N. *Glasgow and the Tobacco Lords*, 1967. Scotland's reward for the Union of 1707.

*Price, J.M. *The Tobacco Trade and the Treasury, 1685-1733* (ms. PhD thesis, Harvard, 1954).
*————. *The Tobacco Venture to Russia: Enterprise, Politics and Diplomacy in the Quest for a Northern Market for English Colonial Tobacco, 1676-1722*, 1961.

Rive, A. *The British Colonial Tobacco Trade* (ms. PhD thesis, Berkeley, 1929).

Rosenblatt, S.M. *The House of John Norton & Sons: A Study of the Consignment Method of Marketing Tobacco from Virginia to England* (PhD thesis, Rutgers, 1960; DA v. 21, p. 2525).

BM – 7 Grain and Flour

Barnes, D.G. *A History of the English Corn Laws, 1660-1846*, 1930 (PhD thesis, Harvard).

Fairlie, S.E. *The Anglo-Russian Grain Trade, 1815-1861* (ms. PhD thesis, London, 1960).

Forbes, H.A.C. and Lee, H. *Massachusetts Help to Ireland During the Great Famine*, 1967. See Sect. AA-3.

Galpin, W.F. *The Grain Supply of England during the Napoleonic Period*, 1925 (PhD thesis, Pennsylvania).

Martin, T.P. *The Influence of Trade in Cotton and Wheat on Anglo-American Relations from 1829 to 1846* (ms. PhD thesis, London, 1922).

Odle, T.D. *The American Grain Trade of the Great Lakes, 1825-1873* (PhD thesis, Michigan, 1952; DA v. 12, p. 180).

*Rothstein, M. *American Wheat and the British Market, 1860-1905* (PhD thesis, Cornell, 1960; DA v. 21, p. 2261).

Surface, F.M. *The Grain Trade during the World War, Being a History of the Food Administration Grain Corporation and the U.S. Grain Corporation*, 1928.

BM – 8   Meat

*Critchell, J.T. and Raymond, J. *A History of the Frozen Meat Trade. An Account of the Development and Present Day Methods of Preparation, Transport and Marketing of Frozen and Chilled Meats*, 1912.

Hanson, S.G. *Argentine Meat and the British Market; Chapters in the History of the Argentine Meat Industry*, 1938 (PhD thesis, Harvard).

Stevens, E.F. *One Hundred Years of Houlders: A Record of the History of Houlder Brothers & Co., Ltd., from 1849 to 1950*, 1950. The line's "reefer" ships were prominent in the refrigerated meat trade, especially from the Argentine to England. See Sect. J-4a.

BM – 9   Timber, Lumber and Other Wood Products

*Albion, R.G. *Forests and Sea Power.* . . . See Sect. L-1.

*Bamford, P.W. *Forests and French Sea Power, 1660-1789*, 1956 (PhD thesis, Columbia). A companion work.

Bryant, R.C. *Lumber: Its Manufacture and Distribution*, 1922.

Calvin, D.D. *A Saga of the St. Lawrence; Timber and Shipping through Three Generations*, 1945.

Carroll, C.T. *The Forest Civilization of New England.* . . . See Sect. AA-1.

*Coman, E.T. and Gibbs, H.M. *Time, Tide and Timber: A Century of Pope and Talbot*, 1949. Leaders in the production and shipping of West Coast lumber.

Defebaugh, J.E. *History of the Lumber Industry of the United States*, 2 v. 1906-07.

Eisterhold, J.A. *Lumber and Trade in the Seaboard Cities of the Old South, 1607-1860* (PhD thesis, U. of Mississippi, 1970; DA v. 31, p. 2816A).

Elchibyoff, I.M. *The United States International Timber Trade in the Pacific Area*, 1949.

Francis, R.J. *An Analysis of British Columbia Lumber Shipments, 1947-1957* (ms. MA thesis, British Columbia, 1961).

Hautala, K. *European and American Tar in the British Market during the Eighteenth and Early Nineteenth Centuries*, 1963.

*Hidy, R.W., et al. *Timber and Men: The Weyerhauser Story*, 1963. West Coast lumber and shipping.

Hunter, H.M. *The United States International Trade in Wood Pulp: A Case Study in International Trade* (ms. PhD thesis, Radcliffe, 1952).

*Latham, B. *Timber: Its Development and Distribution, an Historical Survey*, 1957.

Lord, E.L. *Industrial Experiments in the British Colonies of North America*, 1898 (PhD thesis, Bryn Mawr). Emphasizes official efforts to stimulate naval stores supply.

*Lower, A.R.M. *The North American Assault on the Canadian Forest*, 1938 (PhD thesis, Harvard).

*Malone, J.J. *Pine Trees and Politics: The Naval Stores and Forest Policy in Colonial New England*, 1964. See also Albion above.

McNairn, J. and MacMullen, J. *Ships of the Redwood Coast*, 1945. Lumber-carrying "steam schooners" of the West Coast.

Meany, E.S. *History of the Lumber Industry in the Pacific Northwest to 1917* (ms. PhD thesis, Harvard, 1936).

Newell, G. and Williamson, J. *Pacific Coast Lumber Ships*, 1960.

Perry, P. *The Naval Stores Industry in the Ante-Bellum South, 1789-1861* (ms. PhD thesis, Duke, 1947).

Pratt, E.E. *The Export Lumber Trade of the United States* (U.S. Dept. of Commerce, Misc. Series, No. 67), 1917.

Ryder, D.W. *Memories of the Mendocino Coast*, 1948. Lumber shipments on the California coast. See also McNairn above.

Smith, D.C. *A History of Lumbering in Maine, 1860-1930* (PhD thesis, Cornell, 1965; DA v. 26, p. 5113). Includes the extremely active lumber shipments out of Bangor.

*Wasson, G.S. *Sailing Days on the Penobscot*, 1932, R1949, 1970. Bangor in mid-19th century was the leading lumber port of the world.

Wilson, D.A. *An Analysis of Lumber Exports from the Coast Region of British Columbia to the United Kingdom and United States, 1920-1952* (ms. PhD thesis, Berkeley, 1955).

Wood, R.G. *A History of Lumbering in Maine, 1820-1861* (Univ. of Maine Studies), 1935 (PhD thesis, Harvard).

BM – 10   Coal

Collier, L.B. *A Detailed Survey of the History and Development of the South Wales Coal Industry, c1750 to c1850* (ms. PhD thesis, London, 1941).

Davies, L.N.A. *The History of the Barry Dock & Railways Company in Relation to the Development of the South Wales Coalfield* (ms. MA thesis, Cardiff, 1939).

*Davis, R. *The Rise of the English Shipping Industry in the Seventeenth and*

Eighteenth Centuries, 1963. Includes a wealth of material on the Newcastle coal trade.

Hodges, T.M. *History of the Port of Cardiff in Relation to Its Hinterland, with special reference to the Years 1830-1914* (ms. MEcon thesis, London, 1946).

Makey, W.H. *The Place of Whitehaven in the Irish Coal Trade, 1600-1750* (ms. MSc thesis, London, 1952).

*Nef, J.U. *The Rise of the British Coal Industry*, 2 v. 1932. The standard, comprehensive coverage of the subject.

*Parker, W.J.L. *The Great Coal Schooners of New England, 1870-1909* (Marine Historical Association), 1948. Bituminous, Hampton Roads to Boston and Portland.

Runciman, W. *Collier Brigs and Their Sailors*, 1926.

*Sargent, A.J. *Coal in International Trade*, 1922.

Shipping World Year Book, annual since 1886. For other lists of bunkerage facilities around the world, see Sect. AR.

Smith, R. *Sea-Coal for London: History of the Coal Factors in the London Market*, 1961.

BM – 11   Oil

See also Sect. J-8, on Tankers.

Anderson, J. *East of Suez*, 1968. History of British Petroleum Co. (formerly Anglo-Persian, Anglo-Iranian), since 1907.

Bates, J.L. *The Origins of Teapot Dome; Progressives, Parties and Petroleum, 1909-21*, 1963. The misuse of the naval oil reserves was a prime scandal of the Harding administration, leading to the conviction of the Secretary of the Interior and resignation of the Secretary of the Navy.

Gulbenkian, N. *Portrait in Oil: The Autobiography of Nubar Gulbenkian*, 1965. A particularly sharp and successful Levantine oil operator.

Hakima, A.A. *The Rise and Development of Bahrain and Kuwait*, 1964.

*Hamilton, C.W. *Americans and Oil in the Middle East*, 1962.

Hellner, M.H. *The United States Oil Import Policy* (ms. PhD thesis, American Univ., 1953).

Henriques, R. *Bearsted: A Biography of Samuel, First Viscount Bearsted and the Founder of Shell Transport and Trading Company*, 1960. British edition.

Langebein, L.H. *International Movement of Petroleum Products* (ms. PhD thesis, Pittsburgh, 1960).

*Longrigg, S.H. *Oil in the Middle East: Its Discovery and Development*, 1954, R1961.

Mann, C. *Abu Dhabi: Birth of an Oil Sheikhdom*, 1964.

Noggle, B. *Teapot Dome*. . . . 1962, P1965. See also Bates above.

Odell, P.R. *An Economic Geography of Oil*, 1963.

Pogue, J.E. *Economics of the Petroleum Industry*, 1939.

*Williamson, H.F. and Daum, A.R. *The American Petroleum Industry*. . . . 1959.

BM – 12   Furs

Franchere, G. *Adventure at Astoria*, 1967. See Sect. AD-3.

Kirker, J. *Adventurers to China. Americans in the Southern Oceans, 1792-1812*, 1970. See Sect. AK-1. Sealskins.

McCracken, H. *Hunters of the Stony Sea*, 1957. The Russian sea otter hunters, 1740-1840.

Martin, F.I. *Sea Bears: The Story of the Fur Seal*, 1960.

Moloney, F.X. *The Fur Trade of New England, 1620-1676*, 1931, R1967. See also Roberts below.

Murray, J.E. *The Fur Trade in New France and New England prior to 1645* (ms. PhD thesis, Chicago, 1937; brief 13-page summary, 1938).

*Ogden, A. *The California Sea-Otter Trade, 1784-1848*, 1942 (PhD thesis, Berkeley, 1938).

*Porter, K.W. *John Jacob Astor, Business Man* (Harvard Studies in Business History), 1931 (PhD thesis, Harvard).

*Rich, E.E. *The Hudson's Bay Company, 1670-1870*, 2 v. 1958-61. See comments, Sect. AF-6.

Roberts, W.I. *The Fur Trade of New England in the Seventeenth Century* (ms. PhD thesis, Pennsylvania, 1958). See also Moloney above.

Scamman, C.M. *Marine Mammals of the Northwest Coast*, 1964.

Stevens, W.E. *The Northwest Fur Trade, 1763-1800*, 1928 (PhD thesis, Illinois).

Trelease, A.W. *Indian Affairs in Colonial New York in the Seventeenth Century*, 1960. Expanded from Harvard PhD thesis, *Indian Relations and the Fur Trade in New Netherland, 1600-1664*.

Atwater, F.E. *American Regulation of Arms Exports*, 1941.

Bauer, P.T. *The Rubber Industry: A Study in Competition and Markets*, 1948. Deals chiefly with the period 1930-47.

Borden, N.E., Jr. *Dear Sarah: New England Ice to the Orient and Other Incidents* . . . . 1966.

Bridbury, A.R. *England and the Salt Trade in the Later Middle Ages*, 1955.

Chalk, F.R. *The United States and the International Struggle for Rubber, 1914-1941* (PhD thesis, Wisconsin, 1970; DA v. 31, p. 1721A).

Cummings, R.O. *The American Ice Harvests: A Historical Study in Technology, 1800-1918*, 1949.

Dallas, S.F. *The Hide and Tallow Trade in Alta California, 1822-1846* (PhD thesis, Indiana, 1955; DA v. 15, p. 2435).

Everson, J.G. *Tidewater Ice on the Kennebec River* (Maine Heritage Series V. 1), 1971.

Grindle, R.L. *Quarry and Kiln*. . . . See Sect. AA-2.

Hauk, Z.W. *The Stone-Sloops of Chebeague*. . . . 1949, R1953. Big single-masted craft for carrying Maine granite southward. See Sect. AA-2.

James, M.K. *The Non-Sweet Wine Trade of England during the Fourteenth and Fifteenth Centuries* (ms. DPhil thesis, Oxford, 1952; originally ms. BLitt thesis, entitled *The Gascon Wine Trade*).

Kerr, W.L. *The Malayan Tin Industry to 1914*, 1965.

Lubbock, B. *The Opium Clippers*, 1933, R1967.
————. *The Nitrate Clippers*, 1932, R1966. See Sect. I.

Mathew, W.M. *Anglo-Peruvian Commercial and Financial Relations, 1820-65, with special reference to the Guano Trade* (ms. PhD thesis, London, 1964). See also Kinsbruner, Sect. AH-5c.

Melby, J. *Rubber River: Being an Account of the Rise and Collapse of the Amazon Boom* (ms. PhD thesis, Chicago, 1941). Malaya overtook the Amazon around the time of World War I.

Mitchell, K.M. *United States Canned Foods in International Trade* (ms. PhD thesis, Pittsburgh, 1951).

Moore, E.D. *Ivory, Scourge of Africa*, 1931.

Mushkin, D.J. *The American Colonial Wine Industry: An Economic Interpretation* (PhD thesis, Illinois, 1965; DA v. 27, p. 1997A).

Owen, D.E. *British Opium Policy in China and India*, 1934 (PhD thesis, Yale).

Shineberg, D. *They Came for Sandalwood: A Study of the Sandalwood Trade in the South West Pacific, 1830-1865*, 1967. See also Kirker, Sect. AK-1.

Steadman, M.S. *Exporting Arms: The Federal Arms Exporting Administration, 1935-1945*, 1947.

Stilliard, H.H. *The Rise and Development of Legitimate Trade in Palm Oil with West Africa* (ms. MA thesis, Birmingham, 1938).

Taussig, C.W. *Rum, Romance and Rebellion*, 1930. The rum trade and its influence on New England life. R. Pares' *Yankees and Creoles*, already cited, is also redolent of rum.

Thomas, G.Z. *Richer than Spices*, 1965. Exotic early imports from India. See comments, Sect. AJ-4.

Wilson, C.M. *Empire in Green and Gold: The Story of the American Banana Trade*, 1947. Primarily the United Fruit Co. history.

BN   PASSENGERS AND MIGRATION

BN – 1   Travel Conditions, General

*Abbot, E. *Immigration – Select Documents and Case Records*, 1924. The first group of these original source selections deals with the ocean crossing from Europe to America.
————. *Historical Aspects of the Immigration Problem, Selected Documents*, 1926.

Albion, R.G. *The Rise of New York Port, 1815-1860*, 1939, R1970. Ch. 16, Human Freight.
*————. *Square-Riggers on Schedule*, 1938, R1965. Ch. 9, Thirty Guineas, Wines Included.

Allen, C.R. *Travel and Communication in the Early Colonial Period, 1607-1720* (ms. PhD thesis, Berkeley, 1956).

Babcock, F.L. *Spanning the Atlantic*, 1931. In addition to this history of the Cunard Line, consult the other works on ocean liners in Sect. J-4.

Bateson, C. *The Convict Ships, 1787-1868*, 1959. The conveyance of prisoners from Britain to Australia.

*Bowen, F.C. *A Century of Atlantic Travel, 1830-1930*, 1930. The most useful of Bowen's numerous books.

Cather, T. *Thomas Cather's Journal of a Passage to America in 1836*, 1956. Typical of a useful sort of source too numerous to cite in detail here.

Conant, R. *Mercer's Belles: The Journal of a Reporter*, ed. L.A. Deutsch, 1960. Cargo of would-be brides around the Horn. See comments, Sect. AD-3.

Garrard, J.A. *The English and Immigration, 1880-1910*, 1971.

*Guillet, E.C. *The Great Migration: The Atlantic Crossing by Sailing Ship since 1770*, 1937, RP1963.

International Maritime Consultative Organization, *International Conference on Facilitation of Maritime Travel and Transport*, 1965.

Low, G.W. *Gold Rush by Sea*, ed. K. Harney, 1915. A racy account of a group of passengers rounding the Horn in 1850-51. Numerous other similar accounts are available.

MacDonagh, O. *A Pattern of Government Growth, 1800-1860: The Passenger Acts and Their Influence*, 1961.

Nettle, G. *A Practical Guide for Emigrants to North America . . . with full information respecting . . . matters requisite for the Emigrant to become acquainted with before embarking*, 1850. Typical of numerous such guides.

Parkinson, C.N. *Trade in the Eastern Seas, 1793-1813*, 1937. Ch. 9, Travel on East Indiamen.

Rae, W.F. *The Business of Travel: A Fifty Years Record of Progress*, 1891. Thomas Cook and Son.

*Walpole, K.A. *Efforts to Remedy Abuses on Emigrant Vessels to America*, 1931. In *Transactions of the Royal Society*, 4th Series, XIV.

BN – 2 Migration

The following works deal with various movements which led to considerable ocean travel. The concern here is with conditions leading to "emigration" rather than with the sociological adjustments following "immigration."

Adams, W.F. *Ireland and Irish Emigration to the New World from 1815 to the Famine*, 1932 (PhD thesis, Yale).

Alexander, J.H. *White Indentured Servitude: An American Economic Experience* (PhD thesis, Houston, 1970; DA v. 31, p. 6258).

Appleyard, R.T. *British Emigration to Australia*, 1964.

Blegen, T.C. *Norwegian Migration to America, 1825-1860*, 2 v. 1931-40.

Blumenthal, W.H. *Brides from Bridewell: Female Felons Sent to Colonial America*, 1962.

Booker, H.M. *Efforts of the South to Attract Immigrants, 1860-1900* (ms. PhD thesis, Virginia, 1965).

Bromwell, W.J. *History of Immigration into the United States*, 1856. Includes detailed statistical tables by nationality and port of arrival, 1819-55, summarized in appendix of R.G. Albion, *The Rise of New York Port*.

Carrothers, W.A. *Emigration from the British Isles, with special reference to the Development of the Overseas Dominions*, 1929, R1965.

Conway, A.A. *New Orleans as a Port of Immigration, 1820-1860* (ms. MA thesis, London, 1949).

Cowan, H.I. *British Emigration to North America: The First Hundred Years*, 1928, R1961.

Cumpston, I.M. *The Problem of the Indian Immigrant in British Colonial Policy after 1834*, 1953 (DPhil thesis, Oxford).

Dickson, R.J. *Ulster Emigration to Colonial America, 1718-1778*, 1966 (PhD thesis, Belfast).

Ferenzi, I. and Willcox, W.F., eds. *International Migrations*, 2 v. 1929-31.

Fothergill, G. *Emigrants from England, 1773-1776*, 1964.

Glass, R. *London's Newcomers: The West Indian Migrants*, 1961.

Graham, I.C.C. *Colonists from Scotland: Emigration to North America, 1707-83*, 1956 (PhD thesis, Illinois).

*Handlin, O. *The Uprooted: The Epic Story of the Great Migrations that Made the American People*, 1951 (PhD thesis, Harvard). Also several other writings on the same general subject.

*Hansen, M.L. *The Atlantic Migration, 1607-1860: A History of the Continuing Settlement of the United States*, ed. A.M. Schlesinger, 1940 (PhD thesis, Harvard), RP1961.

Janson, F.E. *The Background of Swedish Immigration, 1840-1930*, 1931 (PhD thesis, Pennsylvania).

Jones, M.A. *American Immigration*, 1961.

Kaminkov, J. and M., comps. *A List of Emigrants from England to America, 1718-1759*, 1965.

Keep, G.P.C. *The Irish Migration to North America in the Second Half of the Nineteenth Century* (ms. PhD thesis, Trinity College, Dublin, 1952).

Lancour, A.H. *Passenger Lists of Ships Coming to North America, 1607-1825*, 1937, R1964. The third edition has been revised and enlarged by Richard Wolf, with list of passenger arrival records.

Lawrence, K.O. *Immigration into Trinidad-British Guiana, 1834-1871* (ms. PhD thesis, Cambridge, 1959). Particularly the importation of East Indian "coolies" following the abolition of slavery. See also Cumpston above and Lubbock below.

Lubbock, B. *Coolie Ships and Oil Sailers*, 1935, R1955. Importation of East Indian and some Chinese laborers for sugar plantations of Mauritius, Trinidad and British Guiana.

Lucas, H.S. *Netherlanders in America: Dutch Immigration to the United States and Canada, 1789-1950*, 1955.
————. *Dutch Immmigrant Memoirs and Selected Writings*, 2 v. 1955.

MacDonagh, O. *Irish Overseas Emigration and the State during the Great Famine* (ms. PhD thesis, Cambridge, 1952). See also Woodham-Smith below.

Macmillan, D.S. *Scotland and Australia, 1788-1850: Emigration, Commerce, and Investment*, 1967.

Madgwick, R.B. *The Quality of Immigration into Eastern Australia before 1851*, 1937 (DPhil thesis, Oxford).

Oldham, W. *The Administration of the System of Transportation of British Convicts, 1763-93* (ms. PhD thesis, Leeds, 1933).

Schrier, A. *Ireland and the American Emigration, 1850-1900*, 1958 (PhD thesis, Northwestern).

Shepperson, W.S. *The Promotion of British Emigration by Agents for American Lands, 1840-1860*, 1954. Based on PhD thesis, Western Reserve, *The British View of Emigration to North America*.

Stephenson, G.M. *A History of American Immigration, 1820-1924*, 1964.

Tyack, N.C.P. *Migration from East Anglia to New England before 1660* (ms. PhD thesis, London, 1951).

Walker, M. *Germany and the Emigration, 1816-1885*, 1964 (Harvard Hist. Monographs).

Wertimer, S. *Migration from the United Kingdom to the Dominions in the Interwar Period, with special reference to the Empire Settlement Act of 1922* (ms. PhD thesis, London, 1952).

Wingerling, O.W. *The Removal of the Acadians from France to Louisiana, 1763-1785* (ms. PhD thesis, Berkeley, 1949).

*Woodham-Smith, C. *The Great Hunger*, 1963. A valuable, best-selling account of the British government's faulty handling of the Irish famine crisis.

For the most extensive of migration movements, see Sect. AI-6, The Slave Trade.

BO MARITIME AND INTERNATIONAL LAW

BO – 1 Maritime Law, General

See also Sect. O-1, Regulations and Mutiny.

Alexander, L.M. *The Law of the Sea*, 1968.

Alford, N.H., Jr. *Modern Economic Warfare (Law and the Naval Participant)*, 1967.

Allen, E.W. *The Treatment of Enemy Merchant Vessels in Port at the Outbreak of War* (ms. PhD thesis, Radcliffe, 1923).

Arzt, F.K. *Marine Laws – Navigation and Safety*, 1953. A broader version of his *Navigation Laws of the United States*.

Baer, H.R. *Admiralty Law of the Supreme Court*, 1963.

Balch, T.W. *The* Alabama *Arbitration*, 1900.

Bartie, R.O. *Introduction to Shipping Law*, 1958.

Beardwood, A. *Alien Merchants in England, 1350 to 1377; Their Legal and Economic Position*, 1931 (DPhil thesis, Oxford).

Benton, E.J. *International Law and Diplomacy of the Spanish-American War*, 1968.

*Boczek, B.A. *Flags of Convenience: An International Legal Study*, 1962. See Sect. J-6.

Bowett, D.W. *The Law of the Sea*, 1967. These lectures deal with modern problems of the continental shelf, community interest, and flags of convenience.

Brown, B.V. *The Status of Armed Merchantmen* (ms. PhD thesis, Radcliffe, 1920).

Burke, W.T. *Ocean Sciences, Technology, and the Future International Law of the Sea*, 1966.

Canfield, G.L. and Dalzell, G.W. *The Law of the Sea: A Manual of the Principles of Admiralty Law for Students, Mariners and Ship Operators*, 1929.

Carver, T.G. *Carriage by Sea*, 11th ed., 1969.

*Chance, E.W. *The Principles of Mercantile Law*, 16th ed., 1961.

Coughlin, F.X.J. *Radar and the Admiralty Law* (ms. PhD thesis, New York Univ., 1951).

*Dana, R.H. *The Seamen's Friend*, 1845 ff, R1970. See comments, Sect. O-1.

DePauw, F. *Grotius and the Law of the Sea*, P1965. The first part of his Dutch edition on Grotius.

Goss, R.O. *Studies in Maritime Economics*, 1968. Essays dealing with seaports as well as ships.

Higgins, A.P. and Colombos, C.J. *The International Law of the Sea*, 5th ed., 1962.

Hilbert, W.E. *The International Rules of the Road at Sea (as interpreted and altered by the courts, and with recommendations regarding desirable changes to modernize the rules)*, 1938 (SJD thesis, Georgetown).

*Hough, C.M., ed. *Reports of Cases in the Vice Admiralty of the Province of New York and in the Court of Admiralty of the State of New York, 1715-1788*, 1925.

Koushnareff, S.G. *Liability of Carriers of Goods by Sea*, 1943 (PhD thesis, Columbia).

Laing, L.H. *Merchant Shipping Legislation and Admiralty Jurisdiction in Canada* (ms. PhD thesis, Harvard, 1935).

*Marsden, R.D., ed. *Select Pleas in the Court of Admiralty* (Selden Society), 2 v. 1894-97.
*————. *Documents Relating to the Law and Custom of the Sea* (Navy Records Society, v. 49, 50), 2 v. 1915-16.

McDougal, M.S. and Burke, W.T. *The Public Order of the Oceans: Contemporary International Law of the Sea*, 1963. "A massive compendium of contemporary international law of the sea," presenting "a heavily documented legal approach to the process of decision."

McFarland, M.E. *Ship's Business and Cargo Loss and Damage*, 1963.

McFee, W. *The Law of the Sea*, 1950. A useful summary of maritime law down through the centuries, by the author of many books on the sea.

Meyers, H. *The Nationality of Ships*, 1967.

Norris, M.J. *The Law of Seamen*, 1951.
————. *The Law of Maritime Personal Injuries, Affecting Harbor Workers, Passengers and Visitors*, 1959.

Piper, D.C. *The International Law of the Great Lakes* (ms. PhD thesis, Duke, 1961).

Proehl, P.O., ed. *Legal Problems of International Trade*, 1959.

*Reiff, H. *The United States and the Treaty Law of the Sea*, 1958. Extensive technical record of American participation in treaty laws from colonial times to 1945, excluding maritime problems in time of war.

Reinow, R. *The Test of the Nationality of a Merchant Vessel*, 1937 (PhD thesis, Columbia).

Rideout, E.S.F. *The Commercial Law of Ancient Athens to 323 B.C.* (ms. PhD thesis, London, 1935).

Robinson, G.H. *Handbook of Admiralty Law in the United States*, 1939.

Sanborn, F.R. *Origins of Early English Maritime and Commercial Law*, 1930.

*Saunders, A. *Maritime Law, Illustrated by the History of a Ship from and Including the Agreement to Build Her until She Becomes a Total Loss*, 1920.

*Senior, W. *Naval History in the Law Courts: A Selection of Old Maritime Cases*, 1927. A delightful little volume.

Smith, E.S. *The Law of Maritime Exploration* (ms. PhD thesis, George Washington, 1954).

*Smith, H.A. *Law and Custom of the Sea*, 3rd ed., 1959.

Steiner, H.J., et al. *International Legal Problems*, 1968.

Ubbelohde, C.W. *The Vice Admiralty Courts of British North America, 1763-1776*, 1960 (PhD thesis, Wisconsin).

Udell, G.G., comp. *Laws Relating to Shipping and the Merchant Marine*, 1969. Covers Sept. 7, 1916 to Oct. 12, 1968.

Ueda, T. *Studies in Shipping as an Enterprise from the Legal Sources of the Medieval and Early Modern Periods* (ms. PhD thesis, Pennsylvania, 1921).

Van der Malen, G.H.J. *Alberico Gentili and the Development of International Law*, 1968.

Williams, R.G. and Bruce, G.A. *A Treatise on the Jurisprudence and Practice of the English Courts in Admiralty*, 3rd ed., 1902.

Wiswell, F.L., Jr. *The Development of Admiralty Jurisdiction and Practice since 1800*, 1971 (PhD thesis, Cambridge).

BO – 2   Neutrality, Contraband, and Prize Law

*Bailey, T.A. *The Policy of the United States toward the Neutrals, 1917-1918*, 1964.

Baker, T.E. *Contraband of War* (ms. PhD thesis, Harvard, 1947).

Benton, E.J. See Sect. BO-1.

Black, T. *Prize Law in World War II* (ms. PhD thesis, UCLA, 1954).

*Briggs, H.W. *The Doctrine of the Continuous Voyage*, 1926 (PhD thesis, Johns Hopkins). See also Gantenbein below.

Devlin, Lord. *The House of Lords and the Naval Prize Bill, 1911*, 1968.

Fenwick, C.G. *The Neutrality Laws of the United States*, 1912 (PhD thesis, Johns Hopkins).

Gantenbein, J.W. *The Doctrine of the Continuous Voyage, Particularly as Applied to Contraband and Blockade*, 1929 (PhD thesis, Columbia). See also Briggs above.

Gerner, J.W. *Prize Law during the World War: A Study of the Jurisprudence of the Prize Courts, 1914-1924*, 1927.

Grönfors, K. *Six Lectures on the Hague Rules*, 1968.

*Grotius, H. *The Rights of War and Peace*, ed. A.C. Campbell, 1901. The classic 17th-century Dutch argument for "freedom of the seas." See also DePauw, Sect. BO-1.

Ho, P.J. *Pacific Blockade, with special reference to Its Use as a Measure of Reprisal*, 1928 (PhD thesis, Illinois).

*Jessup, P.C., et al. *Neutrality: Its History, Economics and Law*, 4 v. 1935-36; Vol. 1, The Origins; 2, The Napoleonic Period; 3, The World War I Period; 4, Today and Tomorrow.

Millikan, G.L. *The Status of Armed Vessels* (ms. PhD thesis, Yale, 1942).

Morrissey, A.M. *Some Legal Economic Aspects of the American Policy of Neutrality, 1914-1918* (ms. PhD thesis, Radcliffe, 1936).

*Pares, R. *Colonial Blockade and Neutral Rights, 1739-1763*, 1938. Special emphasis on the West Indies, his particular sphere of interest.

Percy, Lord E.S.C. *Maritime Trade in War: Lectures on the Freedom of the Seas*, 1930.

Piggott, Sir F.T. *The Freedom of the Seas, Historically Treated* (Foreign Office Handbooks, No. 148), 1920.
*————. *Documentary History of the Armed Neutralities, 1780 and 1800*, 1910.

Potter, P.B. *Freedom of the Seas* (ms. PhD thesis, Harvard, 1918).

*Robinton, M.R. *An Introduction to the Papers of the New York Prize Court, 1861-1865*, 1945.

Soulsby, H.G. *The Right of Search and the Slave Trade in Anglo-American Relations, 1814-1862*, 1933 (PhD thesis, Johns Hopkins).

Taylor, A.E. *The Development of the Economic Blockade: A New Feature in International Relations* (ms. PhD thesis, Pennsylvania, 1934).

BO – 3   Fishery Rights and Territorial Waters

Baxter, R.R. *The Law of International Waterways, with particular regard to Interoceanic Canals,* 1964.

Butler, W.E. *The Law of Soviet Territorial Waters,* 1967.

Chee, C. *The National Regulation of Fisheries in International Law* (PhD thesis, New York Univ., 1964; DA v. 27, p. 812A).

Daggett, A.P. *Fishery Rights in Territorial Waters Secured by International Agreements* (ms. PhD thesis, Harvard, 1931).

Davis, M. *Iceland Extends Its Fishery Limits: A Political Analysis,* 1964.

Fenn, P.T. *The Origin of the Right of Fishery in Territorial Waters,* 1926 (PhD thesis, Harvard).

Foster, H.E. *The Development of Public International Law relating to Fisheries Interests of Selected Major States, 1910-1938* (ms. PhD thesis, Duke, 1941).

Harley, L.R. *Our Diplomatic Relations with Great Britain – The Fisheries* (ms. PhD thesis, Pennsylvania, 1895).

*Jessup, P.C. *The Law of Territorial Waters and Maritime Jurisdiction,* 1927 (PhD thesis, Columbia).

Johnston, D.M. *The International Law of Fisheries; A Framework for Policy-centered Inquiries,* 1965.

Kobayashi, T.J. *The Anglo-Norwegian Fisheries Case of 1951; Its Role in the Transition of the Law of the Territorial Sea* (PhD thesis, Florida, 1960; DA v. 21, p. 2773).

Leonard, L.L. *International Regulation of Fisheries,* 1944 (PhD thesis, Columbia).

Oda, S. *International Control of Sea Resources,* 1963.

Park, J.S. *A Study of Theory and Practice of Territorial Sea, with special reference to the Rights of Fishing in the Selected Areas of Asia* (PhD thesis, New York Univ., 1969; DA v. 21, p. 2351).

Rothney, G.O. *British Policy in the North American Cod Fisheries with special reference to Foreign Competition, 1776-1819* (ms. PhD thesis, London, 1939).

Shalowitz, A.L. *Shore and Sea Boundaries, with special reference to the Interpretation and Use of Coast and Geodetic Survey Data* (U.S. Dept. of Commerce, Coast and Geodetic Survey), 2 v. 1962-64.

Sismarian, J. *The Diversion of International Waters,* 1939 (PhD thesis, British Columbia).

Slouka, Z. *International Custom and the Continental Shelf, a Study of Some Aspects of the Growth of Customary Rules of International Law* (PhD thesis, Columbia, 1965; DA v. 26, p. 4789).

U.S. State Dept. (The Geographer, Bureau of Intelligence and Research, Office of Research in Economics and Science), *Sovereignty of the Seas* (Geographic Bulletin, No. 3). Useful supplement to the law of the sea.

Wolff, T. *Inter-American Maritime Disputes over Fishing in the 20th Century* (ms. PhD thesis, California-Santa Barbara, 1968).

BP   PRIVATEERING, BUCCANEERING AND PIRACY

The borderline between these activities was often hazy. Consult the naval history sections, especially Sects. AV-BC, for additional works on special aspects of these categories.

*Albion, R.G. and Pope, J.B. *Sea Lanes in Wartime: The American Experience*, 1942, R1968. Ch. 5, Pirates, deals with the Barbary and West Indian pirates.

*Andrews, K.R. *Elizabethan Privateering: English Privateering during the Spanish War, 1588-1603*, 1964 (PhD thesis, London).

Arnold-Forster, F.D. *Madagascar Pirates*, 1957.

Belgrave, Sir C. *The Pirate Coast*, 1966. Southern Arabia. See Sect. AJ-3.

Clune, F. and Stephenson, P.R. *The Pirates of the Brig* Cyprus, 1963. Frustrating adventure in the South Seas.

Collier, J. *Pirates of Barataria*, 1966. Louisiana and Gulf.

Course, A.G. *Pirates of the Eastern Seas*, 1966.

Eller, E.M., ed. *Journals of Two Cruises Aboard the American Privateer* Yankee, *by a Wanderer*, 1967.

*Exquemelin, A.O. (Esquemling, J.) *The Buccaneers of America; a true account of the most remarkable atrocities committed of late years upon the Coasts of the West Indies by the Buccaneers of Jamaica and Tortola.* . . . 1684 ff, R1967. Source of much of the information and misinformation about Morgan and others on the "Spanish Main."

Fisher, Sir G. *The Barbary Legend*. See Sect. W-3 for this and other works on the Barbary pirates.

Gerhard, P. *Pirates on the West Coast of New Spain, 1575-1742*, 1960.

*Gosse, P. *The History of Piracy*, 1932. Probably the most satisfactory of the very numerous books on the subject, most of them more lively than scholarly.

Hughes, C.E. *Wales and Piracy: A Study in Tudor Administration, 1500-1640* (ms. MA thesis, Swansea, 1937).

*Jameson, J.F. *Privateering and Piracy during the Colonial Period; Illustrative Documents. . . .* 1923.

Johnson, C. *General History of the Robberies and Murders of the Most Notorious Pirates*, 1724. Possibly the work of Daniel Defoe.

*Kemp, P.K. and Lloyd, C. *The Buccaneers*, P1965. Originally published as *Brethren of the Coast: Buccaneers of the South Seas*, 1960. In contrast to much of the overripe melodrama on the subject, this is an authoritative, but none the less lively, survey by two of Britain's leading naval historians. Includes major Caribbean as well as "South Seas" characters. The first chapter is a useful summary of the status of that group who flourished around 1700. See additional comments, Sect. AX-4.

Lloyd, C. *William Dampier*, 1966. Prominent and semi-respectable.

Lubbock, B. *Bully Hayes, South Seas Pirate*, 1931. See Sect. AL-1.

Maclay, E.S. *A History of American Privateers*, 1863.

Mahan, A.T. *Sea Power in Its Relations to the War of 1812*, 2 v. 1905. Contains a highly critical estimate of the low value of privateering, written a dozen years before submarines demonstrated the full modern possibilities of the *guerre de course*.

Means, P.A. *The Spanish Main, Focus of Envy, 1492-1700*, 1935.

Moore, R.O. *Some Aspects of the Origin and Nature of English Piracy, 1603-1625* (PhD thesis, Virginia, 1960; DA v. 21, p. 2260).

Omerod, H.A. *Piracy in the Ancient World*, 1924.

Piggott, Sir F.T. *The Declaration of Paris, 1856*, 1919. Abolition of privateering by the maritime nations, except the United States, in 1856.

Robinson, W.M. *The Confederate Privateers*, 1928. A mediocre group, not to be confused with the *Alabama* and her commissioned "CSS" associates.

Tarling, N. *Piracy and Politics in the Malay World: A Study of British Imperialism in the Nineteenth-Century South-East Asia*, 1963.

Tugwood, R.M.S. *Piracy and Privateering from Dartmouth and Kingswear, 1540-58* (ms. MA thesis, London, 1953).

Williams, G. *History of the Liverpoool Privateers and Letters of Marque*, 1897, R1966.

Wycherly, G. *Buccaneers of the Pacific*, 1928. From Drake through Dampier to Anson. See also Kemp and Lloyd above.

BQ MARINE DISASTERS

BQ – 1 General

Allen, K.S. *The World's Great Sea Disasters*, 1969. One of the numerous compilations.

*Baldwin, H.W. *Sea Fights and Shipwrecks: True Tales of the Seven Seas*, 1955. Sound and interesting, this well-selected collection of naval and merchant marine disasters is one of the best; too many of the others, like the books on pirates, simply exploit atmosphere without adding anything new.

Croome, A. *Know About Wrecks*, 1965.

Hardwick, J.M.D. and Greenhalgh, M. *The World's Greatest Sea Mysteries*, 1968.

Hoehling, A.A. *They Sailed into Oblivion*, 1959 and P.

Horner, D. *Shipwrecks, Skin Divers, and Sunken Gold*, 1965.

Jeffries, R. and McDonald, K. *The Wreck Hunters*, 1966.

Marx, R.F. *Shipwrecks in Florida Waters*, 1969.

Mielke, O., tr. M. Savelle. *Disaster at Sea: The Story of the World's Greatest Maritime Disasters*, 1950.

Padfield, P. *An Agony of Collisions*, 1966.

Rieseberg, H.E. and Mikalow, A.A. *Fell's Guide to Sunken Treasure Ships of the World*, 1965.

Snow, E.R. *Great Gales and Dire Disasters*, 1952. Other titles in his almost annual output include *Storms and Shipwrecks of New England*, 1943, R1946 ff; *The Vengeful Sea*, 1956; and *New England Sea Tragedies*, 1960. His specialty is the loss of the coastal sidewheeler *Portland* with all hands in an 1898 gale.

Throckmorton, P. *Shipwrecks and Archaeology: The Unharvested Sea*, 1969. See Sect. W-1.

Villiers, A.J. *Posted Missing*, 1956.

BQ – 2 Regional

Boyle, D. *Ghost Ships of the Great Lakes*, 1968. Narratives of 17 vessels that have "gone missing."

Burman, J.L. *Great Shipwrecks . . . Southern Africa*, 1967.

Carter, C. *Cornish Shipwrecks: The North Coast*, v. II, 1970.

Farr, G. *Wreck and Rescue on the Coast of Devon*, 1968.
————. *Wreck and Rescue in the Bristol Channel*, 1967. These series include accounts of the lifeboats involved.

Gibbs, J.A. *Shipwrecks of the Pacific Coast*, 1950, R1963.
————. *Shipwrecks of the Puget Sound Area*, 1955. A 21 x 20 in. map listing 455 shipwrecks with details.
————. *Disaster Log of Ships*. See Sect. AD-1.

Ingram, C.W.N. and Wheatley, P.O. *New Zealand Shipwrecks, 1795-1960*, 3rd ed., 1961.

Larn, R. *Cornish Shipwrecks; The Isles of Scilly*, v. III, 1971.

Larn, R. and Carter, C. *Cornish Shipwrecks: The South Coast*, 1969. See also Noall below.

Lonsdale, A.L. and Kaplan, A.R. *A Guide to Sunken Ships in American Waters*, 1964.

Malster, R. *Wreck and Rescue on the Coast of Devon*, 1968. As in the case of Farr above and Parry below, emphasizes work of the local lifeboats.

Noall, C. *Cornish Lights and Shipwrecks*, 1968.

O'May, H. *Wrecks in Tasmanian Waters*, 1797-1950, 1956.

Parry, H. *Wreck and Rescue on the Coast of Wales*, v. 1, 1969.

Rattray, J.E. *Ship Ashore! A Record of Marine Disasters off Montauk*, 1968.

Small, I.M. *Shipwrecks on Cape Cod*, 1928, R1967.

Snow, E.R. See Sect. BQ-1.

*Stick, D. *Graveyard of the Atlantic: Shipwrecks of the North Carolina Coast*, 1952. See also B.D. MacNeill, *The Hatterasman*, 1958.

BQ – 3   Sailing Vessels

Baas, G.F. *Cape Gelidonya: A Bronze Age Shipwreck* (ms. PhD thesis, Pennsylvania, 1964). See comment, Sect. W-1.

Bradford, G. *The Secret of the* Mary Celeste *and other Sea Fare*, 1966. One of the prime mysteries. See also Fay, C.E., *Mary Celeste. . . .* 1960.

Chase, O. *Shipwreck of the Whaleship* Essex, 1821, RP1963. Sunk by whale. Similar episode recounted in C.C. Sawtell, *The Ship* Ann Alexander *of New Bedford, 1805-1851* (Marine Historical Assn.), 1962.

Duffy, J. *Shipwreck and Empire; Being an Account of Portuguese Maritime Disasters in a Century of Decline*, 1954. See also Sect. AJ-4 for comments on this and on Gomes de Brito, *Tragic History of the Sea*.

Johnson, R.F. *The* Royal George. See Sect. AY-2.

Kirby, P.R. *The True Story of the* Grosvenor, *East Indiaman, Wrecked on the Coast of Pondoland, South Africa on 4 August, 1782*, 1960. The fictional *Loss of the* Grosvenor has nothing to do with this episode.

McKee, A. *The Golden Wreck: The True Story of the Great Maritime Disaster*, 1962. Loss of the British clipper *Royal Charter* homeward bound from Australia, close to Liverpool, with loss of nearly 500 lives and much gold, Oct. 26, 1859.

Mudie, I.M. *The Wreck of the* Admella, 1967. Australia.

Ruben, O. *Minerva Reef*, 1964. Wreck of Tongan cutter on lonely submerged reef, and ordeal of survivors.

Shepard, B. *Lore of the Wreckers*, 1961.

BQ – 4   Steam Vessels

Addison, A.C. *The Story of the* Birkenhead, 1902. Sinking of British transport, with troops observing the "women and children first" principle. Also told by Corbett and Kerr below and by Baldwin, Sect. BQ-1.

Booker, F., et al. *The Wreck of the* Torrey Canyon, 1968. See Sect. J-8.

Brown, A.C. *Women and Children Last: The Loss of the Steamship* Arctic, 1961. Sinking of Collins liner with heavy loss of life (except among crew) after collision in fog.

Corbett, S. *Danger Point: The Wreck of the* Birkenhead, 1962. See also Addison above and Kerr below.

Cowan, E. *Oil and Water: The* Torrey Canyon *Disaster*, 1968. See also Booker above.

Elliott, J.W. *Transport to Disaster*, 1962. See Sect. BC-4.

Gallagher, T. *Fire at Sea: The Story of the* Morro Castle, 1959. Some question his explanation of the fire which caused heavy loss of life off the New Jersey coast on New York-Havana liner, 1934.

Hawkey, A. *H.M.S.* Captain, 1965. Foundering of experimental British ironclad, involving loss of most of 500 aboard. (Warships are included here for peace-time troubles, not involving enemy action.)

Hoehling, A.A. *The Last Voyage of the* Lusitania. See Sect. J-4c.

Hough, G.A., Jr. *Disaster at Devil's Bridge*, P1963 (Marine Historical Assn.). Wreck of coastal liner *City of Columbus* on Gay Head, Martha's Vineyard, in 1884 with heavy loss of life.

Kerr, J.L. *The Unfortunate Ship: H.M. Troopship* Birkenhead, 1961. See also Addison and Corbett above.

Lambert, M., et al. *The* Wahine *Disaster*, 1969. See Sect. AL-4.

Lloyd, J.T.T. *Lloyd's Steamboat Directory and Disasters on the Western Waters*, 1856. Long series of boiler explosions, etc., on river steamers.

Lockwood, C.A. and Adamson, H.C. *Tragedy at Honda*, 1960. See Sect. BF-3.

*Lord, W. *A Night to Remember*. Sect. J-4c.

Marcus, G. *The Maiden Voyage. The* Titanic *Epic from the Embarkation to the Disaster and the Dramatic Aftermath*, 1969. See also Lord above and Oldham and Padfield below.

Moscow, A. *Collision Course: The* Andrea Doria *and the* Stockholm, 1959. Italian luxury liner sunk by Swedish liner near Nantucket.

Oldham, W.J. *The Ismay Line: The White Star Line and the Ismay Family Story*, 1961. Ismay was involved in the *Titanic* disaster which he survived.

Padfield, P. *The* Titanic *and the* Californian, 1965. Argues that Captain Lord of the *Californian* was made a scapegoat.
————. *An Agony of Collisions*, 1966.

Polmar, N. *Death of the* Thresher, 1964. See comments, Sect. BI-3.

Read, G.H. *The Last Cruise of the* Saginaw, 1912. Cruiser wrecked near Midway, 1870.

Stackpole, E.A. *Wreck of the Steamer* San Francisco (Marine Historical Assn.), P1954. Loss of New York-Isthmus mail steamer, with rescue of passengers, troops and crew, Dec., 1853.

Thurston, G. *The Great Thames Disaster*, 1965. Burning of Thames pleasure steamer *Princess Alice*, 1878, after collision, with loss of 640 lives.

Weems, J.E. *The Fate of the* Maine, 1958 and P.

Werstein, I. *The* General Slocum *Incident: Story of an Ill-fated Ship*, 1965. Burning of excursion steamer in New York's East River, June 15, 1904. "Almost as many died on the *General Slocum* as on the *Titanic* or *Lusitania*."

BR SAFETY AT SEA AND SALVAGE

BR – 1 Safety Measures

Arzt, F.K. *Marine Laws – Navigation and Safety*, 1953.

Bennett, A.J. *Ship Fire Prevention*, 1963.

Burnett, W.E. *Fire Down Below*, 1968.

Dalton, J.W. *The Life Savers of Cape Cod*, 1902, R1969.

Dawson, A.J. *Britain's Life-Boats: The Story of Heroic Service*, 1923. For lifeboats also see Sect. BQ-2, Farr, Malster and Parry.

Doner, M.F. *The Salvager: The Life of Captain Tom Reid of the Great Lakes*, 1958.

Francis, J. *A History of Life Saving Apparatus . . . Invented and Manufactured by Joseph Francis*, 1885.

Grossett, H. *Down to the Ships in the Sea*, 1954. Half a century of salvage diving experience.

*Hardy, A.C. *Wreck-S.O.S.; A Story of How Ships Are Wrecked, How They Are Repaired, and What Exists to Save Them*, 1944.

Howarth, P. *Life-Boat Story, Work of the British Royal National Life-Boat Institute*, 1957.

Langmaid, K.J.R. *The Sea, Thine Enemy: A Survey of Coastal Lights and Life Boat Services*, 1966.

Lewis, R. *History of the Lifeboat and Its Work*, 1874.

Lindblad, A.F. *A Critical Analysis of the Factors Affecting Safety and Economy in the Operation of Bulk Freight Vessels of the Great Lakes*, 1924 (PhD thesis, Michigan).

*MacNeill, B.D. *The Hatterasman*, 1958. Excellent account of the American Life-Saving Service at its busiest, around Cape Hatteras. See also D. Stick, *Graveyard of the Atlantic*, 1952.

*Masters, D. *The Plimsoll Mark*, 1955. Samuel Plimsoll's persistent efforts for Parliamentary measures for safety at sea, particularly in the matter of overloading. See also Warner below.

Methley, N.T. *The Life-Boat and Its Story*, 1912.

Nicholl, G.W.R. *Survival at Sea*, 1960. "The development, operation and design of inflatable marine lifesaving equipment, with historic background."

Rushbrook, F. *Fire Aboard*, 1961. An account of shipboard fires and fire prevention.

Shelford, W.O. *Subsunk – The Story of Submarine Escape*, 1960. By a British naval captain who headed the Escape Training School.

Soule, G. *Sea Rescue*, 1966.

Toxopeus, K. *Flying Storm: The Adventures of the Skipper of a Rescue Boat off the Stormy Coast of Holland*, 1954.

*Warner, A.C. *The Plimsoll Agitation: A Chapter in Nineteenth-Century British Social and Maritime History* (ms. PhD thesis, Harvard, 1960).

Waters, J.M. *Rescue at Sea*, 1966. By a leading figure in the U.S. Coast Guard's "Search and Rescue" activity.

Young, D. *The Man in the Helmet*, 1963. Salvage aspect of diving.

BR – 2   Salvage

Bearss, E.C. *Hardluck Ironclad: The Sinking and Salvage of the* Cairo, 1967. Sunk by Confederate mine in the Yazoo River and raised in 1964.

Bowman, G. *The Man Who Bought a Navy*, 1965. See Sect. BE-2.

Brady, E.M. *Marine Salvage Operations*, 1969.

Brooks, E. Turmoil, 1956. The name of a celebrated salvage tug; see also Mowat below.

Burke, E.H. *The Diver's World*, 1966.

*Ellsberg, E. *No Banners, No Bugles*, 1949. One of the United States Navy's leading salvage experts tells of clearing the harbors of Oran, Massawa and other ports of sunken ships. His other works include *On the Bottom*, 1929.

Franzen, A. *The Warship* Vasa – *Deep Diving and Marine Archaeology in Stockholm*, 1962. Salvage of Swedish warship capsized on her maiden voyage in 1628. See also Ohrelius below.

Korn, J. *The Raising of the Queen*, 1961, RP1963. Salvage of the tanker *African Queen* wrecked near the entrance of Delaware Bay, 1958.

Lipscomb, F.W. and Davies, J. *Up She Rises! The Story of Naval Salvage*, 1966.

Marx, R.F. *They Dared the Deep; A History of Diving*, 1967.

Mowat, F. *The Grey Seas Under*, 1959. Career of Nova Scotian salvage tug *Franklin Foundation*, 1930-48.

343

Norris, M.J. *The Law of Salvage*, 1958.

Ohrelius, B. Vasa, *the King's Ship*, tr. M. Michael, 1962. See Franzen above.

*Schultz, C.R. *Inventory of the T.A. Scott Company, Inc., Papers, 1889-1927*, 1964. By the Librarian at Mystic Seaport. This celebrated salvage firm later became Merritt, Chapman, Scott.

Wheeler, G.J. *Ship Salvage*, 1958.

Wildeboer, L.H. *The Brussels Salvage Convention*, 1965.

BS MARITIME HISTORICAL JOURNALS

The American Neptune: A Quarterly Journal of Maritime History, 1941-American Neptune, Inc., Peabody Museum, Salem, Mass. Articles chiefly on American merchant marine. Reviews. Index every five years.

Inland Seas (Great Lakes Historical Society), quarterly, 1945-   . 480 Main Street, Vermilion, Ohio 44089.

The Log of Mystic Seaport, quarterly, 1948-   . Membership in Marine Historical Association, Mystic, Conn. 06355, includes subscription. Articles on American maritime history.

Mariner's Mirror (Society for Nautical Research), quarterly, 1911-   . Membership in Society includes subscription, through the Hon. Secretary, Society for Nautical Research, National Maritime Museum, Greenwich, SE 10, England. Articles on both maritime and naval history, chiefly British. Reviews.

Maritime History, quarterly, 1971-   . David & Charles, South Devon House, Newton Abbot, Devon, England. Book reviews, current notes, articles on sources, etc., annual bibliography of maritime books and articles, in addition to general articles.

The Nautical Magazine: A Magazine for those interested in Ships and the Sea, monthly, 1832-   . Brown, Son, & Ferguson, 52 Darnley St., Glasgow, Scotland. Some historical articles and very comprehensive brief review coverage of "books just received."

Sea Breezes Magazine: The Ship Lover's Digest, monthly, 1919-39, 1946-Charles Birchall & Sons, Ltd., 17 James St., Liverpool, England. Accounts of experiences in sail and steam, chiefly British, and of old steamships and lines.

Steamboat Bill, relating primarily to American Steam and other power vessels, past and present, quarterly, 1939-   . Membership in Steamship Historical Society of America includes subscription: 414 Pelton Ave., Staten Island, N.Y. 10310.

United States Naval Institute Proceedings, monthly, 1874-   . Membership in Institute, Annapolis, Md., includes subscription. Very well illustrated, with occasional articles on naval history, in addition to bibliographical notes, particularly the annual review of year's writings in December issue.

BT MAJOR AMERICAN MARITIME MUSEUMS

MAINE: Penobscot Marine Museum, Searsport 04974
Bath Marine Museum, 963 Washington St., Bath 04530

MASSACHUSETTS: Peabody Museum, 161 Essex St., Salem 01970
Salem Maritime National Historic Sites: Custom House (1819), 168 Derby St;
nearby Derby House (1762), 172 Derby St., Salem 01970
Francis Russell Hart Nautical Museum, Massachusetts Institute of Technolo-
gy, 77 Massachusetts Ave., Cambridge 02139
Whaling Museum and Old Dartmouth Historical Society, 18 Johnny Cake
Hill, New Bedford 02740
Whaling Museum, Maritime Museum, Nantucket 02554
The Peter Folger Museum, Nantucket 02554
Nantucket Life-Saving Museum, Nantucket 02554
Kendall Whaling Museum, Sharon 02067
Marine Museum at Fall River, 70 Water St., Fall River 02721

CONNECTICUT: Mystic Seaport, Marine Historical Assn., Mystic 06355
Submarine Museum, U.S. Naval Submarine Base, Box 157 New London,
Groton 06340 (originally established by Electric Boat Co.)

NEW YORK: South Street Seaport Museum, 16 Fulton St., New York 10038
Museum of the City of New York, Maritime Museum, 1220 Fifth Ave., New
York 10029
New York Historical Society (marine, naval rooms), 170 Central Park West at
77th St., New York 10024
Maritime Museum, Seamen's Bank for Savings, 546 Fifth Ave., New York
10036

PENNSYLVANIA: Philadelphia Maritime Museum, 427 Chestnut St., Philadelphia 19106

MARYLAND: U.S. Naval Academy Museum, Annapolis 21402
Chesapeake Bay Maritime Museum, St. Michaels 21663
Maryland Historical Society (marine wing), 201 W. Monument St., Baltimore
21201

DISTRICT OF COLUMBIA: Smithsonian Institution (transportation, naval
history), Jefferson Drive at 10th St., Washington 20560
Truxtun-Decatur Naval Museum (Naval Historical Foundation), 1610 H St.,
Washington 20006
U.S. Naval Historical Display Center, Building 76, Navy Yard Annex, U.S.
Naval Station, Washington 20390

VIRGINIA: The Mariners Museum, Newport News 23606

OHIO: Great Lakes Historical Society Museum, 480 Main St., Vermillion 44089

MICHIGAN: Dossin Museum of Great Lakes History, 5401 Woodward Ave.,
Detroit 48207

CALIFORNIA: San Francisco Maritime Museum, Foot of Polk St., San Francisco 94109

Maritime Museum Association of San Diego, 1306 North Harbor Drive, San Diego 92101

CANADA: Maritime Museum of Canada, Halifax
Marine Museum of Upper Canada, Exhibition Park, Toronto, 2B
Maritime Museum, 1905 Ogden St., Vancouver 9

For a more complete list, including vessel exhibits, see annual *Nautical Museum Directory*, Quadrant Press, New York, and *Museum Directory of the United States.*

AUTHOR INDEX
and
SUBJECT INDEX

Index of Authors

Hartog, J.de. 76
Harvey, M.L. 113
Hashimoto, M. 288
Haskell, D.C. 254
Hatch, A. 269, 299
Hatch, J. 174
Hattori, V. 193
Haugen, R.N.B. 218
Hauk, Z.W. 134, 136, 326
Hauser, H. 119
Hautala, K. 118, 130, 322
Havighurst, W. 155, 156
Hawes, C.B. 136, 202, 206
Hauk, Z.W. 134, 136, 326
Hawkes, F.A. 306
Hawkey, A. 340
Hawkins, C. 199
Hawkins, R. 94
Hay, R. 76
Hayes, J.D. 262
Hayford, H. 254
Haynes, E.R. 161
Haywood, C.N. 174, 202
Haywood, C.R. 106, 144
Hazard, J.L. 144
Healey, J.C. 63
Healey, J.N. 74
Heaton, H. 160, 318
Heawood, E. 86
Heckstall-Smith, A. 293
Hedges, J.B. 138
Hedges, W. 95
Hegarty, R.B. 20, 21, 202
Heinl, R.D. 7, 227, 284, 301
Hellner, M.H. 324
Helm, T. 291
Helwig, A.B. 146, 164
Hemphill, J.M. 106, 145
Henderson, D. 256
Henderson, W.O. 318
Hendricks, G. 260
Hendry, F.C. 46
Hennessy, M.W. 32, 61
Henningsen, H. 66
Henretta, J.A. 106
Henriques, R. 324
Henry, A.K. 132
Henson, C.T. 254
Herbert, J. 124
Hercher, W.H. 278
Herman, Z. 111
Herreshoff, L.F. 61
Herrick, R.B. 59, 134
Herrick, R.W. 213
Herrick, W.R. 218, 264
Herring, J.M. 99
Hervey, A.J. 76, 238
Herzog, D.R. 64

Hewitt, M.J. 165, 240
Hewson, J.S. 79
Heyerdahl, T. 197
Heyl, E. 28, 35, 37
Hezlet, A. 210, 289
Hickmore, M.A.S. 58
Hidy, R.W. 131, 316, 322
Higgins, A.P. 332
Higgins, T. 272
Higham, C.S. 165
Higham, R.D.S. 44, 51, 277
Highsmith, R.M. 317
Hilbert, L.W. 215
Hilbert, W.E. 332
Hill, H.O. 79
Hill, J.D. 262
Hill, R.N. 37
Hilling, D. 174
Hilton, G.W. 37, 156
Hilton, S.E. 172
Hinsley, F.H. 277
Hinton, R.W.K. 118
Hitchings, A.F. 20
Hitchins, H.L. 79
Ho, P.J. 334
Hobart-Hampden, A.C. 260
Hodges, T.M. 126, 324
Hodson, J.J. 287
Hoehling, A.A. 44, 260, 270,
  272, 273, 338, 341
Hoehling, M. 292
Hoffman, N.J. 146
Hoffman, P.E. 232
Hoffman, R.J.S. 119, 316
Hogan, W.C. 71
Hohman, E.P. 64. 202
Holbrook, S.H. 153
Holden, D.A. 56
Hole, E. 318
Holley, A.L. 53
Holt, E. 191, 252
Holthouse, H. 195
Homans, I.S. 7, 18
Hook, C. 53
Hoole, W.S. 262
Hoon, E.E. 304
Hope, R. 64
Hopkins, A.G. 176
Hopkins, F.N. 8, 313
Horgan, T.P. 48, 250
Horlick, A.S. 139, 311
Horn, A.H. 115
Horn, D. 70, 275
Horner, D. 338
Horrabin, J.F. 99
Horsfall, L.F. 165
Horwood, O.P.F. 178
Hoskins, H.L. 99, 182, 185

Hough, C.M. 139, 332
Hough, F.O. 284
Hough, G.A. 341
Hough, R. 28, 50, 266, 267
  269, 272,
Houk, R.J. 205
Hourani, G.F. 181, 230
Hovgaard, W. 49
Howard, J.L. 49, 300
Howard, M. 285
Howard, R.W. 144, 207
Howard, W.S. 179, 254
Howarth, D. 245, 293
Howarth, P. 342
Howay, F.W. 163
Howe, G.F. 1
Howe, O.T. 31, 32, 151
Howe, S.E. 319
Howell, B.M. 181, 319
Howell, G.C. 205
Howeth, L.S. 99
Howse, D. 79
Hoyle, B.S. 174, 177
Hoyt, E.P. 51, 264, 272, 276
Huck, E.R. 172
Hucul, W.C. 229, 267
Hudson, G.F. 190
Hudson, H. 95
Hudson, J.E. 170
Huebner, G.G. 313
Huebner, S.S. 315
Huff, B.F. 151
Hughes, C.E. 89, 337
Hughes, D.D. 112
Hughes, H. 126
Hughes, J.Q. 125, 310
Hughes, J.S. 128
Hugill, S. 74
Huitt, H.C. 166
Hulderman, B. 41, 119
Hull, A.H. 150
Hull, F. 127
Hulley, C.C. 154
Humboldt, A. 169
Humiston, F.S. 64
Humphreys, R.A. 168, 170,
  172
Hunsberger, W.S. 193
Hunt, L.M. 7
Hunter, H.C. 107
Hunter, H.M. 322
Hunter, L.C. 37, 158
Hunter, W.C. 143
Hunter, W.W. 183
Huntington, G. 74
Huntington, S.P. 213
Huntley, F.C. 165
Hurd, A.S. 107, 266, 274, 307

Stelle, C.C. 190
Stephen, E.P. 279
Stephen, J. 249
Stephens, A.E. 127, 224
Stephens, H.M. 184
Sterling, E.W. 263
Sterling, Y. 268
Steve, F.K. 229, 300
Stevens, E.F. 42, 173, 313, 322
Stevens, H.C. 184
Stevens, M. 312
Stevens, P.H. 54
Stevens, T.A. 62
Stevens, W.E. 153, 325
Stevens, W.O. 210, 251
Stevenson, D.A. 306
Stevenson, R.L. 201
Stewart, C. 40
Stewart, C.L. 153
Stewart, C.S. 255
Stewart, D.A. 152
Stewart, H.B. 84
Stewart, I.M.G. 295
Stewart, J.O. 224
Stewart, L.G. 200
Stewart, P.C. 146
Stewart, R.A. 242
Stewart, W.H. 157
Stewart, W.K. 153
Stick, D. 147, 339
Still, W.N. 58, 259
Stilliard, H.H. 176, 327
Stillman, N.A. 113
Stillson, A.C. 220
Stockhan, J.M. 65
Stockman, J.R. 284
Stokesbury, J.C. 225
Stommel, H. 84
Storey, A. 128, 303
Story, D. 34, 137
Stouppe, W. 68
Stout, N.R. 240
Strachey, W. 95
Strahan, J.H. 224
Strakhovsky, L.I. 275
Straus, R. 73
Strauss, L.L. 299
Strauss, W.P. 196
Street, J.C. 170
Strong, D. 207
Strong, L.A.G. 320
Stuart, C.B. 40
Stuart, F.S. 45
Studley, M.V. 36
Summersell, C.G. 147, 257, 261
Supple, B.E. 123
Surface, F.M. 321

Surface, G.T. 320
Surrey, N.M. 148
Sutherland, L.S. 124, 312
Sutherland, W. 58
Sutton, J.E. 266
Sven-Erik, A. 118
Swain, J.E. 253
Swanborough, C. 52
Swann, D. 307
Swann, L.A. 62, 173, 270
Swanstrom, E.E. 65, 309
Sweetman, J. 275
Swenson, S. 29
Swerling, B.C. 320
Swisher, F. 192
Switzer, D.C. 59, 135, 259
Swygard, K.R. 208
Sykes, P. 86
Syme, J.D. 206
Syrett, D. 222, 242
Szczepanik, E.E. 192
Szulc, T. 302

Talbot, F.A.A. 36
Talbot-Booth, E.C. 22
Tanner, E.C. 138
Tantum, W.H. 68
Tapp, E.J. 200
Tarling, N. 188, 337
Tarn, W.W. 231
Tascher, H. 100
Tate, V. 152, 169
Taussig, C.W. 327
Tawes, L.S. 146
Taylor, A.E. 334
Taylor, E.G.R. 80
Taylor, H.C.D. 317
Taylor, J.C. 288
Taylor, J.D. 84, 111
Taylor, N.M. 257
Taylor, P.S. 65
Taylor, T. 299
Taylor, T.D. 229
Taylor, W.L. 39, 133
Tedder, A.W. 236
Teignmouth, Lord. 305
Teller, W.M. 77
Telley, E. 316
Templeman, F. 316
Tenenti, A. 113
Tenkorang, S. 180
Tennent, J.E. 54
Teonge, H. 77
Terraine, J. 299
Thacker, J.W. 201
Theiss, L.F. 306
Theobald, R.A. 296
Thetford, O. 52
Thibodeaux, E.C. 148, 149

Thiel, J.H. 231
Thoman, R.S. 310
Thomas, A. 162
Thomas, A. 181
Thomas, D.A. 297
Thomas, F.N.C. 224
Thomas, F.P. 220
Thomas, G.Z. 184, 327
Thomas, L. 272, 276
Thomas, N.A. 186
Thomas, P.J. 106
Thompson, E. 207
Thompson, R.P. 146
Thomson, D.B. 206
Thorburn, T. 314
Thorner, D. 186
Thornton, R.H. 8, 108, 120, 313, 314
Throckmorton, A.L. 153
Throckmorton, P. 111, 338
Thorgrimsson, T. 302
Thrupp, S.L. 121, 123
Thurman, M.E. 152, 224
Thurston, G. 341
Tickner, F.J. 188
Timoshen, V.P. 320
Tirpitz, A.P.F. 270
Tod, G.M. 29, 34, 133
Todd, H.H. 259
Todd, J.A. 314
Toland, J. 295
Tolbert, F.X. 260
Tomlinson, H.M. 108, 173, 188
Tonning, O. 116
Tooker, E. 142
Tooley, R.V. 84
Torr, C. 231
Toussaint, A. 181
Towers, G. 316
Towle, E.L. 4, 84, 155, 255
Townsend, M.E. 101
Toxopeus, K. 343
Traung, J.O. 206
Tredree, H.I. 73
Tregoning, K.G. 42, 188
Trelease, A.W. 140, 325
Tremaine, M. 4
Tressler, D.R. 317
Trevor-Roper, H.R. 101
Tripathi, A. 186
True, C.A. 171
Trump, R.M. 148
Tryckare, T. 26
Tsou, S.S. 320
Tsuji, M. 298
Tuchman, B. 271
Tucker, C.D. 54
Tucker, G.N. 224, 251, 284

Subject Index

(This is intended only to facilitate quick location of subjects; only the major entries are indicated, with no attempt to show other incidental references.)

369

370